SEAN O'CASEY

A Bibliography

Also edited by Ronald Ayling

BLASTS AND BENEDICTIONS: ARTICLES AND STORIES BY SEAN O'CASEY

SEAN O'CASEY (MODERN JUDGEMENTS)

The Harvest Festival

A Play in Three Acts.

Caste:

Rev J. Jennings	Rector of St Brendan's.
Rev W. Bishopson	Curate " "
Melville Williamson	A churchwarden
Sir Jocelyn Vane	A Synodsman and leading man of commerce.
Jack Rocliffe	A labourer; afterwards on strike
Tom Nimmo	A Bricklayer
Bill Brophy	A Docker on strike
Simon Waugh	Sexton of St Brendan's.
Mrs Williamson	
Elurie	her daughter
Mrs Rocliffe	Jack's mother.
Mrs Duffy	A Poor Parishioner

Time: The Present.

The first act takes place on Monday, the second on the Friday, and
the third on the Sunday of the same week.

Act 1. Scene: The Drawing-Room of the Williamsons

Act 2. Scene: The Tenement Home of the Rocliffes

Act 3. Scene: The Exterior of St Brendan's Church.

S. Ó Cathasaigh
18, Abercorn Road.
Dublin.

SEAN O'CASEY

A Bibliography

RONALD AYLING
and
MICHAEL J. DURKAN

First published 1978 by
THE MACMILLAN PRESS LTD
London and Basingstoke
Associated companies in Delhi Dublin
Hong Kong Johannesburg Lagos
Melbourne New York Singapore Tokyo

Produced by offset lithography by
UNWIN BROTHERS LIMITED
The Gresham Press, Old Woking, Surrey

A member of the Staples Printing Group

British Library Cataloguing in Publication Data

Ayling, Ronald

    Sean O'Casey
    1. O'Casey, Sean — Bibliography
    I. Durkan, Michael
    016.822'9'12   Z8640

    ISBN 0-333-11348-9

For

Jan and Yvonne

who've done so much to make
this book possible

Contents

Illustrations

Dust Jacket The jacket for this *Bibliography* is a composite montage of the jackets from four of the original six volumes of O'Casey's autobiographies. The author made sketches that were used for each of the six jackets (1939–1954). *Design by Ken Leeder, using material from the book collections of John O'Riordan and Ronald Ayling.*

Frontispiece Holograph opening page and cast list for *The Harvest Festival*. This was O'Casey's second play, begun in 1918, and the earliest dramatic writing by him that is extant (E5). *Henry W. and Albert A. Berg Collection, The New York Public Library (Astor, Lenox and Tilden Foundations).*

1 Broadsheet of 'The Grand Oul' Dame Brittannia' [sic]. This now rare item, printed in 1916, was extremely popular in Dublin during the Great War (A1). Its authorship was probably unknown to most of its readers. Copies such as that reproduced here did not bear the author's name even in the Irish form that he used for his earliest publications. In the version printed in *The Workers' Republic* in 1916 O'Casey used one of his early pseudonyms 'An Gall Fada' (C68). *Henry W. and Albert A. Berg Collection, The New York Public Library (Astor, Lenox and Tilden Foundations).*

2 The three Thomas Ashe pamphlets, published by Fergus O'Connor in 1917 (A2, A3, and A4). *Harvard University (Houghton Library).*

3 The three Wren pamphlets, printed by Fergus O'Connor in 1918 (A5, A6, and A8). *From the collection of Douglas M. Jacobs, Connecticut.*

4 Holograph page opening the second act of *The Harvest Festival* (E5). *Henry W. and Albert A. Berg Collection, the New York Public Library (Astor, Lenox and Tilden Foundations).*

5 A vision of the Great War. Behind the front-line in Flanders, a sketch by O'Casey of the stage setting for Act II of *The Silver Tassie*, drawn while writing the play in 1927 (A14). *Henry W. and Albert A. Berg Collection, the New York Public Library (Astor, Lenox and Tilden Foundations).*

Preface

D. H. Lawrence wanted his introduction to Edward D. McDonald's bibliography of his work to be entitled 'The Bad Side of Books'. Many creative writers would share his suspicion, if not outright hostility to bibliographical compilation. Of his writings he said that 'the voice inside is mine forever. But the beastly marketable chunk of a published volume is a bone which every dog presumes to pick with me.' Bibliographers are not only bone pickers, although they often find the bones and shards from which textual scholars and critics assemble skeletons; they are cataloguers, too, and this leads to further resistance from the properly self-critical author who would prefer many of his pieces to remain undiscovered or, at least, disregarded: he sees his writings treated like so many laboratory specimens pinned down for microscopic examination, all his works – early as well as late, hot-blooded and hastily written rejoinders to the press as well as finely wrought fictions – displayed in order, so that others may label and categorise. As Lawrence told McDonald, with obviously mixed feelings: 'I shall be pleased to get the bibliography, though it frightens me to think of seeing my "works" arrayed against me.'

There is no doubt that Sean O'Casey would have agreed with the following characteristically lively assertion by Lawrence:

> Books to me are incorporate things, voices in the air, that do not disturb the haze of autumn, and visions that don't blot the sunflowers. What do I care for first or last editions? I have never read one of my own published works. To me, no book has a date, no book has a binding. What do I care if 'e' is somewhere upside down, or 'g' comes from the wrong fount? I really don't. . . .
>
> To every man who struggles with his own soul in mystery, a book that is a book flowers once, and seeds, and is gone. First editions or forty-first are only the husks of it. Yet if it amuses a man to save the husks of the flower that opened once for the first time, one can understand that too. It is like the costumes that men and women used to wear, in their youth, years ago, and which now stand up rather faded in museums. With a jolt they reassemble for us the day-to-day actuality of the bygone people, and we see the trophies once more of man's eternal fight with inertia.

O'Casey did not collect first editions of his own or any other writer's books, though he did present inscribed copies of each edition of his writings to his wife and children. However, in his old age he sometimes lamented that he hadn't the time or opportunity to look up his earliest writings, written before he became a full-time professional author, and that he hadn't a record of the many occasional and fugitive pieces printed in journals all over the world. We hope that this bibliography will be useful, then, even in its partial function of being a museum or a fossil collection, but we believe that its scope extends beyond this purpose. We attempt to list as many of O'Casey's hitherto unknown publications as possible as well as to record (in several significant instances) the many revised versions of certain plays. The playwright's extensive revisions – sometimes after, as well as before publication – create the possibility that for textual scholars and critics some editions later than the first one, far from being empty 'husks' of the one true version, will occasionally be of equal or, arguably, more importance than are the first published texts. Donald Gallup reminds us that Ezra Pound sometimes chided bibliographers and collectors for exalting the first edition, with its imperfections, over the last edition, with its corrections and revisions; this practice, similarly, needs to be cautiously reassessed for some of O'Casey's writings. So far, only one published critical dissertation – *Sean O'Casey: Das dramatische Werk* by Heinz Kosok (Erich Schmidt Verlag, Berlin, 1972) – has acknowledged in practical terms the value of comparative textual analysis in studying O'Casey's drama; Dr Kosok's pioneer study could not take into consideration the early unpublished manuscripts and various typescript drafts (see Section E of this book), which were inaccessible when his pioneer thesis was undertaken.

Critical and biographical studies of Sean O'Casey have appeared with some frequency since his eightieth birthday in 1960 but the present book is the first attempt to bring together a full descriptive record of the playwright's published and unpublished writings. In it are described all separate publications by O'Casey; there are also separate checklists of first appearances of individual pieces in books and periodicals, two hundred and twenty-six translations in twenty-five languages published in twenty-nine countries, all known collections of manuscript and typescript material in public institutions, together with details of stage premières and notable stage revivals, phonograph recordings, and ephemera. The descriptive method used will be subsequently discussed; it is intended to provide the information ordinarily needed about twentieth-century books, in a form simple and brief enough to be clearly understood. Descriptions are based upon copies of the items themselves; in exceptional cases where an item has not been examined, however, this information is given in the appropriate entry.

The book's overall structure and its internal ordering within ten separate sections follow basically (though with occasional modifications) what may now be called, in the words of the *Times Literary Supplement*, 'the Soho formula'. We are indeed pleased to acknowledge with gratitude the exacting bibliographical standards established by the Soho series of author bibliographies originally published by Rupert Hart-Davis. Among exemplary works of contemporary bibliographers we owe most to the practice of Dan H. Laurence, Warren Roberts, Alan Denson and Donald Gallup. Moreover, while we differ in emphasis with regard to certain bibliographical theories advanced by Professor Gallup, we nonetheless deeply appreciate his attempts to formulate new biblio-

graphical standards for modern publications. We also owe a large debt to the
theoretical writings of Professor R. B. McKerrow, David F. Foxon, Professor
Fredson Bowers, William B. Todd, and the late John Carter.

Our compilation employs the following format, using ten sections from
A to K (omitting the letter I because it presents practical difficulties in
numbering individual items).

Section A: Books. This section includes books, pamphlets and broadsides
by O'Casey published in England, Ireland and the United States, arranged
chronologically by date of publication and by printings within editions.
Details of the ordering of the material in this section and explanations of
the methods and terms used in the bibliographical descriptions are provided
later in this Preface.

Section B: Contributions to Books and Pamphlets. This section includes titles in
which material by O'Casey constitutes *first publication* or *first book appearance*
outside the pages of a periodical. O'Casey's many contributions to drama
anthologies are thus omitted from this list. The arrangement is by date of
publication. Usually, only the first edition is described with an added note
on subsequent publication in the U.S. if the first edition was issued in England
(and vice versa); later impressions and editions are generally ignored except
where some particular significance attaches to them. We include in this
section a few works that, in some bibliographies, would qualify for Section C,
contributions to periodicals. We define periodicals as journals appearing
with at least a twice-yearly frequency. Thus, had O'Casey contributed to
The Yellow Book, an Illustrated Quarterly, we would have included these entries
in Section C, though Gilcher's *Bibliography of George Moore* puts such contributions in Section B. Certain annual publications that we list in Section B—
examples include *The American Spectator Yearbook* (B6), *The Saturday Book* (B12
and B15), *The Holiday Book* (B20) and *The Socialist Register 1965* (B47)—would
appear in Section C in some bibliographies. As such publications appear
only once a year, however, we list them in the more restricted category.

Section C: Contributions to Periodicals. Materials by O'Casey first printed in
periodicals are arranged chronologically by date of publication. As a rule,
only first periodical appearances have been listed, of contributions not
already printed in book form. Later first periodical publication in, say, the
United States, of a contribution first printed in an English periodical (and vice
versa) has normally been noted only under the first entry. In the later years
of O'Casey's life many of his articles first appeared in Soviet periodicals
(often in an abbreviated form); subsequent republication of these articles
in periodicals is noted whenever the subsequent publication first appeared
in English. All contributions to periodicals later reprinted in books are
noted in both Section C and Section B. Under the heading of periodicals
we include newspapers and other journals which appear at least twice yearly,
as well as occasional publications such as theatre programmes. Interviews
are excluded.

Section D: Translations. This section is arranged primarily by language.
Within each language there are two subdivisions (namely, *Books* and
Periodicals), each in chronological order.

Section E: Manuscripts and Typescripts. This section, like the following five divisions, is not primarily concerned with printed material, strictly speaking, other than the small amount of proof material at the end of Section E. We agree with Professor Gallup's belief that the bibliographer's first responsibility is for printed matter; yet, while recognising that the core of the present book lies in the first four sections, there are also good reasons for believing that Section E contains much important material. The section is arranged in order of, first, holograph material listed chronologically—the chronology of each exercise book or notebook being assessed by the date of the earliest ascertainable item of writing in it—and, secondly, typescript material listed chronologically in order of publication in book form. There are three exceptions within the typescript material: 'Kathleen Listens In' and 'Nannie's Night Out' are listed in order of the date of their composition, which accords with that of their first stage production at the Abbey Theatre, while individual typescripts of articles, stories, and poems that were not printed in O'Casey's books during his lifetime appear in a sequence entitled Miscellaneous Typescripts at the end of the section of typescript material. The section closes with a short checklist of proof material. All the material in Section E is now in libraries or public collections; these sources are named under the individual entries unless the item is in the Berg Collection of the New York Public Library. The latter collection, having acquired both the Sean O'Casey and Fergus O'Connor Papers, has by far the largest collection of O'Casey material in existence. Readers wishing to trace entries by title should use the Index, which we have made as comprehensive as we have thought necessary. Section E does not include letters by O'Casey in public collections.

Section F: Stage Productions. This is a checklist of world stage premières and of first productions (whether amateur or professional) in Ireland, England and the United States. Notable revivals are also acknowledged. The plays are listed alphabetically by title. Films of O'Casey's plays (but not television versions) are appended to Section F.

Section G: Adaptations. Literary, musical and stage versions of O'Casey's works are arranged chronologically by original adaptation.

Section H: Recordings. Commercial recordings of O'Casey's work are arranged chronologically. No material held in private collections is listed.

Section J: Radio and Television Broadcasts. Only broadcasts in which O'Casey himself participated are included. The arrangement is chronological.

Section K: Motion Pictures. The two motion pictures of O'Casey's plays made during his lifetime—*Juno and the Paycock* and *The Plough and the Stars*—are recorded in the appendix to Section F. In Section K we list films in which O'Casey appeared as well as the motion picture, *Young Cassidy*, which was based loosely on autobiographical writings concerning O'Casey's early years.

Perhaps it is best, at this point, to explain the methods and the terms we use in the present work. Such definitions will be especially pertinent with regard to Section A and, to a lesser extent, Section B. In Section A we give the following details: the number of each book or pamphlet by O'Casey, together with details of first and subsequent editions; each edition is described in terms of title-page transcription together with the size of leaf, pagination, binding and publication details. Each entry concludes with notes on the bibliographical significance and publishing history of the work and, wherever ascertainable, a checklist of its contemporary reviews in the English-language press.

Regarding these sub-divisions in Section A, the following more specific definitions may be of help:

Numbering. The numbering system indicates the chronological sequence of the separate publications as well as the edition sequence. Thus A30a indicates that *Rose and Crown* is the thirtieth separate publication (A30), of which entry (a) is the first edition. When no designation of edition is made, it is assumed that there is a single edition only of the title. An *edition* is taken to mean all the copies of a book printed from one setting of type. However, photolithographic versions of a work published under a different publisher's imprint are considered as editions and are so styled.

Title-pages. Although we share the opinion of Professor Gallup—a view that is gradually gaining ground among modern bibliographers—that title-page transcriptions would seldom be essential if publishers could 'be persuaded to pay for easily legible photographic reproductions as illustrations', the fact remains that it is an expensive business and few bibliographies can yet afford the procedure. In the present case, for Sections A and B, title-pages are transcribed in quasi-fascimile. Each line is treated as a separate unit, with line endings indicated by a solidus. Typeface is distinguished as roman or italic. The use of capital and lowercase letters is followed strictly. No distinction is made between capitals and small capitals unless they appear on the same line. The size and weight of the original letters are ignored. All lettering is black unless specifically noted otherwise.

Size of leaf. Size is expressed in centimetres to the nearest half centimetre.

Pagination. In Section A the pagination is included in the collation statement. All pages, including blank ones, are accounted for. Inferential information is enclosed within square brackets. In Section B a simple statement of pagination is given on a separate line, with inferential information again being enclosed within square brackets.

Binding. Cloth colours are described simply. In the transcriptions the lettering on spines when reading vertically is treated as a single line. Book edges are described by the terms *trimmed* and *untrimmed*. The bibliographical importance of dust-jackets in modern book production has been persuasively argued by G. Thomas Tanselle and Donald Gallup. Many librarians and bibliographers still think of book-jackets as a temporary protection to be speedily discarded, and therefore not to be recorded, yet it is surely difficult to disregard Professor Gallup's examples (drawn from books by Thomas Wolfe and Ezra Pound) in which jackets have been solely responsible for identifying editions and (in the many Faber books of poetry to whose jackets T. S. Eliot contributed) for recording writings by authors unobtainable elsewhere. While Professor Tanselle sometimes goes too far in the length and complexity of book-jacket description, we believe that the judicious use of such material is abundantly justified in contemporary bibliography. This is certainly true for the present book because Sean O'Casey himself took great interest in the physical appearance of jackets as well as the books inside them. He contributed to both the design and the text of some of these dust-jackets and, where this is ascertainable, they have been described in some detail in Section A. Two illustrations are given, showing how the jackets he sketched for the first and the last autobiographical volumes—divided by fifteen years in date of publication—bring together in symbolic visual terms the young boy knocking at the door of life and the aged author, on the edge of the doorstep, saluting the future as well as the past.

Publication.   The number of copies printed, the date of publication (that is, the date the book was made available to the public), and the price for which the work was sold on publication are given. Later impressions are indicated with the number of copies printed whenever this information was available. When the number of copies printed is not stated, this is either because the publisher no longer exists or did not respond to enquiries or has a policy of not releasing this type of information. (It is a matter of some scholarly concern that the latter practice seems, from our experience, to be on the increase.) Whenever possible, the firm responsible for the printing is identified in Section A. 'Published privately' refers to a work produced to the order and expense of a private concern and not offered for sale. Unlike D. H. Lawrence, for instance, O'Casey presents few difficulties for the bibliographer in so far as private and pirated editions are concerned.

Notes.   This section is concerned with textual information and the publishing history of each work, not with literary evaluation or criticism. It attempts to identify and clarify bibliographical problems. First-publication material and first-book-appearance material are identified. Notes on the genesis and growth of each book or pamphlet are given from the earliest ascertainable ideas in the author's mind to the process of rewriting and revision before (and sometimes after) publication. In this regard, Warren Roberts's practice in his *A Bibliography of D. H. Lawrence* has been of considerable value.

Reviews.   Here we cite a selection of reviews in English of the work which appeared on its publication. Reviews of stage productions are not included; they may be found in E. H. Mikhail's *Sean O'Casey: A Bibliography of Criticism.*

Our major concern in compiling this bibliography has been to establish the canon of Sean O'Casey's printed works while trying to assure ourselves that the facts assembled are useful to the literary scholar as well as to the book collector and librarian. By preparing a record of his published work and of his manuscript material (including unpublished as well as published writings) we have tried to take the first step towards the much needed textual studies still to be undertaken. The final volume of the *New Cambridge Bibliography of English Literature* gave major prominence to only two dramatists in English in the twentieth century, Sean O'Casey and Samuel Beckett (Shaw, Yeats and Synge were included in the preceding volume). It is our hope that the present book will help stimulate the serious critical and textual attention that such an evaluation implies. Naturally, the value of our book must be determined ultimately by its accuracy and completeness. Any bibliography must be by its nature incomplete, of course, for information is not always made available and unpublished material will subsequently be printed. In the present case, moreover, we are aware of particular as well as hypothetical omissions. The second and third volumes of O'Casey's correspondence have yet to appear and their editor's present concern, with new letters turning up with some frequency, seems to be what to leave out rather than what to include. There will certainly be further discoveries of contributions to periodicals. Some will be in obscure English-language journals while some will probably be found in Eastern European publications. There is no doubt, for instance, that the dramatist wrote a number of articles supporting the Spanish Republican Government during that country's Civil War in the late 1930s. Some of these contributions were written for the Spanish press; others were written for journals outside Spain. We have been unable to trace any of these writings, whose existence is known to us only through contemporary letters by the author; nor have we found the article that one of his letters in the 1930s claims appeared in several Australian papers. Some of these fugitive pieces may well no longer exist; others may yet turn up. It is very likely too that there are more translations still to be unearthed, particularly in countries which were until recently outside the copyright requirements of the Berne convention. While we include in Section E all known manuscripts and typescripts in public collections, it is possible that the National Library of Ireland in Dublin now has in its archives some manuscript material that should be recorded in this section. The *Irish Times* reported (in the issue for May 11, 1976) that the Abbey Theatre directors had 'recently presented a collection of manuscripts and play-scripts to the library'. No details were given and subsequent enquiries have failed to discover whether or not any O'Casey scripts were part of the donation. In these and other matters, additions and corrections to all sections of the present work will be very welcome indeed. We shall be as happy to acknowledge future assistance as, in the next few pages, we are glad to thank many past contributors to this first full-length Sean O'Casey bibliography.

Acknowledgements

So many kind people all over the world have answered enquiries concerning Sean O'Casey's writings that it is impossible to do adequate justice to their invaluable contributions. Many librarians, publishers, friends of the playwright and O'Casey scholars everywhere will recognise in this book their helpful suggestions and information. The authors are deeply grateful for all the unselfish help given to them during more than a decade's work on this bibliography and for the patience of the many contributors who must have begun to fear (as did the publisher!) that the work would never be completed. The following list attempts to name all those who have given assistance but, because the period of research and compilation has been protracted, it is possible that some have been inadvertently overlooked. Omissions should be brought to the attention of the authors for correction in possible future editions.

Sean O'Casey himself gave much help and guarded encouragement in letters and in conversations. His caution was a characteristically unselfish concern: he thought a full-scale bibliography would be too laborious and thankless a task, telling Ronald Ayling that he'd be better off in the sun rather than poring over documents in libraries. Eileen O'Casey's consistent support and practical assistance have been truly invaluable. She allowed Ronald Ayling access to all her husband's private papers, after his death, and this enabled the list of manuscripts and typescripts in Section E to be as full and detailed as it is. Moreover, knowledge of various notebook accounts, in which the dramatist recorded payments for contributions to journals and publishers and for translations published or staged abroad, led to the tracing of hitherto unknown writings which are now listed in Sections B, C and D. Mrs O'Casey's personal interest in the work, moreover, has been of inestimable value.

The patient and long-lasting forbearance as well as encouragement of Mr T. M. Farmiloe is greatly appreciated; indeed, the help of very many of Mr Farmiloe's colleagues at Macmillan, in London and in Basingstoke, has largely helped to make this compilation as detailed and comprehensive as it is. Mr O'Casey was indeed fortunate in having such a company as his major publisher. Professor David Krause gave freely of his time and knowledge. The compilers were given access to letters that Dr Krause will be publishing in the second and third volumes of his collected edition of Sean O'Casey's correspondence and this enabled them to find several published letters that would otherwise have been omitted from Section C. However, it should be made clear that when O'Casey's published or unpublished letters are quoted in this bibliography—as they are frequently in the *Notes* to individual books in Section A—the texts are invariably those of the original letters or of carbon copies of them preserved among the playwright's private papers. None of the quotations used in this book are taken from Dr Krause's three-volume edition of *The Letters of Sean O'Casey*; the *Notes* to Section A had been completed before the first volume appeared in print. The responsibility for transcription from letters and manuscripts must therefore rest with the compilers of this bibliography.

Mr David F. Cheshire helped with material for Section F and that section was typed by Irene Evans with meticulous care. Several details elsewhere in the book have been corrected by Professor Edward H. Mikhail. Mr Robert G. Lowery's encouragement was especially appreciated in the final stages of preparation for the press, when the authors most needed it. Moreover, Mr Lowery published substantial parts of Sections D and E in the *Sean O'Casey Review*, thus enabling readers to offer corrections and additions to the checklist before publication in book form.

Mrs Lola L. Szladits, Curator of the Berg Collection at the New York Public Library, has been particularly helpful in many indirect as well as direct ways. Mr Douglas M. Jacobs has also helped in many valuable respects, generously allowing access to his bookselling catalogues and to letters he received from Sean O'Casey, giving permission for one of his photographs to be reproduced in the present work and—last, but hardly least—introducing Michael J. Durkan and Ronald Ayling to each other, by letter, when he discovered that, unkown to each other, they were both working on an O'Casey bibliography.

That the two compilers remain (so far as can be ascertained) relatively sane is the supreme achievement of the two women to whom this work is dedicated; 'relatively' is said advisedly for Donald Gallup is surely right in warning that 'bibliography can hardly be recommended as an occupation for completely sane persons'.

Whatever the faults of the present publication, its existence in its present form would be unthinkable without major contributions by the above mentioned men and women, and by varied forms of assistance by the following individuals and institutions:

Aguilar S. A. De Ediciones, Madrid; John Allen; W. H. Allen and Company Limited; Allen and Unwin Limited; Alley Theatre, Houston; American Film Institute (Center for Advanced Film Studies); American Russian Institute (Holland Roberts); Angel Records (Brad Engel); Dr Alexander Anikst; Anvil Books (Daniel Nolan); L'Arche, Paris; Elliot Arluck; Professor W. A. Armstrong; Jim Aronson; Allan Aslett; Robert Avery; Michael and Joyce Bailey; Miss Elizabeth Barber; Barnes and Noble; Barrie and Jenkins Limited (John G. Pattisson); the Bayerische Staatsbibliothek, München; Miss Lorraine Beaver; Samuel Beckett; Miss Sally Belfrage; Dr Werner Beyer; Biblioteca da Ajuda, Lisboa; Biblioteca del Ateneo de Madrid; Biblioteca de Cataluña, Barcelona; Biblioteca Communale di Milano, Milan (Anna Maria Rossato);

Biblioteca General da Universidade, Rio de Janeiro (Amelia Rosauro de Almeida); Biblioteca Nacional, Lima, Peru (Graciela Sánchez Cerro); Biblioteca Nacional de Lisboa (Reinalda Catarino Afreixo); Biblioteca Nacional, Madrid (J. Almuderar); Biblioteca Nacional del Uruguay, Montevideo; Biblioteca Nazionale di Berera, Milan; Biblioteca Nazionale Braidense, Milan (L. Pernalla); Biblioteca Nazionale Centrale, Florence; Biblioteca de la Universidad de Madrid; Biblioteka Narodowa, Warsaw (Rafal Kozlowski); Bibliothèque Cantonale et Universitaire, Lausanne; Bibliothèque Nationale, Luxembourg; Bibliothèque Nationale, Paris (Roger Pierrot); George Bidwell; Kenneth Blackwell (Archivist, Bertrand Russell Archives, McMaster University Library); Benjamin Blom, Incorporated; the late Ernest Blythe; the late Guy Boas; Bodleian Library; Boston University Libraries; John Boyd; Dr Birgit Bramsbäck; Dr Otto Brandstädter; George W. Brandt; George Braziller; British Broadcasting Corporation; British Drama League Library (Enid M. Foster); British Institute of Recorded Sound (Sheila Metcalf); the British Library (formerly the British Museum); the British Library of Political and Economic Science (C. G. Allen); the British Museum Newspaper Library, Colindale; Stephen Brook; G. J. Brouwer (Bibliotheek van der Vereeniging Ter Bevordering van de Belangen des Boekhandels, Amsterdam); the late Ivor Brown; Miss Marguerite Buller; Dr Robert Busch; Dr S. Bushrui; Caedmon Records; Cambridge University Library (Alison M. Wilson and C. E. P. Tyrrel); the late Mrs M. Carney; Cassell and Collier Macmillan Publishers, Limited; the late Sir Lewis Casson; CBS Records; Center for Cassette Studies, Incorporated; City of Bristol Libraries; the late Austin Clarke; Cleveland Public Library (Jay W. Beswick); Ken Coates; Cockermouth Public Library (K. Skillen); Gerald Colgan; Collins Publishers (Katherine Craig Brown and K. Duesbury); the late Padraic Colum; Dr L. W. Conolly; Conservatório Dramatica e Musical, São Paulo (José Raymundo Lobo); the late Barney Conway; Cornell University Library; Aileen Coughlan; Coward, McCann and Geoghegan, Incorporated; Mr J. Shum Cox (past librarian, University of Bristol); Elizabeth Coxhead; the late Miss May Craig; Thomas Quinn Curtiss, Cyril Cusack; Sorcha Cusack; Cyril and Methodius National Library, Sofia (Yordanka Parvanova); Czechoslovak Theatrical and Literary Agency (Gustav Bernau); the late Jack Daly; Miss Vera Darlington (librarian of the *Morning Star*); Norris Davidson (literary executor to the Lennox Robinson estate); Mrs Florence Davis; Henry D. Davy; Sean Day-Lewis; Alan Denson; Hon. Thomas C. Desmond; Dr Patrick Destenay; Deutsche Bücherei, Leipzig; Devin Adair Company; Devon County Library; Diogenes Verlag, Zürich (Fredy Barth and Ann E. Suter); the late Geoffrey Dobbie; Dolmen Press; Donnchadh Ó Súilleabháin (An Chomhairle Náisiúnta Drámaíochta); Miss Angela Dormer; Dorset County Library; Dramatic, Artistic and Literary Rights Organization (Pty.) Limited (DALRO), Johannesburg (Paul Roos); Dramatists Play Service, Incorporated (F. Andrew Leslie); Clive E. Driver; Margaret Drummond; Dr Marina Druzina; Dublin Public Libraries (Mairin O'Byrne); Dublin University Press, Limited; Professor Barrows Dunham; Frank Dunlop; Maurice Dunmore; Angela Dyer; Editorial Nova, Buenos Aires; Professor A. C. Edwards; Elizabeth Ellam; the late St. John Ervine; the late Dr Griff Ewer; Exeter City Library; Faber and Faber; W. J. Fairbrother; Gabriel Fallon; the late Gerard Fay; Miss L. Fitzgerald; Francke Verlag; Frances-Jane French; Miss Hannah D. French (formerly reference librarian, Wellesley College, Massachusetts); Samuel French; Dr Elisabeth Freundlich; Leslie Frewin Publishers (Susan Tovy); P. N. Furbank; Professor Donald Gallup; David and Richard Garnett; George Gilmore; the late Mr John D. Gordan (formerly Curator of the Henry W. and Albert A. Berg Collection, the New York Public Library); Robert D. Graff; C. Desmond Greaves; Grosset and Dunlap, Incorporated; André van Gyseghem; Michel Habart; Hammersmith Books; Harcourt, Brace and World, Incorporated; Harper and Row; Harvard College Library (Mary S. Smith); Harvard University, Houghton Library (Suzanne Flandreau, Rodney G. Dennis and Roger Stoddard); Dr R. J. Hayes (past director, National Library of Ireland); Leslie Head; the late George H. Healey, Curator of Rare Books, Cornell University Library; William Heinemann, Limited; Helsinki University Library; James Henderson (New York Public Library); Henschelverlag, Berlin; Mr N. Highan (present librarian of the University of Bristol); Margery J. Hiltz; the late Bulmer Hobson; Hofstra University; Robert Hogan; Holt, Rinehart and Winston; Horizon Press; Sarah Horn; Joyce Huddart; Harry Hutchinson; Hutchinson Publishing Group, Limited; the Henry E. Huntington Library (William Ingoldsby); Independent Broadcasting Authority; Institute for Research and Planning in Science and Education, Tehran; Dr Valentin Iremonger; the *Irish Independent* Library; the *Irish Press* Library (Thomas P. McCann); the *Irish Times* Library; Irish Transport and General Workers' Union, Dublin; Jarrolds Publishers (London) Limited; the Jewish National and University Library, Jerusalem (Mrs Ruth Tronik); John Johansen; the late Augustus John; Denis Johnston; Harold Jones; John Jordan; Kansankulttuuri Oy, Helsinki (Marja Lallo); the late Jim Kavanagh; Libby and Paul Kaye; David Blake Kelly; Mrs E. Kelly; Kensington Public Libraries; The Kerryman Limited; Miss J. R. Kilroe; Mrs Oksana Krugerskaya; Kungliga Biblioteket (Olof von Feilitzer); Landsbókasafn Íslands (National Library of Iceland), Reykjavík; Dan H. Laurence; the League of Dramatists, London; Professor Clifford Leech; Library of Congress; Library and Museum of the Performing Arts, The New York Library at Lincoln Center, New York (Paul Myers, Curator, Theatre Collection, and Donald Fowle); Jack Lindsay; Little, Brown and Company; Wilfrid Lockwood (Cambridge University Library); Louisiana State University (Peter Paul Fuchs); the late Walter Lowenfels; Frances Lubin; Gigi Lunari; Edward H. Mabley; Frank McCarthy; Ralph E. McCoy (director of libraries, Southern Illinois University); Hugh McDiarmid (C. M. Grieve); Peadar MacMaghnais; Macmillan Publishing Company Incorporated; the Richard J. Madden Play Company Incorporated; Miss Pegeen Mair; Dr Lila Maitra; Herbert Marshall; the late Sir Alec Martin; Dr Eva Masnerová; Raymond Massey; Matica Slovenská, Czechoslovakia (Dr Ing. Jaroslav Celko); George Matthews; Merlin Press, Limited; Methuen and Company, Limited; Liam Miller; Ewart Milne; Professor H. Milnes; Ministry of Higher Education and Scientific Research, University of Baghdad (Dr. Husham Al-Chawaf); Professor Christian H. Moe; *Monthly Review Press*; *Morning Star* (formerly the *Daily Worker*); Professor Alton C. Morris; Dr Carmela Moya; Chancellor Franklin D. Murphy; Nancy Murphy; Museum of Modern Art, Film Study Center; Dr Péter Nagy; Koshi Nakanori; National Broadcasting Company Incorporated (Mary Jo O'Hagan); National Diet Library, Tokyo; National Library and Archives, Cairo (A. M. Kahil);

National Library of Greece (Anastasia D. Samsarelou); National Library of Ireland (Patrick Henchy and Alf MacLochlainn); National Library of Peking, Peking; National Széchényi Library, Budapest; John Neville; New American Library, Incorporated; New English Library, Limited; W. A. Newman; Peter Newmark; New York Public Libraries (Berg and Theatre Collections); New York Public Library, Manuscript Division; New York State Library (Susan Lawrence); New York University Press; *Newcastle Evening Chronicle* (D. Foreman); Joseph North; W. W. Norton and Company, Incorporated; Brendan O'Brien; Professor Frank O'Brien; the late Professor George O'Brien; Breon and Shivaun O'Casey; the late Mrs Maude O'Connor; Réamonn O'Corcoráin; Peader O'Donnell; Mícheál ÓhAodha; Dr Ott Ojamaa; Oliver and Boyd, Limited; Lord Olivier; Mrs Mary O'Malley; John and Kate O'Riordan; Országps Széchényi Könyvtar (György Pajkossy); Dr Shotaro Oshima; Österreichische Nationalbibliothek, Vienna (V. O. Thiel); Dr Malcom Page; Professor N. Parker-Jervis; Dr Andrew Parkin; Paul List Verlag, Leipzig (the late Dr. Franke); Peter Owen, Limited; Dr J. H. P. Pafford (formerly Goldsmiths' librarian, University of London); Pan Books, Limited (Kyle Cathie); Professor Roy Pascal; People's Theatre Arts Group (R. A. Watson); Stephen Pezim; the late Professor V. de Sola Pinto; Prentice Hall, Incorporated; the late Dr Alan Price; Putnam and Company; the late Tony Quinn; Radio Telefís Éireann; Randolph-Macon College Library; Readers Union; Guy Rétoré; Rhodes University Library, Grahamstown, South Africa; Elsa Rice; Olive Richardson; Mrs Lennox Robinson; the late Bertram Rota; Paul Rotha; Routledge and Kegan Paul, Limited; the Royal Library, Danish Department, Copenhagen (Hofman Hansen); Miss Teresa Sacco; St. Martin's Press, Incorporated; San Francisco Public Library; Mrs A. Saruchanian; Wolfgang Schuch; Margaret I. Scott (Cambridge University Library); Seámus Scully; Edith Segal-Kamen; Irwin Silber; Miss Betty Sinclair; *Sing Out*; the late Dr Owen Sheehy Skeffington; Slovenská Akadémia Vied, Bratislava; Slovenská Literárna Agentúra, Bratislava (V. Dinková); Jessica Smith; Colin Smythe; the Society of Authors, London; Dr Elaine Sofer; Southern Illinios University Library (Kenneth W. Duckett); Southern Illinois University Press; Dean Thomas F. Staley; the late Professor Walter Starkie; State Library of the Czech Socialist Republic, Prague (Karel Kozelek); the State Library, Pretoria, South Africa (E. Nel); Joseph Stein; Professor A. G. Stock; Suid-Afrikaanse Biblioteek, Cape Town (Dr A. M. Lewin Robinson); Swiss National Library, Berne; Talbot Press, Limited; Don Taylor; Kim Taylor; Tehran Book Processing Centre (Kámrán Fáni); Dr R. Hinton Thomas; the late Dame Sybil Thorndike; Eva Tisell (Nordiska Teaterförlaget AB); Trinity College Library, Dublin; Peter Trower; James and Joanna Turner; Università Cattolica Del S. Cuore, Milan; Université L. Eötvos De Budapest, Budapest; Universitetsbiblioteket, Oslo (Erling Grønland); University of Alberta Library, Edmonton, Canada; University of Bristol Library; University of California, Berkeley (Margaret D. Uridge); Department of Special Collections, University of California, Los Angeles (Brooke Whiting); Library of the University of California, Los Angeles; Library of the University of Damascus, Syrian Arab Republic; University of Kansas Library, Lawrence (Alexandra Mason); University of London Library; University of Missouri Press; University of Texas Library, Austin (Mary M. Hirth); Juvencio Valle (Director de Bibliotecas, Archivos y Museos, Santiago, Chile); Van Nostrand

Reinhold Company; Viking Press, Incorporated; the late Jean Vilar; Robert
Voisin; Wesleyan University Library (William J. Dillon, Ann-Frances Di
Stefano, Ellen T. Hayes and Gertrude McKenna); Arnold Wesker; *West
Cumberland Times and Star*; Dr Richard Whittaker; William Morris Agency
(Jane Chodorov); H. W. Wilson Company; Mrs C. Wojewoda; Miss Julia
Wootten; Dr K. J. Worth; Yale University Library; the late Mrs W. B. Yeats;
Zentralbibliothek, Zürich.

Wesleyan University's generosity in providing Michael Durkan with a
summer research fellowship in 1971, and its annual grants-in-aid of research
is hereby gratefully acknowledged. A post-doctoral fellowship at the
University of Alberta, Edmonton, enabled Ronald Ayling to work on the
present book almost uninterruptedly from 1969 to 1970; the generosity of
the University and the encouragement of Dr R. G. Baldwin, then chairman
of the Department of English there, thus gave much-needed impetus
to Dr Ayling's share in the research. His work was also aided by the co-
operation of the Bursar and staff of Churchill College, Cambridge, during
a year's residence there from 1974–5; the facilities and resources of Clare
Hall, Cambridge, were also of considerable value that year. A small grant
from the Canada Council in 1974 allowed Dr Ayling to work on various
manuscript material. Though this research was not intended to aid the present
bibliography, it did so in various indirect ways and thus what one may call
the inadvertent assistance of the Canada Council (which has done so much
for literary scholarship in Canada in many direct ways) is hereby gratefully
acknowledged.

SECTION A

Books and Pamphlets

This section includes books, pamphlets and broadsides by
O'Casey published in England, Ireland and the United States,
arranged chronologically by date of publication and by
printings within editions. Details of the ordering of the
material in this section and explanations of the methods and
terms used in the bibliographical descriptions are provided
in the Preface.

THE GRAND OUL' DAME BRITANNIA 1916

a. *first edition*
In *The Workers' Republic*, January 15, 1916 (C68)

b. *first separate edition*
The Grand Oul' Dame Brittannia. / (Air: Leather away with the Wattle O.) / [ornamental line]

28.5 × 11cm.

Broadside. Caption title as above, followed by a poem of seven stanzas of eight lines each.
Published January 1916 by Fergus O'Connor, Dublin; number of copies undetermined.

Notes: This ballad was most probably written as a reaction to the news from England, when, in January 1916, conscription legislation was introduced for Great Britain. O'Casey's recollection of the event was written eighteen years later in the preface to *Windfalls* (A16), 'Finally came the crash of the guns in the Great War, and England's hurried and agitated recruiting campaign in Ireland calling on Irishmen of goodwill to go out and fight a fight for little Catholic Belgium. Then "The Grand Oul' Dame Britannia" was written, printed as a "nix job" by friendly printers, and circulated among the various National Societies. Many others followed, all of which have gone down into the limbo of forgotten things. But I often wish that they were alive again, for buried in them are a wild joy and a savage bitterness that I shall never know again.'

It is probable that the publication in *The Workers' Republic* of January 15, 1916 (C68) preceded the broadside publication. Neither author nor publisher is named in the broadside. In *The Workers' Republic* for January 15, 1916 (not January 16, as reported in *Feathers from the Green Crow*), the ballad was published under the pseudonym 'An Gall Fadd' [*sic*], i.e. 'An Gall Fada', which means 'the tall stranger (or foreigner)', a name used occasionally by O'Casey since his first appearance in print in 1907 (C1). Another pseudonym used by O'Casey in his apprentice years was 'Craobh na nDealg' ('the Branch of Thorns', or, 'Thorny Branch') which was used occasionally in articles in the *Irish Worker*. Otherwise his early work was published under the Irish form of his name – Sean O'Cathasaigh – except for the reprint of *Songs of the Wren No. 1* (A5) which gives his name as Sean O'Casey. It was only with the publication of *Two Plays* (A10) by Macmillan in 1925 that he began the regular use of his name as we know it today. He used the Irish form in correspondence with his first publisher, Fergus O'Connor, and with the Abbey directors, at least until his first play was staged there in April 1923. O'Casey himself used sobriquets, e.g. 'the Wren', 'the Green Crow' and 'the Green Searchlight', the latter in reports for readers in the Soviet Union during the Second World War, but was very specific in identifying himself as the author under his real name.

In *Songs of the Wren* No. 1 and No. 2 the O'Casey authorship is acknowledged in the phrase 'By Sean O'Cathasaigh, Author of "The Grand Oul'

Dame Brittannia" '. It seems to have been highly popular in Dublin at the time it appeared. O'Casey included the ballad in his collection of occasional writings, *Windfalls*, in 1934. Lady Gregory had published it in her *Kiltartan History Book* (London, 1926), giving its date as 1917, but did not acknowledge O'Casey as the author; she probably did not know that the newly popular Abbey playwright was the author. Her explanation for including fairly recent songs in her anthology is certainly apt in so far as O'Casey's work is concerned: 'I have added to the book a few of the ballads printed on broadsheets and sung at fairs or markets, that have to do with the English wars in which so many of our people have fought. I give also some that are concerned with the desire and attempts to break away from English rule. And if these are far from having the wildness and beauty of the passionate outcries made in earlier years in the native language, they are as I have called them elsewhere "roughly hammered links in a chain of unequal workmanship" that stretches back to the time when Spenser advised Queen Elizabeth to harry the poets out of Ireland.'

The broadside version is shorter by two verses than that printed in *The Workers' Republic* (C68), and is basically the version published in Lady Gregory's *Kiltartan History Book* (reprinted in 1971 in Volume ix of the Coole Edition of Lady Gregory's Works) and in *Windfalls* (A16). *The Workers' Republic* version was published by Robert Hogan in *Feathers from the Green Crow* (A40). A manuscript version is included amongst the O'Casey Papers in the New York Public Library Berg Collection. In 1966 a phonograph recording of the ballad was made by Tommy Makem and the Clancy Brothers for the CBS Legacy Collection, *The Irish Uprising: 1916–1922*.

2 LAMENT FOR THOMAS ASHE 1917

first edition
Lament for Thomas Ashe / By SEAN O'CATHASAIGH. / [double rule]

18.5 × 12cm.

Broadside. Caption title as above, followed by a poem of four stanzas of eight lines each.
Published September 25–26? 1917 by Fergus O'Connor; number of copies undetermined.

Notes: This is probably the first of the two laments referred to by O'Casey in *Inishfallen, Fare Thee Well* (A27). Thomas Ashe was an Irish patriot who was sentenced to death for his part in the Easter Rebellion of 1916. The sentence was later commuted to penal servitude for life. Under the General Amnesty of June 1917, Ashe was released with the other Republican prisoners. On August 18 he was re-arrested and charged with 'attempting to cause disaffection among the civil population', and was lodged in Mountjoy Jail. On September 18, when demands to be treated as prisoners of war were not met, Thomas Ashe and other Republican prisoners went on hunger-strike. On September 25, Ashe collapsed while attempts were being made at forcible feeding. He was removed to the Mater Hospital where he died about five hours later. O'Casey's obituary tribute to him was published in *Dublin Saturday Post*, October 6, 1917 (C73). Later, in 1949, he was to recall Ashe's death in *Inishfallen, Fare Thee Well* (A27): 'Sean had written two laments for Thomas Ashe, for he had been an old friend of his when both had been pipers; and now, with a Fergus O'Connor, who had published the two laments, he was on his way to the prison to get news as to when the body of the dead man would be allowed out for burial . . . In silence, there they stood, Sean in his old clothes, his broken cap pulled sullenly down over his eyes . . . acting as a chorus to O'Connor chanting in a low whisper Sean's lament for the dead man . . .' It is more than likely that O'Connor was reading from *Lament for Thomas Ashe*. O'Casey's phrase, 'acting as chorus', probably refers to the line 'Thomas Ashe, Thomas Ashe, we are mourning for thee', which serves as a refrain in three of the four stanzas of the lament. The *Lament* also has all the appearances of a hasty printing – ornament, except for a double rule, is absent; omitted too is any reference to the publisher; there is almost no differentiation between stanzas. The broadside was probably printed in a hurry for distribution outside the gaol gates. It was later incorporated in the prose pamphlet *The Sacrifice of Thomas Ashe* (A4b); reprinted in the *Kerry Annual*, 1953. A holograph transcription of the poem is to be found among the Fergus O'Connor Papers (E3).

A3   THOMAS ASHE   1917

first edition
THOMAS ASHE. / [short rule, cross, short rule]

22 × 14cm.

Broadside. Caption title as above, followed by a poem of six numbered
stanzas of five lines each. Printed signature at end of sixth stanza: SEAN
O CATHASAIGH. /; the whole within border of rules. Publisher's imprint
at bottom left outside border: FERGUS O'CONNOR, DUBLIN. /
Published October 1–12? 1917; number of copies undetermined.

Notes: A copy of this broadside was quoted as item 259 in Catalogue no.
14 issued by the American bookseller Mr Douglas Jacobs. The copy offered
for sale by Mr Jacobs has an inscription in O'Casey's hand: 'From Sean
to his beloved Maire. October 12, 1917'. The Maire referred to here is undoubtedly Maire Keating, his first serious love, to whom he dedicated *Juno
and the Paycock* (A11). She appears as Nora Creena in *Inishfallen, Fare Thee
Well* (A27). Several poems, later printed in *Windfalls* (A16) and in *The World
of Sean O'Casey* (B53), were addressed to her. It is reasonable to assume
that the copy of *Thomas Ashe* dedicated to her by O'Casey would have been
presented to her fairly close to its date of publication. This assumption
would place the publication of the broadside in early October. It is much
more elaborately designed and printed than the *Lament for Thomas Ashe* (A2).
The decoration, numbering of stanzas and publisher's imprint all point to
a more leisurely and later publication than for the *Lament*. Reprinted in
I Die in a Good Cause by Sean O Luing (Tralee, 1970). The poem appears
in a holograph transcript among the Fergus O'Connor Papers (E3). It is
not to be confused with the poem of the same title by O'Casey printed in
Bottom Dog on November 3, 1917 (C74).

4 THE STORY OF THOMAS ASHE   1917?

a. *first edition*
[in outline letters] THE STORY / OF / THOMAS ASHE / BY SEAN
O CATHASAIGH. / [ornament] / "God must judge the couple! leave them as they
are / Whichever one's the guiltless, to his glory, / And whichever one the
guilt's with to my story." / —*Browning*. / [ornament] / PRICE—TWOPENCE. /
Published by Fergus O Connor Dublin.

18.5 × 12cm.

[1], title-page as above; [2]–[3], Foreword; [4]–14, text; 15, Afterword; [16],
blank.

White paper covers, the front cover serves as title-page; back cover blank;
lettered and decorated in black; all edges trimmed.
Published November 1917 at twopence; exact date and number of copies
undetermined.

b. *new edition*
THE SACRIFICE / OF / THOMAS ASHE / BY SEAN O' CATHASAIGH. /
[double rule] / "Tom Ashe is a man."—*Jim Larkin*. / [short rule] / "His life was
gentle, and the elements / So mixed in him that Nature might stand up / And
say to all the world 'This was a man!' " / —*Shakespeare*. / [short rule] / "What
danger singly if I stand the ground, / My friends all scattered, all the foes
around? / Yet wherefore doubtful? let this truth suffice: / The brave meets
danger and the coward flies; / To die, or conquer proves a hero's heart; / And
knowing this, I know a soldier's part." / —*Pope*. / [double rule] / FERGUS
O'CONNOR / PUBLISHER, DUBLIN / 1918.

18.5 × 12cm.

[1], title-page as above; 2–16, text.

Issued in stiff grey paper covers; front cover: THE SACRIFICE / [double rule]
OF [double rule] / THOMAS ASHE / [decoration consisting of three sets of six
short lines over two sets of six short lines] / *"Stretched in the dust the dauntless
warrior lies, / And sleep eternal seals his swimming eyes, / Oh, worthy better fate! Oh,
early slain! / Thy Country's friend."* / —POPE. / Price = Fourpence / PUBLISHED
BY FERGUS O'CONNOR, / DUBLIN. / [all above within border of short
rules]; back cover has advertisement for Monument Creameries, Dublin;
lettered and decorated in black.
Published February/March? 1918 at fourpence; exact date and number of
copies undetermined. In a letter of February 17, 1918 to Fergus O'Connor,
O'Casey reminds him, 'You have from me . . . Sacrifice of Thomas Ashe
(Reprint).' It is more probable that he was in fact referring to the new
edition, *The Sacrifice of Thomas Ashe*, regarding it as a reprint of *The Story
of Thomas Ashe*. Later on in the same letter he refers to 'Sacrifice of Thomas
Ashe, 2d line', which indicates that he was indeed regarding it as a reprint of
The Story of Thomas Ashe which had sold for twopence. The selling price for the
new edition was established at fourpence.

Notes: The new edition includes, in addition to *The Story of Thomas Ashe*, the ballad *Lament for Thomas Ashe* (A2), p. 2; 'The Jury's Verdict', pp. 15–16; 'To Thomas Ashe', poem by Anna G. Lang, p. 16. Ashe's death had a great effect on the mood of the Irish people at the time; there was a very real shift of support to the cause for which he had died. Broadsheets, magazines, leaflets and newspapers bore tributes to his memory. In his ballads and in *The Story of Thomas Ashe* O'Casey caught the fervour of the moment, and recorded the sorrow and anger that were felt by the people at this time. Ashe's funeral procession to Glasnevin Cemetery on Sunday, September 30, 1917 was attended by people who came in their thousands from all parts of Ireland. An inquest into the cause of his death opened at the Mater Hospital on September 28 and with adjournments continued until November 1. Among its findings it stated, 'we condemn forcible or mechanical feeding as an inhuman and dangerous operation, and say it should be discontinued.'

In a letter to Harold D. Jones dated February 21, 1961 O'Casey wrote, 'Thanks for the booklet *The Story of Thomas Ashe*. I haven't the original [manuscript]. That was written longhand, pen and ink, no copy was kept, and this original, if existing, can only be among the papers of Fergus O Connor to whom it was sold, with others, and a number of songs for a few pounds—a godsend to me then. . . . I had completely forgotten this Life Story, and can't remember writing [it] even now. All I have in mind were two sets of verses (poetry to me then) around the death of T. Ashe, who was a great friend of mine in the Gaelic League and the Society of Irish Pipers.'

In 1960 University Microfilms of Ann Arbor, Michigan, sought permission to reproduce the Thomas Ashe material photographically by both xerox and microfilm processes. Fergus O'Connor's widow, Maude, asked O'Casey for his advice. His reply was dated March 10, 1960: 'Regarding the request of the University Microfilms Ltd. to film my old work, which interested Fergus in auld lang syne, though I don't think they are worth the trouble, I have no objection whatever for there's nothing to be ashamed of in any of them.' Asked about copyright ownership of writings published by O'Connor, he answered Mrs O'Connor in a letter dated March 16, 1960: 'I sold these things—or most of them, but not the Lament for Thomas Ashe and the other poem about him; I amn't sure about the 'Life' [presumably *The Story of Thomas Ashe*], which, of course, isn't a life at all. Anyway, they are yours to do what you wish with them. I wouldn't think of taking any royalty; so go ahead, dear lady, and do as you wish.' University Microfilms did make arrangements with Mrs O'Connor for photographic reproduction of *The Story of Thomas Ashe*; copies in xerox and in microfilm were made available to purchasers upon request.

In 1918, when O'Casey was writing his pamphlet on the history of the Irish Citizen Army (A9), he recalled *The Story of Thomas Ashe* in the title of the new work, thinking of it as being part of a continuing series: 'It was one of the "stories" planned by me—Story of Ashe, Story of C.A., Story of Tone, Story of John Mitchel, etc. I wrote but the [first] two', he told Ronald Ayling in a letter dated December 29, 1963.

The Sacrifice of Thomas Ashe was reprinted in 1962 in *Feathers from the Green Crow* (A40).

SONGS OF THE WREN NO. 1   1918

first edition

Ꭺṁṗáın Ꭺn 'Oṕeoıƚın. / New Series. No. 1. [all underlined] / SONGS OF THE WREN / By SEAN Ó CATHASAIGH, / Author of "The Grand Oul' Dame Brittannia." / [short double rule, one heavy one light] / Humorous and Sentimental. / [rule] / CONTENTS: / The Man from the "Daily Mail." / Air: "The Girl from the County Clare." / If the Germans Came to Ireland in the / Morning, / Air: "I'm Off To Philadelphia in the Mornin'." / The Demi-Semi Home Rule Bill. / Air: "The Wearin' of the Green." / Mary is Faithful to Me. / Air: "Has Sorrow Thy Young Days Shaded." / As I Wait in the Boreen for Maggie. / Air: "Cnochainin Aerach Chille Mhuire." / "Merrily, merrily, all the day, / Merrily over the stile, a, / A merry heart goes all the way— / A sad one tires in a mile a" / [rule] / PRICE—ONE PENNY. / FERGUS O'CONNOR, PUBLISHER, DUBLIN. / [all above except first and last line within border of three wavy rules, broken twice at top and bottom, broken three times on each side]

18.5 × 11.5cm.

[1], title-page as above; 2–7, text; [8], blank.

White paper covers, the front cover serves as title-page. Published February/ March 1918 at one penny; exact date and number of copies undetermined; reprinted April 1918 (10,000 copies).

Notes: In a letter to Douglas Jacobs dated June 23, 1963, the author explained, 'There is an old Gaelic song "An Dreoilin," the Wren, which if my memory still serves me, was one about the hoped for return of the young Stuart to take his seat on the throne of England.' The title is a nationalist symbol and one which conveys a sense of exile; both elements were to be picked up in the writer's pen-name in the later years of his life, when he became the Green Crow calling raucously to Ireland from the other side of the Irish Sea. Asked by Jacobs to explain 'New Series' on the title-page of the first number, O'Casey replied, ' "The New Series" hinted—again, if my memory serves—at a few previous printings in leaflet form: "Death [*sic*] of Thomas Ashe" and "The G. Oul' Dame Britannia"; so the issue of a little booklet "Songs of the Wren" was a big step forward, or so I thought then. They were written around 1917–18–19.'

Most of the songs in this first number seem to have been written close to the time of publication. 'As I Wait in the Boreen for Maggie' first appeared in *Irish Opinion*, January 12, 1918 (C77); all others appear here in print for the first time. In 'The Man from the Daily Mail', the allusion to 'Conventions in the air' is probably a reference to Lloyd George's Convention of Irishmen that would submit to the Cabinet proposals for the future government of Ireland within the Empire. The Convention began its sittings at Trinity College, Dublin, on July 25, 1917, and after fifty-one meetings made its report on April 5, 1918. In a letter to Fergus O'Connor, the publisher, dated February 13, 1918, O'Casey suggests that *Songs of the Wren* ought to be advertised·in *Irish Opinion*, indicating that the work had been published.

On March 4 he writes 'I hope "The Songs of the Wren" are going well'
In the letter of February 13 he also expresses the wish, 'I think all my
future publications ought to bear on cover the name of Shaun O'Casey,
because many of my friends fail to discover me under the usual title that
appears thereon.' His wishes were honoured in the reprint which gives his
name as Sean O'Casey. For the remaining two titles in the *Songs of the Wren*
series, however, his name is given in each case as Sean O'Cathasaigh. The
reprint omits the publisher's name on the front cover but carries his advertisement on the back cover. It was issued probably April 1918. On March
8, 1918 O'Casey writes to Fergus O'Connor, 'I have seen today the proof
—the cover of the reprint of No 1 Songs of the Wren, & it is most attractive
& splendidly turned out. I really believe you ought to charge 2d for it.
It is really too good value for one Penny. When I compare it with the
rubbish that sells at a penny, the reflection is a painful one.' This was
a matter of contention between them for some time as O'Connor indicates
in his letter of February 17, 1918 to O'Casey: 'Of course the Songs of the
Wren should be a twopenny line but the public would look upon me
as a wholesale robber to charge 2d for a little thing like that'. On April
9 O'Casey writes indicating that the reprint is not yet published. His asking
fee for *Songs of the Wren No. 1* was £2 10s. The *Irish Opinion* for March
16, 1918 reported, 'Fergus O'Connor has published a four-page [*sic*] penny
songsheet, 'Songs of the Wren' by Sean O'Cathasaigh. Humourous and sentimental is the description & they make excellent chorus songs.' All of the
songs with the exception of 'The Man from the Daily Mail' were reprinted
in *Feathers from the Green Crow* (A40).

SONGS OF THE WREN NO. 2   1918

first edition
NEW SERIES No. 2. /   Amáin an Dreoilín . / Songs of the Wren /
HUMOUROUS AND SENTIMENTAL, / To well known Airs. / By Seán
Ó'caThasaigh, / Author of "The Grand Oul' Dame Brittannia." /
CONTENTS: / The Divil's Recruitin' Campaign. / *Air*: "Sargeant Willy Baily."
/ We've Captured the Cave of Machpelah. / *Air*: "Under the Willow Tree." / I
Don't Believe It, Do You? / *Air*: "I've Never been Courting Before." / The
Summer Sun is Tightly Folding. / *Air*: "The Golden Haired Niamh." / Since
Maggie Went Away. / *Air*: "The Auld House." / Merrily, merrily, all the day,
/ Merrily over the stile, a; / A lively heart goes all the way, / A sad one tires in
a mile, a!" / —*Shakespeare*. / PRICE – – ONE PENNY. / PUBLISHED BY /
FERGUS O'CONNOR, DUBLIN. / [all above save for the first line within
border of single rules, with decoration at each corner]

19 × 12.5cm.

[1], title-page as above; 2–7, text; [8], running title: Songs of the Wren,
by Sean O'Cathasaigh. /; publisher's advertisement.

White paper covers, the front cover serves as title-page.
Published April? 1918 at one penny; exact date and number of copies
undetermined.

Notes: This is the second in the series of *Songs of the Wren* written by O'Casey
and published by his friend Fergus O'Connor. The songs in this pamphlet
were probably written within the period November 1917–April 1918. 'We've
Captured the Cave of Machpelah' is a satirical comment on the British occupation of Hebron during the 1914–18 war. Hebron was captured by the British
troops under General Allenby advancing towards Jerusalem. In Hebron
is located the Cave of Machpelah, celebrated as the burial place of Abraham,
Isaac and Jacob. *The Times* reported the fall of Hebron in its issue for
December 8, 1917. O'Casey's songs were usually written quite close to the
events they celebrated. He sent an unpublished poem on the death of John
Redmond, leader of the Irish Parliamentary Party, to O'Connor on March
9, 1918, three days after Redmond's death on March 6. We can therefore
assume that 'We've Captured the Cave of Machpelah' would have been written
in the first half of December 1917. 'Since Maggie Went Away' was probably
written for Maire, his first love, as was 'The Summer Sun is Tightly Folding'.
A manuscript version of 'Since Maggie Went Away' exists in the New York
Public Library's Berg Collection with the title, 'Since Maura Went Away'.
Maire is the lady to whom he later dedicated his first published stage work,
Two Plays (A10). 'The Summer Sun is Tightly Folding' was reprinted with
four additional lines in each stanza in *The World of Sean O'Casey* (B53).
A manuscript version exists in the Berg Collection. 'The Divil's Recruitin'
Campaign' is an anti-conscription song. On April 9, 1918 Lloyd George
announced to the House of Commons the terms of a new Man-Power Bill,
by which conscription could be applied to Ireland by the signing of an
Order in Council at any time. O'Casey's ballad may be a reaction to this

or to the passing of the conscription bill on April 16. 'I Don't Believe It, Do You?' was probably written in late November 1917. The *Dublin Saturday Post* for December 1, 1917 describing the 'O'Toole Concert' held at the Empire Theatre on Saturday, November 24, reported: 'the applause of the night was reserved for Messrs. Smyth and O'Cathasaigh [Sean O'Casey] in the topical song "The Constitutional Movement Must Go On," and, in response to an arís [encore], "I Don't Believe It, Do You?"' A holograph version exists in the Berg Collection (E3). Three songs from this *Songs of the Wren No. 2* were reprinted in *Feathers from the Green Crow* (A40): 'We've Captured the Cave of Machpelah', 'Since Maggie Went Away' and 'The Divil's Recruitin' Campaign'.

ENGLAND'S CONSCRIPTION APPEAL TO IRELAND'S DEAD   1918

first edition
ENGLAND'S CONSCRIPTION APPEAL TO IRELAND'S DEAD / Air—
"Harp and Lion."

18 × 22.5cm.

Broadside. Caption title as above followed by a poem of five stanzas of eleven lines each, printed in double columns separated by a double vertical rule. Printed signature at end of fifth stanza: seán ó catasaig. Published April 1918 by Fergus O'Connor; exact date and number of copies undetermined.

Notes: This anti-conscription song was composed as a protest against the British Government's Bill to enforce conscription in Ireland. The Bill was passed in the House of Commons on April 16, 1918 by 301 to 103 votes. An Anti-Conscription Pledge drawn up by Éamon de Valera was proposed to be taken in every parish on the following Sunday, April 21. Opposition to conscription was so vehement and universal that it was abandoned on June 25, 1918. The same setting, with some leading removed, was used for the poem's subsequent publication in *More Wren Songs* (A8). Reprinted in *Rallying Songs* No. 2, 1918.

MORE WREN SONGS   1918

first edition

ᴀᵯᴚᴀɪɴ ᴀɴ ᴏᴚᴇoɪʟ́ɪɴ / [double rule] / MORE / [double rule] / WREN / [double rule] / SONGS / [double rule] / BY / ꜱᴇᴀɴ ó ᴄᴀᴄᴀꜱᴀɪ̵ꜱ./ [short rule] / Price = Twopence. / [all above within decorative border]

19 × 12.5cm.

[1], title-page as above; [2]–[8], text.

White paper covers, the front cover serves as title-page.
Published April/May? 1918 at twopence; exact date and number of copies undetermined.

Contents:
We Welcom [*sic*] the Aid of Japan
    Reprinted in *Rallying Songs* No 1 and in *Feathers from the Green Crow* (A40).
England's Conscription Appeal to Ireland's Dead
    First appeared as broadside (A7), reprinted in *Rallying Songs* No. 2.
The Bonnie Bunch of Roses, O!
    Reprinted in *Rallying Songs* No. 3 and in *Feathers from the Green Crow* (A40).
    This is a nationalist, anti-conscription song and must not be confused with O'Casey's pro-labour ballad of the same title printed in the *Irish Worker* January 11, 1913 (C10).
The Girl from the County Kildare
    Reprinted in *Rallying Songs* No. 3, in *Feathers from the Green Crow* (A40) and in *The Letters of Sean O'Casey* (A46).

Notes: The songs in this collection were most probably written in April 1918. 'We Welcom the Aid of Japan' is an obvious reference to the joint British and Japanese force of marines, which landed at Vladivostock on April 5, 1918. 'England's Conscription Appeal to Ireland's Dead' and 'The Bonnie Bunch of Roses, O!' are both responses to the British Government's Bill of April 16, 1918 which sought to enforce conscription in Ireland and would have been composed close to that time. 'The Girl from the County Kildare' was sent with a letter of April 10, 1918 to Fergus O'Connor but was returned to O'Casey without any plans for publication. The copy of *More Wren Songs* in the National Library of Ireland bears the accession date of September 7, 1918. We can therefore assume that the pamphlet was published sometime between April 16, and September 7, 1918. The fact that conscription in Ireland was abandoned on June 25, 1918 would narrow the date still further since the two anti-conscription songs would have lost their immediacy and appeal after June 25. It is much more likely that the pamphlet was published at the height of the anti-conscription protest in late April or in May 1918.

This was the last in the *Songs of the Wren* series written by O'Casey and published by Fergus O'Connor. O'Connor published some songs from the series in his *Rallying Songs* Nos 1 – 3 printed in the same year. The relationship between O'Casey and O'Connor, occasionally uneasy, did not survive beyond

1918. For his next publication O'Casey selected a more prestigious publisher. His respect for O'Connor was undiminished, however, as is shown by his surviving correspondence to him. In a letter of March 16, 1960 to the publisher's widow, Maude O'Connor, O'Casey wrote, 'I was sorry to hear of the death of Fergus. He was a fine Irishman, and with Miceal Ó Foley, and others then, were those who kept Ireland from sinking into a shapeless mass of shoneens.' The O'Connor Papers, which include holograph manuscript material of poems, songs and other material by O'Casey printed by O'Connor, together with a number of the playwright's letters to him, are now in the Berg Collection, New York Public Library (E2 and E3).

A9   THE STORY OF THE IRISH CITIZEN ARMY   1919

a. *first edition*
THE STORY OF THE / IRISH CITIZEN ARMY / By P. O CATHASAIGH /
MAUNSEL & CO., LTD. / DUBLIN AND LONDON 1919

18.3 × 12.4cm.

[i], half-title: THE STORY OF THE / IRISH CITIZEN ARMY / ; [ii], blank;
[iii], title-page as above; [iv], blank; [v]–[vi], Preface; [vii], Contents; [viii],
blank; [1]–62, text; [63]–67, Afterword; [68]–72, Appendix.

Paper covers, found in two states, the first state in dove-grey covers, the second
state, and seldom found, in white covers; front cover: THE STORY OF
THE / IRISH CITIZEN ARMY / By P. O CATHASAIGH / [14 lines of text
within border of rules] / MAUNSEL & CO., LTD. / *one shilling net* /;
publisher's list on both sides of back cover and on inside of front cover;
lettered and decorated in black.
Published March 1919 at 1s; number of copies undetermined.

b. *Oriole Chapbooks (photo-offset) edition*
Sean   O'Casey / [swelled   rule] / The / Story   of   the   Irish / Citizen   Army /
[publisher's mark] / *ORIOLE CHAPBOOKS*

19 × 11.5cm.

[i], title-page as above; [ii], publisher's description of book; rest as in first
edition.

Olive paper covers; front cover as title-page; publisher's advertisements on
inside front cover, and on both sides of back cover; lettered and decorated
in brown.
Published in 1970 at $1.25; number of copies printed unavailable.

c. *Talbot Press (photo-offset) edition*
THE STORY OF THE / IRISH CITIZEN ARMY / by P. Ó CATHASAIGH /
(Seán O'Casey) / [publisher's mark] / THE TALBOT PRESS / 89 TALBOT
STREET, DUBLIN 1.

18.5 × 12cm.

[a], half-title: THE STORY OF THE / IRISH CITIZEN ARMY /; [b], edition
statement; [i], blank; [ii], facsimile of front cover of first edition; [iii], title-
page as above; [iv], printing history, copyright; rest as in first edition.

Dark green leather; back cover blank; front cover: [the following within
border of rules] / The Story of / The / Irish Citizen / Army / P. Ó
CATHASAIGH / (Seán O'Casey) /; lettered and decorated in gold; grey end-
papers, all edges trimmed, top edge stained green.
Published March 11, 1971 at £3; 750 copies printed by O'Gorman Ltd,
Galway.

Notes: In the chapter 'Mrs Casside Takes a Holiday' in *Inishfallen, Fare Thee Well*

(A27) the playwright describes in some detail the financial and censorship difficulties he encountered with the publication of his first full-length work: 'It was a tiny booklet . . . and the Dublin publishers, Maunsel & Son, had promised to print it, provided it passed the British Censor. He [O'Casey] was to get fifteen pounds on its day of publication . . . [but] day after day, week after week, passed without showing any sign of the censored manuscript . . . When the manuscript did come back, it was a creased and tangled mass, with Sean's small, cramped longhand heavily underscored on every page with red, green, and blue pencil lines. With his eyes the way they were, it took him a week to get the sheets into orderly rotation. They were curious-looking documents now: the first Censor had encircled with red anything he thought to be dangerous to the British Government, peace, and God's truth; the second Censor, mind superior, went over what had been marked in red, and confirmed whatever he thought damaging by adding a green circle to the red one; and the third, mind *superiorum*, decided, finally, what was indeed dangerous, by encircling the red and green attempts with a lofty blue one of his own. After what seemed to be ages of labour, Sean filled the gaps in, the Censors, with a few more alterations, passed it, and Sean found himself waiting for fifteen pounds.' The tragicomic saga of his attempts to cash the £15 cheque to pay for his mother's last illness and funeral is also recounted in 'Mrs Casside Takes a Holiday'.

In correspondence Miss Frances-Jane French, the historian of Maunsel & Co., notes that the text was submitted to the Irish Press (Military) Censor on September 13, 1918. It was returned to Maunsel & Co. on September 15, 1918 with considerable deletions. On October 24, 1918 Chapter x and the Afterword were resubmitted to the censor and were passed on October 28. Proofs were submitted on October 29, 1918 and were passed the same day by the censor. In letters to Robert Hogan, quoted in *Feathers from the Green Crow* (A40), O'Casey further describes the fortunes of the manuscript at the hands of the military censor. He virtually disowns the work asserting that, because of the rigorous censorship, it was not the work he had written.

In the text of the work itself O'Casey takes care to stress its simple unpretentious nature, 'a humble attempt to reveal some of the hidden things correlative with the origin and development of the Irish Citizen Army.' The *Irish Book Lover* in its issue for April–May 1919 had the following statement: 'Messrs. Maunsel announce "The Story of the Irish Citizen Army," by P. O'Cathasaigh, who was a leading figure in that movement, and traces its formation during the Dublin Strike of 1913–14, and the part which it played in the subsequent history of Ireland.' The playwright always disavowed it as a historical chronicle. In a letter to Ronald Ayling dated December 29, 1963 he explained that it was never meant as an official 'history' of the I.C.A. but was intended to be one of a series, the first of which had been published in 1917 (A4): 'It was one of the "stories" planned by me—Story of Ashe, story of C.A., Story of Tone, Story of John Mitchel, etc. I wrote but the [first] two, for by this time I was thinking of better ways to write, and the Story of the C.A. ended the series.'

The name P. O'Cathasaigh on the title-page has occasioned a good deal of confusion. O'Casey's authorship was generally unknown until the early 1960s. The pamphlet has often been advertised in second-hand book catalogues as one published pseudonymously by the playwright and, as late as 1971, the

Talbot Press, Dublin, reissued the work and explained the 'pseudonym' by
saying that in 1919 'a writer expressing revolutionary ideas could find himself
at the mercy of a ruthless employer'. This is certainly true of the time, but it is
not true for this booklet. P. O'Cathasaigh is a misprint for S. O'Cathasaigh,
the name under which O'Casey had published most of his writings up to 1919.
In a letter to Prionsias Mac An Bheatha dated 1955, printed in the *Irish Times*,
June 2, 1971 (C645), O'Casey wrote, 'Yes, P. O'C and Sean O'C are one. The
"Story" was the first book I had published, so I knew little about proofs. I got
the pages to do, but not the title page. I imagine this wasn't sent because it was
so simple that no error could occur. It was on the title page that the big
mistake appeared. This is how it happened.'

The Appendix reprints the text of several documents: a manifesto
announcing the reorganisation of the Army, a handbill, a membership card;
the Constitution of the Irish Citizen Army; details from the first poster issued
by the Citizen Army Council in 1914. These documents were almost certainly
drafted by O'Casey during his term as honorary secretary of the Irish Citizen
Army. They are reprinted in *The Letters of Sean O'Casey* (A46). The text without
the Appendix was reprinted in *Feathers from the Green Crow* (A40).

Reviews: *The Story of the Irish Citizen Army* was reviewed by T. O'H. in *Irish
Independent*, Mar 17, 1919; by Eimar O'Duffy in *Irish Statesman*, July 12, 1919;
by L.O.B. in *Leader*, July 1971; by R. J. C[asey] in *An Leabharlann*, Sept 1971; by
Annraoi Beechhold in *Eire-Ireland*, autumn 1973.

a. *first edition*

TWO PLAYS / JUNO AND THE PAYCOCK / THE SHADOW OF A GUNMAN / BY / SEAN O'CASEY / MACMILLAN AND CO., LIMITED / ST. MARTIN'S STREET, LONDON / 1925

19 × 13cm.

[a]–[b], blank; [i], half-title: TWO PLAYS /; [ii], publisher's monogram and imprints; [iii], title-page as above; [iv], copyright and printing; v, Contents; [vi], blank; 1–113, *Juno and the Paycock*; [114], blank; 115–[199], *The Shadow of a Gunman*, printer's imprint at foot of [199]; [200], blank.

Grey-green boards with tan cloth spine. White label on front cover within border of rules: TWO PLAYS / SEAN O'CASEY / [all within decorative border]; back cover blank; spine: TWO / PLAYS / . . . / SEAN / O'CASEY [all above on white label within decorative border] / MACMILLAN & CO /; lettered and decorated in green; white end-papers, all edges trimmed; ivory dust-jacket, lettered and decorated in green.

Published February 10, 1925 at 7s 6d; 1500 copies printed by R. & R. Clark, Ltd, Edinburgh; reprinted December 1925, February, April and July 1926, 1927 and 1930.

Notes: The reprint of December 1925 and subsequent reprints omit the preliminary blank pages and have the variant preliminary pagination: v, dedication: TO / MAURA / AND TO / THE ABBEY THEATRE /; [vi], blank; vii, Contents; viii, details of first production and cast of *Juno and the Paycock*. At this time also details of first production and cast of *The Shadow of a Gunman* were included on p. 114. For the July 1926 and subsequent reprints, the frontispiece portrait of O'Casey by Augustus John was added. The portrait had been exhibited in the Chenil Gallery earlier in the year. The request had been made in a letter from O'Casey received on May 19, 1926 by Macmillan and Co., 'Augustus John has just painted a picture of me which I should very much like to have as a frontispiece to any new edition of "Two Plays" & "The Plough & the Stars." ' The dedication 'To Maura and to the Abbey Theatre' was retained in later editions of *Juno and the Paycock* (A11) but was dropped by the author in *Five Irish Plays* (A17), and in *Collected Plays*, vol. 1 (A29), although he retained other dedications to individual plays in the four volumes of *Collected Plays* (A29).

b. *American edition*

TWO PLAYS / JUNO AND THE PAYCOCK / THE SHADOW OF A GUNMAN / BY / SEAN O'CASEY / New York [in Gothic type] / THE MACMILLAN COMPANY / 1925 / *All rights reserved*

19 × 13cm.

[i], half-title: TWO PLAYS /; [ii], publisher's imprints; [iii], title-page as above; [iv], copyright, publication, printer's imprint; [v], Contents; / [vi], blank; [1]–199, text; [200], blank.

Green cloth; front cover has border of blind rules, decoration within blind-stamped oval border; back cover blank; spine: TWO / PLAYS / [decoration] / O'CASEY / MACMILLAN / .————. /; lettered and decorated in gold; white endpapers, top and bottom edges trimmed, front edge untrimmed; yellow dust-jacket, lettered and decorated in brown. Published February 10, 1925 at $2.25; 15,000 copies printed by J. J. Little and Ives Company, New York; reprinted January 1927, 1929.

Notes: With this work, O'Casey began his long association with Macmillan. Both plays had had prior stage performances at the Abbey Theatre, Dublin, *Juno and the Paycock* on March 3, 1924, *The Shadow of a Gunman* on April 12, 1923. In a letter of February 29, 1924 to Lady Gregory, O'Casey writes, 'I am glad to say that I expect The Gunman and Juno (in one volume) to be published shortly. I have just signed an agreement with Macmillan & Co.' On July 7, 1924 the manuscript was sent to the publishers. Macmillan requested James Stephens, the Irish author, to write a preface for the book. In a letter to Stephens dated September 28, 1924 O'Casey supported this request, 'As a Playwright I will be honoured if you should do as Messrs Macmillan suggest; as a Buttie I shall be delighted.' The preface, however, did not materialise. The publishers had little to say of this new author. The dust-jacket of the English edition carries two simple statements on the front flap: 'These plays have been produced with great success at the Abbey Theatre, Dublin. An eminent critic considers them the best and most promising work by a new man which has come from Ireland for some time, and Mr. James Stephens calls the author "the greatest dramatic find of modern times." '

The dust-jacket of the American edition cites the 'vivid portrayal of the recent chaos in Ireland, with fears, suspicions, rumours of violence, murder, and sudden death on every hand. Die-hards, Black and Tans, and the innocent victims of fruitless loyalties live again in these scenes from common life in a land where death seemed always lurking just outside the door.'

Reviews: *Two Plays* was reviewed in *Times Literary Supplement*, Feb 19, 1925; in *Irish Truth*, Feb 21, 1925; by M. Mac C. in *Sunday Independent* (Dublin), Feb 22, 1925; by T. C. M[urray] in *Irish Independent*, Feb 23, 1925; in *Waterford Evening News*, Feb 24, 1925; by A. E. Malone in *Dublin Magazine*, Mar 1925; in *Irish Sketch*, Mar 1925; in *Irish Times*, Mar 6, 1925; by George Russell (AE) in *Irish Statesman*, Mar 7, 1925; in *New York Times Book Review*, Mar 8, 1925; by Donald Douglas in *New York World*, Mar 8, 1925; by A. N. M. in *Manchester Guardian*, Mar 10, 1925 and in *Manchester Guardian Weekly*, Mar 13, 1925; by F. W. B. in *Boston Transcript*, Mar 14, 1925; in *Spectator*, Mar 14, 1925; by W. J. Lawrence in *Irish Statesman*, Mar 15, 1925; by J. R. Towse in *New York Evening Post and Literary Review*, Mar 21, 1921; by D. F. in *Christian Science Monitor*, Mar 24, 1925; by B. Dobrée in *Nation and Athenaeum*, Mar 28, 1925; by C. E. Lawrence in *Bookman*, Apr 1925; in *Calendar of Modern Letters*, Apr 1925; in *Irish Book Lover*, Apr 1925; in *Times of India*, Apr 8, 1925; in *New Statesman*, Apr 18, 1925; by A. E. Malone in *Irish Tribune*, May 7, 1925; by Padraic Colum in *Theatre Arts*, June 1925; by Stark Young in *New York Times*, June 14, 1925; by Joseph Campbell in *Saturday Review*, Aug 29, 1925; by William Dawson in *Studies*, Sep 1925; by James Agate in *Sunday Times*, Nov 1925; by Ivor Brown in *Saturday Review*, Nov 21, 1925; by D. McCarthy in *New Statesman*, Nov 28, 1925; by H. Shipp in *English Review*, Jan 1926; in *London Mercury*, Feb 1926; in *Catholic Times*, Mar 21, 1926; in *Bookman*, May 1926; by A. E. Malone in *Irish Tribune* (Cork), May 7, 1926; in *Criterion*, May 1927; in *Dial*, Mar 1928.

A11 JUNO AND THE PAYCOCK   1925

a. *first edition*
In *Two Plays*, 1925 (A10)

b. *first separate edition*
JUNO AND THE / PAYCOCK / BY / SEAN O'CASEY / MACMILLAN AND
CO., LIMITED / ST. MARTIN'S STREET, LONDON / 1928

17 × 11cm.

[i], half-title: JUNO AND THE PAYCOCK /; [ii], Macmillan monogram and
imprints; [iii], title-page as above; [iv], copyright, publication details, printer's
imprint; v, dedication: TO / MAURA / AND TO / THE ABBEY THEATRE /;
[vi], blank; vii, details of first production and cast; [viii], blank; 1–113, text;
[114], blank; [115]–[116], titles in The Caravan Library.

Maroon cloth; monogram SOC blind stamped on front cover within triple-
rule blind border at outer edges; back cover blank; spine: [ornament] /
JUNO / AND THE / PAYCOCK / SEAN / O'CASEY / [ornament] / MAC-
MILLAN & C⁰ / [ornament] /; spine lettered and decorated in gold; white
endpapers, all edges trimmed; orange dust-jacket, lettered and decorated in
black.
Published February 1928 at 3s 6d; 2000 copies printed by R. & R. Clark, Ltd,
Edinburgh; reprinted October 1928, June 1930, February 1937 (O'Casey
commented on this reprint in a letter dated January 29, 1937 to Harold
Macmillan, 'I like the blue cover on Juno, and think it much prettier
than the original reddish-brown one.'), January 1945; reissued in the New
Eversley Series 1946, 1947, 1948; reissued in Macmillan's Pocket Library
Series and with the St Martin's imprint added in 1954, 1955.

c. *acting edition*
JUNO AND THE / PAYCOCK / A Tragedy in Three Acts / BY / SEAN
O'CASEY / Copyright 1925 (A—814996) by Macmillan / Copyright 1932
(Acting Edition) by Samuel French, Ltd. / *All rights reserved* / [on left hand
side of vertical rule:] London / SAMUEL FRENCH, LTD. / Publishers / 26
SOUTHAMPTON STREET / STRAND, W.C.2 / [on right hand side of vertical
rule:] New York / SAMUEL FRENCH, INC. / Publishers / 25 WEST 45th
STREET

21.5 × 14cm.

[1], title-page as above; [2], fees, licence, costumes and wigs information,
printer's imprint; [3], cast of London production on November 16, 1925 at
the Royalty Theatre; [4], scene, period; 5–61, text; [62], blank; 63, words and
music of Boyle's songs; [64], blank; 65–7, property and furniture plots; 68,
lighting plot.

Blue paper covers; lettered and decorated in black; all edges trimmed.
Published October 24, 1932 at 2s 6d; 1000 copies printed by Butler &
Tanner Ltd, Frome and London; reprinted eleven times. French's Acting
Edition no. 2406.

Notes: The play was first produced at the Abbey Theatre, Dublin on March 3, 1924 directed by Michael J. Dolan. It was an immediate success with the audience. It was awarded the Hawthornden Prize for 1926 in spite of O'Casey's refusal to send a copy of the play for the competition or for inspection. Lady Gregory was the main speaker at the presentation in the Aeolian Hall, London. On receiving the Prize of £100 from Lord Oxford, O'Casey was asked to speak. Lady Gregory records in her *Journals* (B19) that O'Casey '. . . made first a little speech in Irish and then just simple thanks in English . . .' One of the stanzas quoted by Mary Boyle in Act III is from a poem by O'Casey, 'A Walk with Eros', first published in *Windfalls* (A16).

The Macmillan edition was a reprint of the text in *Two Plays* (A10). The acting edition was prepared by O'Casey himself, as related in *Rose and Crown* (A30), '. . . and, now, busy typing, cutting, and cutting his plays into a new form . . .' Bernard Shaw in a letter had advised against the selling of the amateur rights to Samuel French Ltd, but O'Casey's financial situation forced the sale. Many stage directions are added, mostly brief indications of movement or tone of voice, as well as a few minor changes in dialogue. Notable among the latter is the substitution of a different song for Mrs Madigan in the party scene in the second act. In the acting edition her song is changed from 'If I were a Blackbird' to Thomas Moore's 'The Young May Moon'. In Act III, the concluding three speeches of the scene between Mary Boyle and Jerry Devine are omitted. There is a more detailed description of the stage setting for Act II, and there are several additional instructions giving guidance to directors and actors, and adding a few comic touches to the stage business.

In the original version of the play, before publication, O'Casey had written an extra scene for the third act in which he described the actual shooting of Johnny. This scene was cut out during rehearsals for the original production. Details of this change and a number of others are recorded in '*Juno and the Paycock*: A Textual Study' by Ronald Ayling, *Modernist Studies*, II, 1 (1976). The play was subsequently reprinted in *Five Irish Plays* (A17), *Juno and the Paycock* and *The Plough and the Stars* (A26), *Collected Plays* (A29), *Selected Plays* (A32), *Three Plays* (A36) and *The Sean O'Casey Reader* (A45).

Juno and the Paycock, a motion picture, was released in 1930. It was directed by Alfred Hitchcock for British International. Barry Fitzgerald, Maire O'Neill, Edward Chapman, Sidney Morgan and Sara Allgood starred in the film.

A recording of *Juno and the Paycock* by Cyril Cusack Productions, Ireland, was made in Dublin in June 1955. The cast included Siobhán McKenna, Cyril Cusack, Seamus Kavanagh, Maire Kean, Godfrey Quigley, May Craig, Harry Brogan and others and was issued by Angel Records (35275–6) on February 27, 1956. The recording included a spoken introduction by O'Casey (B30). The text of the Introduction is included in the 'Programme Notes' (12 pp.) in the container. The recording was reissued on Seraphim Records on May 29, 1967. Released in the United Kingdom on EMI's HMV series.

A musical play, *Juno*, based on O'Casey's work, with book by Joseph Stein, music and lyrics by Marc Blitzstein, was completed in 1958. O'Casey wrote two songs for the musical. In the accompanying letter to Joseph Stein dated October 8, 1956 he said, 'I'm afraid, I've little talent for this special work, but I present them to you as (I think) the best I could do.' The play opened 'on the road' in Washington, D.C., with Shirley Booth, Melvyn

Douglas and Jack McGowran playing the principal parts. It underwent many revisions and the director, Vincent J. Donehue, was replaced by José Ferrer in an attempt to have a strong play ready for the Broadway début. It opened at the Winter Garden Theater, New York, on March 9, 1959. Reviews generally were unfavourable, Brooks Atkinson in the *New York Times*, March 15, 1959 remarked on the musical's failure to capture 'the biting humor and the blistering tragedy' of the original. The closing notice, effective at the end of the week, was posted on Monday, March 16, 1959.

The musical saga was taken a stage further when an adaptation of Blitzstein's *Juno*, entitled *Daarlin' Juno*, was given a trial production by the Williamstown Theatre Festival (Virginia) in the summer of 1974; it was revived at the Long Wharf Theatre, New Haven (Connecticut) from May 14 to June 11, 1976. The adaptation, made by Richard Maltby Jr and Geraldine Fitzgerald, contained additional lyrics by Maltby and the music was arranged and adapted by Thomas Fay. Directed by Arvin Brown, the play starred Geraldine Fitzgerald as Juno Boyle and Milo O'Shea as Captain Boyle. The Long Wharf programme note contained a conversation with Brown and Maltby in which the following dialogue explained the work's origins: 'Blitzstein's *Juno* came out in early '59. He had begun to write it in 1957–58, the year after *My Fair Lady* appeared. In Blitzstein's first conception, his *Juno* was to be a small, intimate show. But then, perhaps influenced by *My Fair Lady's* sensational success, Blitzstein's piece became transformed into something else, into an over-blown Broadway musical. His *Juno* was not successful, because it was in the wrong mode. Could you explain "the wrong mode"? In the Broadway expansion of Blitzstein's score, much of the original quality of his music and his lyrics got lost. Now we're working on our own show, *Daarling Juno*, as if Blitzstein were still alive. Luckily, tapes are available from his first score for *Juno*. On the other hand, the album of the actual Broadway production of *Juno* reveals considerable changes from Blitzstein's first intention. So you've gone back to Blitzstein's beginning? Yes, and in fact, the original score, preserved on the tapes, has become a kind of underground classic. Thanks to the tapes, Blitzstein's original vision has survived. What would you say about the relation of Blitzstein's first score to O'Casey's play? That first score had O'Casey's play inside it. But by the time the show reached Broadway, the O'Casey quality had somehow disappeared. Now, at Long Wharf, we're uncovering the O'Casey play within the score. We're restoring both play and music.'

THE SHADOW OF A GUNMAN   1925

a. *first edition*
In *Two Plays*, 1925 (A10)

b. *acting edition*
THE SHADOW OF / A GUNMAN / A Tragedy in Two Acts / BY SEAN
O'CASEY / COPYRIGHT 1926 (A—890233) BY MACMILLAN / COPYRIGHT 1932
(ACTING EDITION) BY SAMUEL FRENCH, LTD. / *All rights reserved* / [on left hand
side of vertical rule:] LONDON / SAMUEL FRENCH, LTD. / PUBLISHERS / 26
SOUTHAMPTON STREET / STRAND, W.C.2 / [on right hand side of
vertical rule:] NEW YORK / SAMUEL FRENCH, INC. / PUBLISHERS / 25 WEST
45TH STREET

21.5 × 14cm.

[1], title-page as above; [2], fees, licence, costumes and wigs information,
printer's imprint; [3], cast of London production on May 27, 1927 at the
Court Theatre, scene, period; [4], blank; 5–46, text; 47, stage diagram; 48,
property and furniture plot, lighting plot.

Blue paper covers; lettered and decorated in black; all edges trimmed.
Published October 17, 1932 at 2s 6d; 1000 copies printed by Butler & Tanner
Ltd, Frome and London. French's Acting Edition no. 1946.

Notes: The Shadow of a Gunman was written in 1922. In a letter of April 10, 1922
to Lennox Robinson, O'Casey tells of the beginning: 'I am gathering together
the material for "On the Run" and have already started it.' The title *On the
Run* was abandoned before the play's first production in Dublin. In a letter of
May 22, 1937 to Kurt Wittig and quoted in *Sean O'Casey als Dramatiker* (B7) he
tells of the change: '"On the Run" was first title thought of; there happened
to be a play in existence already of that name, so, for copyright reasons, the
better name was given.' By October 9, 1922 the playwright reports progress to
Robinson: 'The draft of the first act is finished and most of the second . . . It
deals with the difficulties of a poet who is in continual conflict with the
disturbances of a tenement house, and is built on the frame of Shelley's
phrase, "Ah me, alas, pain, pain ever, forever".' On November 17, 1922 he
finally reported to Robinson, 'I have just completed "On The Run." It is a
tragedy in two acts—at least I have called it so. The play is typed—not
faultlessly, I'm afraid—but the result is obviously immeasurably above my
fiendish hand-writing. I have to thank you and Lady Gregory for the self-
sacrifice displayed by the reading of such a manuscript as "The Crimson In
The Tri-colour." ' Unfortunately, the Abbey Theatre director was at that time
on holiday in Spain; he did not return to Dublin until December. However,
O'Casey had left the typescript of the play with the theatre's secretary, J.H.
Perrin, and it is therefore likely that the managing director of the theatre read
it before Robinson did. This is suggested by the way Robinson opens his letter
dated February 26, 1923: 'I am very glad to say that Mr. Yeats likes your play
"On the Run" very much and we shall try and put it on before the end of our
season. Lady Gregory hasn't read it yet but I am sure her opinion of the play

will be the same as Mr. Yeats. The play will need a little cutting here and there. I like it very much myself.' The fifth play by O'Casey to be submitted to the Abbey, *The Shadow of a Gunman* was first performed at that theatre on April 12, 1923. The play was an instant success and O'Casey's reputation was made almost overnight. It was the third of his plays to appear in London, following *Juno and the Paycock* and *The Plough and the Stars*; it was first staged there on May 27, 1927.

In this acting edition, the dialogue is the same as in *Two Plays* (A10), but the stage directions are fuller and more detailed. As with *Juno and the Paycock* (A11), O'Casey's financial situation forced the sale of the amateur rights to Samuel French. He records the story in *Rose and Crown* (A30), 'The play agents, French and Son, had offered three hundred pounds for the world amateur rights of his Irish plays, provided a prompt copy of each play was given to them; and Sean and Eileen . . . were now busy in the bungalow making out three [copies] of them . . .' The playwright's wife in *Sean* (B68) describes the event, 'Unwillingly, we accepted the offer for the play rights; and Samuel French asked us to do prompt-copies, with a series of stage plans that I produced with great labour after we had taken hours and hours to draw and measure them, a task we loathed.'

The three verses quoted by Davoren in the play were subsequently published as part of two poems, 'A Walk with Eros' and 'Sunshadows', in *Windfalls* (A16). This is the only separate publication of the play. It was subsequently reprinted in *Five Irish Plays* (A17), *Collected Plays* (A29), *Selected Plays* (A32) and in *Three Plays* (A36).

THE PLOUGH AND THE STARS 1926

a. *first edition*
THE PLOUGH AND / THE STARS / A TRAGEDY IN FOUR ACTS / BY / SEAN O'CASEY / WITH A PORTRAIT / MACMILLAN AND CO., LIMITED / ST. MARTIN'S STREET, LONDON / 1926

19 × 13cm.

[i], half-title: THE PLOUGH AND THE STARS /; [ii], publisher's monogram and imprints; frontispiece, portrait of O'Casey by P. Tuohy; [iii], title-page as above; [iv], copyright, printing; [v], dedication: TO THE GAY LAUGH OF MY MOTHER / AT THE GATE OF THE GRAVE /; [vi], blank; vii, first production, cast, producer; viii, characters, scenes, time; 1–[137], text, printer's imprint at foot of [137]; [138], blank; 1–4, publisher's advertisements; [5]–[6], blank.

Grey-green boards with tan cloth spine; white label on front cover within border of rules: THE / PLOUGH / AND THE / STARS / [all within decorative border]; back cover blank; spine: THE / PLOUGH / AND THE / STARS / ... / SEAN / O'CASEY / [all above on white label within decorative border] / MACMILLAN & CQ /; lettered and decorated in green; white endpapers, top edge trimmed and stained green, other edges untrimmed; ivory dust-jacket lettered and decorated in green.
Published February 1926 at 5s; 2000 copies printed by R. & R. Clark, Ltd, Edinburgh; reprinted April 1926 (2000 copies), July 1926 (1000 copies), 1927 (1000 copies), 1930 (1000 copies), 1935 (1000 copies); 3000 copies were issued in February 1937 in the Caravan Library in the same setting, at 2s 6d. In the July 1926 and subsequent reprints, the frontispiece portrait by Tuohy was replaced by the Augustus John portrait; the Caravan Library issue does not contain either portrait.

b. *American edition*
THE PLOUGH AND / THE STARS / A TRAGEDY IN FOUR ACTS / BY / SEAN O'CASEY / New York [in black letter type] / THE MACMILLAN COMPANY / 1926 / *All rights reserved*

19 × 13cm.

[i], half-title: THE PLOUGH AND THE STARS /; [ii], publisher's monogram and imprints; [iii], title-page as above; [iv], copyright, publication date, printer's imprint; [v], dedication as in first edition; [vi], blank; vii, first production, cast, producer; viii, characters, scenes, time; 1–136, text.

Green cloth; front cover has design blind stamped within single ruled blind border at outer edges; back cover blank; spine: [rule] / THE / PLOUGH / AND / THE / STARS / [ornament] / O'CASEY / [centred dot] MACMILLAN [centred dot] / [rule] /; lettered and decorated in gold; cream endpapers, all edges trimmed; yellow dust-jacket, lettered and decorated in brown.
Published April 6, 1926 at $1.50; 2000 copies printed by Ferris Printing Co.; reprinted October 15, 1935.

c. *acting edition*

THE PLOUGH AND / THE STARS / A Tragedy in Four Acts / BY / SEAN
O'CASEY / COPYRIGHT 1926 (A–890233) BY MACMILLAN / COPYRIGHT 1932
(ACTING EDITION) BY SAMUEL FRENCH, LTD. / *All rights reserved* / [on left hand
side of vertical rule:] LONDON / SAMUEL FRENCH, LTD. / PUBLISHERS / 26
SOUTHAMPTON STREET / STRAND, W.C.2 / [on right hand side of vertical
rule:] NEW YORK / SAMUEL FRENCH, INC. / PUBLISHERS / 25 WEST 45TH
STREET

21.5 × 14cm.

[1], title-page as above; [2], fees, licence, costumes and wigs information,
printer's imprint; 3, cast of production on May 12, 1926 at the Fortune
Theatre, London, scene, period; [4], blank; 5–70, text; 71, lighting plot;
72–9, property and furniture plot; 80, notes.

Blue paper covers, lettered and decorated in black; all edges trimmed.
Published October 24, 1932 at 2s 6d; 1000 copies printed by Butler & Tanner,
Frome and London; reprinted eight times. French's Acting Edition no. 625.

Notes: The original title for the work was *The Easter Lily Aflame* but this was
soon deposed in favour of the name of the banner of the Irish Citizen
Army: as the author wrote in the *New York Times*, December 4, 1960 (C544),
'It was this flag that fired in my mind the title for the play; and the events
that swirled around the banner and that of the Irish Volunteers, the Tricolor
of green, white and orange . . . gave me all the humour, pathos and dialogue
that fill the play.'

The Plough and the Stars was written between October 1924 and August
1925. O'Casey had thought of the play earlier, as shown in his letter of July
22, 1924 to Lady Gregory: 'I am working at Penelope's Lovers, but have not
yet started the more ambitious play "The Plough & the Stars."' In a further
letter some time in October 1924, he tells her, 'I am anxious to start work
on "The Plough and the Stars" which, dealing with Easter Week, will bring to
our remembrance "old unhappy, far off days, and battles long ago."' By
February 22, 1925 he was 'working slowly at "The Plough and the Stars."' On
August 12, 1925 he again writes to Lady Gregory, 'Today, I have to type the
Caste [*sic*], and then, after a final look at the Script, bring it with hope to
the Abbey Theatre Directorate. I have really worked very hard at it for the
last few months, and am glad the "Labourer's task is o'er" – for the present.'
On September 9, 1925 he wrote the good news to Macmillan & Co.: 'You
may be interested to hear that a new four act tragedy of mine – "The Plough
and the Stars" – has been accepted by the Abbey Theatre, and that Mr. Yeats,
Lady Gregory and Mr. Robinson think it a fine play, possibly the best work I
have yet done.' At the same time, the directors feared the work was too
outspoken, sexually, and wanted some changes in dialogue and the deletion of
the song at the end of Act II (it was retained in the printed text). The
dramatist wrote to Lady Gregory on September 11, 1925, 'I am going up on
Sunday to Mr Yeats to speak about some cuts in my play . . . I've no objection
to cuts made by him, or you or Mr. Robinson. My little song, I think, has to go.
Speaking, to me across the telephone, Mr. Yeats said he thought "The Plough"
a wonderful play, and I am very pleased to rank with you, and Yeats, Robinson
and Synge in the great glory of the Abbey Theatre.' Subsequently on

November 1, he told the same correspondent, 'I have altered the love scene in the first act of "The Plough," and the alteration has eliminated any possibly objectionable passage.'

The play opened at the Abbey Theatre, Dublin, on Monday, February 8, 1926. It was rumoured that the new play would provoke protest and violence. Michael J. Dolan refused to direct the play, a chore which was handled by Lennox Robinson. Casting too was a problem, as O'Casey tells in a letter of February 10, 1926 to Sarah Allgood, 'We had a little bit of trouble when the play was being cast, Miss Crowe objecting to a good deal of the dialogue in her part (grand dialogue too) & May Craig had to take her place.' All tickets for the opening night, as well as for some of the following nights, were sold out shortly after the play was advertised. It was enthusiastically received on the first three nights. On the fourth night, Thursday, February 11, rioting broke out during the Rosie Redmond scene. On the entrance of the flag into the pub, the police had to be called to restore order. O'Casey defended the play in letters to the *Irish Times*, February 19 (C101), and to the *Irish Independent* on February 20 and February 26 (C102), and also in a public debate on March 1, 1926. *The Plough and the Stars* was also attacked in the correspondence columns in the Dublin newspapers, but survived to become O'Casey's most popular play and one of the best loved plays in the Abbey Theatre repertoire.

Gabriel Fallon in his *Sean O'Casey, the Man I Knew* (B48) remarks that much of the dialogue of O'Casey's rejected script *The Crimson and* [sic] *the Tri-Colour* had found its way into *The Plough and the Stars*, but he may have been thinking of the one-act play 'The Cooing of Doves'. O'Casey has described in the *New York Times*, December 4, 1960 (C544) how the latter work, rejected earlier by the Abbey Theatre, 'now formed the much-praised second act of [*The Plough and the Stars*] . . . it went in with but a few minor changes.' Two characters from *The Crimson in the Tricolour*, however, were developed into significant figures in *The Plough and the Stars*, as O'Casey explained in a letter to Jack Carney dated March 28, 1942: ' "Crimson in the Tricolour" . . . had in it a character posed on A[rthur] Griffith, [and] a Labour Leader, mean and despicable . . . and the "noble proletarian" in it was later "The Covey" in *The Plough and the Stars*, as was a carpenter who developed into "Fluther." '

Although all editions of *The Plough and the Stars* contain the short episode with The Woman from Rathmines in Act III, the author himself in later years regarded it as redundant. He requested the Abbey Theatre to remove it from their productions of the play. In the essay 'Overture', in *The Green Crow* (A34), he criticised the scene, saying that the Woman 'had neither rhyme nor reason for being there; a character that was in every way a false introduction; one who could have no conceivable connection with any of the others from the play's beginning to the Play's end.'

Patrick Tuohy, the artist for the original frontispiece portrait, was born in Dublin in 1894. He painted some of his contemporaries at a time when they were little known. He did portraits of James Joyce and his father, and James Stephens among others. O'Casey was not satisfied with the Tuohy portrait as a frontispiece and on May 19, 1926 he wrote to Macmillan and Co., 'Augustus John has just painted a picture of me . . . The picture is a wonderful work, & it must, if at all possible, be added to the "Two Plays," & supersede the one done by Tuohy in "The Plough & the Stars." ' Writing to Gabriel

Fallon a few days earlier on May 13 he remarks, 'Augustus John says Tuohy's picture of me is a splendid drawing of somebody else.' The Caravan Library issue did not have a frontispiece portrait. It was issued at the time of the public release of the film version.

The Plough and the Stars was O'Casey's fifth play to be produced at the Abbey Theatre, and was the first of his plays to be published separately. It was introduced on the front cover of the dust-jacket of the English edition as follows: 'This play, recently produced at the Abbey Theatre, Dublin, is by the author of *Juno and the Paycock* and *The Shadow of a Gunman*.' *The Plough and the Stars* was subsequently reprinted in *Five Irish Plays* (A17), in *Juno and the Paycock and The Plough and the Stars* (A26), in *Collected Plays* (A29), in *Selected Plays* (A32), in *Three Plays* (A36) and in *The Sean O'Casey Reader* (A45).

The Plough and the Stars, a motion picture with script adapted by Dudley Nichols, was released in January 1937. It was directed by John Ford, produced by Cliff Reid and Robert Sisk for RKO-Radio. Barbara Stanwyck, Preston Foster, Barry Fitzgerald, Una O'Connor and Dennis O'Dea starred in the film.

Dublin Song, an opera in three acts based on O'Casey's *The Plough and the Stars*, with libretto by Edward Mabley and music by Elie Siegmeister, was first produced at Louisiana State University on March 16, 1959. It had its European première at the Grand Théâtre Municipale, Bordeaux, in March 1970, directed by Roger Lalande.

Reviews: *The Plough and the Stars* was reviewed by Ivor Brown in *Saturday Review*, Apr 10, May 22, 1926; in *Times Literary Supplement*, Apr 15, 1926; by Y. S. in *Irish Truth*, Apr 17, 1926; in *Catholic Herald*, Apr 17, 1926; by J. R. Towse in *New York Evening Post Literary Review*, Apr 24, 1926; by T. P. O'Connor in *T. P.'s and Cassell's Weekly*, Apr 24, 1926; by S. R. Littlewood in *Bookman* (London), May 1926; by George Russell in *Irish Statesman*, May 1, 1926; in *Northern Whig* (Belfast), May 1, 1926; by W. P. Eaton in *New York Herald Tribune Books*, May 16, 1926; by Brooks Atkinson in *New York Times Book Review*, May 16, 1926; by St John Ervine in *Observer*, May 16, 1926; in *Catholic Times*, May 21, 1926; in *Living Age*, May 22, 1926; by N. G. Royde-Smith in *Outlook* (London), May 22, 1926; by D. McCarthy in *New Statesman*, May 29, 1926; in *Nation* (London), May 29, 1926; in *Spectator*, May 29, 1926; by H. Shipp in *English Review*, June 1926; by Padraic Colum in *Saturday Review of Literature*, June 12, 1926; in *Contemporary Review*, July 1926; in *Dublin Magazine*, July–Sep 1926; by M. Waldman in *London Mercury*, July 1926; in *Independant* (Boston), Sep 18, 1926; by George Jean Nathan in *American Mercury*, Oct 1926; in *Booklist*, Nov 1926; by W. M. C. In *Queen's Quarterly*, Apr–June 1927; in *Criterion*, May 1927; by Oliver M. Saylor in *Saturday Review of Literature*, Dec 10, 1927.

THE SILVER TASSIE   1928

a. *first edition*
THE SILVER TASSIE / A TRAGI-COMEDY / IN FOUR ACTS / BY / SEAN
O'CASEY / WITH A PORTRAIT OF THE AUTHOR BY / EVAN WALTERS
/ MACMILLAN AND CO., LIMITED / ST. MARTIN'S STREET, LONDON /
1928

19 × 13cm.

[i], half-title: THE SILVER TASSIE /; [ii], publisher's monogram and
imprints; frontispiece, portrait of O'Casey by Evan Walters; [iii], title-page as
above; [iv], copyright, printer's imprint; [v], dedication: TO / EILEEN / WITH
THE YELLOW DAFFODILS / IN THE GREEN VASE /; [vi], blank; vii,
acknowledgement to Messrs Francis, Day & Hunter for use of music; viii,
characters, scenes; 1–132, text; 133–40, Songs and Chants in the Play.

Grey-green boards with tan cloth spine; white label on front cover within
border of rules: THE / SILVER TASSIE / SEAN O'CASEY / [all within
decorative border]; back cover blank; spine: THE / SILVER / TASSIE / . . . /
SEAN / O'CASEY [all above on white label within decorative border] /
MACMILLAN & Cº /; lettered and decorated in green; white endpapers, top
edge trimmed and stained green, other edges untrimmed; ivory dust-jacket
lettered and decorated in green.
Published June 12, 1928 at 7s 6d; 3000 copies printed by R. & R. Clark,
Ltd, Edinburgh; reprinted 1929 (2000 copies), 1930 (1000 copies).

b. *American edition*
THE SILVER TASSIE / *A TRAGI-COMEDY IN FOUR ACTS* / BY / SEAN
O'CASEY / New York [in black letter type] / THE MACMILLAN COMPANY /
1928 / *All rights reserved.*

19 × 13cm.

[i], half-title: THE SILVER TASSIE /; [ii], publisher's monogram and
imprints; frontispiece, portrait of O'Casey by Evan Walters; [iii], title-page
as above; [iv], copyright, publication, setting, printer's imprint; [v], dedication;
[vi], blank; [vii], acknowledgement to Milton Weil Music Company for use
of music; viii, characters, scenes; 1–131, text; [132] blank; 133–40, Songs
and Chants in the Play.

Green cloth; border of blind rules on front cover; back cover blank; spine:
[rule] / THE / SILVER / TASSIE / [ornament] / O'CASEY / –MACMILLAN– /
[rule] /; lettered and decorated in gold; white endpapers; top and bottom
edges trimmed, front edges untrimmed.
Published July 3, 1928 at $1.75; 2307 copies printed by the Cornwall Press,
Inc.; set up by Brown Brothers Linotypers.

Notes: The Silver Tassie must rank as the most crucial of O'Casey's plays
since it severed his connections with the Abbey Theatre, and left him a
playwright without a theatre. The play was written between the end of 1926

and the beginning of 1928. On August 14, 1926 he writes to Macmillan and Co. that he 'will probably commence a new play shortly', and on December 24, 1926 he says in a letter to Lady Gregory 'I am now—very tranquilly—working on a new play.' To Gabriel Fallon on January 5, 1927 he sends a letter saying 'The Play writes well—a double event of a joking pun. Haven't much of it done yet.' By April 25 the first act was finished, and he was starting on the second. On September 14, 1927 he wrote again to Fallon: 'I have just altered a good deal of the second act—an idea came to me after I had passed the middle of the act, & I liked it so well that I felt that idea was meant to leaven the whole lump. I start the third act tomorrow & afterwards the fourth act, & then revision, & then an exultant weariness.'

The Silver Tassie was finished by February 1928 when O'Casey wrote to Lady Gregory: 'I'll send a copy to The Abbey, and will send a copy to no-one else till I get word that the play has been received . . . I hope it may be suitable, and that you will like it. Personally, I think the play is the best work I have yet done. I have certainly put my best into it, and have written the work solely because of love and deep feeling that what I have written should have been written. . . . Most of the Second Act is to be sung. A good deal to Gregorian chant, and some to the airs of songs and a hymn.' On March 8, 1928 the playwright wrote to Macmillan: 'I have just finished my new play, "The Silver Tassie", and am having it typed in a better way than I have done it. As soon as this is done, I want to have a talk with you about the publication of musical notation in the volume (a good deal of the second act is to be sung to Gregorian chant) and some airs that I have joined to words of my own. I hope you may find the play acceptable—I myself am satisfied, and think the work by far the best I have yet done.' Having submitted the work to the Abbey Theatre for production, the dramatist wrote to Lennox Robinson on April 5, 1928: 'Assuming acceptance of "The Silver Tassie," I send above list of those whom I imagine would fill the principal parts of the play.' The Abbey's rejection of the play sparked a heated correspondence which was published in the *Observer*, June 3, 1928 (C107) and several other newspapers; a more comprehensive selection of letters between O'Casey and the Abbey directors appeared in the *Irish Statesman* for June 9, 1928 (C109). O'Casey had submitted the letters to Macmillan and Co. suggesting that they be printed as a preface to the published play. Daniel Macmillan replied in a letter dated May 10, 1928, 'We have read through your correspondence with the Abbey Theatre people with great interest, but we think that on the whole it would be a mistake to publish it in the book as a preface, so I am returning it to you.' Most of the documents relating to the play were printed in the appendix to Robert Hogan's *The Experiments of Sean O'Casey* (B39) and in *The Letters of Sean O'Casey* (A46). O'Casey's defence of the play 'A Stand on *the Silver Tassie*' which he sent to W. B. Yeats on November 23, 1935 is printed in Saros Cowasjee's *Sean O'Casey, The Man Behind the Plays* (B45). *Rose and Crown* (A30) and *Blasts and Benedictions* (A44) both contain further views of O'Casey on the play.

The Silver Tassie was the first of his plays to be published without a prior production. It was first played at the Apollo Theatre, London, on October 11, 1929. The production was designed by Augustus John and directed by Raymond Massey. Lady Gregory, after seeing the London presentation, said in a letter to Yeats which she records in her *Journals* (B19), 'I am troubled because having seen the play I believe we ought to have accepted it.' On August 12, 1935 the play was performed at the Abbey Theatre, Dublin.

The frontispiece by Evan Walters was specifically recommended by the playwright in a letter of March 31, 1928 to Macmillan: 'A young artist friend of mine—who, if he lives, will make his name—would, I think, do a charcoal sketch portrait as a frontispiece for the book, & I should like to know what you think of the suggestion. There is no doubt of the young fellow's genius, & a sketch by him in my book might help to bring notice to his work, and the drawing would add to the publication.' Eileen O'Casey in her book *Sean* (B68) refers to the dedication: 'In the spring I always filled a large green vase with daffodils. Sean, who looked forward to this, dedicated the book of the *Tassie* to "Eileen, with the yellow daffodils in the green vase." '

The text of the play was revised for its subsequent publication in *Collected Plays* (A29) where the text is described as a 'Stage Version'. The alterations owe a great deal to the playwright's co-operation with Raymond Massey on the 1929 London production. A copy of the text of the London 1928 edition with the author's manuscript corrections for the *Collected Plays* revision is in the Berg Collection, New York Public Library. The stage version of *The Silver Tassie* was reprinted in *Selected Plays* (A32), *Three More Plays* (A42) and *The Sean O'Casey Reader* (A45).

Reviews: *The Silver Tassie* was reviewed in the *Irish Times*, June 14, 1928; by Ivor Brown in *Manchester Guardian*, June 18, 1928; in *Irish News* (Belfast), June 23, 1928; by Ivor Brown in *Saturday Review*, June 23, 1928; by Sylvia Lynd in *Daily News* (London), June 27, 1928; by A. E. Malone in *Irish Book Lover*, July-Dec. 1928; by W. A. Darlington in *Daily Telegraph*, July 5, 1928; in *Times Literary Supplement*, July 5, 1928; in *Yorkshire Evening Post* (Leeds), July 7, 1928; by St John Ervine in *Observer*, July 8, 1928; by A. Newsome in *New Age*, July 12, 1928; by Y. O. [George Russell] in *Irish Statesman*, July 21, 1928; in *An Poblacht*, July 28, 1928; in *Boston Transcript*, Aug 11, 1928; in *Independent* (Boston), Aug 18, 1928; in *New York Evening Post Literary Review*, Sep 1, 1928; by M. S. P. in *Dublin Magazine*, Oct-Dec 1928; by Jane Dransfield in *Saturday Review of Literature*, Dec 15, 1928; in *Criterion*, Apr 1929.

A15   WITHIN THE GATES   1933

a. *first edition*
WITHIN THE GATES / A PLAY OF FOUR SCENES / IN A LONDON
PARK / BY / SEAN O'CASEY / MACMILLAN AND CO., LIMITED / ST.
MARTIN'S STREET, LONDON / 1933

19 × 12.5cm.

[i], half-title: WITHIN THE GATES /; [ii], publisher's monogram and
imprints; [iii], title-page as above; [iv], copyright, printer's imprint; v, Notes
for Production; vi, notes for front curtain; vii, characters; viii, scenes; 1–169,
text; [170], blank; [171], text title: MUSIC TO THE PLAY /; [172], blank;
173–203, Music to the Play; [204], blank.

Grey-green boards with tan cloth spine; white label on front cover within
border of rules: WITHIN / THE GATES / SEAN O'CASEY / [all within
decorative border] /; back cover blank; spine: WITHIN / THE / GATES / . . .
/ SEAN / O'CASEY [all above within decorative border on white label]
/ MACMILLAN & Cº /; lettered and decorated in green; white endpapers,
top edge trimmed and stained green, other edges untrimmed; ivory dust-jacket,
lettered and decorated in green.
Published November 24, 1933 at 7s 6d; 2000 copies printed by R. & R.
Clark, Ltd, Edinburgh; reprinted 1934 (1500 copies).

b. *American (offset) edition*
WITHIN THE GATES / A PLAY OF FOUR SCENES / IN A LONDON PARK
/ BY / SEAN O'CASEY / NEW YORK / THE MACMILLAN COMPANY /
1934

19 × 13cm.

[i], half-title; WITHIN THE GATES /; [ii], publisher's monogram and
imprints; [iii], title-page as above; [iv], copyright, printer's imprint; v, Notes
for Production; vi, notes for front curtain; vii, characters; viii, scenes; 1–169,
text; [170], blank; [171], text title: MUSIC TO THE PLAY /; [172], blank;
173–203, Music to the Play; [204], blank.

Green cloth; border of blind rules on front cover; back cover blank; spine:
WITHIN / THE / GATES / . / O'CASEY / MACMILLAN / ⊔ . /; lettered and
decorated in gold; white endpapers, top and bottom edges trimmed, front
edge untrimmed.
Published January 16, 1934 at $1.75; 5200 copies printed by The Polygraphic
Company of America, New York; reprinted May 1934, November 1934,
January 1935, February 1935.

Notes: In her book *Sean* (B68), Eileen O'Casey tells of the inspiration for *Within
the Gates*: 'Since he reached London, Hyde Park, and Speakers' Corner
especially, had stirred his imagination, and he intended to write a play of four
seasons that would be set entirely in the Park.' The work was initially entitled
'The Green Gates'. He had begun it in 1928 shortly after completing *The Silver
Tassie* (A14). In the essay 'No Flowers for Films', in *The Green Crow* (A34),

O'Casey tells of setting out to do 'a film of Hyde Park, London, its life, its colour, its pathos, its pattern; its meaning to the rest of England.' Mrs O'Casey describes the progress in *Sean*: 'Originally he had imagined it as a film in which everything, from flower-beds to uniforms, would be stylised. Beginning at dawn and ending at midnight, to the soft chime of Big Ben in the distance, it would be "geometrical and emotional, the emotions of the living characters to be shown against their own patterns and the patterns of the Park." Having got so far, he wrote to Alfred Hitchcock, and when Hitchcock and his wife dined with us Sean explained his ideas to an apparently responsive hearer. Hitchcock and he talked excitedly. They parted on the same terms, with the prospect of another immediate meeting, and Sean never heard again.' The playwright's account of this episode appears in 'A Long Ashwednesday' in *Rose and Crown* (A30). A rough draft of O'Casey's highly stylised film scenario is among his manuscripts in the Berg Collection, New York Public Library. After Hitchcock's failure to follow up his initial interest O'Casey then turned the film into a play which became *Within the Gates*.

On October 5, 1932 the dramatist told George Jean Nathan in a letter: 'I am working on my new play; but the work is hard, and the going is damned slow.' The following year, in another letter to Nathan, dated May 30, he picks up the same refrain: 'I am working hard towards the completion of my new play, *Within the Gates*. It is the hardest job that I have ever attempted, making me exclaim with Yeats, "my curse on plays that have to be set up in fifty ways." All the action takes place in a Park; it is in four scenes, Spring (morning), Summer (noon), Autumn (evening) and Winter (night), so, to keep the action in the Park, and keep it going, is a job. There will be music, songs sung singly and in chorus, and though the work may not be a great one, or even fine, I'm sure it will be interesting.' Two months later, on July 23, 1933 he wrote to Macmillan and Co., 'I have just finished a new play called "Within the Gates." '

The dilemma of an experimental playwright deprived of what he most needed – theatrical production of each new work prior to publication so that he might better understand the practical problems involved and have an opportunity to solve them – is one with which O'Casey was continually faced from *The Silver Tassie* (A14) onward. The situation adversely affected the writer in two ways: firstly, there was the difficulty of publishing revised versions of the plays once they had been printed and, secondly, there was the reluctance of theatre managers to stage work that had been in print for some time. It is the latter problem which occasioned the playwright's lament to George Jean Nathan on November 30, 1933: 'Alas, you will know by now that the play has been published. I had no chance to postpone the publication, for I was in desperate need of the advance royalties given by Macmillan. I have had a bad two years of it, and they came just in time. It can't be helped now, and I can only hope the publication of the play won't harm the production there [in the United States] or here [England].' His fears were unfounded in this case; *Within the Gates* was staged the following year in both countries. In another regard, however, his worst fears were realised with the play's first presentation. In *Rose and Crown* (A30), writing of this period of his life, he describes the dangers facing a pioneer in drama: he 'knew that the more he tried to put into a play, the less chance he'd have of a production in England, so he had to decide whether he would model a play so as to squeeze it towards triviality, or persist in experimental imagination, and suffer for it. On the other hand, if he did get a production of an experimental play, he would be forced to submit to a rag-and-tag one, one that would be cheapened so much that half the life would be gutted out of it. The English critics, by and large, would measure the play by its furtive, underhand performance, so giving the play no chance of a better and deserving production in the future.' When *Within the Gates* was first staged – at the Royalty Theatre, London, on February 7, 1934 – it was, in the view of O'Casey and many of the critics, a lifeless 'rag-and-tag' production. Financially, the production was a failure; O'Casey had less than twenty pounds after expenses and the play closed after twenty-eight performances. The American production opened at the National Theatre on October 22, 1934, directed by Melvyn Douglas, and featuring Lillian Gish and Bramwell Fletcher. O'Casey visited New York for the première. The play had a run of one hundred and one performances before closing on January 12, 1935. A projected tour of Philadelphia, Boston, Providence and ten other cities was abandoned at the end of the Philadelphia engagement. While it was playing in Philadelphia, Mayor Mansfield of Boston asked that the performances scheduled for Boston be cancelled. A hearing before the Board of Censorship in Boston supported the mayor's view, and the play was returned to New York where it ran for a further forty performances. O'Casey, in an article in the *New York Times* for Sunday, October 21, 1934 (C155), the day before the play opened in New York, described what he was trying to do in the play and outlined the symbolism of each character. Other interpretations and defences of the play by O'Casey were published in 'The Cutting of an Agate' in *The Flying Wasp* (A18), in the *Daily Princetonian*, January 10, 1935 (C157), in essays collected in *Blasts and Benedictions* (A44) and in *The Letters of Sean O'Casey* (A46).

The 'stage version' printed in *Collected Plays* (A29), *Selected Plays* (A32), and in *The Sean O'Casey Reader* (A45), incorporated changes made by O'Casey after the London and New York productions. On May 5, 1946 O'Casey told George Jean Nathan, 'At the moment I'm revising *Within the Gates*; trying to knit it closer together. As you know, I was never satisfied with it.' The changes were of a radical nature. The number of characters was reduced from twenty-seven to twenty; some scenes, speeches and songs were eliminated or changed; the character of the Bishop was made more sympathetic. For details of the specific changes, see R. Mary Todd, 'The Two Published Versions of O'Casey's "Within the Gates" ', *Modern Drama*, x, (1967–8) 346–55. A letter of November 8, 1959 to Miss Jane Rubin summarises some of the practical problems presented by even the simplified stage version (his American agent was arguing for an off-Broadway production of *Within the Gates*): 'This play is the most difficult play I have written from every point of view: the number of characters, the music, the acting. It isn't an off-Broadway show, for it needs a fine chorus of singers, a large stage, and a variety of costumes.'

On October 5, 1932, while still wrestling with the problems presented by the play, O'Casey confided to Nathan, 'My wife has just read O'Neill's *Mourning Becomes Electra*, and the play has made a powerful impression on her. I will not read it till I have finished my own, for if I did, I know my mind should be full of it for months, and this influence would be a handicap to my own thoughts. But the temptation to read it is growing stronger every day, and in the end, I suppose I shall yield, and curse O'Neill for being such a powerful writer.' O'Casey did indeed succumb and, though there is little or no discernible influence to be detected in the play itself, a production note that prefaces *Within the Gates* concludes: 'The above idea of a front curtain was derived from Eugene O'Neill's suggestion of a front curtain for his great play, *Mourning Becomes Electra.*'

The music to the play, which is described in the published book as 'composed and adapted by Herbert Hughes', is referred to by O'Casey in a letter dated May 15, 1954 to Thomas Mark of Macmillan: 'Even the airs in WITHIN THE GATES which Mr. Hughes attributed to himself are all mine.' This statement is borne out by his letter of July 23, 1933 to Macmillan and Co. – 'At present I'm awaiting the notation of the airs for the songs in the play. Otherwise it is ready' – and by a letter to Nathan of July 27, 1933, speaking of the airs of the songs in *Within the Gates*: 'They are modifications, done by myself, from Irish folk tunes.'

Reviews: *Within the Gates* was reviewed in *The Times*, Nov 28, 1933; by Howard Spring in *Evening Standard*, Nov 30, 1933; by John Shand in *Sunday Referee*, Dec 3, 1933; in *Times Literary Supplement*, Dec 7, 1933; in *Irish Times*, Dec 16, 1933; by T. C. Murray in *Irish Press*, Dec 19, 1933; by Ivor Brown in *Manchester Guardian Weekly*, Dec 22, 1933; by Brooks Atkinson in *New York Times Book Review*, Dec 31, 1933; by A. G. Stock in *Socialist Review*, Jan 1934; by George Jean Nathan in *Vanity Fair*, Jan 1934; by St John Ervine in *Observer*, Jan 7, 1934; in *Time and Tide*, Jan 27, 1934; by W. P. Eaton in *New York Herald Tribune Books*, Jan 28, 1934; by V. Geddes in *New Masses*, Jan 30, 1934; by Richard Rees in *Adelphi*, Feb 1934; by D. Verschoyle in *Spectator*, Feb 16, 1934; by Desmond McCarthy in *New Statesman and Nation*, Feb 17, 1934; by Hugh MacDiarmid in *Scots Observer*, Feb 17, 1934; by Horace Reynolds in *Saturday Review of Literature*, Mar 3, 1934 and Nov 3, 1934; by Elinor Hughes in *Boston Herald*, Mar 25, 1934; in *Dublin Magazine*, Apr–June 1934; by A. Dukes in *Theatre Arts*, Apr 1934; by Florence Codman in *Nation*, Apr 25, 1934; by Osbert Burdett in *London Mercury*, May 1934; by H. T. E. Perry in *Yale Review*, June 1934; by J. J. H. in *Irish Book Lover*, July–Aug 1934.

A16   WINDFALLS   1934

a. *first edition*
WINDFALLS / STORIES, POEMS, AND PLAYS / BY / SEAN O'CASEY /
MACMILLAN AND CO., LIMITED / ST. MARTIN'S STREET, LONDON /
1934

18 × 12.5cm.

[i], half-title: WINDFALLS /; [ii], publisher's monogram and imprints; [iii],
title-page as above; [iv], copyright, printer's imprint; v-vii, Preface; [viii],
blank; ix–x, Contents; [1]–[201], text, printer's imprint at foot of [201]; [202],
blank.

Green cloth; front cover: WINDFALLS / SEAN O'CASEY / [all incorporated
in design with scroll, fruit-tree and fruit]; back cover blank; spine:
WINDFALLS / SEAN / O'CASEY / [all above incorporated in design of sky,
birds, fruit-tree branch and fruit] / MACMILLAN /; lettered and decorated
in gold; white endpapers; top edge trimmed and stained green, other edges
untrimmed.
Published October 16, 1934 at 7s 6d; 3000 copies printed by R. & R. Clark,
Ltd., Edinburgh.

b. *American edition*

WINDFALLS / STORIES, POEMS, AND PLAYS / BY / SEAN O'CASEY / NEW
YORK / THE MACMILLAN COMPANY / 1934

18 × 13cm.

[i], half-title: WINDFALLS /; [ii], publisher's monogram and imprints; [iii],
title-page as above; [iv], copyright, printing, publication, printer's imprint;
v–vii, Preface; [viii], blank; ix–x, Contents; [1]–202, text.

Red cloth; front cover: WINDFALLS / SEAN O'CASEY /; back cover blank;
spine: WINDFALLS / [ornament] / O'CASEY / MACMILLAN /. /; lettered
and decorated in gold; white endpapers, top and bottom edges trimmed, top
edge stained yellow, front edge untrimmed; dust-jacket in orange, cream and
brown.
Published October 16, 1934 at $1.75; 2000 copies printed by The Stratford
Press, Inc., New York.

Contents:

FIRST FALL
Wisdom and Life
    First appeared in *Time and Tide* June 23, 1934 (C151).
A Walk with Eros
    Verses from this poem are quoted in *Juno and the Paycock* (A11) and in
    The Shadow of a Gunman (A12).
Chosen Life
Sunshadows
    Verses from this poem are quoted in *The Shadow of a Gunman*.

The Garland
A revised version of the poem which appeared under the title 'To Maire'
in *The World of Sean O'Casey* (B53).
Thoughts of Thee
Reprinted with a slightly different fifth stanza in *The World of Sean O'Casey*
(B53).
Bonnie Mary

SECOND FALL

Gold and Silver Will Not Do
In her book *Sean* (B68), Eileen O'Casey recounts how the original manu-
script version, using the name Eileen throughout, was presented to her by
the dramatist on July 14, 1929. A few alterations were made for this
published version including the omission of Mrs O'Casey's name through-
out the prose poem. A brief passage from the original version is quoted in
Sean.
The Dreamer Dreams of God
She Will Give Me Rest
First appeared in *Time and Tide*, July 7, 1934 (C153).

A FALL FROM AN IRISH TREE

The Grand Oul' Dame Britannia
First appeared in *Workers' Republic*, January 15, 1916 (C68), from which
version it differs in minor ways and has one less verse. Also published
as a broadside becoming O'Casey's first separately published work (A1).

FALLS IN A HIGH WIND

I Wanna Woman
Reprinted in *The Green Crow* (A34) and in *The Sean O'Casey Reader* (A45).
The Star-Jazzer
Reprinted in *The Green Crow*.
The Job
Reprinted in *The Green Crow*.

A FALL IN A GENTLE WIND

A Fall in a Gentle Wind
This revised version first appeared in *Life and Letters* December 1933 (C136).
The original version first appeared under title 'Mollser' in *Irish Statesman*,
April 25, 1925 (C96). Reprinted in *The Green Crow*.

FALLS IN AN IDLE WIND

The End of the Beginning: A Comedy in One Act
Reprinted in *Five Irish Plays* (A17), *Collected Plays* (A29), *Five One-Act Plays*
(A37).
A Pound on Demand: A Sketch in One Act
Reprinted in *Five Irish Plays*, *Collected Plays*, *Five One-Act Plays*.

Notes: The contents of *Windfalls* were written over a long period, 1916–34. The poems in the section 'First Fall' were written under the influence of the girl who is called Nora Creena in the chapter 'The Girl He Left Behind Him' in *Inishfallen, Fare Thee Well* (A27). The relationship lasted from 1917 to 1926, and it was to this girl, Maura, that he dedicated *Juno and the Paycock* (A11). The typescript drafts of poems in 'First Fall', among the O'Casey Papers in the Berg Collection of the New York Public Library, show a number of significant changes from the published texts. There are many additions and deletions in 'A Walk with Eros'; the version in *Windfalls* has sixty-nine stanzas while the original typescript contains eighty-three. 'Sunshadows', which was originally entitled 'Sunlight and Shadow', has a number of word changes. There are minor alterations in 'Chosen Life', with one extra stanza in the unpublished text.

Except for 'The Grand Oul' Dame Britannia' (A1, 1916), all the other pieces in *Windfalls* were written between 1925 and 1934. The three pieces in 'Second Fall' were almost certainly written between 1929 and 1933, while the author was composing *Within the Gates*. Two of the three are love poems while the third is a tribute to 'the Dreamer, brave singer of songs.' In all three we find strong echoes of the Authorized Version of the Bible, particularly Psalms and the Song of Songs. In form and subject matter alike, these occasional writings have much in common with the lyrics in *Within the Gates* while the protagonist in that play is called the Dreamer. The original title for 'Gold and Silver Will Not Do' was 'Everlasting Appleblossom'. The typescript of 'The Dreamer Dreams of God', among the O'Casey Papers in the Berg Collection, contains minor changes from the printed version.

The playwright records in the preface to *Windfalls* that 'the three short stories [in 'Falls in a High Wind'] were an effort to get rid of some of the bitterness that swept into me when the Abbey Theatre rejected *The Silver Tassie*.' The extent of O'Casey's anger, which is not reflected within the stories themselves, is shown in his original title to this section: 'Falls in a Fierce Gale'. In a letter of October 28, 1929 to Gabriel Fallon, O'Casey writes: 'Just finished a short story—it isn't a story—The Star Dance—who says Yeats?' This is obviously the story 'The Star-Jazzer', entitled 'The Star Jazz' in the original typescript. 'I Wanna Woman' was originally accepted for publication by the editor of *Time and Tide* in 1933, but had to be cancelled when the printer refused to set up the text. In several issues, during May and June 1933, O'Casey's right to be published was defended by writers such as W. B. Yeats, Wyndham Lewis, Sylvia Townsend Warner, Arthur Waugh, Naomi Mitchison, Harold Laski and Desmond MacCarthy. In sending the story to Macmillan and Co. for inclusion in *Windfalls*, O'Casey wrote in a letter of June 30, 1934: 'Enclosed is the short story, "I Wanna Woman" with the passages marked by Mr. Desmond MacCarthy modified. I sincerely hope the changes will be suitable—they are much more discreet than the original passages.' The typescript of this story among the O'Casey Papers in the Berg Collection includes three short passages that were deleted in the printed version.

O'Casey's preface to *Windfalls* explains why the new plays were included in a section entitled 'Falls in an Idle Wind': the 'two One-Act Sketches were written when funds were low, to bring in a little money, but no attempt was made to market them, and so they shiver among the unemployed.' Both were written for Arthur Sinclair in the hope that they could be used as music-hall comedy turns but the Irish actor preferred to tour England and the United States in already proven Irish plays including O'Casey's Dublin trilogy. 'The End of the Beginning' (originally entitled 'Power House God') is O'Casey's adaptation of a popular folk tale. The original typescript, among the O'Casey Papers in the Berg Collection of the New York Public Library, includes a scene in which Alice Lanigan appears. She is described as 'About thirty-five. Good looking; well shaped plump legs, and fond of showing them. Has a name for carrying on with the men.' This character and the scene in which she partici-pates are cut completely in the published text. 'A Pound on Demand' was based on a story related to the playwright by Gabriel Fallon; a short story with the same title is included among the O'Casey Papers in the Berg Collection, New York Public Library.

O'Casey originally proposed the idea for this gathering of material, old and new, in a letter of July 23, 1933 to Macmillan and Co: 'I'm thinking of making a volume called "Windfalls," consisting of some poems written some years ago, two humorous one act sketches – one of which is written and the other on the way – and a few short stories.' The English and American editions of *Windfalls* were published simultaneously on October 16, 1934. The American edition was published at this time to take advantage of the publicity attending on O'Casey's visit to New York for the first American production of *Within the Gates* (A15) at the National Theatre on October 22. Proofs of the English edition were sent to New York on September 14. It was decided, however, to print the American edition from type following, in a general way, the style of the English edition. O'Casey's copy of the American edition was sent to him on October 10, 1934, 'hot off the press, greatly rushed but not a bad job' according to a letter from George Brett, of the Macmillan Company, now in the Manuscript Division of the New York Public Library.

Reviews: *Windfalls* was reviewed by Desmond MacCarthy in *Sunday Times*, Oct 28, 1934; in *Times Literary Supplement*, Nov 8, 1934; by St John Ervine in *Observer*, Nov 11, 1934; in *Spectator*, Nov 16, 1934; by Horace Gregory in *New York Herald Tribune Book Review*, Nov 25, 1934; by Peter M. Jack in *New York Times Book Review*, Nov 11, 1934; in *Theatre Arts*, Dec 1934; by W. H. in *Time and Tide*, Dec 1, 1934; by Samuel Beckett in *Bookman*, Christmas 1934; by Ernest Boyd in *American Spectator*, Jan 1935.

A17   FIVE IRISH PLAYS   1935

first edition

FIVE / IRISH PLAYS / JUNO AND THE PAYCOCK / THE SHADOW OF A
GUNMAN / THE PLOUGH AND THE STARS / THE END OF THE
BEGINNING / A POUND ON DEMAND / SEAN O'CASEY / WITH A
PORTRAIT OF THE AUTHOR / MACMILLAN and CO., LIMITED / ST.
MARTIN'S STREET, LONDON / 1935

19 × 12.5cm.

[i], half-title: FIVE IRISH PLAYS /; [ii], publisher's monogram and imprints;
frontispiece, photograph of Sean O'Casey by Elliott & Fry, Ltd; [iii], title-page
as above; [iv], copyright, printer's imprint; v, dedication: TO / GEORGE
JEAN NATHAN / DRAMATIC CRITIC / WITHOUT FEAR AND WITHOUT
REPROACH /; [vi], blank; vii, Contents, Frontispiece; viii, first production
and cast of *Juno and the Paycock*; [1]–[409], text, printer's imprint at foot
of [409]; [410], blank; [411]–[412], list of O'Casey's works published by
Macmillan.

Green cloth; front and back covers blank; spine: FIVE / IRISH / PLAYS /
[ornament] / SEAN / O'CASEY / [all above incorporated in design of
proscenium arch, harp, shamrocks, masks] / MACMILLAN /; lettered and
decorated in gold; white endpapers, all edges trimmed.
Published October 29, 1935 at 7s 6d; 2000 copies printed by R. & R. Clark,
Ltd, Edinburgh; reprinted 1940 (1000 copies).

Notes: The original dedication to his mother for *The Plough and the Stars* is
retained, but that 'to Maire and the Abbey Theatre' for *Juno and the Paycock* is
omitted and was not subsequently restored for later editions. Although
O'Casey made many alterations for the acting editions of the three plays (*Juno
and the Paycock*, *The Shadow of a Gunman*, and *The Plough and the Stars*), published
in 1932, none of these changes are incorporated in the texts published in *Five
Plays*. The texts of 'The End of the Beginning' and of 'A Pound on Demand'
are identical with those published in *Windfalls* (A16). There was no American
edition.

Reviews: *Five Irish Plays* was reviewed by T. C. Murray in *Irish Press*, Nov 19,
1935; and by E. Shackleton in *Time and Tide*, Nov 23, 1935.

THE FLYING WASP 1937

a. *first edition*
The / FLYING WASP / A LAUGHING LOOK-OVER OF WHAT HAS / BEEN SAID ABOUT THE THINGS OF THE / THEATRE BY THE ENGLISH DRAMATIC / CRITICS, WITH MANY MERRY AND AMUS- / ING COMMENTS THEREON, WITH SOME / SHREWD REMARKS BY THE AUTHOR ON / THE WISE, DELICIOUS, AND DIGNIFIED / TENDENCIES IN THE THEATRE OF TO-DAY / *by* / SEAN O'CASEY / There is a nest of wasps that must be / smoked out because it is doing the / theatre infinite harm. MR. J. AGATE. / LONDON / MACMILLAN & CO. LTD. / 1937

18.8 × 12.5cm.

[i], half-title: THE FLYING WASP /; [ii], publisher's monogram and imprints; [iii], title-page as above; [iv], copyright, printer's imprint; v–vi, Contents; vii–xiii, Overture; [xiv], blank; 1–[201], text, printer's imprint at foot of [201]; [202], blank.

Yellow cloth; front and back covers blank; spine: THE / FLYING / WASP / SEAN / O'CASEY / [all above on two silver panels within black borders] / MACMILLAN /; lettered in black; white endpapers; top edge trimmed, other edges untrimmed; yellow dust-jacket, lettered and decorated in black.
Published March 5, 1937 at 6s; 2000 copies printed by R. & R. Clark, Ltd, Edinburgh.

b. *Benjamin Blom (photo-offset) edition*
The / FLYING WASP / A LAUGHING LOOK-OVER OF WHAT HAS / BEEN SAID ABOUT THE THINGS OF THE / THEATRE BY THE ENGLISH DRAMATIC / CRITICS, WITH MANY MERRY AND AMUS- /ING COMMENTS THEREON, WITH SOME / SHREWD REMARKS BY THE AUTHOR ON / THE WISE, DELICIOUS, AND DIGNIFIED / TEN-DENCIES IN THE THEATRE OF TO-DAY / *by* / SEAN O'CASEY / There is a nest of wasps that must be / smoked out because it is doing the / theatre infinite harm. MR. J. AGATE. / Published By / BENJAMIN BLOM, INC.

21 × 13cm.

[a]–[b], blank; [i], half-title: THE FLYING WASP /; [ii], blank; [iii], title-page as above; [iv], details of publication, publisher's imprint, Library of Congress card number, printing; v–vi, Contents; vii–xiii, Overture; [xiv], blank; 1–[201], text; [202]–[204], blank.

Red cloth; front and back covers blank; label on spine: [line of short vertical rules] / THE / FLYING / WASP / . / SEAN / O'CASEY / BLOM / [line of short vertical rules] /; lettered and decorated in black; white endpapers, all edges trimmed.
Published December 1971 at $10.75; number of copies undetermined.

Contents:

Overture

A revised and expanded version was published in *The Green Crow* (A34).

The Public Death of Shakespeare

First appeared in *Time and Tide*, July 13, 1935 (C163); reprinted with the addition of an introductory paragraph in *The Green Crow*.

National Theatre Bunkum I

First appeared in *Time and Tide*, Oct 12, 1935 (C168); reprinted in *The Green Crow*.

National Theatre Bunkum II

First appeared in *Time and Tide*, Nov 9, 1935 (C169); reprinted in *The Green Crow*.

England, Say When

Reprinted in *The Green Crow*.

The Cutting of an Agate

An expansion of a letter which originally appeared under the title 'Within the Gates' in *Sunday Times*, Feb 18, 1934 (C145).

Three Cheers for Noah

First appeared in *Time and Tide*, Aug 10, 1935 (C164).

Murdher in the Theatre

First appeared in *Time and Tide*, Oct 10, 1936 (C185); reprinted in *The Green Crow*.

Mr. Ervine's Cry for the Critics

Sainte-Beuve, Patron of Poor Playwriters, Pray for Us!

First appeared in *Time and Tide*, May 9, 1936 (C179); the opening originally appeared as a letter under the title 'Agate, O'Casey and Coward' in *Sunday Times*, Mar 1, 1936 (C175).

It's All Very Curious, Isn't It?

Poor Pinero Passes By

Green Goddess of Realism

Reprinted in *The Green Crow*.

Coward Codology: I, Cavalcade

An abbreviated version first appeared in *Time and Tide*, Jan 11, 1936 (C173); reprinted in *The Green Crow*.

Coward Codology: II, Design for Dying

Reprinted in *The Green Crow*.

Coward Codology: III, Excelsior Ingenium

Reprinted in *The Green Crow*.

Shakespeare Lives in London Lads

First appeared in *Time and Tide*, Apr 18, 1936 (C177); reprinted in *The Green Crow*.

Critici Infallibilibombast

First appeared under the title 'Pontiffs of the Theatre' in *Fortnightly*, Oct 1936 (C183); reprinted in part under the title 'Critica Silentio Luna' in *The Green Crow*.

Let the Wheel Turn

First appeared in *Time and Tide*, Feb 1, 1936 (C174).

Pro-per Proscenium

Reprinted in *The Green Crow*.

Hail, Columbia!
    First appeared in *Time and Tide*, Aug 1, 1936 (C182).

Notes: This collection of essays gives O'Casey's views on critics and the theatre. On March 8, 1937 he described it, in a letter to George Jean Nathan, as his 'first, and most probably last, effort in Dramatic Criticism'; it was not the last, however, as critical writings were to be published subsequently in *The Green Crow* (A34), *Under a Colored Cap* (A41) and in *Blasts and Benedictions* (A44). The dust-jacket has the additional sub-title: Essays on the Modern Theatre, which (as O'Casey said in a letter to Nathan on May 4, 1937) was 'Macmillan's genteel touch'.

    Writing to Nathan on October 28, 1936 O'Casey says of the work, 'I expect my little book—an onslaught on the critics here . . . an effort to confound them out of the words of their own mouths—called "The Flying Wasp", will appear in January next. I will send you the first copy printed. Between ourselves, Macmillan jibbed a little at it, and gave me some fatherly advice to keep it back, saying that it would make many enemies. They said something about "brawling in church", and fell silent when I told them that the first to create a brawl in church was Jesus Christ. . . . I shouldn't have bothered only I thought something ought to be done to prepare a way for some young Nathan that may be growing up here in the theatre of today, to show him that true criticism is greater than a mere job'. Later, in a letter of March 27, 1938 to the same correspondent, the playwright confessed: 'I am altogether too vehement to be a good critic. I can't keep calm . . . However, I think *The Flying Wasp* did some good'.

    Commenting on the cover in a letter of January 29, 1937 to Harold Macmillan, O'Casey wrote, 'I think I like the YELLOW cover suggested for "The Flying Wasp" better than the BLACK one. It is, I think, brighter, and suggests the idea quite as well. If the book meant the death of the critics (which God fulfil), then the Black cover would be more suitable. But God for His own good reasons, will go on trying us in this vale of tears, and He will let the critics live on longer, perhaps to give them a further chance to make their souls'. Most of the essays had already been published, less than half appear in print here for the first time. There was no American edition in 1937. The Macmillan Company, New York, imported a hundred bound copies of the English edition in March 1937 for sale in the United States; Benjamin Blom, Inc. (New York) reissued the book in 1971. Much of the material in *The Flying Wasp* was later collected in *The Green Crow*.

Reviews: *The Flying Wasp* was reviewed in *Times Literary Supplement*, Mar 13, 1937; by James Agate in *John O'London's Weekly*, Mar 19, 1937; in *The Times*, Mar 19, 1937; by George Warrington in *Country Life* (London), Mar 20, 1937; by James Agate in *Sunday Times*, Mar 21, 1937; by T. C. Murray in *Irish Press*, Mar 23, 1937; by D. Verschoyle in *Spectator*, Mar 26, 1937; by D. Walker-Smith in *English Review*, May 1937; by Gabriel Fallon in *Irish Monthly*, May 1937; by P. C. T. in *Irish Book Lover*, May–June 1937; by J. S. Collis in *London Mercury*, May 1937; by Brooks Atkinson in *New York Times*, June 6, 1937; by P. M. Jack in *New York Times Book Review*, June 13, 1937; in *Dublin Magazine*, July–Sep 1937; by L. A. MacKay in *Canadian Forum*, July 1937; by W. P. Eaton in *New York Herald Tribune Book Review*, Oct 10, 1937; by B. Hewitt in *Quarterly Journal of Speech*, Dec 1937.

A19   I KNOCK AT THE DOOR   1939

a. *first edition*
I KNOCK / AT THE DOOR / *Swift Glances Back / at Things That Made Me* /
BY / SEAN O'CASEY / *Knock, and it shall be opened unto you* / LONDON /
MACMILLAN & CO. LTD / 1939

22 × 14cm.

[i], half-title: I KNOCK AT THE DOOR /; [ii], blank; frontispiece, portrait
photograph: MRS. SUSAN CASSIDE IN GALA DRESS / The relics of oul'
dacency, the dhress me mother wore /; [iii], title-page as above; [iv], copyright,
printer's imprint; [v], dedication: TO / BREON AND NIALL /; [vi], blank;
vii, Contents; [viii], blank; 1–[269], text; [270], printer's imprint; [271],
publisher's list of works by Sean O'Casey; [272], blank.

Buff cloth; front and back covers blank; spine: I / KNOCK / AT THE / DOOR
/ [ornament] / SEAN / O'CASEY / [all above on maroon panel within grey,
maroon and gold borders] / MACMILLAN /; lettered and decorated in
maroon and gold; white endpapers, all edges trimmed; dust-jacket in red,
grey and white, depicts on front the young O'Casey knocking on a door in
a panel on a Celtic cross.
Published March 3, 1939 at 10s 6d; 2110 copies printed by R. & R. Clark,
Ltd, Edinburgh; reprinted April 1939 (2120 copies).

b. *American (offset) edition*
I KNOCK / AT THE DOOR / *Swift Glances Back / at Things That Made Me* / BY
/ SEAN O'CASEY / *Knock, and it shall be opened unto you* / NEW YORK / THE
MACMILLAN COMPANY / 1939

21.5 × 14cm.

[i], half-title: I KNOCK AT THE DOOR /; [ii], publisher's monogram and
imprints; frontispiece, portrait photograph: MRS. SUSAN CASSIDE IN GALA
DRESS / The relics of oul' dacency, the dhress me mother wore /; [iii], title-
page as above; [iv], copyright, printing; [v], dedication; [vi], blank; vii,
Contents; [viii], blank; 1–[269], text; [270]–[272], blank.

Grey cloth; front and back covers blank; spine: I / KNOCK / AT THE /
DOOR / [ornament] / SEAN / O'CASEY / [all above on maroon panel within
grey, maroon and gold borders] / MACMILLAN /; lettered and decorated in
maroon and gold; white endpapers, all edges trimmed.
Published July 18, 1939 at $2.50; 2000 copies printed.

c. *Readers Union edition*
[rule] / SEAN O'CASEY / [rule] / I Knock AT / The Door / [rule] / *Swift
Glances Back at Things / That Made Me* / [rule] / KNOCK AND IT SHALL BE
OPENED UNTO YOU / [rule] / London 1943 [solidus] Readers Union
[solidus] Macmillan & Co / [heavy rule]

18.5 × 12.5cm.

[i], half-title: I Knock At The Door / [rule] /; [ii], frontispiece, portrait photograph: MRS. SUSAN CASSIDE IN GALA DRESS / The relics of oul' dacency,

the dhress me mother wore /; [iii], title-page as above; [iv], dedication, details
of production and printing; [v], Contents; [vi], blank; 1–241, text; [242],
blank. The pasted down endpapers at front and back are conjugate respectively with pp. 21–2 and 215–16; the fly leaves at front and back are conjugate
respectively with pp. 19–20 and 213–14.

Orange-brown cloth; front and back covers blank; spine: [double rule] /
O'Casey / [double rule] / I / Knock / At / The / Door / [heavy rule] /
[publisher's mark, in green] /; lettered and decorated in silver; white endpapers, all edges trimmed.
Published in 1943 for sale to its members only by Readers Union Ltd; printed
by Butler & Tanner Ltd, Frome, Somerset, England; number of copies
undisclosed.

d. *American edition reset*
I Knock / AT THE DOOR / *Swift Glances Back* / *At Things That Made Me* / BY /
Sean O'Casey / *Knock, and it shall be opened unto you* / NEW YORK / THE
MACMILLAN COMPANY / *1949*

21 × 14cm.

[i], half-title: *I Knock at the Door* /; [ii], Books by Sean O'Casey; frontispiece,
portrait photograph: MRS. SUSAN CASSIDE IN GALA DRESS / The relics
of oul' dacency, the dhress me mother wore /; [iii], title-page as above;
[iv], copyright, printing; [v], dedication; [vi], blank; [vii], Contents; [viii],
blank; [ix], fly-title: *I Knock at the Door* /; [x], blank; 1–294, text.

Tan cloth; front and back covers blank; spine: I Knock / AT THE / DOOR /
[ornamental line] / O'CASEY / MACMILLAN /; lettered and decorated in
green; white endpapers, all edges trimmed.
Published September 6, 1949 at $3.50; 3036 copies printed. Five hundred
copies of this edition were imported by Macmillan and Co. Ltd, London,
for sale in England. This edition was used to reproduce the text for *Mirror
in My House* (A35). The text was also used, without the frontispiece photograph, for the Macmillan Paperbacks edition MP9 which was published
March 14, 1960 at $1.45 in an edition of 10,111 copies. This edition was
also licensed to Liberty Book Club for its September 1950 selection.

e. *Panther Books edition*
I KNOCK AT THE DOOR / SWIFT GLANCES BACK / AT THINGS THAT
MADE ME / BY / SEAN O'CASEY / Knock, and it shall be opened unto you /
PAUL LIST VERLAG LEIPZIG

19.5 × 11.5cm.

[1], half-title: PANTHER BOOKS · PAUL LIST EDITION / A Collection
of British and American Writers / [publisher's mark] / SEAN O'CASEY · I
KNOCK AT THE DOOR /; [2], Books by Sean O'Casey; [3], title-page as
above; [4], publisher's imprint, dedication, copyright, sales information,
printing; [5], Contents; [6], blank; 7–[240], text.

Stiff paper wrappers in rust and white; lettered and decorated in black and
white; all edges trimmed; dust-jacket in rust and white, design identical
with covers.

Published April 1955 at 1.85DM; 5000 copies printed to commemorate the author's seventy-fifth birthday.

Notes: This was the first in the series of six autobiographical volumes published between 1939 and 1954. The idea had been long in O'Casey's mind. In a letter to Macmillan and Co. dated August 14, 1926 he says, 'I have thought of writing a book reminiscent of my experiences.' In an essay, 'Sidelighting on Some "Pictures"', published in the *New York Times*, September 16, 1956 (C458), he tells how the autobiography was begun without any set plan. Between writing plays, while his family slept, he sat down and wrote 'of past experiences—the molds in which myself was made.' Beginning in the late 1920s with a few sketches of his early childhood, and writing in the first person, the playwright had no thought of the sequence assuming its eventual epic proportions. In October 1930, in an entry in one of his notebooks, O'Casey outlined a plan for a volume of seventeen short stories, the ideas for some of them being clearly autobiographical. On and off, from 1930 onward he was engaged in writing what he called 'biographical sketches', or, in the words in which he described the first book of autobiography, writing 'stories' about 'what I saw and heard and felt during the first eleven or twelve years of my life.' These stories or events appear in one continuous narrative in several exercise books, undivided by chapter or title. Sometimes there is no break at what is, in the published version, the end of a volume. In one exercise book for instance, the unbroken narrative sequence contains the final chapters of *I Knock at the Door* (A19) and the opening ones of *Pictures in the Hallway* (A22); another contains a long draft which eventually became nine chapters in *Rose and Crown* (A30) and ten chapters in the following book, *Sunset and Evening Star* (A31). Gradually, however, the work took on a life of its own, demanding expression on a scale much larger than the one volume originally envisaged; moreover, to distance himself from the experiences related and give the narrative a novel-like texture, O'Casey finally decided to write in the third person. It was a long time before the author himself realised the full magnitude of the autobiographical sequence he was creating.

In a letter to William J. Maroldo of August 10, 1962 the author declared: 'As for my own "Auto-biography," it was not first conceived as such, but just as incidents I had experienced. Indeed, three of them appeared in print before the idea of a biography came into my head.' The first autobiographical episode was published in the *American Spectator*. When George Jean Nathan asked for a contribution for the journal, O'Casey sent him 'A Protestant Kid Thinks of the Reformation'. It was printed in the issue for July 1934 (C152), and met with such success that, as the author wrote in the *New York Times* September 16, 1956, 'The biography started in earnest.' The story was considerably expanded for its appearance in *I Knock at the Door*. 'His Father's Dublin Funeral' appeared in *English*, 1936 (C172) and was subsequently enlarged to become the chapter 'His Father's Funeral'. 'The Dream School' chapter is a slightly expanded version of 'The Dream School: A Story', which appeared in the *Yale Review*, June 1937 (C192). The chapter 'A Child of God' had been submitted to the *Yale Review* by Horace Reynolds on O'Casey's behalf, but was withdrawn at the playwright's request when Macmillan and Co. had decided on the publication of *I Knock at the Door*. On February 19, 1937 he wrote to Peter Newmark, 'I am doing a little with my "Autobiography." Have just finished a chapter on "Sunday-school & church," ending—not beginning—with the text, "And God said let there be light & there was light." ' This was probably the chapter which was published under the title 'A Child of God'. In January 1938 he wrote to Macmillan and Co., 'I have a few things in hand (doing something with a play, and a few fantastic pages of biography), but they haven't reached the stage yet that would interest a publisher.'

Once the author got down in earnest to the work, however, the writing went smoothly. Many years later, in a letter of August 10, 1962 to William J. Maroldo, O'Casey explained that when 'the idea came to me' it soon 'grew expansively out and down deep, so that a letter I have before me, from Macmillan's dated July 1938, tells me the material sent in [amounted to] 60,000 words. They thought that amount would make a book, but would prefer 75,000 words. I evidently sent word saying material was plentiful (the ideas were growing), and that I would send in additional chapters; for a following letter from them says "they are glad to hear that you will find no difficulty in sending further material." ' By June 21, 1938 he was completing the manuscript, as he wrote to Harold Macmillan: 'I'll do my best to add the 15,000 words wanted. I've already done two sketches— "The Tired Cow" and "The Street Sings," with another—"Vandhering Vindy Vendhor"—well on the way. A few more should make a volume.' He was also having trouble with the title as he indicates in the same letter: 'I'm not satisfied with the title "The Green Blade;" and I am trying to think of another—"Father of the Man," or "Of Such is the Kingdom of Heaven"—too long? "Studies" in Autobiography seems to have too much of a scholastic touch about it for me. I'll have to try to make the sub-title simpler.' A fuller explanation for his change of mind was made in the same letter to William J. Maroldo: 'I first intended to take titles for the work from "First the Green Blade, then the Corn, then the Full Corn in the Ear"; but the rapid development of what I was conceiving in my mind, additional ideas crowding in after the conception of previous ideas, made me alter the titles to the present ones which top the various volumes.' In any case, work on the first volume progressed so well that proofs were sent to O'Casey in September 1938. He had moved to Devon that same month and was to spend the rest of his life in this area.

In a letter of October 7, 1938 to Harold Macmillan the author says something of the book and indicates his plans for future volumes: 'The Book—the 23 chapters or sections is an organic whole—at least I hope it is—; and the whole book is autobiographical from Alpha to Omega, of the first twelve years of my life [1880–92]. I have thought of two more volumes: "Come On In," and the third "The Lighted Room." The second to consist of what happened till I joined the Irish Movement, & the last to deal with all or most of what happened afterwards.' Subsequently, in a letter of December 21, 1938 to the publicity department of Macmillan he asks, 'If you can, don't use the word "Biography"—what a detestable word it is—, for the Saxon "Lifestory" is far better and much more musical.' Further comments by the author are also found on the dust-jacket of the 1939 English edition of *I Knock at the Door*: 'This is the story of the first twelve years of the author's life, full of sound, sometimes full of fury, and always signifying a lot ... The book discloses the life of a boy in the Dublin

Streets, a Dublin School, a Dublin Church; in scene and conversation the squalor and glamour of a mean and splendid city is, presented, wearing again in drab and sparkling colours the strange patterns that went to make the man.'

O'Casey himself wrote the descriptive matter and suggested the design for the dust-jacket of the English edition, as he was to do for the subsequent five volumes. He submitted various designs and sketches for the dust-jacket: writing to L. E. Carroll, Macmillan and Co., on January 21, 1939 he says, 'Here's another suggestion with the head of a Celtic Cross forming the whole design; instead of, as in the other, the head and shaft. On this are Nelson's Pillar, Lion and Unicorn, Queen Victoria, Parnell & a Church; centre, Arms of Dublin; below, boy knocking at door; & underneath this, the tired cow & a group of children playing "ring." '

Punctuation was a point of difference between O'Casey and his publishers, the playwright maintaining that he 'must allow the rhythm or lilt to flow free.' On July 20, 1938 he wrote to Harold Macmillan: 'I've been thinking and thinking over your anxiety about punctuation . . . I'm no innovator—I wish I was—; this has been done years & years & years ago. In some parts of the book, the usual method is impossible—it would murder the lilt of the sentences . . . Perhaps, we could come to some compromise—there is, of course—a lot in what you say—; but in many parts of the book conventional punctuation's impossible.'

Later volumes in O'Casey's autobiographical sequence were criticised for their alleged excessive wordplay in the manner of James Joyce, but the author argued that this element was a consistent feature of the work from the very beginning. In a letter to Ralph Thompson dated December 8, 1948 he wrote: 'This piece called A PROTESTANT KID THINKS OF THE REFORMATION . . . was first welcomed by the Editor of *The American Spectator*, George Jean Nathan, and his Associate Editors—who, I think were E. O'Neill, T. Dreiser, E. Boyd, and Sherwood Anderson, years before I began work definitely on the biographical venture. The piece in question is, I think, a Joycean effort, or would be called one, or is pricked with a Joycean influence, though it was written in a full flood of spontaneity. So, it would appear, it was from eminent minds in your Country that I got a first encouraging clap for a "Joycean" indiscretion.'

The Panther Books edition of *I Knock at the Door* was issued by the Leipzig publisher, Paul List, in 1955 in the firm's series of British and American Writers. On the front flap of the dust-jacket the publisher states: '*I Knock at the Door* is autobiography. It is history. It is poetry . . . Panther Books proudly presents this new edition . . . to honour the birthday and the man, and his deep and unshaken belief in mankind's ability to build a better world.'

I Knock at the Door was reprinted in *Mirror in My House* (A35a), in *Autobiographies* (A35b) and in *Autobiography* (A35c). Excerpts were published in *The Sean O'Casey Reader* (A45).

A version in English for the use of sixth forms in secondary schools, prepared by O. Truevtseva and L. Shifulina, was published in 1959 in Leningrad by the State Text Book Publishing House of the Soviet Union Ministry of Education. An adaptation of *I Knock at the Door*, designed for a staged reading by six voices, was prepared by Paul Shyre and presented at YM-YWHA Poetry Center, New York, on March 18, 1956. The adaptation,

in two acts, was published by Dramatists Play Service Inc. in 1958. A typescript
is in the Theater Collection, New York Public Library.

Reviews: *I Knock at the Door* was reviewed by P. C. T. in *Irish Book Lover*,
Jan-Feb 1939; in *Listener*, Feb 16, 1939; by Sean O'Faolain in *London Mercury*,
Mar 1939; by D. H. V. in *Spectator*, Mar 3, 1939; in *The Times*, Mar 3,
1939; in *Times Literary Supplement*, Mar 4, 1939; by Ivor Brown in *Manchester
Guardian*, Mar 7, 1939; by G. W. Stonier in *New Statesman*, Mar 11, 1939;
by Oliver St John Gogarty in *Observer*, Mar 12, 1939; by Howard Spring
in *Evening Standard*, Mar 16, 1939; by Desmond MacCarthy in *Sunday Times*,
Mar 19, 1939; by Montagu Slater in *Daily Worker* (London), Apr 5, 1939;
by A. C. [Austin Clarke?] in *Dublin Magazine*, Apr–June 1939; by Brooks
Atkinson in *New York Times*, Apr 9, 1939; by V. S. Pritchett in *Christian Science
Monitor*, Apr 15, 1939; by Max Wood in *Fortnightly*, June 1939; by Desmond
MacCarthy in *Living Age*, June 4, 1939; by Eleanor Godfrey in *Canadian Forum*,
July 1939; in *Christian Century*, July 12, 1939; by Ralph Thompson in *New
York Times*, July 18, 1939; by Louis Kronenberger in *New Yorker*, July 22,
1939; by Shaemas O'Sheel in *New York Herald Tribune Book Review*, July
23, 1939; by Horace Reynolds in *New York Times Book Review*, July 23, 1939;
in *Time*, July 24, 1939; by Ruth Page in *Boston Transcript*, July 29, 1939; by
Ernest Boyd in *Saturday Review of Literature*, July 29, 1939; by Edith J. Isaacs in
Theatre Arts, Aug 1939; by J. Cambridge in *Sunday Worker*, Aug 13, 1939; in
New Republic, Aug 16, 1939; by Padraic Colum in *Yale Review*, Sept 1939; by
Katherine Brégy in *Catholic World*, Oct 1939; by Shaemas O'Sheel in *New
Masses*, Oct 17, 1939.

A20   THE STAR TURNS RED   1940

first edition
THE   STAR   /   TURNS   RED   /   BY   /   SEAN   O'CASEY   /   LONDON   /
MACMILLAN & CO. LTD / 1940

20 × 14cm.

[i], half-title: THE STAR TURNS RED /; [ii], blank; [iii], title-page as above;
[iv], copyright, printer's imprint; [v], dedication: TO / THE MEN AND
WOMEN / WHO FOUGHT / THROUGH THE GREAT DUBLIN LOCK-
OUT / IN NINETEEN HUNDRED AND THIRTEEN /; [vi], acknowledge-
ment: *My thanks to Brigid Edwards / for setting down the music* /; vii, Contents;
[viii], blank; [1]–[184], text, printer's imprint at foot of [184].

Red cloth; front and back covers blank; spine: THE / STAR / TURNS /
RED / [star in outline] / SEAN / O'CASEY / MACMILLAN /; lettered and
decorated in gold; white endpapers, all edges trimmed; ivory dust-jacket
lettered and decorated in black and red.
Published February 15, 1940 at 7s 6d; 2000 copies printed by R. & R. Clark,
Ltd, Edinburgh.

Notes: This play, dedicated to the Dublin Strikers of 1913, presents not the
conflict between labour and capital, but rather that between Communism and
Fascism. The note on the dust-jacket, almost certainly written by the playwright, describes it as 'A new play by Sean O'Casey that plunges into the
turmoil between the Fascists, a Church with her eyes on the earth, and the
trumpet-call claims of the militant workers.' On April 22, 1960 O'Casey wrote
to Sally MacDermott, Society of Authors, concerning the play: '*The Star Turns
Red* was written 1937–38, after the unfortunate defeat of Republican Spain by
Franco, helped by Hitler & Mussolini. Venturing to foresee what might
happen, I wrote the play to try to awaken all to the menace of Nazism.'
    Many of the ideas, characters and incidents in the work had been in the
author's mind for a number of years. Several Dublin trade-union officials
known to O'Casey provide material for their counterparts in the play; in
particular, the dominant figure of Red Jim undoubtedly owes much to the
character of 'Big Jim' Larkin. As early as October 9, 1922 O'Casey told
Lennox Robinson, 'I was thinking of writing a play around Jim Larkin—
The Red Star—in which he would never appear though be responsible for all
the action.' Red Jim is a strongly felt and seen presence in *The Star Turns Red*,
in fact, but it is interesting to note that the technique of the unseen character
who profoundly influences the dramatic action is one employed in several later
O'Casey plays – *The Drums of Father Ned* is an example. On February 23, 1940
the author told Jack Carney, a friend and former colleague of Larkin, that he
wanted to send the labour leader a copy of the play, adding 'I suppose
different people will read different interpretations into the characters. As a
matter of fact, they're all composite—bar Red Jim—and, if it be a sketch of
our Jim, then it's a pale one [compared] to the real Red Jim.'
    The first intimation of the play appears in a letter to George Jean Nathan on
March 8, 1937: 'I haven't started a new play yet. I am a little tired of all the

rows that my plays [have] caused. I haven't written one yet that didn't create a blaze . . . and I really hate quarreling although I like an argument as well as the next one. I am thinking about a play to be called *The Star Turns Red*—Star of Bethlehem, that is—but amn't sure that I'll go on with it, for it would sure cause another bloody big row!' The playwright had started the work by the summer of that year, but progress was slow; his reluctance is explained in a striking passage in a letter to Nathan dated June 28, 1938: 'The play is as it was when I last wrote to you. At present I'm writing four more chapters to make a vol. [*I Knock at the Door*] to be published by Macmillans—they're waiting for it, and when this is done, then, with the help o' God—the play. Though things are so curious in the theatre, I'm not over anxious to come into contact with it again. I dread the dumb look of reproach in so many eyes when a play's a financial failure; and I don't expect any play of mine to be a financial success. However, the new play, success or no, has got be written; and maybe, more when that's done.' By December 9 he was able to report to Nathan, 'The chief news is . . . that I am in the middle—more than the middle—of the new play: First Act and Second Act done; Third Act nearly so; and Fourth partly. Out of a huge mountain of chaos, order is, I think, beginning to appear.' To the same correspondent he wrote on January 13, 1939: 'I have just finished *The Star Turns Red* and have but to add a line or two, and go through it once more to see and feel (or try to, rather) how it moves.' A typescript of the play was sent to Nathan on February 8, 1939 with the following declaration: 'I hope you'll see something in it. As well as being something of a confession of faith, it is, I think, a play; and, possibly, the best of its kind which has been written—which isn't saying a lot. There are, anyhow, some good lines in it. It is, I think, much more compact than "Within The Gates"; though I don't yet know just how much of the verse form ought to go to a play dealing with present-day life. There was too much singing in "Within The Gates," or, maybe, as is most probably, the singing was in the wrong place; or the chanting, or whatever we can call it. The action takes place during the last few hours of a Christmas Eve; and by this means, I've managed, I think, to give an ironical twist here and there. And I've tried to give a symbolism in the coloring of the 4 scenes, as you will see.' O'Casey revised the play in the light of Nathan's subsequent criticisms, some of which are apparent from O'Casey's letter of April 4, 1939: 'I've made a few alterations in the play, trying to make it appear that one Priest is the Red Priest of the Politicians, and the other the Brown Priest of the Poor; have brought in Kian again twice; and have made the girl a consistent (with a moment's lapse) upholder of the Red Star.'

O'Casey delayed publication, telling Harold Macmillan in a letter dated March 7, 1939, 'I have finished a new play—"The Star Turns Red," have sent two copies to America, hoping for a production there. I don't think I'll try for publication till a production comes my way—if it does come—, as there are usually a few things to change in Rehearsal; and these changes are not there to do in the book when the play has once been printed.' The production did not materialise in the United States. In England the play was performed at the Unity Theatre, London, on March 12, 1940 a month *after* its publication; it was revived at the same theatre in 1946. An American publication of the play was declined by the Macmillan Company, which feared the public temper of the country at the time – the time of the Nazi-Soviet Pact and the Russo-Finnish War.

Something of the author's retrospective opinion of *The Star Turns Red* may be gleaned from a letter of March 8, 1951 to Anne Munro-Kerr, League of Dramatists, concerning a possible East German production: 'I am looking forward to having this play done as I have a very warm corner in my heart for it, though it isn't by any means as good a work as some other plays I have done.' His reservations about it had been voiced nearer its publication, when he told Jack Carney on February 23, 1940, 'Glad you like the play; but it isn't (as a play) all you think it is.' On May 8, 1942 he wrote to the same correspondent: 'By the way, [James Agate] calling *Star Turns Red* a masterpiece shows him down; it isn't anything like one; I wish it were. It has a fine third scene [act], and good bits, here and there; but a masterpiece — no.' Nearly twenty years later, on October 27, 1961, he wrote to Miss Teresa Sacco in answer to an enquiry about possible rights for a French translation of the work: 'I'd like to rewrite [it], but haven't time, and lack interest in it.'

Passages and scenes were cut for the revised version published in 1949 in *Collected Plays* (A29), which constituted its sole subsequent publication. A copy of the 1940 edition with the playwright's corrections and additions for the *Collected Plays* edition is in the Berg Collection, New York Public Library.

Reviews: *The Star Turns Red* was reviewed by J. J. Hogan in *Studies*, Mar 1940; by Ivor Brown in *Manchester Guardian*, Mar 1, 1940; by Derek Verschoyle in *Spectator*, Mar 15, 1940; by W. A. Darlington in *New York Times*, Mar 24, 1940; by Richard Prentis in *John O'London's Weekly*, Mar 29, 1940; by A. Digges in *Irish Freedom*, Apr 1940; in *Times Literary Supplement*, Apr 13, 1940; by Ashley Dukes in *Theatre Arts*, June 1940; in *Dublin Magazine*, July–Sep 1940; by Benjamin Brooks in *Nineteenth Century*, Aug 1940.

PURPLE DUST   1940

a. *first edition*
PURPLE DUST / A WAYWARD COMEDY / IN THREE ACTS / BY / SEAN
O'CASEY / LONDON / MACMILLAN & CO. LTD / 1940

19.5 × 13cm.

[i]–[ii], blank; [iii], half-title: PURPLE DUST /; [iv], blank; [v], title-page as
above; [vi], printer's imprint, copyright; [vii], dedication: TO / SHIVAUN /;
[viii], characters, scenes, time; 1–[175], text; [176], blank; [177]–181, Music to
the Play; [182], printer's imprint; [183]–[184], publisher's list of works by
Sean O'Casey.

Blue cloth; front and back covers blank; spine: PURPLE / DUST / [star] /
SEAN / O'CASEY / MACMILLAN /; lettered and decorated in gold; white
endpapers, all edges trimmed; light grey dust-jacket lettered and decorated in
purple.
Published November 19, 1940 at 6s; 2000 copies printed by R. & R. Clark,
Ltd, Edinburgh.

b. *acting edition*
PURPLE / DUST / BY SEAN O'CASEY / [star] / A PLAY IN THREE ACTS /
[star] / DRAMATISTS / PLAY SERVICE / INC. [all above incorporated in
design consisting of seven vertical rules, seven horizontal rules, seven vertical
rules]

19.5 × 13cm.
[1], title-page as above; [2], copyright, acting rights, publisher's acknowledgement, sound effects records; 3, details of the Cherry Lane 1956 production,
scenes; [4], blank; 5–83, text; 84–7, music to the play; 88, Scene Design;
89–94, property, costume, light and sound plots; [95]–[96], publisher's
advertisements.

Stiff purple paper covers; lettered and decorated in black; all edges trimmed.
Published December 16, 1957 at $1.25; 1000 copies printed; reprinted
April 1, 1964 (1000 copies).

Notes: Introducing *Purple Dust* to an American audience on the occasion of its
New York stage début, O'Casey wrote in the *New York Herald Tribune*, December
23, 1956: 'This play was written eighteen years ago—two years before World
War II.' It was completed in the first half of 1940. In a letter to George
Jean Nathan of November 28, 1939 the author writes that he has begun
a second volume of autobiography and is 'attempting a sort of comedy to
be called, I think, "Purple Dust," and which I hope may be done, or
nearly done, early on in the new year.' On January 13, 1940 he wrote
to Peter Newmark: 'I am hard at work on "Purple Dust," a joke in three
acts.' On February 4 he told George Jean Nathan that he was busy 'finishing'
the work. Ten days later he declared to the same correspondent that *Purple
Dust* was, 'in some ways, an odd play', adding 'At first it was just to be
a skit on the country; but it changed a little into, maybe, a kind of an

allegorical form. The idea crept into my head after a visit to a family living in a Tudor House here; suffering all kinds of inconveniences because of its age and history; going about with lanterns, and eating in semi-gloom. Terrible torture for the sake of a tumbledown house with a name! I've never gone there since. I was perished with the cold, and damaged with the gloom. . . . I hope you'll find something in it. A lot of the humour is, I think, pretty broad, and a little exaggerated; but we Irish are fond of adding to things.' A version of the play must have been completed by this time and typescript copies sent to Nathan and O'Casey's American agent, Richard Madden. A letter from the dramatist to Nathan dated March 31, 1940 says, 'Dick [Madden] mentioned a few overdone [passages] in "Purple Dust"; and I'm going to look them over to see what parts would be best to knock out of them.' The same letter also gives his response to the critic's judgement: 'I am, of course, very glad and very proud of your good opinion of "Purple Dust." I was somewhat uncertain about the play myself. I knew there were good passages in it, and that it was odd—that's the word I thought of—; but was afraid to fancy it had more than those things in it.' The emphasis on its 'oddness' possibly explains the subtitle of 'Wayward Comedy' that was eventually added to the title-page. A letter to Morley Horder on April 8 confirms that he has 'just finished a new play'. The playwright was clearly not satisfied with the version, however, as a letter of June 24 to Peter Newmark indicated: 'I've just ended, roughly, the last act of "Purple Dust." I'm writing an alternative end; then I'll think for a while; & so eventually choose which will be the better one.' Even after publication in England on November 19, 1940 significant changes were made to the play, including the printing of a slightly different conclusion to the last act in an acting edition issued in 1957; it is possible that this was one of the alternative endings mentioned in the letter to Newmark. Earlier in 1940 the Macmillan Company, New York, had expressed an interest in publishing the play but, on receiving the reader's report and considering the temper of the times, coupled with the desire not to offend the strong pro-British sentiment in the country, it was decided not to go ahead with an American edition. Two hundred and fifty bound copies of the English edition were imported for sale in the United States.

O'Casey hoped for a stage production of *Purple Dust* before it was published; as with his other plays from *The Silver Tassie* (A14) onward, this hope was to be unrealised. The world première was on December 16, 1943 at the People's Theatre, Newcastle upon Tyne. Its first professional production was in November 1945 at the Liverpool Playhouse by the Northern Company of the Old Vic. The author had not had the opportunity of working on the play in collaboration with a stage company before it was reissued in Volume III of his *Collected Plays* (A29) in 1951. For this reprinting, a number of minor revisions were made and additional dialogue added to Act III (pp. 106–10). In the first half of 1953 the American producer, Sam Wanamaker, gathered together a cast and rehearsed the play in preparation for a London opening. The playwright actively co-operated with the director, attending rehearsals and rewriting scenes and dialogue. On March 11, 1953 he reported to George Jean Nathan: 'I've written four new songs for *Purple Dust*, asked for by Sam Wanamaker; two said to be "amusing," and two I like myself, which can be printed; kinda folk songs: "The Ruined Rowan Tree," and "How I Grieve for the Time When my Heart was Mine Own." ' After a tour of the north of England and an appearance in Edinburgh, the venture was abandoned through lack of financial support. O'Casey wrote to Wanamaker on June 5, 1953, upon hearing he was still trying to interest businessmen in the production: 'Never have I put so much energy into a play before, before writing it, writing it, and during rehearsals, and I dont relish the idea of putting a lot more into it. So I think better to cry quits. By the way, I've just come across notes on royalties received from the old Liverpool production; they were £75 and £69, which seems to say it done fairly well here, with a far less fine production.' Not all this intensive work was wasted. Some of the revisions and the songs were used in the text presented off-Broadway in 1956. In the meantime, the revisions of 1953 were further examined the following year when O'Casey corresponded with a New York director who hoped to produce the play there. As a result of practical suggestions on both sides, O'Casey was able to report to Nathan on November 22, 1954: 'I've amended it a good deal, cutting out two episodes that were dull and pointless, and though it isn't yet what it could be, I think it is better than it was.' Through lack of financial backing, once again, the projected production did not materialise and it was not until December 1956 that *Purple Dust* opened at the Cherry Lane Theater, New York. This presentation settled down for what was a record run for an O'Casey play – fourteen months. Its first appearance in London was at the Mermaid Theatre in 1962 when it was the opening play in that theatre's 'Sean O'Casey Festival'. This production was reviewed by Harold Hobson in the *Sunday Times*, August 19, 1962 and by Kenneth Tynan in the *Observer* of the same date. O'Casey's reaction to their reviews is expressed in the essay 'Purple Dust in Their Eyes' in *Under a Colored Cap* (A41).

The text used for the 1957 Acting Edition was the revised version which had been used in the New York production. It includes the song 'The Ruined Rowan Tree' which first appeared in print in *Chanticleer*, summer 1956 (C455), but not the other three songs O'Casey wrote for the play in 1953. This version of the play was reprinted in the anthology *The Genius of the Irish Theater* published by the New American Library in 1960, edited by Sylvan Barnet, Morton Berman and William Burto. The text in *Three More Plays* (A42) is that printed in *Collected Plays* (A29) with a change introduced into Act II. This change (pp. 180–1 in *Three More Plays*) was first published in the 1957 Acting Edition. It is the only one of the many alterations in that edition to be reprinted. The text of *Purple Dust* included in *Three More Plays*, like that of *Red Roses for Me* in the same volume, would thus appear to be the final printed version approved by the playwright.

The note on the dust-jacket of the 1940 edition, almost certainly written by the playwright himself, declared '*Purple Dust* may be called an O'Casey Pastoral, flushed by symbolism, marked by mad fun, with method in the madness; satire that laughs at philosophy gushing from the mouth of uninnocent fools, and at the end, a thunderclap of realistic and comic philosophy . . . The play laughs at those who see beauty in old things just because they are old. It shows how dismal a thing it is to try to live beside things and traditions that have passed away forever; and how futile it is to try to answer a faintly-blown bugle call that is but an imagined echo of bygone days; showing in [a] half funny, half savage way the river of time sweeping away the last little heap of purple dust.' In 1942, when

Red Roses for Me (A23) was published, O'Casey thought *Purple Dust* inferior
to it. Subsequently he came to have a much higher regard for his 'wayward
comedy', perhaps because he could see that the direction in which it led was
towards *Cock-a-Doodle Dandy* (A28). In the *New York Herald Tribune* of December
23, 1956 the dramatist stressed, 'There are no politics as such in this play; its
foundation, its roof, floor, windows and doors are built out of laughter',
adding, 'The play isn't an attack on England, not even on any particular
class in the country. . . . It is to some extent, a symbolic play, and uncon-
sciously, a prophetic one too. The auld hoose, beloved by so many for so
long, is in a bad way; old things are passing away, and new things are
appearing in the sky, on the horizon, and right here in the middle of us.
The house is falling, and we hardly know where to start to pick up the
bits. . . . Within the symbol and the prophecy is woven slapstick and rhythm,
a song here, a little dance there, some comic manners of man.' *Purple Dust*
was reprinted in *Collected Plays* (A29), in *Selected Plays* (A32), in *Three More
Plays* (A42) and in *The Sean O'Casey Reader* (A45).

Reviews: *Purple Dust* was 'previewed' by George Jean Nathan in *Esquire*,
Sep 1940 and in *Liberty*, Oct 12, 1940; it was reviewed in *Times Literary Supplement*, Nov 23, 1940; in *Irish Times*, Dec 14, 1940; by T.C. Murray in *Irish
Press*, Dec 20, 1940; in *Manchester Guardian*, Dec 31, 1940; in *Dublin Magazine*,
Jan–Mar 1941; by Denis Johnston in *Bell*, Jan 1941; by Edward Farrer
in *Life and Letters Today*, Jan 1941; by L. A. G. Strong in *Spectator*, Jan 17,
1941; by W. P. Eaton in *New York Herald Tribune Book Review*, Feb 9, 1941;
by Ivor Brown in *Observer*, Mar 16, 1941; by John J. Hogan in *Irish Book
Lover*, Sep 1941; in *Studies*, Sep 1941; in *English*, spring 1955.

2 PICTURES IN THE HALLWAY 1942

a. *first edition*
PICTURES / IN THE / HALLWAY / BY / SEAN O'CASEY / [all above in outline letters] / *Time flies over us, but leaves its shadow behind* / *New York* / THE
MACMILLAN COMPANY [in outline letters] / 1942 [in outline letters] / [all
above within decorative border]

21.5 × 14.5cm.

[i], half-title: PICTURES IN THE HALLWAY /; [ii], Books by Sean O'Casey;
frontispiece photograph: SEAN O'CASSIDE, GAELIC LEAGUER, IN HIS
SUNDAY BEST; [iii], title-page as above; [iv], copyright, printing, setter's
imprint, printer's imprint; [v], dedication: TO / THE MEMORY OF / THE
REV. E. M. GRIFFIN B.D., M.A. / ONE-TIME RECTOR OF ST.
BARNABAS, DUBLIN / *A fine scholar; a man of a many-branched* / *kindness, whose*
sensitive hand was the first / *to give the clasp of friendship to the author.* /; [vi], blank;
[vii], Contents; [viii], blank; [ix], fly-title: PICTURES IN THE HALLWAY; [x],
blank; 1–356, text; [357]–[358], blank.

Grey cloth; front and back covers blank; spine: O'CASEY / [ornament] /
PICTURES / IN THE / HALLWAY / [ornament] / *MACMILLAN* / .⊔. /;
lettered and decorated in green; cream endpapers, all edges trimmed, top edge
stained green; dust-jacket in green, black and white.
Published February 17, 1942 at $2.75; 2000 copies printed by The Ferris
Printing Co., set up by Brown Brothers Linotypers.

b. *English edition*
PICTURES / IN THE HALLWAY / BY / SEAN O'CASEY / *Time flies over us,*
but leaves its shadow behind / LONDON / MACMILLAN & CO. LTD / 1942

21.5 × 13.5cm.

[i], half-title: PICTURES IN THE HALLWAY /; [ii], Books by Sean O'Casey;
frontispiece, photograph: SEAN O'CASSIDE, GAELIC LEAGUER, CLAD IN
HIS SUNDAY BEST /; [iii], title-page as above; [iv], copyright, printer's
imprint; [v], dedication: TO / THE MEMORY OF / THE REV. E. M.
GRIFFIN, B.D., M.A. / ONE-TIME RECTOR OF ST. BARNABAS,
DUBLIN. / A FINE SCHOLAR: A MAN OF A MANY-BRANCHED
KINDNESS, / WHOSE SENSITIVE HAND WAS THE FIRST / TO GIVE THE
CLASP OF FRIENDSHIP / TO THE AUTHOR /; [vi], blank; vii, Contents;
[viii], blank; 1–[345], text, printer's imprint at foot of [345]; [346], blank;
[347]–[348], publisher's list of works by Sean O'Casey.

Olive cloth; front and back covers blank; spine: PICTURES / IN THE /
HALLWAY / [ornament] / SEAN / O'CASEY / [all above on blue panel
within grey-blue and gold borders] / MACMILLAN /; lettered and decorated
in green and gold; white endpapers, all edges trimmed; dust-jacket in green
and white.
Published February 20, 1942 at 15s; 2500 copies printed by R. & R. Clark,
Ltd, Edinburgh.

c. *first edition reset*

Pictures / IN THE HALLWAY / BY / *Sean O'Casey* / *Time flies over us, but leaves its shadow behind* / NEW YORK / THE MACMILLAN COMPANY / *1949*

21 × 14cm.

[i], half-title: *Pictures in the Hallway* /; [ii], Books by Sean O'Casey; frontispiece, photograph: SEAN O'CASSIDE, GAELIC LEAGUER, IN HIS SUNDAY BEST /; [iii], title-page as above; [iv], copyright, printing; [v], dedication to the Rev. E. M. Griffin; [vi], blank; [vii], Contents; [viii], blank; [ix], fly title: *Pictures in the Hallway* /; [x], blank; 1–373, text; [374], blank.

Tan cloth; front and back covers blank; spine: Pictures / IN THE / HALL- / WAY / [ornamental line] / O'CASEY / MACMILLAN / ; lettered and decorated in green.

Published September 6, 1949 at $4.00 (500 copies were imported by Macmillan and Co. for sale in Great Britain); reprinted 1952 (1250 copies, without the frontispiece). In 1950 this edition was licensed to Liberty Book Club, New York for distribution to its membership. The text was also reproduced, omitting the frontispiece, for the Macmillan Paperbacks edition, MP10, which was published on March 14, 1960 at $1.65 in an edition of 10,000 copies.

Notes: The enthusiasm which greeted *I Knock at the Door* (A19) spurred O'Casey into continuing his life story. On November 28, 1939, he wrote to George Jean Nathan that he was at work on the new volume and that the probable title would be 'Rough House'. In a letter to Peter Newmark dated March 30, 1940 he says, 'I am busy on my autobiography, (now isn't lifestory a better word than that?) & hope to have most of another volume done by the end of the year.' The following day he tells Nathan: 'I am still working on the second book of my life. I have ten chapters done; and I think some of them are very good.' The work proceeded steadily but the author was worried by the worsening war situation, with increasing air raids on Britain and heavy ship losses. In a letter of April 24, 1941 to Jack Carney he says: 'For the last few months I've typed more than ever in my life. Had to. I wanted to make sure of the MS. for second volume of "I Knock at the Door"; so I typed copies of twenty chapters, threefold: one for the U.S.A., one for Macmillans of London, and one for meself. So they'll hardly be bombed in three places at once. Three or four more chapters should do the trick. And I've never learned to dictate. Couldn't do it even to a letter.'

Pictures in the Hallway was completed in the first half of 1941. Writing to Peter Newmark on July 9, 1941 he tells him, 'I have just finished the second biograph vol. to be called "Pictures in the Hallway." I've overshot the mark in amount of material, writing over 100,000 words; I have now, I fear, to think of what can come out to make it sell for less than a quid.' A week earlier, on July 1, he told Daniel Macmillan: 'I have been surprised that the stuff I sent in was so full of words. I have since looked over and looked over the list of chapters, and find it undesirable to evict any of them from their holding. They, one by one, follow the years, and any of them would be out of place in any succeeding volume. I had thought of four [books] altogether, with the last one to be called, "The Clock Strikes

Twelve." What the intervening one may be called, God only knows; if indeed any other thing can be written. If there be, it will be per ardua ad astra with a vengeance. However, I can drop out the last chapter—"He Paints His First Picture," and end the volume with the part that gives the title to the book: "Pictures in the Hallway." ' The latter arrangement was followed and 'He Paints His First Picture' was omitted; it remains unpublished and no trace of it was to be found among the playwright's papers at his death.

The time sequence covered by *Pictures in the Hallway* is roughly 1892 to 1905. The dust-jacket of the English edition, almost certainly written by the playwright himself, describes the book: 'We are shown how O'Casside first touched the hand of Shakespeare; and how he first came close to the living theatre in a playhouse that is now the main part of the Abbey Theatre. We find him thrusting himself into the presence of Milton and other fine minds, seeking, in face of obstacles, and even perils, the rich and daring company of great men . . . The visit to Kilmainham Jail, the lordly fight in the Cat 'n Cage, ending in a flight from the police, the glow of the demonstration in Dublin streets voicing its sympathies with the Boers mingle with the Te Deum and the steady roll of the Orange drums . . . We find him, too, working for Harmsworth and heaven, hand in hand; and we are shown how colour and line and form swept into his life through the pictures of Constable and Fra Angelico. Dublin in her deep shade and glittering sun strikes up her drum again as Sean O'Casside sails down her stream of life in a gold canoe.' The phrase 'in a gold canoe' takes us forward to his next published work *Red Roses for Me* (A23) which owes a great deal to *Pictures in the Hallway*. O'Casey had originally intended that *Red Roses for Me* should be entitled 'At Sea in a Gold Canoe'.

In a letter to Macmillan and Co. dated July 1, 1941, the author wrote that he was sending 'a photo of myself when I had grown from a gasún into a bouchal. Could this be given as a frontispiece? I wanted, if possible, a picture of The Rev. E. M. Griffin, a Rector of a parish I lived in for a long time, a very dear friend of mine, and a beautiful character, inset, too; but although I've written his daughter whom I taught in Sunday School (God forgive me!) for a photo, she tells me she has but a snapshot of her father (he has been dead quite a while; but his memory is very vivid with me still) . . . I think I shall dedicate the volume to this dear friend of mine.' This arrangement was followed. Subsequently, O'Casey obtained a photograph of Griffin from his son and this was used as the frontispiece for the next autobiographical volume, *Drums Under the Windows* (A24).

O'Casey's letter to Macmillan of July 1, 1941 also announced his intention of sending a design for the dust-jacket of *Pictures in the Hallway*, as he had done for *I Knock at the Door*. The front of the dust-jacket has at the top two angels blowing trumpets; in the middle Milton and Shakespeare are on either side; at the bottom King William and an Orangeman beating a drum face Patrick Sarsfield and a worker carrying a flag. On the spine there are two illustrations, one showing a church, round tower and a Celtic cross, the other portraying a figure (O'Casey) seated under a tree.

Seeing a pre-publication copy of the book on February 18, 1942, O'Casey wrote to Daniel Macmillan: 'I am very pleased with the format, inside & out, of "Pictures in the Hallway." I think the cover looks very dignified & graceful.

I am downright glad that the book appealed to you so much. I think it
better, on the whole, than "I Knock at the Door"; though that thought may
be due to the illusion that the more you write, the better you get.' Later,
in a letter dated May 17, 1942, the playwright told George Jean Nathan,
'I am so glad that you liked my new book, Pictures in the Hallway, and
how much rest your fine opinion of it gave to me. . . . To keep my head
from flying too high, I see James Stern, in the New Republic, has said
some stern things . . . He's kind enough to say that the chapter "I Strike a
Blow" has grand writing, but "the road leading there is monotonous and
mighty long in which O'Casey dismally recalls the years." There's me for
you! thinking the years recorded grand effort and the will to live . . . Some
[critics] think that the talk of St. Patrick to the Irish and the Protestant Kid's
Idea of the Reformation was got from Finnegans Wake; but I have a recollection of writing the latter fourteen years ago, and of being encouraged to
go on by a fellow named G. J. Nathan publishing it eight or nine years
ago in THE AMERICAN SPECTATOR; and saying it was good:'

   The American edition of *Pictures in the Hallway* in this case preceded the
English edition by three days, despite the fact that it was set up and printed
using the proofs of the English edition. In selecting *Pictures in the Hallway*
for distribution to its membership in 1950, Liberty Book Club feared that
its readers would be offended by the apparent anti-semitic references in pp.
102–4 of the reset edition (A22c). Liberty therefore proposed changes
involving the pages in question as well as a relocation of the frontispiece.
In a letter to Daniel Macmillan, dated February 8, 1950, O'Casey rejected
the proposals, saying, 'I have carefully read the parts proposed to be cut . . .
Mr. Greenberg is a very acceptable human being. In fact, he was a very
decent man, and nothing said of him, shows him to be different. Anyway,
I have no racial prejudices—bondman or free, Jew or Gentile are equal
with me. I, therefore, can't see my way to cut out the passages named.' Liberty
Book Club offered the unchanged text to its membership as its March 1950
selection.

   The quotation on the title-page of the book is from Ralph Waldo Emerson.
'Royal Risidence', a chapter based on a visit made as a youngster with his
uncle to Kilmainham Jail, was published in abbreviated form in the *Virginia
Quarterly Review*, winter 1940 (C229). The chapter 'Cat 'n Cage' first appeared
also in the *Virginia Quarterly Review*, summer 1940 (C244).

   Pictures in the Hallway was reprinted in *Mirror in My House* (A35a), in *Autobiographies* (A35b) and in *Autobiography* (A35c). Excerpts were printed in *The Sean
O'Casey Reader* (A45).

   An adaptation of *Pictures in the Hallway*, by Paul Shyre, designed for a staged
reading was first presented at the YM-YWHA Poetry Center, New York, on
May 27, 1956. The text was published by Samuel French Inc. in 1957. A
recording by the cast of the September 1956 production at the Playhouse New
York, was issued by Riverside Records, RLP 7006–7. Another adaptation for a
staged reading by Patrick Funge and David Krause was first presented at the
Lantern Theatre, Dublin, on August 4, 1965; it has not been published.

Reviews: *Pictures in the Hallway* was reviewed by G. W. Stonier in *New Statesman
and Nation*, Feb 28, 1942; by Ivor Brown in *Observer*, Mar 1, 1942; by Robert
Van Gelder in *New York Times*, Mar 7, 1942; in *Times Literary Supplement*,

Mar 7, 1942; by A. S. W. in *Manchester Guardian*, Mar 13, 1942; by Patrick Kavanagh in *Irish Times*, Mar 14, 1942; by Lewis Gannett in *New York Herald Tribune*, Mar 19, 1942; by Ernest Boyd in *Saturday Review of Literature*, Mar 21, 1942; by Jenny Ballou in *New York Herald Tribune Book Review*, Mar 22, 1942; by Horace Reynolds in *New York Times Book Review,* Mar 22, 1942; by Stephen Gwynn in *Time and Tide*, Mar 28, 1942; by James Stern in *New Republic*, Mar 30, 1942; by Brooks Atkinson in *New York Times*, Apr 5, 1942; by John Brophy in *John O'London's,* Apr 10, 1942; by Charles A. Brady in *America,* Apr 11, 1942; in *New Yorker*, Apr 11, 1942; by S. Sillen in *New Masses*, Apr 21, 1942; by N. E. Monroe in *Catholic World*, May 1942; by Elizabeth Bowen in *Spectator*, May 1, 1942; by Maurice Devane in *Dublin Magazine*, July–Sep 1942; in *Listener*, July 2, 1942.

A23   RED ROSES FOR ME   1942

a. *first edition*
RED ROSES / FOR ME / *A Play in Four Acts* / BY / SEAN O'CASEY / "You may
break, you may shatter the vase, if you will, / But the scent of the roses will
hang round it still." / LONDON / MACMILLAN & CO. LTD / 1942

19.5 × 13cm.

[i], half-title: RED ROSES FOR ME /; [ii], Books by Sean O'Casey; [iii], title-
page as above; [iv], acknowledgement to Brigid Edwards for setting down the
airs to the songs, printer's imprint; copyright; [v], dedication: TO / Dr. J. D.
CUMMINS / IN MEMORY OF THE GRAND CHATS / AROUND HIS
SURGERY FIRE /; [vi], characters, scenes, time; 1–156, text; 157–[160], words
and music for the songs; [161], printer's imprint; [162], blank.

Red cloth; front and back covers blank; spine: RED / ROSES / FOR / ME /
[star] / SEAN / O'CASEY / MACMILLAN /; lettered and decorated in gold;
white endpapers, all edges trimmed; grey dust-jacket lettered and decorated in
red.
Published November 17, 1942 at 6s; 1990 copies printed by R. & R. Clark,
Ltd, Edinburgh; reprinted 1943 (1260 copies); 1944 (2000 copies); 1947 (1000
copies).

b. *American (offset) edition*
RED ROSES / FOR ME / *A Play in Four Acts* / BY / SEAN O'CASEY / "You may
break, you may shatter the vase, if you will, / But the scent of the roses will
hang round it still." / NEW YORK / THE MACMILLAN COMPANY / 1943

20.3 × 13.5cm.

[i], half-title: RED ROSES FOR ME /; [ii], Books by Sean O'Casey; [iii],
title-page as above; [iv], copyright, printing; [v], dedication to Dr J. D.
Cummins; [vi], blank; [vii], acknowledgement to Brigid Edwards; [viii],
characters, scenes, time; 1–156, text; 157–[160], words and music for the
songs.

Blue-grey cloth; front and back covers blank; spine lettered lengthwise:
SEAN O'CASEY [star] RED ROSES FOR ME [star] MACMILLAN /; lettered and
decorated in yellow; white endpapers, all edges trimmed; dust-jacket in red
and white.
Published January 18, 1944 at $2.00; 2600 copies printed; there were two
printings.

c. *acting edition*
RED ROSES / FOR ME / BY SEAN O'CASEY / [star] / A PLAY IN FOUR
ACTS / [star] / DRAMATISTS / PLAY   SERVICE / INC. [all above incorporated in design consisting of seven vertical rules, seven horizontal rules,
seven vertical rules]

20 × 13cm.

[1], title-page as above; [2], copyright, acting rights, sound effects records;

3–4, details and cast of the Booth Theater (New York) production, scenes, time; 5–76, text; 77–8, scene designs; 79–80, words and music for the songs; 81–2, property plot; [83]–[84], lists of publisher's plays.

Stiff red paper covers; lettered and decorated in black; all edges trimmed. Published August 22, 1956 at 90 cents; 1000 copies printed. In this version (which was not proof-read by O'Casey) there are two misprints on p.3. On p.4 the time is incorrectly indicated as 'A little while ago. 1913', the only edition in which the specific time 1913 was so listed. It is possible that this erroneous information was taken from the programme for the New York production of December 1955 – January 1956. In all other editions the dramatist wanted a vague suggestion of time as indicated by the phrase, 'A little while ago'. It is therefore fair to assume that the date 1913 is an erroneous interpolation for this text only. The contract with Dramatists Play Service was signed on March 28, 1956, two months after the play closed in New York for want of a theatre.

Notes: *Red Roses for Me* was completed early in 1942. It had been in the author's mind from the beginning of the Second World War, as a letter of November 28, 1939 to George Jean Nathan indicates (O'Casey was in the middle of writing *Purple Dust* at the time): 'I have had to put off, for the time being, my vague scheme for a new play. The times are too bad.' A year later, on October 29, 1940, before the war made its full impact on that part of south-west England in which O'Casey lived, he confided to Nathan, 'I have been a little disturbed by the war. It upsets the regular way of living. As well, I'm a member now of the Editorial Board of *The Daily Worker*, and these, and three kids, fill up a lot of time. But I am working at "the Biography" [*Pictures in the Hallway*], and in a chapter just written, I've included a song, that I like, called "She Carries a Rich Bunch of Red Roses for Me." I have a few thoughts swimming around in my head for another play, too; and hope things will let them grow into a decision.' At this time the ideas for the play were vague and there was no thought that the song would have an important place in the play and even provide its eventual title. It is no accident that the first intimation of the play should be in this context, for it is generally regarded as his most autobiographical drama. The work clearly owes a great deal to the playwright's experience in writing *Pictures in the Hallway* (A22) during the same period. Several episodes in the drama – notably the transformation scene in Act III – closely parallel episodes related in the second autobiographical volume. The main plot of a young worker killed in a strike, and the realisation of his relationship with his mother and with his friend, the rector of a Protestant Church in Dublin, are elements in *Red Roses for Me* that were originally the basis of O'Casey's unpublished play, *The Harvest Festival* (1918– 19) (B71), the manuscript of which is in the Berg Collection, New York Public Library. On April 18, 1942 O'Casey told George Jean Nathan, 'The play is built in a wholly new way on a theme sent many years ago to the Abbey Theatre by the name of *The Harvest Festival*. Of course, there was little or nothing then to the play; though I think this one isn't bad.' In an earlier letter to Nathan, dated February 19, 1942, the dramatist wrote: 'I have written out the rough copy (four acts) of a proposed new play, to be called, I think, *At Sea in a Gold Canoe*. But I'm not yet sure of the title.' On March 10 he told the same correspondent that he had completed the second autobiographical book, adding 'I dread looking forward to writing the next volume. To get a rest, I'm trying to write a play . . . calling it "At Sea in a Gold Canoe"; but I've since changed the name to "Red Roses for Me," a strange change for a name to take.' In a letter to Daniel Macmillan on April 29, 1942 O'Casey writes, 'Enclosed with this note is the MS of the play . . . RED ROSES FOR ME . . . I myself think it a finer play than PURPLE DUST; but that opinion doesn't go far.' The American drama critic, George Jean Nathan, preferred *Purple Dust* to *Red Roses for Me* (as eventually O'Casey was to do), and it was this fact which made the playwright quote comparative sales figures in a letter dated July 12, 1943; 'Strangely enough, [*Purple Dust*] hasn't sold well—a little over a hundred copies in the U.S.A. and about 700 here; though *Red Roses* has sold out a second edition [impression].' The latter work was further reprinted in 1944 and 1947.

The background to the play is not the 1913 Dublin Lock Out, as many critics have claimed, but an earlier rail strike in Ireland. This is explicitly stated by the playwright himself in a programme note for a production of the play performed at the University of California at Los Angeles in May 1964 (C596): 'Though the play is dedicated to the gallant men and women who took part in the long and bitter fight for freedom to join the Union of their choice, under the leadership of the great Jim Larkin, the play doesn't deal with that Lockout, but with a strike of Railwaymen of the British Isles long before Jim Larkin was known to any Irish worker.' However, the 1911 Rail Strike in Dublin (when O'Casey still worked for the G.N.R.I.) may also be relevant. The Rev. E. Clinton in the play is said to be modelled on the Rev. H. Fletcher and on the Rev. E. M. Griffin. The playwright himself in a letter of February 21, 1942 told Nathan that the original man was Griffin: 'My new play (if it ever be finished) has a clergyman (Protestant) in it . . . He's a character I drew, oh, thirty years ago [actually, twenty-four], in a play called "The Harvest Festival". . . and, in a hazy way, I have remembered something of what was written, and have made him a part of the play. He's modelled on a dear dead friend of mine— I have dedicated "Pictures in the Hallway" to him—, and stands up for the antagonistic element in his parish—as he did for me.' The bigoted vestry member, Dowzard, was a real-life character who was the subject of O'Casey's article 'Dowzard: the Hector of the Quays' in *Irish Worker*, December 20, 1913 (C43). Mrs Breydon is identified with O'Casey's mother, Ayamonn with O'Casey himself and Sheila with Maura, his early love and the girl to whom he dedicated *Juno and the Paycock*. Writing to Thomas Mark of Macmillan on May 15, 1954 concerning the music O'Casey says, 'The air [of the song "Red Roses for Me"] is semi-Traditional, that is I took it from an air known as "Eamonn a' Cnuic," "Ned o' the Hill"; but altered it to suit the words, as I did with many others in various plays. The words are my own as they are in all songs except those obviously by others.' The origin of another air in the drama emerges from a letter O'Casey wrote to Jack Carney on March 2, 1942: 'I'm always a little jealous of [a] fellow having a song I don't know. However, I've written a song "The Scab" to your air, and it will appear in the play I'm trying to write now.' He included the words with his letter, adding the inscription, '*The Scab* by S. O'Casey, from Jack Carney's singing of the air.' The song appears in all versions of the play except the 1956 Acting Edition.

Red Roses for Me was first produced at the Gaiety Theatre, Dublin, on

March 15, 1943 and was the first full-length work of O'Casey to have its première in his native city since *The Plough and the Stars* in 1926; the Abbey Theatre did not stage it until 1967, after the author's death. The English première occurred ten days after the Dublin opening – on March 25, 1943 – at the People's Theatre, Newcastle upon Tyne. Its first London performance was at the Embassy Theatre on February 26, 1946, where it beat all records for the Embassy up to that time, according to a letter of Sir Bronson Albery to Cyril Cusack, quoted in *Sean O'Casey, the Man Behind the Plays* by Saros Cowasjee (B45). It was produced on Broadway at the Booth Theatre, December 28, 1955 – the first full-length O'Casey play to reach New York since *Within the Gates* (A15), twenty-one years previously. There had been an amateur production in Boston in 1944 by the Tributary Theatre. O'Casey made minor revisions to the play in 1946 after witnessing the London production. These changes – mainly cuts in Act IV – were incorporated into the 1951 version of the play printed in Volume III of the *Collected Plays* (A29). The dramatist made further alterations, in addition to those incorporated in the *Collected Plays* text, for the 1955 New York presentation. A number of revisions were made to each of the four acts, particularly additions to Acts III and IV, and these were included in the Dramatists Play Service acting edition printed in 1956. Subsequently, in 1964, when invited by Macmillan and Co. to supervise a new paperback edition of *Three More Plays* (A42), O'Casey selected *Red Roses for Me* to be one of them; for the text he chose to follow that printed in *Collected Plays* with the addition of a short scene first printed in the 1956 version. The additional episode appears on pages 281–2 of the 1965 collection. The text of *Red Roses for Me* that appears in *Three More Plays* may thus be regarded as the final 'authorised' version of the work.

O'Casey himself composed the text for the dust-jacket of the 1942 English edition, in the course of which he writes, '. . . though in this play he [O'Casey] is in a gentler mood than is usual, there are fierce things in it as well as gentleness. The play is woven out of many moods, forming a coloured pattern of lively life. Especially to be noted is the Dublin Street Scene near the River Liffey. A thing of black and scarlet, silvered with song. The characters are clearly, and sometimes vividly painted in rich dancing dialogue . . .' The dust-jacket of the 1944 American edition included the following: '. . . "Red Roses for Me" is a blend of realism and mysticism . . . The symbolic passages of the play allow its author to use a poetical language unhampered by the limitations of everyday conversation, and, as in O'Casey's other plays, that language is magnificent. Even the beggars rise at times to a superb beauty of speech. Indeed, hardly another contemporary playwright has achieved such high poetry in drama.' The quotation on the title-page of the first English and American editions is taken from Thomas Moore's 'Farewell! But Whenever'. It does not appear in subsequent editions. *Red Roses for Me* was collected in *Collected Plays*, vol. III (A29), in *Selected Plays* (A32), in *Three More Plays* (A42) and in *The Sean O'Casey Reader* (A45)

Reviews: *Red Roses for Me* was reviewed by G. W. Stonier in *New Statesman and Nation*, Nov 14, 1942; by H. A. Milton in *Reynolds News*, Nov 22, 1942; in *Irish Press*, Dec 3, 1942; by A. D. in *Manchester Guardian*, Dec 4, 1942; in *Spectator*, Dec 25, 1942; in *Times Literary Supplement*, Jan 9, 1943; in *The Times*, Jan 9, 1943; by M. M. in *Bell*, Feb 1943; by Sheila May in *Dublin*

Magazine, Apr–June 1943; by Sylvia Townsend Warner in *Our Time*, Apr 1943; in *Theatre Arts*, Oct 1943; by Horace Reynolds in *New York Times Book Review*, Jan 30, 1944; by Edmund Wilson in *New Yorker*, Feb 5, 1944; by George Mayberry in *New Republic*, Feb 14, 1944; by W. P. Sears in *Churchman*, Mar 1, 1944; by John Kelleher in *New Republic*, Mar 20, 1944; in *Christian Century*, Mar 22, 1944; in *Theatre Arts*, Apr 1944; by W. P. Eaton in *New York Herald Tribune Book Review*, Apr 30, 1944; by Eric Bentley in *Partisan Review*, spring 1945.

DRUMS UNDER THE WINDOWS   1945

a. *first edition*
DRUMS   UNDER / THE / WINDOWS / BY / SEAN   O'CASEY / *Study   that house. / I think about its jokes and stories.* / LONDON / MACMILLAN & CO. LTD / 1945

21.5 × 14cm.

[i], half-title: DRUMS UNDER THE WINDOWS /; [ii], Books by Sean O'Casey; frontispiece, photograph: THE REV. E. M. GRIFFIN, B.D., M.A. / who by refusing to be either Orangeman or Freemason, kept the door of / the Church open for all to enter /; [iii], title-page as above; [iv], copyright, dedication to Dr Michael O'Hickey, printer's imprint; v, Contents; [vi], blank; 1–[340], text; [341], blank; [342], printer's imprint; [343]–[344], free endpaper, blank, conjoint with 333–4; [345], pasted-down endpaper, blank, conjoint with 331–2.

Grey cloth; front and back covers blank; spine: DRUMS / UNDER / THE / WINDOWS / [ornament,   drum   and   drumsticks] / SEAN / O'CASEY / [all above on red panel surrounded by borders of gold, grey and red] / MACMILLAN /; lettered and decorated in gold and red; cream endpapers at front, all edges trimmed; dust-jacket in red, grey and white, design on front incorporates a marching pipe band observed by George Bernard Shaw and W. B. Yeats on a background representing O'Connell Street, Dublin.
Published October 16, 1945 at 15s; 8,300 copies printed by R. & R. Clark, Ltd, Edinburgh.

b. *American edition*
Drums under the / Windows / BY / *Sean O'Casey / Study that house. / I think about its jokes and stories.* / NEW YORK / THE MACMILLAN COMPANY / 1946

22 × 14cm.

[i]–[ii], blank; [iii], half-title: *Drums under the Windows* /; [iv], Books by Sean O'Casey; frontispiece, photograph: THE REV. E. M. GRIFFIN, B.D., M.A./ who, by refusing to be either Orangeman or Freemason, kept the door of / the Church open for all to enter /; [v], title-page as above; [vi], copyright, printing; [vii], dedication to Dr Michael O'Hickey; [viii], blank; [ix], Contents; [x], blank; [xi], fly title: *Drums under the Windows;* [xii], blank; 1–[431], text; [432]–[436], blank.

Blue cloth; front and back covers blank; spine: [double rule] / [decorative rule] / DRUMS / UNDER THE / WINDOWS / [short decorative rule] / O'CASEY / [decorative rule] / [double rule] / MACMILLAN /; lettered and decorated in yellow; white endpapers, all edges trimmed.
Published May 7, 1946 at $4.50; 3000 copies printed; reprinted 1955; in 1950 this edition was licensed to Liberty Book Club, New York, for use as the August1950 selection for its membership; the text was also used without the frontispiece photograph for the Macmillan Paperbacks edition, MP30, which was published September 12, 1960 at $1.65 in an edition of 9940 copies.

Notes: Drums Under the Windows was written between 1942 and mid-1944. On March 10, 1942 O'Casey confessed to George Jean Nathan: 'I dread looking forward to writing the next volume. To get a rest, I'm trying to write a play [*Red Roses for Me*].' Two months later, on May 17, he told the same correspondent, 'I am so glad that you liked my new book, Pictures in the Hallway . . . I have started notes for a further volume; but I am so much occupied with many things that only God knows when it'll be well on the way.' On June 26, 1942 the dramatist wrote to Nathan: 'In the midst of many interruptions, I'm trying to get together a few chapters of the 3d volume of biography which I think I'll call Drums Under the Window.' The following year, in a letter to Jack Carney dated August 26, O'Casey said: 'I am doing a little with a new volume of "Biography." I've got about nine chapters done, which leaves me about fourteen more to do.' The writing proceeded steadily so that by February 8, 1944 the playwright could express the hope that the book would be completed that year. On June 9, 1944 in a letter to Daniel Macmillan he says: 'I have almost chosen the title DRUMS UNDER THE WINDOWS for this number. I will send on the other chapter as soon as it is done. I was thinking of writing a short FLASH FORWARD to describe my thoughts at the present time (some of them anyway), and so give an unusual end to it. I think I shall finish it off with a fourth volume to be called THE CLOCK STRIKES TWELVE.' On February 1, 1944 he had sent seven chapters to the Macmillan Company, New York, for safe keeping; on May 29, 1944 a further five chapters were sent; and on July 12 he was able to inform Jack Carney, 'I've sent in the ms. for another volume of biography and comment—*Drums under the Windows*, and have started work on another play [*Oak Leaves and Lavender*].'

This third volume of the playwright's life-story covers approximately the period 1905–16. The title of the book (the author used both *Window* and *Windows* in comments both before and after its publication) was most probably suggested by a phrase from W. B. Yeat's letter to O'Casey dated April 20, 1928 rejecting *The Silver Tassie* (A14). Of O'Casey's early work the poet said: 'You were interested in the Irish civil war, and at every moment of those plays wrote out of your own amusement with life or your sense of its tragedy; you were excited, and we all caught your excitement; you were exasperated almost beyond endurance by what you had seen or heard as a man is by what happens *under his window*, and you moved us as Swift moved his contemporaries' (our italics). *Drums Under the Windows* is dedicated 'To Dr. Michael O'Hickey, a Gael of Gaels, one-time Professor of Irish in Maynooth College. In a fight for Irish, he collided with arrogant Irish bishops, and was summarily dismissed without a chance of defending himself; taking the case to Rome, he was defeated there by the subtlety of the bishops, helped by a sly Roman Rota, ending his last proud years in poverty and loneliness. Forgotten, unhonoured, unsung in Eire, here's a Gael left who continues to say Honour and Peace to your brave and honest soul, Michael O'Hickey, till a braver Ireland comes to lay a garland on your lonely grave.' O'Casey regarded O'Hickey as a martyr and tells his story at length in this volume. He and Jim Larkin, the labour leader, are the heroes of the book.

In a letter of July 8, 1945 to Lovat Dickson of Macmillan and Co., O'Casey asserts: 'Prefatorily, let me say that in DRUMS UNDER THE WINDOW,

I primarily aim at doing something that Yeats might call "unique"; that the whole work will be a curious biography, entirely, or almost so, different from anything else of its kind; and, in its way, a kaleidoscopic picture of the poorer masses as they surged around one who was bone of their bone and flesh of their flesh.' The dust-jacket of the first edition carries the following description written by the author himself: 'Here in DRUMS UNDER THE WINDOWS, we get the third part of the author's experiences in the life of Dublin, itself fiercely and humorously dodging, charging, and dancing in and out through the revolving life of the world. Here he is, flitting about Dublin streets, under black and amber skies, to be changed soon to a rosy red when they are lit up by the frantic fires of Easter Week. The old green banners are superseded by the gayer ones of the Gaelic League and Republicans, and high among these flies the flag of the Plough and the Stars carried by the Irish Citizen Army. Drums beat outside every door and under every window, so that old men again see visions and young men dream dreams . . . In all this ferment, stir, light, and darkness, the author found time to close the eyes of his favourite brother, Tom, and hurry his dead sister into the grave. We see all this excellent, fanciful, and drab life move inexorably to one focus, to merge finally into the smoke and flame of revolt. A further volume, to be called *The Clock Strikes Twelve*, is to end the story.' The 'further volume' was called *Inishfallen, Fare Thee Well* (A27) and O'Casey went on to write not one but three further volumes of his life story.

Macmillan's solicitor was concerned about possible 'actionable' passages in the book before publication. O'Casey, in a letter of July 8, 1945 to accompany comments made on the points raised by the solicitor, remarked: 'I shouldn't care to have that solicitor looking over my shoulder while I work, even were I writing prayer or hymn. Reluctantly, I let the little "bawdy" song go as you suggest.' The latter lyric originally ended the chapter entitled 'Song of a Shift', when the fish seller who has attacked W. B. Yeats for obscenity breaks into a ballad that begins 'Oh, sailor Tom came home to wed . . .' Advance proofs of *Drums Under the Windows* contained the song: an uncorrected copy of page proofs among the O'Casey Papers in the Berg Collection of the New York Public Library bears on its cover the inscription in the playwright's handwriting, 'Page 150 Song of the Fish hawker silenced. Macmillans didn't like it.' It remains unpublished. Otherwise, the author rejected most of the solicitor's suggestions and only a few names were altered in deference to any possible objections. Liberty Book Club in considering *Drums Under the Windows* for distribution to its membership objected to the use of the word 'nigger' in the phrase 'work like a nigger' (American edition p. 2) and asked if the word could be changed. On being advised of this O'Casey said he would be willing to have the word changed to 'coolie' or 'trojan'. In copies distributed to its membership by the Liberty Book Club the word became 'trojan'.

As with the two previous volumes of the autobiography, the playwright himself designed the dust-jacket. In a letter of September 4, 1944 to H. Cowdell of Macmillan and Co. he gives the plan for the dust-jacket: 'I like the idea of an indication of buildings to the right of the picture (where a figure meant to be Yeats stands), as if the turbulence of the marching drummers and pipers was hurrying them out of the picture. The main idea,

I think, is the dominance of the drummers and pipers, in stature, over what looks like a toy town. The pillar in [the] distance is meant to be Nelson's in Dublin; and the figure on left, looking over the buildings, is meant to be that of Shaw. For the "spine" is a sketch of a drum, flanked by Easter lilies—symbol of Rising in Easter Week—a crossed pick and shovel, and a rayed circle, cap-badge of the Irish Volunteers; if a right Red Hand—which would symbolize the Irish Citizen Army—could be inserted in centre of rayed circle, I should be glad.' Writing to Daniel Macmillan on November 6, 1945, after publication of the book, he says: 'I do [like the book] very much; though the design on the jacket (mine own) isn't, I'm afraid, quite so good as the previous two. The book itself is near as good as a book can be.' The following month, on December 17, he tells Jack Carney: 'I have been told by Macmillans that Drums Under the Windows is sold out. Curious that, for neither of the previous two [volumes] had such a quick sale.'

The frontispiece photograph of Rev. E. M. Griffin, the dramatist's friend and benefactor, had originally been sent on July 10, 1941 for inclusion in *Pictures in the Hallway* (A22). O'Casey had received the photograph from Griffin's son and had dedicated *Pictures in the Hallway* to his old friend. The quotation on the title-page is from *Purgatory* by W. B. Yeats.

Drums Under the Windows was collected in *Mirror in My House* (A35a), in *Autobiographies* (A35b), and in *Autobiography* (A35c). Excerpts were published in *The Sean O'Casey Reader* (A45).

An adaptation of *Drums Under the Windows*, designed for a staged reading by seven voices, was prepared by Paul Shyre and presented at the Cherry Lane Theatre, New York, on October 13, 1960. The adaptation in two acts was published by Dramatists Play Service, Inc. in 1962. Another adaptation for a staged reading by Patrick Funge and David Krause was presented at the Lantern Theatre, Dublin, on July 21, 1970; it remains unpublished.

Reviews: *Drums Under the Windows* was reviewed by Allen Hutt in *Daily Worker*, Oct 17, 1945; by J. Betjeman in *Daily Herald*, Oct 25, 1945; by G. W. Stonier in *New Statesman and Nation*, Oct 27, 1945; by George Orwell in *Observer*, Oct 28, 1945; by M. J. MacManus in *Irish Press*, Nov 1, 1945; by St John Ervine in *Spectator*, Nov 2, 1945; by W. J. W. in *Irish Times*, Nov 3, 1945; by Desmond MacCarthy in *Sunday Times*, Nov 4, 1945; by Louis MacNeice in *Time and Tide*, Nov 10, 1945; by N. N. in *Irish Independent*, Nov 12, 1945; in *Times Literary Supplement*, Nov 17, 1945; in *Sunday Independent*, Nov 18, 1945; by John Edgell in *Our Time*, Dec 1945; by Sean O'Faolain in *The Bell*, Dec 1945; by E. M. B. in *Irish Democrat*, Dec 1945; by Roibeárd ó Faracháin in *An Iris*, Dec 1945; by R. M. Fox in *Forward*, Dec 22, 1945; by Austin Clarke in *Dublin Magazine*, Jan–Mar 1946; in *Listener*, Jan 31, 1946; by Kathleen O'Brennan in *America*, Feb 2, 1946; by Gerald W. Johnson in *New York Herald Tribune*, May 7, 1946; by William McFee in *New York Sun*, May 7, 1946; by Orville Prescott in *New York Times*, May 8, 1946; by Rolfe Humphries in *Nation*, May 11, 1946; by Frank J. Hynes in *Saturday Review of Literature*, May 11, 1946; by Horace Reynolds in *New York Herald Tribune Book Review*, May 12, 1946; by Richard Sullivan in *New York Times Book Review*, May 12, 1946; in *Newsweek*, May 13, 1946; in *Time*, May 13, 1946; by Richard Watts in *New Republic*, June 10, 1946; by S. Finkelstein in *New Masses*, June 11, 1946; by P. J. O'Donnell in *Catholic World*, July 1946; by T. Q. Curtiss in *Theatre Arts*, Aug 1946; by Padraic Colum in *Yale Review*, autumn 1946; by Brooks Atkinson in *New York Times*, Sep 22, 1946; by William D'Arcy in *Catholic Historical Review*, Jan 1947; by Robert B. Heilman in *Quarterly Review of Literature*, 1947.

5 OAK LEAVES AND LAVENDER   1946

a. *first edition*
OAK LEAVES / AND LAVENDER / OR / A WARLD ON WALLPAPER / BY /
SEAN O'CASEY / LONDON / MACMILLAN & CO. LTD / 1946

19.5 × 13cm.

[i], half-title: OAK LEAVES AND LAVENDER /; [ii], Books by Sean O'Casey;
[iii], title-page as above; [iv], copyright, printer's imprint; [v], dedication:
TO / LITTLE JOHNNY GRAYBURN / WHO, IN HIS SAILOR SUIT,
PLAYED FOOTBALL / WITH ME ON A CHALFONT LAWN / AND
AFTERWARDS GALLANTLY FELL / IN THE BATTLE OF ARNHEM /; vi,
Characters in Order of Appearance; vii, scenes, time; [viii], blank; 1–158,
text; 159–[163], words and music of the songs; [164], printer's imprint; [165]–
[166], free endpaper, blank, conjoint with 155–6; [167], pasted down endpaper,
blank, conjoint with 153–4.

Green cloth; front and back covers blank; spine: OAK / LEAVES / AND /
LAVENDER / [star] / SEAN / O'CASEY / MACMILLAN /;   lettered   and
decorated in gold; white endpapers, all edges trimmed; pale blue dust-
jacket, lettered and decorated in green.
Published April 30, 1946 at 6s; 6000 copies printed by R. & R. Clark, Ltd,
Edinburgh; reprinted May 1947 (2000 copies).

b. *American (offset) edition*
OAK LEAVES / AND LAVENDER / OR / A WARLD ON WALLPAPER / BY /
SEAN O'CASEY / NEW YORK / THE MACMILLAN COMPANY / 1947

18.5 × 12.5cm.

[a]–[b], blank; [i], half-title: OAK LEAVES AND LAVENDER /; [ii], Books
by Sean O'Casey; [iii], title-page as above; [iv], copyright, printing; [v], dedication to Johnny Grayburn; vi, Characters in Order of Appearance; vii, scenes,
time; [viii], blank; 1–158, text; 159–[163], words and music of the songs;
[164]–[166], blank.

Brown cloth; front and back covers blank; spine lettered lengthwise: *O'Casey*
[ornament] Oak Leaves and Lavender [ornament] *Macmillan* /; lettered and
decorated in gold; cream endpapers, all edges trimmed; pale blue dust-
jacket lettered and decorated in brown.
Published April 8, 1947 at $2.50; 2827 copies printed.

Notes: *Oak Leaves and Lavender* was written in 1944. On February 8 of that
year O'Casey told George Jean Nathan that he hoped to finish *Drums Under
the Windows* 'this year', adding, 'Then, I might start on a play, possibly
a war-play—that's how my thoughts go at the moment.' On July 12 he
wrote to Jack Carney: 'I've sent in the ms for another volume of biography
and comment—*Drums Under the Windows*, and have started work on another
play.' Later, in an undated letter to Nathan, he reported, 'I have written
and typed out roughly 60 pages of ideas and dialogue for a new play;
and when I've done near as many more, I'll try to put it into shape. It's

what you call a "Boom Boom" play, though there are no "Boombs" in it. I imagine, in ways, it may be an odd play. I was going to call it "Roll Out the Barrel", but have decided to change it to "A Warald on Wallpaper." There will be a good deal of what I think to be humour (I hope I'm right) in it; and this will be pointed with a few attempts at seriousness.' On October 8, 1944 he was sufficiently advanced to tell the same correspondent, 'I expect to finish my new play—A Warald on Wallpaper—in a fortnight or so . . . I don't imagine it is in any way like most plays (like any) written around the war. It is largely a Comedy (or Farce), and is (will be) inscribed to Cuchullain, the legendary hero, who, having tied himself to a stake that he might die upright in front of his enemies, laughed long at the comic aspect of a raven slipping about in the blood that had flown from his wounds. The play opens with a prelude [with] shades of eighteenth-century sparks and their ladies dancing a slow minuet, and wondering in a ghostly way at what is happening. They end the play, too; and between these two appearances, the major play is written. There is ne'er a bang in it anyway: I don't care a lot now for these bangs, though I had them often enough in my earlier plays; and can't cavil at anyone having them in his.'

The playwright informed Jack Carney on November 7, 1944 that the play was completed. Writing to Daniel Macmillan on November 15, 1944, O'Casey tells him, 'I have written another play . . . It is called A WARALD ON WALLPAPER, I think it good work, if my judgment be worth a damn.' The manuscript of the play was sent to the publisher on November 22, 1944. The first draft was called 'Roll Out the Barrel', the title of a popular song during the Second World War. Later it was entitled 'Warald on Wallpaper', a punning reference to a phrase in W. B. Yeat's letter rejecting *The Silver Tassie* (A14), when the poet wrote that in a good play, 'The whole history of the world must be reduced to wallpaper in front of which the characters must pose and speak.' In a letter to Daniel Macmillan of October 2, 1945 O'Casey writes, 'Looks as if there would be a history round the title of my last play. I clean forgot you were concerned with the change of name. It's like this—Bronson Albery of New Theatre, who has the play under contract, wrote, as well as you, complaining of the name, and asking me to change it. After rejecting many—for instance "Mobled Hours," I came to "Oak Leaves and Lavender," which you and he liked. So far, so good; and I forgot all about it. Long after Mr. Albery wrote again, saying all who read the play preferred the original name of "Warld on Wallpaper"; and he begged me to change it back again. Forgetting you, I agreed, though Mrs. O'Casey likes the second name much better. It is certainly more musical; but not so full of meaning. But I can't keep changing it back and for'ard; so once and for all, I change it to "Oak Leaves and Lavender; or A Warld on Wallpaper." I am writing to Mr. Albery that the play will be published under this title.' In a letter of November 4, 1945 to Bronson Albery the playwright states, 'WORLD ON WALLPAPER wouldn't do at all—there's no meaning in it. There is, of course, in WARLD ON WALLPAPER—that is world-war on wallpaper, by telescoping two words into one. I strongly beseech you let the prettier name ['Oak Leaves and Lavender'] go for the name of the play. As a matter of fact, I added a few phrases to the proofs of the play so as to bring the oak leaves theme to a closer connection with it.'

The printed text was not dedicated to Cuchulain, as originally intended, but to Johnny Grayburn who, about twelve years previously, had been a playmate of O'Casey's son Breon. In *Inishfallen, Fare Thee Well* (A27) the playwright writes of Lieutenant John Grayburn 'who died holding a Rhine bridge at Arnhem', for which gallantry he was awarded the Victoria Cross. In his autobiography he links this latter-day hero with another one to whom he had dedicated early examples of his literary work, the Irish nationalist Thomas Ashe (A2–A4), 'So there these two lie, but a few moments or so apart from each other; the one who died for Ireland's humanity, the other who died for the world's; the one in the grey-green of an Irish Volunteer, the other in the muddy-yellow of England's battledress: both now lost, swallowed up in the greed of eternity.'

The playwright's desire for a production before publication and his concern at his inability to see his plays in performance prior to printing is expressed in his letter of April 23, 1945 to Peter Newmark: 'I've written a war play, called Oak Leaves & Lavender, or, A Warld on Wallpaper . . . But when will it be done? I've now 4 major plays, & none of them have as yet got a professional performance.' *Oak Leaves and Lavender* attracted little attention and has had but one stage production in English – that at the Lyric Theatre, Hammersmith, on May 14, 1947; it was regarded by the dramatist as the worst professional staging of any of his works. Its first stage production was in Sweden at the Helsingborgs Stadsteater in 1946. The critics generally rank it with *The Star Turns Red* (A20) as among his least successful works.

In a letter of August 24, 1946 to the Macmillan Company, New York, the dramatist describes the play as 'an O'Casey tribute . . . to the big fight waged here [in England] against Nazi domination.' On January 3, 1947 he wrote to Miss M. E. Barber, Society of Authors: 'Oak Leaves would hardly be welcomed in Germany, for the mood of the play towards Germany is the mood of all of us to her in 1941, during the big bombing of our cities and towns.' In a letter of January 17, 1959 to Kaspar Spinner and published by Spinner in his *Die alte Dame sagt: Nein*! (B42), O'Casey also had this to say about the work: 'A lady had been pestering me at the time about the truth of "British-Israel," the curious creed making the British (& Irish, Scots, & Welsh) the Chosen People of God. Earlier, before I tried to write anything, I was in a campaign in Ireland to prevent some of their people rooting up our Hill of Tara looking for the Ark of the Covenant; and so I wanted to satirize them.' The play received relatively little attention from the critics on its publication. The playwright himself came to have little regard for it, as a letter dated May 28, 1947 to his eldest son indicated. Attempting to cheer Breon after a personal disappointment, he wrote: 'Every certain and well-developing life leaves a lot of failures behind it; for a good life is one of insistent trying, and to try always is to fail often; though such a life usually succeeds, somehow, someway, in the end. I myself have left more failures behind me (what others called failures) than I bother to sit down to count. Even today, I leave behind me the failure of *Oakleaves and Lavender*; having learned a lot from it, which I hope may serve me in the future. Indeed, I hope it won't be the last "failure", for if it should be, it would mean I'd try nothing else again. It is nothing—relatively—than the occasional failure of a match to strike. We just strike another one.' Perhaps he was able to write in this reasonably self-assured way because he had by this time completed his next play *Cock-a-Doodle Dandy* with its exuberant return to an Irish setting and Irish themes. This supposition appears to be borne out by a passage in one of the playwright's essays in which, commenting on *Cock-a-Doodle Dandy*, he wrote, 'like Joyce, it is only through an Irish scene that my imagination can weave a way' (*New York Times*, Nov 9, 1958, C503).

Oak Leaves and Lavender was reprinted, unrevised, in the fourth volume of *Collected Plays* (A29).

Reviews: *Oak Leaves and Lavender* was reviewed by T. C. Murray in *Irish Press*, Apr 25, 1946; by J. C. Trewin in *John O'London's Weekly*, May 3, 1946; in *Times Literary Supplement*, May 4 and 11, 1946; by Valentin Iremonger in *Irish Times*, May 18, 1946; by G. W. Stonier in *New Statesman and Nation*, May 25, 1946; by J. B. Priestley in *Our Time*, June 1946; by A. Farjeon in *Time and Tide*, June 8, 1946; by John Collier in *New Theatre*, July 1946; by Ewart Milne in *Irish Democrat*, Aug 1946; by A. J. Levanthal in *Dublin Magazine*, July–Sep 1946; by Horace Reynolds in *New York Times Book Review*, May 11, 1947; in *San Francisco Chronicle*, May 11, 1947; in *Christian Century*, May 14, 1947; by George Freedley in *Library Journal*, May 15, 1947; by W. P. Eaton in *New York Herald Tribune Book Review*, May 25, 1947.

A26   JUNO AND THE PAYCOCK AND THE PLOUGH AND THE   1948
      STARS

first edition
JUNO AND THE PAYCOCK / AND / THE PLOUGH AND THE STARS / BY
/ SEAN O'CASEY / With Introduction and Notes by / GUY BOAS, M.A. /
MACMILLAN AND CO., LIMITED / ST. MARTIN'S STREET, LONDON /
1948

17.5 × 11cm.

[i], half-title: THE SCHOLAR'S LIBRARY / *General Editor:*– GUY BOAS, M.A. /
JUNO AND THE PAYCOCK / AND / THE PLOUGH AND THE STARS /:
[ii], blank; [iii], title-page as above; [iv], copyright, printing; v, Contents; [vi],
blank; vii–xi, Introduction; [xii], blank; [1]–163, text; [164], blank; 165–[169],
Notes, printer's imprint at foot of [169]; [170]–[172], List of Titles in The
Scholar's Library.

Green cloth; front and back covers blank; spine: [triple rule] / JUNO / AND
THE / PAYCOCK / & / THE PLOUGH / AND THE / STARS / SEAN /
O'CASEY / [winged head ornament] / MACMILLAN / [triple rule] / ; lettered
and decorated in gold.
Published July 23, 1948 at 4s; 3000 copies printed by R. & R. Clark, Ltd,
Edinburgh; reprinted 1951 (3000 copies), 1954 (3000 copies), 1956 (5000
copies), 1957 (5000 copies), 1958 (5000 copies), 1959 (10,000 copies), 1962
(10,185 copies), 1964 (7575 copies), 1965 (10,203 copies), 1966 (10,137 copies),
1969 (7500 copies), 1970 (10,000 copies), 1971 (11,000 copies).

Notes: These are the two great Dublin plays: *Juno and the Paycock* (A11), first
published in 1925, and *The Plough and the Stars* (A13), first published in 1926.
They are the most popular O'Casey plays in performance; the printing history
of this edition testifies to the plays' great popularity also with the book-buying
public. The text was reset for this edition only and issued in Macmillan's
Scholar's Library. The 1957 reprint bears the misleading note: 'First issued
together in Macmillan's Pocket Library 1957'. The 1957 Pocket Library issue
was an exact reprint of the 1948 text omitting the 'Introduction' and 'Notes'.
For the 1965 and subsequent reprints, a 'Biographical Note' (pp. xi–xii) by
Guy Boas was added.

INISHFALLEN FARE THEE WELL   1949

a. *first edition*
INISHFALLEN / FARE THEE / WELL / BY / SEAN O'CASEY / *The wheel of th'*
wagon's broken, / *It ain't goin' to turn no more;* / *The wheel of th' wagon's broken,*
/ *An' there's weeds round th' ranch-house door.* / LONDON / MACMILLAN & CO.
LTD / 1949

21.5 × 14cm.

[i], half-title: INISHFALLEN, FARE THEE WELL /; [ii], Books by Sean
O'Casey; frontispiece, photograph: THE ROOM IN THE DUBLIN TENE-
MENT HOUSE WHERE THE FIRST THREE PLAYS WERE WRITTEN /;
[iii], title-page as above; [iv], copyright, printing; [v], dedication: TO /
WALTER McDONALD, D.D. / PROFESSOR OF THEOLOGY IN ST.
PATRICK'S / ROMAN CATHOLIC COLLEGE, MAYNOOTH, / FOR
FORTY YEARS; A GREAT MAN / GONE, AND ALMOST FORGOTTEN; /
BUT NOT QUITE FORGOTTEN /; [vi], blank; vii, Contents; [viii], blank;
1–[307], text; [308], printer's imprint.

Grey cloth; front and back covers blank; spine: INISHFALLEN / FARE
THEE / WELL / [ornament] / SEAN / O'CASEY / [all above on green panel
within grey, green and gold borders] / MACMILLAN /; lettered and decorated in green and gold; white endpapers, all edges trimmed; dust-jacket
in grey, green and white; on the front, scenes and personalities in the book
are depicted as panels in a stained glass window, on the spine, there are
three panels showing scenes from O'Casey's own experience.
Published January 28, 1949 at 16s; 5000 copies printed by R. & R. Clark,
Ltd, Edinburgh.

b. *American edition*
Inishfallen / FARE THEE WELL / BY / *Sean O'Casey* / *The wheel of th' wagon's*
broken, / *It ain't goin' to turn no more;* / *The wheel of th' wagon's broken,* / *An' there's*
weeds round th' ranch-house door. / NEW YORK / THE MACMILLAN COM-
PANY / *1949*

21 × 14cm.

[i]–[ii], blank; [iii], half-title: *Inishfallen, Fare Thee Well* /; [iv], Books by Sean
O'Casey; frontispiece, photograph: The Room in the Dublin Tenement Where
the First Three Plays Were Written; [v], title-page as above; [vi], copyright,
printing; [vii], dedication to Walter McDonald; [viii], blank; [ix], Contents; [x],
blank; 1–396, text; [397]–[398], blank.

Buff cloth; front and back covers blank; spine: Inish- / fallen / FARE / THEE /
WELL / [decorative line] / O'CASEY / MACMILLAN /; lettered and decorated
in green; white endpapers, all edges trimmed; dust-jacket in green and white
with photograph of O'Casey by Ben Pinchot on back.
Published February 21, 1949 at $4.75; 5031 copies printed; reprinted 1956;
Book Find Club, New York, selected *Inishfallen, Fare Thee Well* in the same
year for distribution to its membership – it was issued without the frontispiece

and the dedication to Walter McDonald was also omitted; the text was also used, without the frontispiece for the Macmillan Paperbacks edition, MP29, which was published September 12, 1960 at $1.65 in an edition of 10,071 copies.

Notes: Inishfallen, Fare Thee Well was written between 1945 and 1947. In the blurb for the dust-jacket of the previous volume of the series, *Drums Under the Windows* (A24), O'Casey had written: 'A further volume, to be called *The Clock Strikes Twelve* is to end the story.' A letter to Jack Daly dated November 26, 1946 speaks of working 'at the "last" vol. of Biography. It will end at the time when I leave Ireland for England. "The last glimpse of Eireann." ' The following year, in a letter of March 14, the playwright informed George Jean Nathan: 'I have just finished another vol. of biography, which ends this work for awhile. I end it when I leave Ireland and am calling it (I had a trying time thinking of a title; Clock Strikes Twelve was used as a title a few months ago here) "Goodbye at the Door." '

Neither The Clock Strikes Twelve nor Goodbye at the Door was used as a title. On April 15, 1947 the playwright gives his final choice for title in a letter to Macmillan: 'I have completed the MS for another biographical vol. to be called, I think, INISHFALLEN FARE THEE WELL; and I shall be glad if you would let me know whether or no I may send it on to you. This vol. ends the series with the author's departure for England.' The title is taken from one of Thomas Moore's Irish Melodies (ninth number) entitled 'Sweet Innishfallen, fare thee well'. Macmillan's desire to see the manuscript was expressed in Lovat Dickson's letter of April 16 to O'Casey. The eighteen chapters were sent to Mr Dickson on April 18 together with several sketches for the dust-jacket.

The book covers approximately the years 1917–26, beginning with his mother's death and ending with his decision to leave Ireland. The dust-jacket of the English edition, almost certainly written by the author himself, describes the book as one which 'recreates with his unique blend of grim realism and poetic imagery the Ireland of the days when, as he recalls, death lounged by the corner of every Dublin street, or waited in the primrose-spangled country lanes. It depicts the turbulence of the Black and Tans, the uneasy truce, the dispute over the treaty, and the bitter feud that raged between its supporters and the Republicans ... In other pages the author writes of more peaceful things, of visits to Lady Gregory's home, Coole Park in Galway ... Others of her circle are met as the author enters into the life of the Abbey Theatre ... We catch a glimpse of Yeats, "a banner without an army," but always trailing a silvery shadow behind him ... The book shows O'Casey bidding a long farewell to his mother, as she leaves her life of toil for an everlasting holiday; to his brother Michael; to a girl for whom he had a deep admiration; and at last to Ireland herself, and, though this was not foreseen, to the Abbey Theatre.' The dust-jacket of the American edition has this to say of the work: 'Like Mr O'Casey's other biographical volumes, *Inishfallen, Fare Thee Well* is written in the third person, recording the thoughts, opinions and experience of one Sean Casside, a Dublin firebrand who became a writer. The new volume takes him through the years when the Abbey Theatre put on *Juno and the Paycock* and *The Plough and the Stars* to the time when he left Ireland forever in self-imposed exile.

It includes a masterly sketch of his mother's death in a moldy tenement and of her poverty-stricken funeral, and a memorable character portrait of Lady Gregory—"a robin with the eye of a hawk." '

As with each of the preceding three autobiographical volumes, the author himself designed the book's dust-jacket. On April 18, 1947 he sent Macmillan 'sketches for a possible jacket, with three additional thumnail [*sic*] ones for the spine'; twelve months later he was still engaged in correspondence with the firm on the same subject, telling H. Cowdell on April 8, 1948: 'I have but a few comments to make [on the sketch for the dust-jacket]. I think the face of "St. Patrick" ought to be more masklike, more stern-looking; a face indifferent to all things outside of its own thought—if it can be done. The face of "Chesterton" is inclined a little to the left; I think the face of "Belloc," on the opposite side, should, to balance the picture, be a little inclined to the right.' The playwright's instructions were followed closely. The design for the front of the dust-jacket incorporates a church window representing personalities and scenes. The top circular window has a 'stern-looking' St. Patrick; directly beneath, the faces of Chesterton and Belloc are inclined to the left and the right respectively; underneath is the face of de Valera; three vertical windows depict a religious procession, a street battle, and a book-burning scene.

The frontispiece is a photograph of the interior of O'Casey's room at 422 North Circular Road, Dublin, taken about March 1924. The Irish theatre critic and a former member of the Abbey Theatre Company, Gabriel Fallon, who appears in the photograph on the mantelpiece, describes the photograph and the circumstances of its taking in his *Sean O'Casey, the Man I Knew* (B48), pp. 78–9. The chapter 'The Raid' had already been published as 'The Raid, an Autobiographical Sketch' in *The Mint*, edited by Geoffrey Grigson (B18). Some of the material in the chapters 'Blessed Bridget o' Coole' and 'Where Wild Swans Nest' appeared originally in the article 'Lady of Coole' in the *Saturday Book* (B15), published seven years previously.

The book was given the 'Page One Award' in 1949 by the Newspaper Guild of New York. The citation read: 'To Sean O'Casey for his autobiography, the most recent volume of which is *Inishfallen, Fare Thee Well*, a superb work by a writer of genius too little recognized in this country.'

Inishfallen, Fare Thee Well was reprinted in *Mirror in My House* (A35a), in *Autobiographies* (A35b) and in *Autobiography* (A35c). Excerpts were published in *The Sean O'Casey Reader* (A45).

An adaptation for the stage by Patrick Funge and David Krause was produced at the Lantern Theatre, Dublin, on July 24, 1972. It shared the stage with the authors' adaptations of *Pictures in the Hallway* and *Drums under the Windows* in a production which lasted for six and three-quarter hours. It has not been published.

Reviews: *Inishfallen, Fare Thee Well* was reviewed by M. J. MacManus in *Irish Press*, Jan 27, 1949; by Austin Clarke in *Irish Times*, Jan 29, 1949; by L. A. G. Strong in *Observer*, Jan 30, 1949; by Desmond MacCarthy in *Sunday Times*, Jan 30, 1949; by Gerard Fay in *Manchester Guardian*, Feb 1, 1949; by Allen Hutt in *Daily Worker* (London), Feb 3, 1949; by Sean O'Faoláin in *John O'London's*, Feb 4, 1949; by Una Pope-Hennessy in *Spectator*, Feb 4, 1949; by Bruce Bain in *Tribune*, Feb 4, 1949; by Annabel Farjeon in

Time and Tide, Feb 5, 1949; by Harold Nicolson in *Daily Telegraph* Feb 11, 1949; by Louis MacNeice in *New Statesman*, Feb 19, 1949; in *Times Literary Supplement*, Feb 19, 1949; by Horace Gregory in *New York Herald Tribune Book Review*, Feb 20, 1949; by Orville Prescott in *New York Times*, Feb 22, 1949; by Hayter Preston in *Cavalcade*, Feb 26, 1949; by N. N. in *Irish Independent*, Feb 26, 1949; in *New Yorker*, Feb 26, 1949; by Brooks Atkinson in *New York Times*, Feb 27, 1949; in *Time*, Feb 28, 1949; by Gabriel Fallon in *Irish Monthly*, Mar 1949; by Horace Reynolds in *Saturday Review of Literature*, Mar 5, 1949; by Leo Kennedy in *Chicago Sun*, Mar 17, 1949; in *Christian Science Monitor*, Mar 24, 1949; by Joseph Wood Krutch in *New York Times Book Review*, Mar 27, 1949; in *Dublin Magazine*, Apr-June 1949; by Charles J. Rolo in *Atlantic*, Apr 1949; by Charles Humboldt in *Masses and Mainstream*, Apr 1949; by Alec Digges in *Irish Democrat*, Apr 1949; by W. Gallacher in *Labour Monthly*, Apr 1949; by Hugh MacDiarmid in *New Theatre*, Apr 1949; by J. W. Bogan in *Springfield Republican*, Apr 24, 1949; in *Catholic World*, May 1949; by H. M. in *Drama* (London), May 1949; by Fred Urquhart in *Our Time*, May 1949; by Marshall Wingfield in *Christian Century*, May 4, 1949; by P. S. O'Hegarty in *Irish Book Lover*, June 1949; by Walter O'Hearn in *America*, June 11, 1949; by Robert Greacen in *Irish Writing*, July 1949; by Horace Reynolds in *Yale Review*, Sep 1949.

COCK-A-DOODLE DANDY   1949

first edition
COCK-A-DOODLE / DANDY / BY / SEAN O'CASEY / LONDON /
MACMILLAN & CO. LTD / 1949

20 × 13cm.

[i], half-title: COCK-A-DOODLE DANDY /; [ii], blank; [iii], title-page as
above; [iv], copyright, dedication to James Stephens, printing; v, Characters
in the Play; [vi], scenes; 1–102, text; 103–4, words and music for the songs;
[105], printer's imprint; [106], blank.

Blue cloth; front and back covers blank; spine: COCK- / A- / DOODLE /
DANDY / SEAN / O'CASEY / MACMILLAN /; lettered in gold; white
endpapers, all edges trimmed; white dust-jacket lettered in blue.
Published April 8, 1949 at 6s; 2000 copies printed by R. & R. Clark, Ltd,
Edinburgh; reprinted October 1949 (1000 copies).

Notes: The play was written in 1947. In a letter to Daniel Macmillan dated
August 20, 1947 O'Casey ends with the news, 'At the moment, I am trying
to hammer out another play – one with a curious title—COCKADOODLEDOO!'
On September 10 he told Jack Carney, 'I've set myself down to do another
play, and have a good deal of it drafted out. I'm not sure yet how it'll
go. Its *mise en scene*—grand things, these foreign phrases—is Ireland.' The
same day he wrote to George Jean Nathan that the play will, 'if it be
successful, hit at the present tendency of Eire to return to primitive beliefs,
and Eire's preoccupation with Puritanism. I hope it will be gay, with a
sombre thread of seriousness through it.' On October 31, 1947 he again
writes to Daniel Macmillan and notes in the course of the letter: 'I have
almost finished my new play, and have decided to call it *Cockadoodle Dandy*.'
He gave the same news to Jack Carney on the same day, adding, 'Possibly
cause a row.' On the same date he provided further information in a letter
to Nathan: 'I've almost finished my play, and am calling it "Cockadoodle
Dandy." I'm afraid it's a kind of Morality play, with Evil and Good con-
tending with each other; but, I think, on different lines [from orthodox
morality drama]. In fact, I'm thinking of giving it the sub-title of "An
Immorality Play in Three Scenes." I don't quite know what to think of
it myself.' Subsequently, he wrote to Nathan on September 18, 1954 after
finishing the next full-length play (A33): 'I entirely agree that *The Bishop's
Bonfire* would have been a better play had *Cock* never been written. That
play, possibly by accident, came out in a very colourful way, and it is
damned hard to get up to its standard.'
    The manuscript of *Cock-a-Doodle Dandy* was sent to Macmillan and Co. on
January 12, 1948. O'Casey regarded it as 'my favourite play; I think it is my
best play', in an essay 'O'Casey's Credo' in the *New York Times*, November 9,
1958 (C503), reprinted in a fuller version in *Blasts and Benedictions* (A44). In this
essay the author declares that 'The play is symbolical in more ways than one.
The action manifests itself in Ireland, the mouths that speak are Irish mouths;
but the spirit is to be found in action everywhere.' He adds, 'The Cock in the

play, of course, is the joyful active spirit of life as it weaves a way through the Irish scene.' O'Casey emphasises in the same article that 'in spite of the fanciful nature of the play, almost all the incidents [in it] are factual.' A letter to George Jean Nathan, dated December 27, 1949 illustrates this claim: 'The odd thing is that everything in the play "happened" in Ireland—the man killed by the priest for the reasons given; the woman, dragged to the priest for "going with a married man"; the priest's threat to "put her in her coffin," if she didn't leave the place; the 40 shillings fine for a kiss; even the gouging out of "Larry's eye" by the thumb of a demon, and the priest telling the father to get his demonised daughter "off to America" appeared in De Valera's paper, "The Irish Press." I've records of them all. Poor oul' Eire!' An incomplete twenty page typescript, entitled 'A Crow for Cockadoodle Dandy', is among the dramatist's papers in the Berg Collection, the New York Public Library. Written in 1947–8, it gives further documentation of the play's Irish background.

The play was dedicated 'To James Stephens, the Jesting Poet with a Radiant Star in's Coxcomb'. Writing to Daniel Macmillan on April 25, 1950, O'Casey explains the dedication: 'I wonder why is it that James Stephens writes no longer? It is a great pity.' The Macmillan Company, New York, did not publish *Cock-a-Doodle Dandy* feeling that it would not have a large sale in the United States. O'Casey was very disappointed at this decision, and felt that the play should be offered to an American publisher other than the Macmillan Company. Daniel Macmillan wrote on August 27, 1948 asking O'Casey to reconsider his idea of offering the play to another American publisher, pointing out that the Macmillan Company had offered to buy copies of the English edition for sale in the United States. O'Casey agreed to abandon his idea of an American edition. The Macmillan Company subsequently imported 891 copies of the English edition for sale in the United States. For its publication in *Collected Plays* (A29), vol IV, O'Casey made one change as recorded in his letter of June 27, 1950 to H. Cowdell of Macmillan: 'There is one correction to be made in COCKADOODLE DANDY in which a short speech is given to a wrong character on p. 62. There at the very bottom of the page, the remark given to the Messenger should be given to Michael, as is done in the original script.'

The play was first produced in December 1949 at the People's Theatre, Newcastle upon Tyne. It has been rarely staged since that time. In the fifties it was produced in January 1950 at the Arena Theater, Dallas, by Margo Jones; in October 1958 at the Playhouse Theater, Toronto; in November 1958 at the Carnegie Playhouse, New York; in September 1959 the English Stage Company presented it at the Edinburgh Festival (after a trial run at the Theatre Royal, Newcastle), afterwards transferring the production to the Royal Court Theatre, London. It was produced in January 1969 by the APA-Phoenix Repertory Company at the Lyceum Theatre, New York. The play had its Irish première on November 28, 1972 by the Tipperary Dramatic Society in the Gaiety Theatre, Tipperary. *Cock-A-Doodle Dandy* was collected in *Collected Plays* (A29) vol. IV, and in *The Sean O'Casey Reader* (A45).

Reviews: *Cock-A-Doodle Dandy* was reviewed by Austin Clarke in *Irish Times*, Apr 15/16, 1949; by Gerard Fay in *Manchester Guardian*, May 13, 1949; in *The Times Literary Supplement*, May 27, 1949; by Alec Digges in *Irish Democrat*,

June 1949; by E. C. in *New Theatre*, June 1949; by Walter O' Hearn in *America*, June 11, 1949; by Robert Greacen in *Irish Writing*, Oct 1949; by Ivor Brown in *Observer*, Jan 8, 1950; by Horace Reynolds in *New York Times Book Review*, Feb 19, 1950; by R. M. H. in *Christian Science Monitor*, Feb 25 and 27, 1950; by W. P. Eaton in *New York Herald Tribune Book Review*, Apr 9, 1950; by W. R. W. in *San Francisco Chronicle*, Apr 9, 1950.

COLLECTED PLAYS   1949–51

VOLUME I

first edition

SEAN O'CASEY / [ornamental rule] / COLLECTED PLAYS / *Volume One* / JUNO AND THE PAYCOCK / THE SHADOW OF A GUNMAN / THE PLOUGH AND THE STARS / THE END OF THE BEGINNING / A POUND ON DEMAND / LONDON / MACMILLAN & CO. LTD / 1949

20 × 13cm.

[i], half-title: COLLECTED PLAYS /; [ii], blank; [iii], title-page as above; [iv], copyright, printing; v, *Contents*; [vi], blank; [1]–314, text, printer's imprint at foot of 314.

Maroon cloth; front and back covers blank; spine: COLLECTED / PLAYS / VOLUME / ONE / [asterisk] / SEAN / O'CASEY / MACMILLAN /; lettered and decorated in gold; ivory endpapers, all edges trimmed; dust-jacket in ivory and grey, lettered in maroon.

Published November 11, 1949 at 12s 6d; 2000 copies printed by R. & R. Clark, Ltd, Edinburgh; reprinted 1950 (2790 copies), 1952 (3000 copies), 1957 (3000 copies, St. Martin's imprint added), 1963 (2020 copies), 1967 (1500 copies), 1971 (1500 copies).

Notes: All the plays in this volume had been previously published, *Juno and the Paycock* and *The Shadow of a Gunman* in 1925 in *Two Plays* (A10); *The Plough and the Stars* in 1926 (A13); 'The End of the Beginning' and 'A Pound on Demand' in 1934 in *Windfalls* (A16). There are no substantial alterations in the texts printed in *Collected Plays*. In checking the text of *The Plough and the Stars* for this volume, O'Casey came across a misprint that had persisted in all editions (except for the acting edition published by Samuel French in 1932, A13c) from 1926 onwards. On p. 208 he corrected 'Shan Vok Vok' to 'Shan Van Vok'. In the first act of *The Plough and the Stars* there is a brief addition to a stage direction on p. 190: 'While this dialogue is proceeding, and while Clitheroe prepares himself, Brennan softly whistles "the Soldiers' Song!" ' This addition was first introduced into the acting edition of the play, but the other changes in that version (mostly deletions) are not retained in the collected edition.

This volume differs from subsequent ones in the series – particularly the second and third volumes – in the significant matter of revision and emendation. In most cases the later plays needed changes (some of them quite substantial ones) when reprinted, whereas the earlier plays in Volume I required very little. O'Casey put the problem in a nutshell when commenting on George Jean Nathan's criticism of the American theatre's neglect of his work. Dated June 17, 1949, the playwright's letter was written only five months before the first two volumes of *Collected Plays* were issued: 'What about my own countrie? It's near three years since any play of mine appeared on the Abbey stage; &, I believe it will be a long time before one does . . . They produced the plays—"Gunman," "Plough" & "Juno"—before publication, & so gave me the power through rehearsals, to amend or alter. Since then, all my plays have had to be published before production; I've had no aid from rehearsals, & so each—except "Cockadoodle Dandy," I think—needed touching here and there.' In the *Collected Plays* edition, the author attempted to introduce these alterations into the printed texts and the result is most marked in the second and third volumes. However, in the case of two plays in Volume III – *Purple Dust* and *Red Roses for Me* – stage productions in the 1950s occasioned further significant textual changes after the collected edition had been published.

VOLUME II

SEAN O'CASEY / [ornamental rule] / COLLECTED PLAYS / *Volume Two* / THE SILVER TASSIE / WITHIN THE GATES / THE STAR TURNS RED / LONDON / MACMILLAN & CO. LTD / 1949

20 × 13cm.

[i], half-title: COLLECTED PLAYS; [ii], blank; [iii], title-page as above; [iv], copyright, printing; v, *Contents*; [vi], blank; [1]–354, text, printer's imprint at foot on 354.

Maroon cloth; front and back covers blank; spine: COLLECTED / PLAYS / VOLUME / TWO / [asterisk] / SEAN / O'CASEY / MACMILLAN /;   lettered and decorated in gold; ivory endpapers, all edges trimmed; dust-jacket in ivory and grey, lettered in maroon.
Published November 11, 1949 at 12s 6d; 2000 copies printed by R. & R. Clark, Ltd, Edinburgh; reprinted 1950 (2790 copies), 1952 (3000 copies), 1958 (2000 copies, St Martin's imprint added).

Notes: The plays in this volume had all been published previously. Writing to his American agent, Richard Madden, on February 6, 1948, O'Casey said of the second volume of *Collected Plays*, 'All [three] plays have been amended. *Within the Gates* has been altered considerably, and made, I think, much more tight and easy [for stage performance].' Earlier, before the idea of a collected edition had been suggested by either dramatist or publisher, O'Casey wrote a letter dated August 29, 1947 in which he asked Daniel Macmillan 'Would it be good to issue a vol. holding the three plays—"Within the Gates," "The Silver Tassie," and "The Star Turns Red?" I have rewritten "Within the Gates," making a stage version of it, and so, I think, simplifying its production a good deal, and improving it. The alterations are so many that, I think, it would need a new printing. That was one big reason why I wished to see you. There would be far less alterations of the other two plays.'

In this volume the texts of both *The Silver Tassie* and *Within the Gates* are described as 'stage versions'. In *The Silver Tassie* there are many changes from the text published in 1928 (A14), made in the light of subsequent stage performance; O'Casey worked closely with the director of the 1929 London production of the play, Raymond Massey, and these alterations owe much to this co-operation. The entire production "Notes" (p. 3) are here printed for the first time. There are both omissions from and additions to Susie Monican's dialogue on p. 7, and another speech by her is deleted on p. 11. Several slight changes in Act II are to be found on pp. 36, 37, 45 and 56; while several verses from the soldiers' chants are omitted, including the deletion of one stanza on p. 43, three further stanzas on p. 52, and two on p. 53. In Act III, there is a brief addition to a stage direction on p. 68, and two extra speeches are introduced on p. 76. In Act IV there are several minor, but significant, changes to the dialogue and songs on pp. 93 and 103.

The text of *Within the Gates* embodies extensive revisions to the original 1933 edition (A15). No other play of O'Casey was so drastically altered after publication. The changes were made as a result of the playwright's observations of both the London and particularly the New York production in 1934 and in the light of George Jean Nathan's criticisms. In a letter to Ronald Ayling dated September 23, 1957 O'Casey said, 'I changed the method of "W. T. Gates" after New York production. Some of the play appeared to me to be very dull, due, I think, to the absence of the chief characters [in some scenes]. I tried to adjust this by the newer version.' Although contemplated earlier, the actual revisions were not made until 1946. On May 5 of that year the author wrote to Nathan: 'At the moment I'm revising *Within the Gates*; trying to knit it closer together. As you know, I was never satisfied with it. I have already altered the first two acts a lot.' In the new version of *Within the Gates* there are seven less individual characters while each of the four scenes, though retaining the same essential plot-sequence and structure, is rewritten. Much of the original dialogue is altered, several new episodes are substituted for ones in the original version, three entirely new lyrics (the Gardener's Song, the Salvationist's hymn, the Old Woman's ballad of the Irish Dragoon) are substituted in place of three in the 1933 text. The changes are too extensive to be listed in detail here. Fuller information is contained in R. Mary Todd's 'The Two Published Versions of O'Casey's "Within the Gates"', *Modern Drama*, x (1967–8) 346–55. Writing to Daniel Macmillan on October 11, 1947 O'Casey speaks of his dissatisfaction with the music: 'I am enclosing with this note the amended script of WITHIN THE GATES. Some of the songs have been altered and I will send the music later on. Otherwise the music remains as it was; but, in the new vol., perhaps it would be better to put in only the bare tunes—the orchestration given is, I fear, not good; so that, should it ever be done again, the Producer may be able to add a better and more simple orchestral addition.'

The text of *The Star Turns Red* is substantially that first published in 1940 (A20) except for the following changes: the Red Priest is now the Purple Priest; there are additions to the end of Kian's speech in Act I, p. 251, and to those of the Old Man and Joybell in Act IV at the top of p. 343; there are alterations in the dialogue between the Brown Priest and Red Jim in Act II, pp. 295–6; the principal deletion is that of a short scene from Act IV, p. 339, extending from the Lady Mayoress's speech, 'You'll be able to sing your little song now, dear, with an easy mind', up to her 'Albert, darling, you sang it beautiful!' A note on the dust-jacket for Volume II says: 'These plays have been unobtainable for some time, and certain important revisions to facilitate stage productions have been made for this edition.' O'Casey in a letter to George Jean Nathan, dated June 17, 1949, wrote 'I've done a lot to W. the Gates, some to Silver Tassie and The Star Turns Red to be issued soon in one vol.'

VOLUME III

SEAN O'CASEY / [ornamental rule] / COLLECTED PLAYS / *Volume Three* / PURPLE DUST / RED ROSES FOR ME / HALL OF HEALING / LONDON / MACMILLAN & CO. LTD / 1951

20 × 13cm.

[i], half-title: COLLECTED PLAYS /; [ii], blank; [iii], title-page as above; [iv], copyright, printing; v, *Contents*; [vi], blank; [1]–274, text; printer's imprint at foot of 274.

Maroon cloth; front and back covers blank; spine: COLLECTED / PLAYS / VOLUME / THREE / [asterisk] / SEAN / O'CASEY / MACMILLAN /; lettered and decorated in gold; white endpapers, all edges trimmed; dust-jacket in ivory and grey, lettered in maroon.
Published July 17, 1951 at 12s 6d; 5000 copies printed by R. & R. Clark, Ltd, Edinburgh; reprinted November 1957 (1500 copies, St. Martin's imprint added), 1962 (1523 copies), 1967 (1500 copies).

Notes: Of the three plays in this volume, 'Hall of Healing' appears here in print for the first time. O'Casey wrote three one-act plays in a short space of time spanning 1949 and the early part of 1950. At the time – as he told George Jean Nathan on December 11, 1949 – he thought of separate publication for them: 'I am working on the biography [*Rose and Crown*], and, as well, I'd like to publish a book of one-act plays. I've done two already—as you know—I finished another a month ago—"Hill of Healing" —and am just finishing the rough ms. of a second, with a third simmering in my mind. These, I hope, will keep my hand and heart in playwriting, while I go on with the biography.' By March 1, 1950 he was able to tell Nathan that he had finished all three short plays. The plan for a book of one-act plays was temporarily abandoned when O'Casey's publisher suggested their inclusion in the collected edition. On April 25, 1950 the playwright wrote to Daniel Macmillan, 'I like your idea of including the [three] new one-act plays in the third and fourth volumes of Collected Plays. The one comment I have to make is that while the first two vols. contain three three-act plays, the two following will contain only two three-act plays and a one-act play ... There may be a few pages less, for I want to make a few cuts in RED ROSES FOR ME and PURPLE DUST.' Eventually, 'Hall of Healing' was printed in Volume III in company with one three-act and one four-act play; while 'Bedtime Story' and 'Time to Go' were published in Volume IV together with two three-act dramas.
The text of *Purple Dust* is, basically, that first printed in 1940 (A21). There are a number of minor alterations on pp. 16, 25, 26, 31, 39, 42–4, 63, 70, 81, 90, 103, 116; and more substantial additions to the dialogue in Act III on pp. 106–10. It was only after publication of this text in the collected edition that O'Casey was actively involved in rehearsals of *Purple Dust*. This experience led to extensive changes being made in 1953; the following year saw the playwright revising the script still further as a result of correspondence with a group of theatre people who planned (unsuccessfully) to produce the work in New York. The radically revised version was eventually presented in that city in 1956, however, and printed there in 1957 (A21b). However, when the

dramatist came to supervise the next new printing of *Purple Dust* in England – in *Three More Plays* (A42) – he decided to follow the text of the *Collected Plays* (A29) edition, with but one change carried over from the 1957 acting version; this alteration is found in Act II, pp. 180–1 in *Three More Plays*.

There are no radical changes in the text of *Red Roses for Me* in *Collected Plays*. The 1942 edition (A23) is followed with minor changes in the dialogue on pp. 140 and 219. The two men trapped in their musical instruments during the police attack (1942 ed. pp. 142–5) are omitted and the Scab song is now sung before instead of after the entrance of Dowzard and Foster. The dramatist did not witness the 1943 Dublin presentation but he saw the 1946 London one, which – as he told George Jean Nathan on March 20, 1946 – was three quarters good and one quarter bad. His experience of the play on stage made him make some changes while the play was still running (it was twice transferred to other London theatres) though he was unable to have them introduced at the time. He wrote to Bronson Albery on May 12, 1946: 'I am, of course, very glad that RED ROSES is going to the New, and, after that, to Wyndham's. As Joxer would say, "Be God, that's good news!" I agree with you about the wisdom of leaving this time well enough alone. All the actors must be set in their parts by now, and it would be unwise, and unfair, to disturb them. So we must wait for some more favourable time to introduce the improvements, for improvements I hope the revisions may be.' It is most probable that the minor changes that were incorporated into the 1951 *Collected Plays* version were the revisions mentioned in the letter to Albery. Subsequently, O'Casey made fuller minor revisions to all four acts of the play, with significant additions in Act III; these were used in the 1955 New York production and printed in the Dramatists Play Service edition the following year. In the final 'authorised' version of *Red Roses for Me*, printed in *Three More Plays* (A42), the dramatist returned to the *Collected Plays* text with the addition of a short episode in Act III that was first introduced into the 1956 acting edition (see *Three More Plays*, pp. 281–2).

'Hall of Healing', sub-titled 'A Sincerious Farce in One Scene', was completed in 1949. On June 29 of that year O'Casey wrote to Daniel Macmillan to tell him 'I'll be sending the one-act play ['Hall of Healing'] to you as soon as I get it back from a typing agency.' On September 15, 1949 he wrote to Peter Newmark: 'I've written a one-act play on an experience long ago in a Dublin Poor-Law Dispensary—"Hall of Healing".' Lady Gregory in her *Journals 1916–1930* (B19), p. 320, describes an incident similar to that upon which the play is based; it was related to her by a hospital sister who knew O'Casey. Many years later, on March 21, 1958, O'Casey wrote to Ronald Ayling, 'The version the Sister gave to L.G. of my experience in hospital is incorrect.' He added: 'Hall of Healing wasnt furnished from experiences in St. Vincent's Hospital, but from a Poor Law Dispensary in North William Street, N. Strand, Dublin. The old cod was just as I draw him; so was the doctor, so are the patients. The episode of the three bottles actually occurred. I mentioned this Dispensary in one of my books; but fearing a libel action, I gave the name of the good doctor to the bad one. Afterwards, I got a letter from the doctor's daughter saying how she rejoiced that her father wasnt what people thought him to be; that she herself even thought him to be the reverse of what I said he was! I didn't try to deliver the poor girl from her illusion.' The chapter 'The Hill of Healing' in

I Knock at the Door (A19) provides further details utilised in writing the play; the title of the chapter (Hill and not Hall of Healing) was in fact originally that given to the latter work. Subsequently, an O'Casey letter of July 9, 1958 to Jane Rubin refers to the play: 'Hall of Healing is more real [than "End of the Beginning"]—all incidents in it happened before my eyes.'

VOLUME IV

SEAN O'CASEY / [ornamental rule] / COLLECTED PLAYS / *Volume Four* / OAK LEAVES AND LAVENDER / COCK-A-DOODLE DANDY / BEDTIME STORY / TIME TO GO / LONDON / MACMILLAN & CO. LTD / 1951

20 × 13cm.

[i], half-title: COLLECTED PLAYS /; [ii], blank; [iii], title-page as above; [iv], copyright, printing; v, *Contents*; [vi], blank; [1]–294, text; [295], printer's imprint; [296]–[298], blank.

Maroon cloth; front and back covers blank; spine: COLLECTED / PLAYS / VOLUME / FOUR / [asterisk] / SEAN / O'CASEY / MACMILLAN /; lettered and decorated in gold; white endpapers, all edges trimmed; dust-jacket in ivory and grey, lettered in maroon.
Published July 17, 1951 at 12s 6d; 5000 copies printed by R. & R. Clark, Ltd, Edinburgh; reprinted October 1958 (2000 copies, St Martin's imprint added), 1964, 1967.

Notes: The two one-act plays in this volume, 'Bedtime Story' and 'Time to Go', are here published for the first time. According to a letter to George Jean Nathan, 'the rough ms.' of 'Time to Go' was nearing completion on December 11, 1949, by which time the other one-act play was already 'simmering' in O'Casey's mind. In a further letter to Nathan on March 1, 1950 he reports, 'I managed to finish the one-act play "Bedtime Story" . . . I think "Time to Go" is good, though I'm not sure. It is, again, realism touched with fancy. "Bedtime Story" is out of my usual manner, a comedy, fanciful in a way, too; but wholly unlike either "Time To Go" or "Hall of Healing."' ' Typescripts were sent to Macmillan and Co. soon afterwards and the publisher decided to include the three plays in the third and fourth volumes of the *Collected Plays*, as a letter from the playwright to Daniel Macmillan on April 25, 1950 acknowledges. Subsequently, in a letter to H. Cowdell of Macmillan dated June 27, 1950, O'Casey writes: 'I understand that Vol. 4 will contain the following plays, OAKLEAVES AND LAVENDER, COCK-ADOODLE DANDY, TIME TO GO and BEDTIME STORY. Am I to send in the books of the first two plays (you have the typescript of the other two)? I did think of giving a change to OAKLEAVES AND LAVENDER, but I am so busy that I have no time to spare for the work. There is one correction to be made in COCKADOODLE DANDY in which a short speech is given to a wrong character on page 62.' Since submitting typescripts of the two one-act plays, O'Casey had some changes he wished to make. In a letter to Macmillan dated February 21, 1951 he writes, 'I wonder would it be possible to get Galley Proofs of the one-act plays (for the 4th vol.), TIME TO GO and BEDTIME STORY? I have a few additions to make in both of these; but, if it isn't possible to get Galley Proofs, it can't be helped now. Perhaps, some of these could be put in the Page Proofs?' In an early typescript, now among the Nathan Papers in Cornell University, 'Bedtime Story' is subtitled 'An Immorality Farce in One Act'. It was eventually printed with the sub-title 'An Anatole Burlesque in One Act', an allusion to Arthur Schnitzler's series of *Anatol* sketches, which O'Casey admired and with which 'Bedtime Story' has affinities. O'Casey's burlesque is a satiric handling of a bedtime incident that actually happened to a friend of his. 'Time to Go' is subtitled 'A Morality Comedy in One Act'. In *Sunset and Evening Star* (A31) the playwright claims that 'Time to Go', like 'The End of the Beginning', is 'founded on another Irish folk-tale'.

Reviews: Collected Plays was reviewed in *Times Literary Supplement*, Dec 9, 1949; by Gerard Fay in *Manchester Guardian*, Dec 28, 1949; by Clifford Odets in *New York Times Book Review*, Feb 5, 1950; by John Garrett in *Spectator*, Feb 24, 1950; by Francis Russell in *Christian Science Monitor*, Feb 25, 1950; by Gerard Fay in *Manchester Guardian* Aug 15, 1951; by Brooks Atkinson in *New York Times*, Sep 16, 1951; in *Times Literary Supplement*, Sep 21, 1951; by Robert Friedman in *Daily Worker* (New York), Oct 3, 1951.

ROSE AND CROWN   1952

a. *first edition*
ROSE AND CROWN / BY / SEAN O'CASEY / *This is the porcelain clay of humankind* / LONDON / MACMILLAN & CO. LTD / 1952

21.5 × 14cm.

[i], half-title: ROSE AND CROWN /; [ii], Books by Sean O'Casey; frontispiece, photograph: EILEEN CAREY, 1926 /; [iii], title-page as above; [iv],
copyright, printing; [v], dedication: TO THE YOUNG OF ALL LANDS, /
ALL COLOURS, ALL CREEDS; / Shadows of beauty. / Shadows of power; /
Rise to your duty- / This is the hour! /; [vi], blank; vii, Contents; [viii], blank;
1–[307], text, printer's imprint at foot of [307]; [308]–[312], blank.

Olive grey cloth; front and back covers blank; spine ROSE / AND / CROWN /
[ornament] / SEAN / O'CASEY / [all above on red panel surrounded by
borders of gold, red and olive grey] / MACMILLAN /; lettered and decorated
in red and gold; white endpapers, all edges trimmed; dust-jacket in green,
black and white with design of rose and crown on front, skyscraper and
frog on spine.
Published July 4, 1952 at 21s.; 5000 copies printed by R. & R. Clark, Ltd,
Edinburgh.

b. *American edition*
Rose / and Crown / BY / *Sean O'Casey* / *This is the porcelain clay of humankind* /
NEW YORK / THE MACMILLAN COMPANY / 1952

21 × 13.5cm.

[i], half-title: *Rose and Crown* /; [ii], Books by Sean O'Casey; frontispiece photograph: EILEEN CAREY, 1926 /; [iii], title-page as above; [iv], copyright,
printing; [v], dedication as in first edition; [vi], blank; [vii], Contents; [viii],
blank; 1–323, text; [324]–[326], blank.

Dark blue cloth; front cover: Rose and Crown /; back cover blank; spine:
Rose / and / Crown / [ornamental line] / O'CASEY / MACMILLAN /; lettered
and decorated in red; white endpapers, all edges trimmed; dust-jacket in
teal blue and white.
Published October 28, 1952 at $4.75; 4000 copies printed. This edition was
licensed to Liberty Book Club, New York, for use as the April 1953 selection
for Liberty's membership; the text was also used without the frontispiece
photograph for the Macmillan Paperbacks edition, MP42, which was
published March 27, 1961 at $1.45 in an edition of 10,000 copies.

Notes: *Rose and Crown* was written between 1947 and 1951. In a letter to
Daniel Macmillan, dated August 29, 1947, O'Casey tells of his plans for
'writing a further vol. dealing with my arrival in England, and carrying
it on, maybe, to the day that now is.' On October 31, 1947 he writes again
to Daniel Macmillan: 'The Vol. on my impressions since I came to England
will take a lot of thinking about; but I may try to start it soon in a rough
way. It would be, I think, a more thoughtful one, and less exciting, which

may be a bad or a good thing. I'm not sure.' The work occupied much
of his time during the following three years. Writing to Ralph Thompson
on December 3, 1948—in a letter subsequently printed in part in the *New
York Times Magazine*, December 26, 1948 (C368)—the playwright says: 'At
the moment, I am jotting down thoughts and incidents for another vol. which
will, of course, open up in England, with a pen in one hand and a spy-glass
in the other—to take an odd look at Eirinn through.' On January 16, 1951
he informed Daniel Macmillan: 'I've written a lot of a 5th vol. biography,
& now fear I shan't be able to end it without another one . . . I've quite
a lot to do yet—I'm now setting down remarks on my visit to America
in 1933 [his visit was actually made in 1934]—say 9 or 10 additonal chapters
to end the work. I propose to call the next vol. "Rose and Crown." ' The
manuscript was sent to Daniel Macmillan on February 15, 1951: 'It brings
me to 1933–34 having just left the United States for home . . . What do you
think of the title? "Rose and Thorn" might be more realistic, but I imagine,
wouldn't suit any of the chapters as a title.'

This, the fifth volume of O'Casey's life-story, covers approximately the
period 1926–35. The dust-jacket of the first edition contains the following
description of the book, almost certainly written by O'Casey himself: 'It
brings O'Casey to England to stand among the alien corn, and like it. He
marries an Irish girl, and makes a home there . . . But stormy days were
still before him. There was the dispute with the Abbey Theatre about the
rejection of *The Silver Tassie*; a bigger row later with the clerics and their
press; and the tumult in America about *Within the Gates*, which was banned
in Boston and other cities. Pictures are given of American life in New York
and Pennsylvania, where O'Casey made many friends. Well-known and
famous figures pass us by . . . Sean visits Ireland, and plays his first and
last game of croquet against Yeats on the poet's lawn. He visits Yeats again
in his lodgings in London, where the poet is working at his anthology;
his affection goes to the sick man, and, finally, saying goodbye, he doesn't
know that he has given a last farewell to Ireland's great poet and great
man.' The dust-jacket of the American edition describes the work: '*Rose
and Crown* takes O'Casey to England where he "was to be shown off, a new
oddity, an odd wonder; a guttersnipe among the trimly-educated and the
richly-clad; the slum dramatist, who, in the midst of a great darkness,
had seen a greater light." In London he discovered that the City was packed
with playwrights who wrote assorted plays, serious plays, sunny plays, sad
plays, all sorts. It was here that he learned "how easy it is to write a
play to be staged; how hard to write one to be remembered" . . . With great
candor and discernment O'Casey draws graphic portraits of famous figures,
Baldwin, Churchill, MacDonald, H. G. Wells, Carson and that "hulk
of a man," Alfred Hitchcock, pass us by, moving as if in a film, with a
stained-glass window for a screen.'

As with the two preceding volumes in the series, the publisher was
apprehensive about possible legal action in connection with incidents in
the narrative. In a letter to Daniel Macmillan of March 7, 1951 O'Casey
wrote of *Rose and Crown*: 'I don't think there is anything libellous in it.
I certainly had no feeling of writing any thing so derogatory while I was
working at it. If I be inclined to libel anyone, I am inclined to libel
myself. But, as you wisely say, it is better to make as sure as assurance

can be by getting a lawyer to look over it. I am sure that no one can write anything worth a damn without annoying someone: Joyce did; Yeats did; Hardy did; and so did Tennyson. And Jesus annoyed a crowd of people. However, I havn't written anything just to annoy, but simply wrote down what I felt I must write down. And that was done, not to annoy any person, but to free myself from annoying God. Of course, some of my conceptions may be wrong—nay, all of them may be so—but they are all honest; though that isnt saying that they are true or proper. Let a man examine himself, says St. Paul, and I have done this often, and most often when I am writing, so as to try to prevent anything malicious creeping in to what I am setting down.' His letter ended: 'I thought of giving an Inn Sign as title to each of the chapters, and would like to brood a little over the idea'; this plan was subsequently abandoned.

The dust-jacket, designed by O'Casey, has alternate bands of green and black incorporating, on the front, a rose on the upper black band and a crown on the lower black band, linked by rose branches. The spine has on the upper black panel a skyscraper, a reference to his New York visit in 1934; the lower black panel portrays a frog, an allusion to the Dublin production of *The Silver Tassie* and its reception by the critics, described in the chapter 'The Friggin Frogs'.

The chapter 'A Gate Clangs Shut' had previously been published in *Irish Writing*, December 1950 (C400). A frontispiece photograph shows Eileen Carey, who became Mrs Sean O'Casey on September 23, 1927. The quotation on the title-page is from *Don Sebastian* by John Dryden, Act I, Scene i.

Rose and Crown was reprinted in *Mirror in My House* (A35a), in *Autobiographies* (A35b), and in *Autobiography* (A35c). Excerpts were published in *The Sean O'Casey Reader* (A45).

Reviews: *Rose and Crown* was reviewed by Peter Quennell in *Daily Mail*, July 5, 1952; in *The Times*, July 9, 1952; by T. A. Jackson in *Daily Worker*, July 10, 1952; by Louis MacNeice in *Observer*, July 13, 1952; by Gerard Fay in *Manchester Guardian*, July 15, 1952; by Austin Clarke in *John O'London's*, July 18, 1952; in *New Statesman and Nation*, July 26, 1952; by Brian Inglis in *Spectator*, Aug 1, 1952; in *Times Literary Supplement*, Aug 1, 1952; by Harold Hobson in *Christian Science Monitor*, Aug 28, 1952; by Brooks Atkinson in *New York Times Book Review*, Sep 14, 1952; by Niall Carroll in *Irish Press*, Sep 23, 1952; by Val Mulkerns in *Bell*, Oct 1952; by Eric Bentley in *New Republic*, Oct 13, 1952; by Gabriel Fallon in *Irish Monthly*, Nov 1952; by Robert Greacen in *Irish Writing*, Nov 1952; by F. E. Faverty in *Chicago Sunday Tribune*, Nov 2, 1952; by W. P. Eaton in *New York Herald Tribune Book Review*, Nov 2, 1952; by Horace Reynolds in *New York Times Book Review*, Nov 2, 1952; by R. M. Hammond in *Christian Science Monitor*, Nov 6, 1952; in *New Yorker*, Nov 8, 1952; in *Time*, Nov 10, 1952; in *Daily Worker*, (New York), Nov 13, 1952; by Maurice Valency in *Saturday Review*, Nov 15, 1952; by C. J. Rolo in *Atlantic*, Dec 1952; by Joseph Carroll in *Theatre Arts*, Dec 1952; by Donagh MacDonagh in *Drama*, winter 1952; by Charles Humboldt in *Masses and Mainstream*, Jan 1953; by Marie A. Updike White in *South Atlantic Quarterly*, Jan 1954.

A31   SUNSET AND EVENING STAR   1954

a. *first edition*

SUNSET / AND EVENING STAR / BY / SEAN O'CASEY / *You cannot prevent the birds of sadness from / flying over your head, but you can prevent them / building nests in your hair.* / CHINESE PROVERB / *I'm gonna wash 'em all outa ma hair.* / LONDON / MACMILLAN & CO. LTD / 1954

22 × 14cm.

[i], half-title: SUNSET AND EVENING STAR /; [ii], Books by Sean O'Casey; frontispiece, photograph by Alfred Eris: THE O'CASEYS / NIALL BREON SEAN SHIVAWN EILEEN /; [iii], title-page as above; [iv], copyright, publisher's imprints, printing; [v], dedication: TO / My dear Friend / HUGH MACDIARMID / Alba's Poet and one of Alba's / first men /; [vi], blank; vii, Contents; [viii], blank; 1–[312], text, printer's imprint at foot of [312].

Olive cloth; front and back covers blank; spine: SUNSET / AND / EVENING / STAR / [ornament] / SEAN / O'CASEY / [all above on maroon panel with olive, gold and maroon borders] / MACMILLAN /; lettered and decorated in maroon and gold; white endpapers, all edges trimmed; dust-jacket, designed by O'Casey, in black, red and white, represents an old man with walking stick coming through door in panel of Celtic Cross, with drinking glass in hand, a tree almost denuded of leaves with some leaves falling, on a sunset background.
Published October 29, 1954 at 21s; 3000 copies printed by R. & R. Clark, Ltd, Edinburgh; reprinted 1954 (1500 copies).

b. *American edition*
Sunset / and Evening Star / BY / *Sean O'Casey* / *You cannot prevent the birds of sadness from / flying over your head, but you can prevent them / building nests in your hair.* / CHINESE PROVERB / *I'm gonna wash 'em all outa ma hair.* / NEW YORK / THE MACMILLAN COMPANY / *1954*

21 × 14cm.

[i], half-title: *Sunset and Evening Star* /; [ii], Books by Sean O'Casey; frontispiece, photograph of the O'Caseys by Alfred Eris; [iii], title-page as above; [iv], copyright notice, printing; [v], dedication to Hugh MacDiarmid; [vi], blank; vii, Contents; [viii], blank; [ix], fly title: *Sunset and Evening Star* /; [x], blank; 1–339, text; [340]–[342], blank.

Black cloth; front cover: Sunset and / Evening Star /; back cover blank; spine: Sunset / and / Evening / Star / [ornamental line] / O'CASEY / MACMILLAN /; lettered and decorated in teal green; white endpapers, all edges trimmed; dust-jacket lettered and decorated in white and teal green.
Published November 9, 1954 at $4.75; 4989 copies printed; this edition was licensed to the Book Find Club, New York, for use as the March 1955 selection for its membership; the text was also used without the frontispiece photograph for the Macmillan Paperbacks edition, MP43, which was published March 27, 1961 at $1.45 in an edition of 10,000 copies.

Notes: This is the sixth and final volume in the life-story series which was begun in 1939 with *I Knock at the Door* (A19). It was completed early in 1953 and delivered to the publisher in April of that year, while O'Casey still lived in Totnes, Devon. In 1954, before the book was published, he moved to Torquay, Devon, which was to be his home for the final ten years of his life. As late as May 7, 1951 – in a letter to George Jean Nathan – the author still referred to this last volume as 'Goodbye at the Door', the title he had initially given to *Inishfallen, Fare Thee Well* (A27) when that book was planned as the final one in the autobiographical sequence. 'Goodbye at the Door' was presumably intended to round off, verbally, the series that began with O'Casey knocking at the door of life. This idea, eventually dropped from the title, is picked up visually on the dust-jacket of *Sunset and Evening Star* which itself echoes that on the dust-jacket of *I Knock at the Door*, both designed by the writer. In the earlier design a young boy is shown rapping at the door superimposed on a large Celtic cross; in the later one, an old man drinks a farewell toast to life outside a half open door with the same cross in the background. The title eventually chosen is the opening line of Tennyson's well-known valedictory poem 'Crossing the Bar'.

Dedicated to Hugh MacDiarmid, the Scottish poet, the work covers the period 1936–53. It is described on the dust-jacket of the English edition as follows: 'The concluding volume of Sean O'Casey's remarkable auto-biographical series is written, as it were, under the mute compassion of the evening star. The book opens on his return from the United States, and brings us up to the present . . . Life, as seen through O'Casey's eyes, and perhaps more markedly in this last volume, wears all its masks, gay, sad, ridiculous and terrible; but life, we are reminded, is young, and has plenty of time to make good.' The American dust-jacket reads, '*Sunset and Evening Star* is the sixth and presumably the last volume of Sean O'Casey's autobiography – one of the great creative works of our time. In it he looks back lovingly and without regrets on the past fifteen years, beginning with his return from America and his settling in Battersea . . . these were the years in which his great talents, lying in obscurity in plays which were never produced, burst forth in the glorious prose of his autobiography . . . As Sean O'Casey was writing this unforgettable story of his life, England was blanketed in the darkness of war. The light of his descriptive genius has never shone more brilliantly than in these black years when, from his home in Totnes, he watched Plymouth being pounded to fiery bits . . . The book ends fittingly with a glorious tribute to his native Ireland, and with a salute to Life, to the past, the present and the future.'

Thus the long sequence – begun in a relatively modest way as a series of 'sketches' of childhood experience, as 'a few fantastic pages of biography', according to a letter of January 1938 addressed to Harold Macmillan – is here completed after attaining an epic compass unimagined by the author at its commencement. As he told William J. Maroldo in a letter dated August 10, 1962: 'it grew as it was written, changing to the long and varied work that grew out of the first fragile green blade.' However, in another significant regard the final volume, like its predecessors, realises the strange and diverse elements that O'Casey claimed for the work from the very beginning. In a letter of May 4, 1937 to George Jean Nathan he wrote that the Dream School episode (subsequently included in the first volume) was 'autobiographical and unconventional', adding the prophecy, 'My autobiography'll be a curious thing, if I ever get to the end of it.' It is difficult to dispute that in this respect, if no other, each book in the narrative sequence lives up to the author's expectation. As for its end, it could be argued that *Sunset and Evening Star* was not his final piece of autobiographical writing. Three contributions to *Under a Colored Cap* (A41) – 'Under a Colored Cap, Part One' ('An Army with Banners'), 'Under a Colored Cap, Part Two' and 'Under a Greenwood Tree He Died' – depict events at both the beginning and the end of O'Casey's long life.

The Chinese proverb quoted on the title-page of *Sunset and Evening Star* was on a Christmas card which O'Casey received from Eric and Doris Leach. In a letter of December 21, 1953 to Doris Leach, O'Casey says, 'I am using the Chinese Proverb as a Quotation on the top of my next (and last) biographical book – Sunset and Evening Star.' George Orwell had reviewed *Drums Under the Windows* in *Observer*, October 28, 1945 and had dealt with it very harshly. O'Casey devotes the chapter 'Rebel Orwell' to an attack on Orwell, which many critics felt was too vindictive. O'Casey himself was sensitive to this criticism, as is indicated by his letter of November 20, 1954 to Doris Leach: 'They [the critics] don't seem to realize that the worst things said about him in the book, come, not from me, but from his friends, nay, his lovers.' In the same chapter the name T. C. Murray is omitted from the collected English edition of the *Autobiographies* (A35b), and from *Autobiography* (A35c); it is retained in all American editions. The frontispiece photograph of the O'Casey family was described by O'Casey in a letter dated March 16, 1954, to Mr De Wilton of the Macmillan Company, as 'a glossy photo of the O'Casey family—the unholy family—taken by an American Alfred Eris . . . about six year ago.'

Part of the chapter 'Childermess' was based on a letter by O'Casey published in *Time and Tide*, July 6, 1935 (C162). The poem to Walt Whitman in the final chapter 'And Evening Star' first appeared under the title 'Saintly Sinner Sing for Us' in *New Statesman and Nation*, December 16, 1950 (C401); this chapter also includes part of a letter 'The Red Ticket' which first appeared in *Irish Times*, December 28, 1951 (C405). Part of the chapter 'Outside an Irish Window' had already appeared under the title 'Jeeps, be Jeepers', in *New Statesman and Nation*, July 18, 1953 (C420), and was to be used later as part of the dialogue in Act II of *The Bishop's Bonfire* (A33).

Sunset and Evening Star had better sales than any of the autobiographies, doing well in both British and American markets. Granville Hicks, who acted as reader for the Macmillan Company, in the course of his report recommending publication made the interesting suggestion of publishing the complete autobiography in one volume, if possible revised and condensed by O'Casey himself. Later in the year, O'Casey received a letter from Mr De Wilton of the Macmillan Company, dated November 5, 1954, thanking him for his letter concerning John Gassner's suggestion of an edited one-volume edition of the biographies. Though the Macmillan Company brought out a two-volume edition, *Mirror in My House* (A35a), in 1956, this was an unedited and unabridged text. The nearest equivalent to Hick's idea appears in *The Sean O'Casey Reader* (A45), where selections from the six books are chosen by Brooks Atkinson; the bulk of this anthology is not autobiographical narrative, however, but dramatic writings.

Sunset and Evening Star was collected in *Mirror in My House*, in *Autobiographies*, and in *Autobiography*. Excerpts were published in *The Sean O'Casey Reader*.

Reviews: *Sunset and Evening Star* was reviewed by W. L. in *Irish Independent*, Oct 30, 1954; by T. C. Worsley in *New Statesman*, Oct 30, 1954; in *The Times*, Oct 30, 1954; in *Sunday Independent*, Oct 31, 1954; by Philip Bolsover in *Daily Worker*, Nov 4, 1954; in *Times Literary Supplement*, Nov 5, 1954; by Austin Clarke in *Irish Times*, Nov 6, 1954; by H. L. Morrow in *Irish Press*, Nov 13, 1954; by Austin Clarke in *Time and Tide*, Nov 13, 1954; by W. P. Eaton in *New York Herald Tribune Book Review*, Nov 14, 1954; by Brooks Atkinson in *New York Times Book Review*, Nov 14, 1954; by Ivor Brown in *Observer*, Nov 14, 1954; in *Time*, Nov 15, 1954; by Horace Gregory in *Saturday Review*, Nov 20, 1954; by Horace Reynolds in *Christian Science Monitor*, Nov 24, 1954; by Gerard Fay in *Manchester Guardian*, Nov 26, 1954; by Harold Clurman in *Nation*, Nov 27, 1954; by Granville Hicks in *New Leader*, Nov 29, 1954; by John Jordan in *Irish Writing*, Dec 1954; by Donald A. Pitt in *San Francisco Chronicle*, Dec 5, 1954; by Padraic Colum in *New Republic*, Dec 27, 1954; by J. C. Trewin in *Drama*, winter 1954; by C. J. Rolo in *Atlantic*, Jan 1955; by Milton Howard in *Masses and Mainstream*, Jan 1955; by Richard Findlater in *Tribune*, Jan 28, 1955; by Gerald Weales in *Commentary*, Feb 1955; by Guy Boas in *English*, spring 1955; by V. S. Pritchett in *New Yorker*, Apr 16, 1955; by Hugh Corbett in *Books Abroad*, summer 1955; by E. J. West in *Educational Theatre Journal*, Dec 1955; by Marie A. Updike White in *South Atlantic Quarterly*, Apr 1956; by K. F. in *Irish Book Lover*, July 1956.

A32   SELECTED PLAYS   1954

first edition
Selected Plays of / SEAN O'CASEY / Selected and with Foreword / by *the Author* /
Introduction / by *John Gassner* / GEORGE BRAZILLER [solidus] NEW YORK [solidus]
1954

20 × 30.5cm.

[a]–[b], blank; [i], half-title: SELECTED PLAYS OF / *Sean O'Casey* /; [ii],
blank; frontispiece, photograph of O'Casey by Alfred Eris; [iii], title-page
as above; [iv], copyright, acknowledgements, performance and translation
rights, manufacture; v–xxi, Introduction by John Gassner; [xxii], blank;
xxiii–xxiv, A Word From O'Casey; xxv–xxviii, Foreword; xxix, Contents;
[xxx], blank; [1]–794, text; 795–6, words and music for songs in *Time to
Go*; 797–800, Chronological Table of O'Casey's Plays.

Green cloth with tan cloth spine; back cover blank; front cover has facsimile
of O'Casey's signature in gold; spine: [decorative rule] / [the following four
lines on black panel] *Selected / Plays of* / sean / o'casey / [decorative rule] /
George Braziller /; lettered and decorated in gold; white endpapers, all
edges trimmed, top edge stained yellow; dust-jacket lettered and decorated
in grey, white and yellow with photograph of O'Casey on front.
Published October 1954 at $5.00, the copyright copy was deposited on October
20; number of copies undisclosed; reprinted 1956.

Contents: Introduction: Genius Without Fetters by John Gassner – A Word
From O'Casey: On Playwriting – Foreword: Before Curtain-Rise – *The Shadow
of a Gunman* (1925) – *Juno and the Paycock* (1925) – *The Plough and the Stars*
(1926) – *The Silver Tassie* (1928) – *Within the Gates* (1933) – *Purple Dust* (1940) –
Red Roses for Me (1942) – *Bedtime Story* (1951) – *Time to Go* (1951) – chronological Table of O'Casey's Plays.

Notes: This collection of plays, selected by O'Casey, was intended by the
publisher as a celebration of the playwright's seventieth birthday. Neither
he nor George Braziller knew, when planning the event, that his actual
age in 1954 was seventy-four. As a number of critical studies claimed (and
as some still do), O'Casey was under the impression he was born in 1884;
it was not until he had to produce a birth certificate in order to fulfil a
contract requirement for stage production in France, some time in 1954, that
he learned he was four years older than he thought he was. A surprising
omission is *Cock-A-Doodle Dandy* (A28) which O'Casey has often referred to
as his favourite play. Gassner in his 'Preface' quotes O'Casey as saying he
did not know why he selected these particular titles, and continues: 'The nine
plays represent my varying mood in outlook on life and in the varying
manners and techniques of the stage.' The plays had all been published
previously. Although this is one of the rare occasions on which a separately
published O'Casey title appeared without a Macmillan imprint, the texts
of the plays are in fact reproduced from the Macmillan *Collected Plays* (A29)
setting. In *The Silver Tassie* the statement that it is a 'Stage Version' is omitted,

as are also the 'Notes' for production given in Volume II of *Collected Plays*. Similarly, both are also omitted from the present printing of *Within the Gates*, although they are included in Volume II of *Collected Plays*. 'A Word From O'Casey: On Playwrighting', and 'Foreword: Before Curtain-Rise', appear here in print for the first time. The latter was reprinted under the title 'A Word Before Curtain-Rise' in *Blasts and Benedictions* (A44).

Reviews: *Selected Plays* was reviewed by Horace Reynolds in *Christian Science Monitor*, Nov 24, 1954; by George Freedley in *Library Journal*, Jan 1955; by E. J. West in *Educational Theatre Journal*, Dec 1955.

A33   THE BISHOP'S BONFIRE   1955

a. *first edition*
THE BISHOP'S / BONFIRE / *A Sad Play within the Tune of a Polka* / BY / SEAN
O'CASEY / *Cad dhéanfamaoid feasta gan adhmad,* / *Atá deire na g-coillte ar lár.* /
ᵢLONDON / MACMILLAN & CO LTD / 1955

19.5 × 13cm.

[i], half-title: THE BISHOP'S BONFIRE /; [ii], blank; frontispiece, Sean
O'Casey from a portrait by Breon O'Casey; [iii], title-page as above; [iv],
copyright, publisher's imprints, printing; [v], dedication: TO SUSAN GONE /
AND SUSAN HERE /; [vi], blank; [vii], details and cast of first production;
[viii], Characters, scenes, time; 1–121, text; 122–4, words and music for the
songs, printer's imprint at foot of 124.

Green cloth; front and back covers blank; spine: THE / BISHOP'S
/ BONFIRE / [star] / SEAN / O'CASEY / MACMILLAN /; lettered and
decorated in gold; white endpapers, all edges trimmed; green dust-jacket,
lettered and decorated in green and maroon.
Published June 24, 1955 at 8s 6d; 2000 copies printed by R. & R. Clark,
Ltd, Edinburgh; reprinted July 1955 (1000 copies), November 30, 1961 (2000
copies of which 1000 were in paper). The frontispiece was omitted in the
1961 reprint.

b. *American (offset) edition*
THE BISHOP'S / BONFIRE / *A Sad Play within the Tune of a Polka* / BY / SEAN
O'CASEY / *Cad dhéanfamaoid feasta gan adhmad,* / *Atá deire na g-coillte ar lár.* /
New York / THE MACMILLAN COMPANY / 1955

20 × 13cm.

[i], half-title: THE BISHOP'S BONFIRE /; [ii], publisher's imprints; frontispiece, Sean O'Casey from a portrait by Breon O'Casey; [iii], title-page as
above; [iv], copyright, printing; [v], dedication: TO SUSAN GONE / AND
SUSAN HERE /; [vi], blank; [vii], details and cast of first production; [viii],
characters, scenes, time; 1–121, text; 122–4, words and music for the songs.

Light blue cloth; back cover blank; front cover: The Bishop's Bonfire;
spine lettered lengthwise top to bottom: *SEAN O'CASEY Thě* BISHOP'S
BONFIRE *MACMILLAN;* lettered in yellow; white endpapers, all edges
trimmed; light brown dust-jacket, lettered in light brown and white.
Published August 30, 1955 at $3.00; 2500 copies printed.

Notes: The Bishop's Bonfire was written in the first four months of 1954. On
January 4 that year O'Casey wrote to George Jean Nathan: 'Have started a
new play—but God knows if I'll ever finish it—"The Bishop's Bonfire." '
Writing to Mr De Wilton of the Macmillan Company, O'Casey, on March 16,
reports that work on the play is proceeding, and by April 12 he is able
to tell Nathan that the play is completed. This news is conveyed to De
Wilton in a letter dated May 7, 1954. The writing can be regarded as fairly
rapid, especially as the playwright was not in good health at this time.

On June 21, 1954 he sent the play to Mr Lovat Dickson of Macmillan and Co., telling him he was also sending a copy to the Macmillan Company, New York, 'who are interested in it, and may ask for the American licence. I think it a good work, quite quietly, but it doesn't follow that others who read it may think the same as I do.' Both companies decided to publish the play. The dramatist confided to Nathan on August 1: 'It isn't a sensational play in any way; but, maybe, has a few moments of pathos and comedy. It's hard for a playwright to judge his own work, or the work of other playwrights either. God help us, we can't do without the critics, grumble how we may.' The next month, on September 18, he responded to Nathan's criticisms of the work in the following terms: 'I entirely agree that *The Bishop's Bonfire* would have been a better play had *Cock* never been written. That play, possibly by accident, came out in a very colourful way, and it is damned hard to get up to its standard. However, I can safely say that *The Bishop's Bonfire* was the best I could do in the mood of the moment. It is gratifying, too, very gratifying to know you think it has some good writing and genuine humorous characterization. Hurrah! for these even aren't easy to do.'

O'Casey, in a letter of November 26, 1954 to Doris Leach, discussed the prospects of a stage production: 'between ourselves I have a fine chance of this one being done in Dublin . . . I shouldn't be surprised at a storm over this play either.' On January 8, 1955 he told Nathan: 'It is more plausible in Dublin than the more gay and imaginative *Cock*: there was no hope for that one [there].' Writing to Peter Newmark on February 7, 1955 – three weeks before the Dublin production – O'Casey describes the work, warningly: 'It's an outspoken play, with a good deal of humour, and some sad moments.' The play had its first presentation by Cyril Cusack Productions at the Gaiety Theatre, Dublin, on February 28, 1955, directed by Tyrone Guthrie. The production was an exciting event. The *Standard*, a weekly paper published in Dublin, in two articles before the play opened, set the climate for controversy, and expressed its opposition to the production of the play. The production itself called forth the applause and boos of the pro- and anti-O'Casey factions. It ran for five weeks before giving way to a previously scheduled season of opera. O'Casey modified the dialogue in places as a result of the Dublin production. Macmillan and Co. (London) sent to New York page proofs of the English edition incorporating the changes. The Macmillan Company (New York) used the proofs to produce its own edition.

The play is dedicated to the author's mother and to his daughter, Shivaun. The frontispiece portrait is a black and white reproduction of an oil painting of the playwright by his son Breon; it was not used in the 1961 reprint. The quotation on the title-page is explained in a letter of March 24, 1955 to Thomas Mark of Macmillan and Co.: 'The Irish motto is the first two lines of a famous and rather lovely, Irish lament; one for the loss of chieftains fled away from Ireland to France and Spain; the beginning of the flight of the "Wild Geese." The best English I can think of is—

> What shall we do for timber
> Now that the last tree in the forest is down?'

The dust-jacket of the English edition describes the play: 'O'Casey's latest three-act play brings us down again to rural Ireland at a time when all are busy providing a colourful welcome to a Bishop about to pay a visit

to the little town he was born in. There are gorgeous goings-on to entertain
him in the house and home of Councillor Reiligan, the big man who owns
all the body and half the soul of the little town of Ballyoonagh.' The
dust-jacket of the American edition has this to say of the work: 'Against
this busy and excited background, O'Casey has placed·his magnificently conceived characters, who, in the rush of preparations, reveal the hilarious
comedy and startling tragedy of their lives, and at the same time unknowingly
present, as well-drawn dramatic personalities must always do, a profound
and moving commentary on life.' Writing to Tarlach O'Huid on June 25,
1955 the playwright refers to the speech of the Railway Porter who appears
in Act II: 'I'm sure you never heard a Railway Porter talk as the one did in
THE BONFIRE—though I know one, a Louis Blad of Dublin, who could
talk, and knew Shakespeare and Shelley quite well; and who was an eloquent
blatherer when he had drink taken.' Some of the dialogue in Act II is adapted
from the chapter 'Outside an Irish Window' in *Sunset and Evening Star* (A31),
a chapter which had already appeared under the title 'Jeeps, be Jeepers'
in *New Statesman and Nation*, July 18, 1953 (C420). O'Casey did not contem-
plate any changes for the 1961 reprint. In a letter of June 30, 1961 he writes
to Macmillan and Co.: 'I can't think of anything to amend in The Bishop's
Bonfire, though if I was starting it, it might be a lot different. I think that
about all [my] plays already written, never satisfied.' The published play
was recommended to its members by the Book Society, London.

Reviews: *The Bishop's Bonfire* was reviewed in *Times Literary Supplement*, July 8,
1955; by John Jordon in *Irish Writing*, summer 1955; by Brooks Atkinson in *New
York Times Book Review*, Sep 11, 1955; by P. L. Adams in *Atlantic*, Oct 1955; by
George Freedley in *Library Journal*, Nov. 1, 1955.

THE GREEN CROW   1956

a. *first edition*
The Green Crow / SEAN O'CASEY / *New York* / GEORGE BRAZILLER, INC. /
1956

21 × 14cm.

[i], title-page as above; [ii], copyright, manufacture, Acknowledgments; iii,
Preface; [iv], blank; v–vi, Contents; vii–xvi, Foreword; [1] fly-title: *The Flying
Wasp* /; [2], blank; 3–303, text; [304], blank.

Black cloth; outline drawing of crow stamped in green on front cover;
back cover blank; spine: O'CASEY [in green] / *The* [in white] / *Green* [in white] /
Crow [in white] / BRAZILLER [in green] /; white endpapers, all edges trimmed,
top edge stained green; dust-jacket in green, white and black, incorporating
crow in design on front cover.
Published March 1956 at $3.95, deposited for copyright March 18, 1956;
number of copies undisclosed. A photo-reprint was published by Grosset
& Dunlap in the Universal Library series (UL-37) in April 1958 at $0.95;
15,000 copies were printed; reprinted January 10, 1961.

Contents:

Foreword
PART ONE: THE FLYING WASP
Overture
  A much revised and rewritten version of the essay with the same title in
  The Flying Wasp (A18).
The Public Death of Shakespeare
  First appeared in *Time and Tide*, July 13, 1935 (C163); identical with the
  reprint in *The Flying Wasp* (A18) except for the addition of the introductory
  paragraph in this case.
National Theater Bunkum
  First appeared in *Time and Tide*, Oct 12 and Nov 9, 1935 (C168 and C169);
  three short paragraphs are added at the beginning, otherwise the essay is
  identical with that of the same title in *The Flying Wasp* (A18).
England, Say When
  First appeared in *The Flying Wasp* (A18).
Murdher in the Theater
  First appeared in *Time and Tide*, Oct 10, 1936 (C185); reprinted in *The
  Flying Wasp* (A18).
Critica Silentio Luna
  This essay uses material taken from three articles in *The Flying Wasp* (A18)
  as follows: 'It's All Very Curious, Isn't It?', 'Critici Infallibilibombast' and
  'Poor Pinero Passes By'.
Green Goddess of Realism
  First appeared in *The Flying Wasp* (A18).
Coward Codology: I. Cavalcade
  An abbreviated version first appeared in *Time and Tide*, Jan 11, 1936 (C173);
  an expanded version was first published in *The Flying Wasp* (A18).

Coward Codology: II. Design for Dying
    First appeared in *The Flying Wasp* (A18).
Coward Codology: III. Excelsior Ingenium
    First appeared in *The Flying Wasp* (A18).
Shakespeare Lives in London Lads
    First appeared in *Time and Tide*, Apr 18, 1936 (C177); reprinted in *The Flying Wasp* (A18).
Pro-Per Proscenium
    First appeared in *The Flying Wasp* (A18).
Bonfire under a Black Sun

PART TWO: ON DIVERSE SUBJECTS

The Arts among the Multitude
    First appeared *7 Arts*, 1954 (B26).
Always the Plough and the Stars
    First appeared in *New York Times Book Review*, Jan 25, 1953 (C417).
Tender Tears for Poor O'Casey
    Slightly revised version of that which first appeared in *Irish Writing*, June 1947 (C343).
No Flowers for Films
    First appeared in *Leader Magazine*, Feb 19, 1949 (C374).
A Whisper about Bernard Shaw
    First appeared as 'Vpolgolosa o Bernarde Shou' in *Britansky Soyuznik*, July 21, 1946 (C328). This is its first appearance in English.
Bernard Shaw: An Appreciation of a Fighting Idealist
    First appeared in *New York Times Book Review*, Nov 12, 1950 (C399).
'St. Patrick's Day in the Morning'
    A shorter version was published in *New York Times Magazine*, Mar 15, 1953 (C418) under the title 'St. Pathrick's Day'.
The Flutter of Flags: A Healthy Pride
    First appeared in *Saturday Night*, July 24, 1954 (C426)
The Power of Laughter: Weapon Against Evil
    First appeared in *Saturday Night*, Oct 3, 1953 (C421)
Come to the Fair
    First appeared in *Saturday Night*, Dec 25, 1954 (C430) under the title 'Philosophy of Despair—A Modern Sickness'.

PART THREE: WINDFALLS: FOUR SHORT STORIES

I Wanna Woman (1934)
The Star-Jazzer (1934)
The Job (1934)
A Fall in a Gentle Wind
    This revised version first appeared in *Life and Letters*, Dec 1933 and was collected in *Windfalls* (A16). The original version first appeared in *Irish Statesman*, Apr 25, 1925 (C96) under the title 'Mollser'.

b. *English edition*
SEAN O'CASEY / [short rule] / *The* [in green] / *Green Crow* [in green] / [publisher's device] / W. H. ALLEN / LONDON / 1957 [all above within border of rules surrounded by decorative border]

22 × 14cm.

[1], half-title: The Green / Crow / [outline drawing of crow] /; [2], blank; [3], title-page as above; [4], printer's statement and imprint; [5]–[6], Contents; [7], Preface; [8], Acknowledgments; 9–16, Foreword; [17], fly title: *The Flying Wasp*; [18], blank; 19–278, text; [279]–[280], blank.

Black cloth; outline drawing of crow stamped in green on front cover; back cover blank; spine: [swelled rule] / *The / Green / Crow* / [swelled rule] / Sean / O'Casey / [publisher's device] / W. H. / ALLEN /; spine lettered and decorated in gold; white endpapers, all edges trimmed; dust-jacket in green, white and black incorporating crow in design on front cover.
Published February 11, 1957 at 21s; number of copies unknown.

Contents:

The same as in the first edition with the addition of the following in PART TWO: ON DIVERSE SUBJECTS:

Shaw – Lord of a Century
    First appeared under the title 'G. B. Shaw: The Lord of a Century', in *New York Times*, July 22, 1956 (C456).
Playwright in Exile
    First appeared under the title 'O'Casey: Playwright in Exile', in *New York Times*, Dec 25, 1955 (C449).

Notes: In a letter dated June 2, 1955 to Mr De Wilton of the Macmillan Company, O'Casey writes that he has been working for some time on a collection at George Braziller's suggestion. According to the letter, the collection was to consist 'of various things scattered in Journals, plus reprinting of some of the articles in THE FLYING WASP, with the three short stories that appeared in WINDFALLS.' Braziller had urged O'Casey to use 'Collected Prose' as the title for the book. The playwright refused, on the grounds that such a title could only be used if the autobiographical prose writings were represented. He also said that 'Collected Prose' or 'Collected Essays', another suggestion, sounded formal and academic, whereas he did not pretend to be an essayist, but a writer of occasional articles and songs. In a letter to Ken Coates dated July 1, 1955 and published in *Socialist Register*, 1965 (B47), O'Casey refers to the forthcoming publication: 'The Flying Wasp has long been out of print. The critics didn't like it, and no wonder. At the moment, oddly enough, I am going over it again, for it is to be published—or so the prospect goes—with other articles of mine, in a volume to be issued by a New York publisher.' The dust-jacket of the American edition describes the book: 'Here is O'Casey–self styled "green crow"–writing on the theatre: its critics, playwrights and productions; its failures and its future. Here also are four of O'Casey's remarkable short stories – stories which capture the warm humanity that makes his plays what they are . . . There is an appreciation of Shaw, a riotous critique of Noël Coward's work, and pieces on Dublin, on O'Casey's latest play, *The Bishop's Bonfire*, and on his peculiar experiences with the films.' The dust-jacket of the English edition describes the book as 'A more informal O'Casey perhaps than usual, commenting on the theatre, its failures and its future; expressing his views on films, critics, Noël Coward; writing about himself and subjects and persons dear to him – Shakespeare, Dublin,

108   *Books and Pamphlets*

Shaw; laughter, and flags, for example.' O'Casey himself in the preface to the book describes it as 'a nest of Ids and Trends, made up of a few short stories and articles, written on divers occasions; added to a laughing look-over of things said about the Theater, here and elsewhere; besides some merry and amusing comments thereon; including a squint and a few quips at Irish notice-writers (popularly called critics); accompanied with a skirl of shrewd remarks made by the Author on the tendencies of the theater of today.' The collection includes thirteen of the twenty-four pieces from *The Flying Wasp* (A18); the four short stories are from *Windfalls* (A16). Apart from the much rewritten 'Overture' and 'Critica Silentio Luna', only 'Bonfire Under a Black Sun' was written especially for this collection. It is interesting to note that W. H. Allen acted as the publisher for the English edition; Macmillan considered the collection would have little commercial value in the nineteen-fifties.

Reviews: The Green Crow was reviewed by Brooks Atkinson in *New York Times Book Review*, Mar 18, 1956; by William Hogan in *San Francisco Chronicle*, Mar 22, 1956; in *Time*, Mar 26, 1956; by Frederick E. Faverty in *Chicago Sunday Tribune*, Apr 8, 1956; by Walter P. Eaton in *New York Herald Tribune Book Review*, May 6, 1956; by Max Cosman in *Theatre Arts*, July 1956; by H. Popkin in *Kenyon Review*, autumn 1956; by John Wain in *Observer*, Feb 10, 1957; by Alan Dent in *News Chronicle*, Feb 14, 1957; in the *Times*, Feb 14, 1957; in *Times Literary Supplement*, Feb 15, 1957; by J. MacC. in *Daily Worker* (London), Feb 21, 1957; by J. P. Henderson in *New Statesman and Nation*, Feb 23, 1957; by J. W. Lambert in *Sunday Times*, Feb 24, 1957; by Joe MacColum in *Irish Democrat*, Apr 1957; by Peter Green in *Time and Tide*, Apr 6, 1957; by E. J. West in *Educational Theatre Journal*, May 1957; in *Listener*, May 9, 1957; by A. T. in *Manchester Evening News*, Mar 14, 1957.

AUTOBIOGRAPHIES   1956

a. *first edition*

VOLUME I

MIRROR / IN MY HOUSE / *The Autobiographies of* / SEAN O'CASEY / TWO VOLUMES / *VOLUME ONE* / I KNOCK AT THE DOOR / PICTURES IN THE HALLWAY / DRUMS UNDER THE WINDOWS / *"Go some of you and fetch a looking-glass."* / *NEW YORK* / THE MACMILLAN COMPANY / *1956*

21 × 14cm.

[i], title-page as above; [ii], copyright; frontispiece; [iii], title-page for *I Knock at the Door*; [iv], copyright, printing; [v], dedication; [vi], blank; [vii], Contents; [viii], blank; 1–294, text of *I Knock at the Door*; [i], half-title: *Pictures in the Hallway*; [ii], blank; frontispiece; [iii], title-page; [iv], copyright, printing; [v], dedication; [vi], blank; [vii], Contents; [viii], blank; 1–373, text of *Pictures in the Hallway*; [374], blank; [i], half-title: *Drums Under the Windows*; [ii], blank; frontispiece; [iii], title-page; [iv], copyright, printing; [v], dedication; [vi], blank; [vii], Contents; [viii], blank; 1–431, text of *Drums Under the Windows*; [432]–[436], blank.

Black cloth; front cover at bottom right: I KNOCK AT THE DOOR / PICTURES IN THE HALLWAY / DRUMS UNDER THE WINDOWS /; back cover blank; spine striped in gold and green on black: MIRROR IN / MY HOUSE / *The* / *Autobiographies* / *of* / SEAN O'CASEY / *VOLUME ONE* / MACMILLAN /; lettered in gold; cream endpapers, all edges trimmed, top edges stained black.

VOLUME II

MIRROR / IN MY HOUSE / *The Autobiographies of* / SEAN O'CASEY / TWO VOLUMES / *VOLUME TWO* / INISHFALLEN, FARE THEE WELL / ROSE AND CROWN / SUNSET AND EVENING STAR / *"Go some of you and fetch a looking-glass."* / *NEW YORK* / THE MACMILLAN COMPANY / *1956*

21 × 14cm.

[i], title-page as above; [ii], copyright; frontispiece; [iii], title-page for *Inishfallen, Fare Thee Well*; [iv], copyright, printing; [v], dedication; [vi], blank; [vii], Contents; [viii], blank; 1–396, text of *Inishfallen, Fare Thee Well*; [i], half-title: *Rose and Crown*; [ii], blank; frontispiece; [iii], title-page for *Rose and Crown*; [iv], copyright, printing; [v], dedication; [vi], blank; [vii], Contents; [viii], blank; 1–323, text of *Rose and Crown*; [324], blank; [i], half-title: *Sunset and Evening Star*; [ii], blank; frontispiece; [iii], title-page for *Sunset and Evening Star*; [iv], copyright, printing; [v], dedication; [vi], blank; [vii], Contents; [viii], blank; 1–339, text of *Sunset and Evening Star*; [340]–[344], blank.

As Volume I, except for the substitution of the three titles *INISHFALLEN, FARE THEE WELL*; *ROSE AND CROWN*; and *SUNSET AND EVENING STAR* on front cover; together with the substitution of *VOLUME TWO* on spine.

The two volumes were issued together as a boxed set with two photographs of O'Casey by W. Suschitzky on the sides of the box.

Published October 1, 1956 at $20.00; 3900 sets printed. Macmillan and Co. Ltd acted as agents in London offering sets at £8 8s.

Notes: On October 30, 1954 O'Casey wrote to Mr De Wilton of the Macmillan Company to say: 'Gassner suggested that an edited 1 volume book of all the biographical books be published when *Sunset* has appeared and has fully achieved its normal sale.' *Sunset and Evening Star* (A31) had been published on October 29, 1954 in London and in New York on November 9, 1954. The idea was acceptable to the Macmillan Company and on September 29, 1955 a proposal was made to O'Casey that the six biographical volumes be published in two volumes in the autumn of 1956. The volumes would be boxed as a set; 3500 sets would be published with a pre-publication price of $16.00 and a post-publication price of $18.00—the selling price was actually established at $20.00. On November 20 O'Casey agreed to the proposal. Production was completed by July 1956 and on July 13 a set was mailed to the playwright. In a letter of August 21 to Mr Budlong of the Macmillan Company he gave his impression of the work: 'They are the handsomest pair of books I've seen during my lifetime. The whole format is delightful.' Writing to O'Casey on October 4, 1956 Mr De Wilton reported brisk sales, especially in New York. The demand fell off, however, and eventually in July 1960 the publishers asked and were granted O'Casey's permission to lower the price to $10.95 because of the discouraging sales. The quotation on the title-page is from Shakespeare's *King Richard II*, Act IV, line 268.

The text was reproduced from the American editions of the biographies as follows: *I Knock at the door* (A19d, 1949), *Pictures in the Hallway* (A22c, 1949), *Drums Under the Windows* (A24b, 1946), *Inishfallen, Fare Thee Well* (A27b, 1949), *Rose and Crown* (A30b, 1952), and *Sunset and Evening Star* (A31b, 1954).

'Young Cassidy', a motion picture based on certain portions of *Mirror in My House*, was released in March 1965. The screenplay was by John Whiting. Entitled 'A John Ford Film', it was directed by Jack Cardiff. It was produced by Robert D. Graff and Robert Emmett Ginna for Sextant Films Ltd, and presented by Metro-Goldwyn-Mayer. The motion picture starred Maggie Smith, Rod Taylor, Michael Redgrave and Flora Robson. O'Casey disliked certain scenes in the screenplay and rewrote some of them; his revisions were mostly ignored in shooting the film. A copy of the script 'O'Casey Revision December 1963' is in the Wesleyan University Library.

Reviews: *Mirror in My House* was reviewed by Granville Hicks in *New Republic*, Oct 22, 1956; in *New York Herald Tribune Book Review*, Oct 28, 1956; by George Freedley in *Library Journal*, Dec 1, 1956; by David H. Greene in *Commonweal*, Jan 25, 1957; by John O'Shaughnessy in *Nation*, Mar 16, 1957; in *Theatre Arts*, Apr 1957; by Marvin Magalaner in *Sewanee Review*, winter 1957.

b. *English edition*

VOLUME I

SEAN O'CASEY / AUTOBIOGRAPHIES / I / *I KNOCK AT THE DOOR* / *PICTURES IN THE HALLWAY* / *DRUMS UNDER THE WINDOWS* / LONDON / MACMILLAN & CO LTD / 1963

17 × 11.5cm.

[i], half-title: SEAN O'CASEY / AUTOBIOGRAPHIES / VOL. I /; [ii], titles in St. Martin's Library; [iii], title-page as above; [iv], publisher's imprints, edition statements, copyright notice, printing; v–[vi], Contents; [1]–666, text, printer's imprint at foot of 666.

Stiff paper covers; decorated in black, white, pink and green; lettered in black and white.

Published August 8, 1963 at 12s 6d; 20,000 copies printed by R. & R. Clark, Ltd, Edinburgh.

VOLUME II

SEAN O'CASEY / AUTOBIOGRAPHIES / II / *INISHFALLEN, FARE THEE WELL / ROSE AND CROWN / SUNSET AND EVENING STAR* / LONDON / MACMILLAN & CO LTD / 1963

17 × 11.5cm.

[i], half-title: SEAN O'CASEY / AUTOBIOGRAPHIES / VOL. II /; [ii], titles in St. Martin's Library; [iii], title-page as above; [iv], publisher's imprints, edition statements, copyright notice, printing; v–[vi], Contents; [1]–665, text, printer's imprint at foot of 665; [666], blank.

Stiff paper covers; decorated in black, white, pink and green; lettered in black and white.

Published August 8, 1963 at 12s 6d; 20,000 copies printed by R. & R. Clark, Ltd, Edinburgh.

Notes: The proposal for a two-volume paperback edition of the six auto-biographies was made in a letter of October 2, 1962 to O'Casey from T. M. Farmiloe of Macmillan and Co. In his letter Farmiloe indicated that the title preferred for the work was *Autobiographies*, that an index should be provided for the work, and that the frontispieces should be omitted. O'Casey in his letter of October 9 expressed himself 'Content with suggested title by your Sales Department. Between ourselves, I have not cared a lot for "Mirror in My House" for a long time.' On October 22 the directors of Macmillan decided against an index. In a letter of October 18 to T. M. Farmiloe O'Casey gives his ideas for a cover design: 'The central idea is myself leaning lazily against the railings of Nelson's Pillar; at bottom, a piper in one corner, a prelate in the opposite one. Above in one corner are the 3 Leopards of England, opposite, the ship carrying me from Ireland. Two youngsters are admiring the great Pillar.' In the same letter he deprecates his own design: 'I don't think much of the design, and think a bright abstract design would be better.' The cover did not incorporate O'Casey's ideas but was acceptable to him as he infers in his letter of July 17, 1963 to T. M. Farmiloe: '[The volumes] look odd but pleasant (like the biographies them-selves odd pleasant and unpleasant). They are very easy to handle, and the design is quietly colorful and oddly attractive. As books go now, they are worth the price, at any rate from the point of view of the print, the binding, and general format: the text must be left to the judgment of the readers.'

The text was reset for this edition and incorporates some corrections, mainly misspellings. Slight changes were made in the text of *Inishfallen, Fare Thee Well*, vol. II, p. 179. They concern remarks on A. E. attributed to C. P. Curran. In this edition the remarks are reduced to one sentence. The rest of the paragraph is set in roman type, not in italic as in previous editions, to indicate that the words are those of O'Casey and not those of Mr Curran. Writing to T. M. Farmiloe on October 21, 1962, O'Casey describes the work: 'It is really more than one Biography, it is one of the child, the youth, the young man, the old one; of a Gaelic Leaguer, a Republican, a Socialist, a Dramatist, &c, here & there, of a damned fool – many forms of one life.'

Reviews: *Autobiographies* was reviewed by John Wain in *Observer*, Aug 11, 1963; by Padraic Fallon in *Irish Times*, Aug 17, 1963; in *Times Literary Supplement*, Sept 6, 1963; by Robert Nye in *Scotsman*, Sep 7, 1963; by Florence O'Donoghue in *Tablet*, Sep 7, 1963; by Valentin Iremonger in *Spectator*, Sep 27, 1963; in *The Times*, Oct 3, 1963; by Philip Hengist in *Punch*, Oct 30, 1963.

c. *Pan Books edition*

VOLUME I

AUTOBIOGRAPHY / VOLUME 1 / *I KNOCK AT THE DOOR* / SEAN O'CASEY / [publisher's mark] / UNABRIDGED / PAN BOOKS LTD: LONDON

18 × 11cm.

[1], half-title, details of *Autobiography*, details of cover photgraph; [2], listing of other O'Casey titles in Pan Books, Conditions of Sale; [3], title-page as above; [4], publication details, International Standard Book Number, rights reservation notice, printer's imprint; [5], Contents; [6], blank; [7], fly title: *I KNOCK AT THE DOOR / Knock, and it shall be opened unto you / To Breon and Niall /*; *[8], blank; [9]–191, text; [192], list of Irish authors published by Pan Books.*

Paper covers; colour photograph 'Quais' by Evelyn Hofer reproduced on covers; lettered and decorated in black, red, white and blue.
Published March 5, 1971 at 30p; 30,000 copies printed by Richard Clay (The Chaucer Press), Ltd, Bungay, Suffolk.

VOLUME II

AUTOBIOGRAPHY / VOLUME 2 / *PICTURES IN THE HALLWAY* / SEAN O'CASEY / [publisher's mark] / UNABRIDGED / PAN BOOKS LTD: LONDON

18 × 11cm.

[1], half-title, details of *Autobiography*, details of cover photograph; [2], listing of other O'Casey titles in Pan Books, Conditions of Sale; [3], title-page as above; [4], publication details, International Standard Book Number, rights reservation notice, printer's imprint; [5], Contents; [6], fly title: *PICTURES IN THE HALLWAY / Time flies over us, but leaves its shadow behind /* [five line dedication to the memory of Rev. E. M. Griffin] /; [7]–240, text.

Paper covers; colour photograph 'Hubrand Bridge' by Evelyn Hofer reproduced on covers; lettered and decorated in black, red, white and blue.

Published March 5, 1971 at 30p; 30,000 copies printed by Richard Clay (The Chaucer Press), Ltd, Bungay, Suffolk.

VOLUME III

AUTOBIOGRAPHY / Book 3 / *DRUMS UNDER THE WINDOWS* / SEAN O'CASEY / [publisher's mark] / UNABRIDGED / PAN BOOKS LTD: LONDON

18 × 11cm.

[1], half-title, details of *Autobiography*, details of cover photograph; [2], listing of other O'Casey titles in Pan Books, Conditions of Sale; [3], title-page as above; [4], publication details, International Standard Book Number, rights reservation notice, printer's imprint; [5], Contents; [6], fly title, quotation from 'Purgatory' by W. B. Yeats, dedication to Dr Michael O'Hickey; [7]– 287, text; [288], listing of works by O'Casey and Frank O'Connor published by Pan Books, with notes.

Paper covers; colour photograph 'Arran Quay' by Evelyn Hofer reproduced on covers; lettered and decorated in black, red, white and blue.
Published March 3, 1972 at 35p; 25,000 copies printed by Richard Clay (The Chaucer Press), Ltd, Bungay, Suffolk.

VOLUME IV

AUTOBIOGRAPHY / Book 4 / *INISHFALLEN, FARE THEE WELL* / SEAN O'CASEY / [publisher's mark] / UNABRIDGED / PAN BOOKS LTD: LONDON

18 × 11cm.

[1], half-title, details of *Autobiography*, details of cover photograph; [2], listing of other O'Casey titles in Pan Books, Conditions of Sale; [3], title-page as above; [4], publication details, International Standard Book Number, rights reservation notice, printer's imprint; [5], Contents; [6], blank; [7], fly title, quotation from song, dedication to Walter McDonald; [8], blank; [9]– 286, text; [287], listing of works by O'Casey and Frank O'Connor published by Pan Books, with notes; [288], list of publisher's titles in 'Autobiography and True Adventure'.

Paper covers; colour photograph 'Mountjoy Square' by Evelyn Hofer repro- duced on covers; lettered and decorated in black, red, white and blue.
Published March 3, 1972 at 35p; 25,000 copies printed by Richard Clay (The Chaucer Press), Ltd, Bungay, Suffolk.

VOLUME V

AUTOBIOGRAPHY / BOOK 5 / *ROSE AND CROWN* / SEAN O'CASEY / [publisher's mark] / UNABRIDGED / PAN BOOKS LTD: LONDON

18 × 11cm.

[1], half-title, details of *Autobiography*; [2], listing of other O'Casey titles in Pan Books, Conditions of Sale; [3], title-page as above; [4], publication

details, International Standard Book Number, rights reservation notice, printer's imprint; [5], Contents; [6], blank; [7], quotation from Dryden's *Don Sebastian*, dedication; [8], blank; [9]–240, text.

Paper covers; colour photographs of inn sign and Young's Rose and Crown Inn on front and back covers; lettered in black and white.

Published March 9, 1973 at 40p; 16,000 copies printed by Richard Clay (The Chaucer Press), Ltd, Bungay, Suffolk.

VOLUME VI

AUTOBIOGRAPHY / BOOK 6 / *SUNSET AND EVENING STAR* / SEAN O'CASEY / [publisher's mark] / UNABRIDGED / PAN BOOKS LTD: LONDON

18 × 11cm.

[1], half-title, details of *Autobiography*; [2], listing of other O'Casey titles in Pan Books, Conditions of Sale; [3], title-page as above; [4], publication details, International Standard Book Number, rights reservation notice, printer's imprint; [5], Contents; [6], blank; [7], Chinese proverb and quotation which originally appeared on title-page of first edition (A31), dedication to Hugh MacDiarmid; [8], blank; [9]–236, text; [237]–[240], publisher's advertisements.

Paper covers; colour photograph of sunset scene on covers; lettered in white.

Published March 9, 1973 at 40p; 16,000 copies printed by Richard Clay (The Chaucer Press), Ltd, Bungay, Suffolk.

Notes: The Pan Books edition was published over three years, 1971–3, two volumes appearing in March of each year. A 'Special Correspondent' writing in the *Irish Times* of March 26, 1971 had this to say, among other things, about the Pan Books edition: 'The title "Autobiography", of course, is wildly misleading, for these volumes are really a strange rainbowed fantasia of fact, dream-fulfilment and paying off of old scores.' The publisher describes the *Autobiography* as: 'essential reading for a proper appreciation of this major Irish dramatist whose plays were among the most exciting developments in modern drama', adding that O'Casey was 'recreating in Volume 1 the days of his Dublin childhood. Volume 2 tells of his coming to manhood and includes episodes later used by the playwright in *Red Roses for Me.*'

The third and fourth volumes were reviewed by a 'Special Correspondent' in the *Irish Times* of March 30, 1972. The publisher writes of *Drums Under the Windows*: 'Here are a nationalist's views of his country and countrymen from 1906 to that "rare time of death in Ireland" – Easter, 1916. From his stay in hospital came people and incidents for *The Silver Tassie*, and out of his personal experiences of Dublin during the Rising arose *The Plough and the Stars*.' Of *Inishfallen, Fare Thee Well* the publisher says: 'The memorable days of Ireland's Independence and Civil War – the background to *Juno and the Paycock* and *The Plough and the Stars* – heralded O'Casey's early triumphs at the Abbey Theatre. This fourth volume vividly recreates the personalities of the era and lists the grievances which made him leave Dublin for England in 1926.'

The fifth and sixth volumes were reviewed in the *Irish Times* of March

29, 1973. The publisher writing of *Rose and Crown* describes the events covered in the book: 'In 1926 O'Casey came to London to receive the Hawthornden Prize for *Juno and the Paycock*, and never returned to Ireland. The crowded years that followed saw his marriage to the lovely young actress, Eileen Carey, the mounting controversy over *The Silver Tassie*, and his eventual visit to America for the staging of *Within the Gates*.' Speaking of *Sunset and Evening Star* the publisher says: 'In this final volume reminiscences of his friendship with Shaw and of life in Devon during World War Two mingle with rebellious indignation at organized religion and true concern for the people of Ireland. The autobiography ends eleven years before O'Casey's death from a heart attack in 1964.'

Reviews: *Autobiography* was reviewed in *Observer* Mar 7, 1971 (vols 1–2); in *Irish Times* March 26, 1971 (vols 1–2); by Sean McMahon in *Irish Press*, May 15, 1971 (vols 1–2); by Ian Aitken in *Teacher's World* (London) June 4, 1971 (vols 1–2); in *Irish Times*, Mar 30, 1972 (vols 3–4); in *Irish Times*, Mar 29, 1973 (vols 5–6); in *Books and Bookmen*, June 1973 (vols 5–6).

A36   THREE PLAYS

first edition

THREE PLAYS / BY / SEAN O'CASEY / JUNO AND THE PAYCOCK / THE
SHADOW OF A GUNMAN / THE PLOUGH AND THE STARS / LONDON
/ MACMILLAN & CO LTD / 1957

17 × 11.5cm.

[i], half-title: THREE PLAYS /; [ii], titles in St Martin's Library; [iii], title-
page as above; [iv], publisher's imprints, copyright, date of issue in St Martin's
Library, printer's imprint; [v], Contents; [vi], blank; [1]–218, text.

Stiff paper covers; lettered and decorated in red, black and cream.
Published April 4, 1957 at 3s in the St Martin's Library series; 40,000 copies
printed by Richard Clay and Co. Ltd, Bungay, Suffolk; reprinted 1960 (10,000
copies, including 5000 copies for St Martin's Press), 1961 (10,000 copies),
1962 (20,000 copies); reprinted in the Papermac series (P85) 1966 (30,377
copies), 1967 (30,000 copies), 1968 (30,000 copies), 1969 (30,000 copies).

Notes: The plays in this volume, O'Casey's earliest printed full-length works,
written and produced in Dublin, established him as a dramatist. They are
his most popular dramatic works, in both the number of stage performances
and of copies printed. 'Juno and the Paycock' and 'The Shadow of a Gunman'
were first printed in 1925 (A10); 'The Plough and the Stars' was first printed
in 1926 (A13). The texts of the *Three Plays* are identical to those printed
in the first volume of *Collected Plays* (A29).

FIVE ONE-ACT PLAYS 1958

first edition
FIVE / ONE-ACT PLAYS / BY / SEAN O'CASEY / THE END OF THE BEGINNING / A POUND ON DEMAND / HALL OF HEALING / BEDTIME STORY / TIME TO GO / LONDON / MACMILLAN & CO LTD / 1958

17 × 11.5cm.

[1], half-title: FIVE ONE-ACT PLAYS /; [2], titles in St. Martin's Library; [3], title-page as above; [4], publisher's imprints, date of issue in St. Martin's Library, printing; [5], Contents, performance and permissions notice; [6], blank; [7]–160, text, printer's imprint at foot of 160.

Stiff paper covers; lettered and decorated in red, black and cream.
Published February 28, 1958 at 3s as no. 18 in the St Martin's Library series; 20,000 copies printed by Richard Clay and Co. Ltd, Bungay, Suffolk (5000 copies issued in special covers for St Martin's Press, New York); 10,000 copies reprinted 1962 (4000 copies issued as P84 in the Papermac series); 10,000 copies reprinted in 1966 in the Papermac series with joint Macmillan and St Martin's Press imprint.

Notes: This collection brings together in a single volume the one-act plays written by O'Casey up to 1958, with the exception of 'Kathleen Listens In' and 'Nannie's Night Out' which the playwright did not wish published, though he was subsequently persuaded by Robert Hogan to allow their inclusion in *Feathers from the Green Crow* (A40) in 1962. 'The End of the Beginning' and 'A Pound on Demand' were first printed in *Windfalls* (A16) in 1934. The other three works were first printed in *Collected Plays*, vols 3–4 (A29) in 1951: 'Hall of Healing' in vol. 3; 'Bedtime Story' and 'Time to Go' in vol. 4.

The playwright had had the idea for a separate volume of his short plays as early as December 11, 1949 when he wrote to George Jean Nathan: 'I am working on the biography [*Rose and Crown*], and, as well, I'd like to publish a book of one-act plays.' In the same letter he speaks of having two already done – presumably 'The End of the Beginning' and 'A Pound on Demand' – and adds, 'I finished another a month ago— "Hill of Healing"—and am just finishing the rough ms. of a second, with a third simmering in my mind.' On March 1, 1950 he tells the same correspondent that the latter is now completed: 'I managed to finish the one-act play "Bedtime Story." . . . I think "Time to Go" is good, though I'm not sure. It is, again, realism touched with fancy. "Bedtime Story" is out of my usual manner, a comedy, fanciful in a way, too; but wholly unlike either "Time to Go" or "Hall of Healing." ' The plan for a book of one-act plays was temporarily abandoned when O'Casey's publisher suggested their inclusion in the Collected Edition. On April 25, 1950 the playwright wrote to Daniel Macmillan: 'I like your idea of including the [three] new one-act plays in the third and fourth volumes.'

The considerable range in dramatic form and subject matter of the five one-act plays in this collection is indicated by the diverse descriptions given by their author. 'The End of the Beginning: A Comedy in One Act' is O'Casey's adaptation of a well-known folk tale. St John Ervine thought it the funniest one-act play in the English language. 'A Pound on Demand', sub-titled 'A Sketch in One Act', is the playwright's knock-about treatment of a friend's anecdote. 'Hall of Healing: A Sincerious Farce in One Scene' is based on actual events with which O'Casey was familiar, as he told Jack Daly in a letter dated July 11, 1949: 'Have written a one-act play to keep my hand in—experience of mine in a Dublin Poor Dispensary, the time you and I and Will Kelly were alive on the Dublin streets.' 'Bedtime Story' (subtitled 'An Immorality Farce in One Act' in an early typescript among the Nathan Papers in Cornell University) is described as 'An Anatole Burlesque in One Act' in a tribute to Arthur Schnitzler's series of *Anatol* sketches, with which it has affinities. On another level of seriousness altogether, 'Time to Go: A Morality Comedy in One Act' is closer in dramatic style and fantasy to a play like *Cock-a Doodle Dandy* (A28), completed two years earlier. The author's comparative evaluation of these works may be gleaned from a letter of July 9, 1958 to his agent in the United States, Jane Rubin: 'Forgot to choose between 'End of the Beginning' & 'Hall of Healing.' Fact is, I prefer either 'Time To Go' or 'Bedtime Story', both better plays than the two mentioned. However, if Cheryl [Crawford] wants either of the first two, then I think 'Hall of Healing' is more real—all incidents in it happened before my eyes; the other is merely an adaptation of [a] world-wide folktale.'

O'Casey wrote only one further one-act play subsequent to this collection: 'The Moon Shines on Kylenamoe' was published as one of three plays in the volume entitled *Behind the Green Curtains* (A39) in 1961.

THE DRUMS OF FATHER NED   1960

a. *first edition*
In *Theatre Arts Magazine*, May 1960 (C528)

b. *first separate edition*
THE DRUMS / OF FATHER NED / *A Mickrocosm of Ireland* / BY / SEAN
O'CASEY / LONDON / MACMILLAN & CO LTD / NEW YORK [centred dot]
ST MARTIN'S PRESS / 1960

19.5 × 13cm.

[i], half-title: THE DRUMS OF FATHER NED /; [ii], blank; frontispiece,
photograph of the Lafayette Little Theatre Company that gave the play its
first performance; [iii], title-page as above; [iv], copyright, publisher's
imprints, printing; [v], dedication; [vi], blank; vii, details of first production;
viii, characters, scenes, time of the play; ix, note on drum roll; [x], poem
of fourteen lines beginning: This comedy's but an idle, laughing play;
1–105, text; 106–9, words and music for the songs; [110], printer's imprint.

Stiff paper covers; design on front cover incorporates biretta and drums;
photograph of O'Casey on back cover; lettered and decorated in light blue,
black and white.
Published June 16, 1960 at 8s 6d; 3000 copies printed by R. & R. Clark, Ltd,
Edinburgh.

c. *American (offset) edition*
THE DRUMS / OF FATHER NED / BY / SEAN O'CASEY / ST MARTIN'S
PRESS / NEW YORK

20 × 13.5cm.

[a]–[d], blank; [i], half-title: THE DRUMS OF FATHER NED /; [ii], blank;
frontispiece, photograph of the Lafayette Little Theatre Company that gave
the play its first performance; [iii], title-page as above; [iv], copyright, Library
of Congress card number, manufacture, affiliated publishers; [v], dedications;
[vi], blank; vii, details of first production; viii, characters, scenes, time of
the play; ix, note on drum roll; [x], poem of fourteen lines beginning:
This comedy's but an idle, laughing play /; 1–105, text; 106–9, words and
music for the songs; [110]–[114], blank.

Black cloth with aqua cloth spine; front and back covers blank; spine:
[lettered lengthwise, top to bottom] sean o'casey *The Drums of Father Ned*
ST MARTIN'S /; lettered in black; white endpapers, all edges trimmed.
Published Aug 29, 1960 at $2.95; 2015 copies printed.

Notes: The Drums of Father Ned was written in 1957. Almost six months after
the death of his younger son, Niall, O'Casey wrote to George Jean Nathan
in a letter dated May 9, 1957: 'To keep my mind from brooding over our
boy, I have set out to try to write a comedy, with my head among the clouds
rather than the stars; a play of common language, but, I hope, with some
humor in it. It's called "The Night is Whispering." ' On June 14 a letter

to Jane Rubin, his American agent, tells her: 'As for the NEW PLAY, it will be a long time before it is finally shaped.' Writing on July 2, 1957 he informs her he will send on the manuscript of the new play after completion, 'but I don't think you will be interested. It is something of a frolic against the background of the Irish Tóstal.' Later the same month, in a letter dated July 22, O'Casey could tell Nathan that he had 'almost finished' the play, adding that it was 'not one of my best; a comedy written against the back-ground of the Irish Tóstal; but not one that will foment a desire on anyone's part to hand out a laurel leaf. I wrote it, I suppose, to help me keep from thinking of things that can never be forgotten; but, I think there is some humour in it; and for this, God will forgive me. Anyway, it was the best I can do at my age, and in my present mood.' Three days later the dramatist informed David Greene that the work was 'not half so good as the Cockadoodle theme, maybe not even as good as the BONFIRE, but it has some amusing moments (I hope), and is played against the background of Tóstal activities, with a theme of courage and the doing of things—"dis-pensing harvest, sowing the To-be" as Tennyson put it.' The play was com-pleted during the summer and on August 22 he reported to Teresa Sacco, of Macmillan and Co, 'I have finished a three-act comedy, not much, but possibly interesting to the Irish; it's called *The Night of Whispering*, and is a comedy right through, with, perhaps, a serious undertone or overtone, or something.' By the time O'Casey wrote to Ronald Ayling on September 20, the work's eventual title had been selected; in this letter the playwright once again stressed the positive philosophy behind the play: 'It, to some extent, answers your question of "ultimate despair". I have never despaired, and I don't think I ever shall.'

On November 1, 1957 he told Jane Rubin that the play would have its première during the Irish festival, An Tóstal, in May 1958. Negotiations for this presentation had been conducted with Brendan Smith, the festival director, who had expressed his committee's (and his own) delight with the play – a drama written about An Tóstal to be staged at An Tóstal. In October 1957 the playwright wrote to Smith with a suggestion for a change in Act II: 'Some time ago, Eileen (Mrs O'Casey) read THE DRUMS OF FATHER NED, and, talking about it a little, later on, said she didn't like the taking of the money episode between Skerighan and Bernadette. She thought that an Irish girl could be hardly so sophisticated (big word), so ready to seize a chance. Thinking over it, I think she is right. Irish girls (or Irishmen) arent clever at taking advantage of a condition of things which would mean money if they were a bit more brassy. They find it hard to make a bargain—bar at cattle fairs, where everyone is doing it. Alone, they are pretty hopeless; or dealing with one whom they know. They refuse what they are longing to take. Even the occasional lass on Leicester Sqr. isn't in it with her other-race competitors. We arent good for standing up for our right[s], unless they are political ones, and when dealing with these, too, we lose sense, and become frenzied. So I send you herewith the amended part of the play, and shall be glad if you would give it to the Director chosen to set the play out on the stage.' Amended or not, the play was not destined to be staged in Dublin for another nine years. On January 8, 1958 the author wrote to Jane Rubin: 'I daresay you have heard that my latest play to be done by the Tóstal Festival in Dublin during May, has fallen on a spot of bother.'

The 'spot of bother' forced the cancellation of the Dublin production and of the Dublin Theatre Festival that year. It is well documented by Robert Hogan in *The Experiments of Sean O'Casey* (B39) pp. 129–44, and by David Krause in *Sean O'Casey, the Man and His Work* (B37), pp. 212–24.

After plans for the Dublin production fell through, O'Casey was anxious to have the play staged elsewhere, as he explained in a letter of February 27, 1958 to Anne Munro-Kerr: 'I want to see if a possible production be given somewhere so that, if any little change be needed, I can do this before sending [the script] for publication.' In the meantime, he discussed the play in correspondence with Robert Hogan, who wrote to him on March 8, 1958: 'It is a fine play. Skerighan and Reverend Fillifogue are two of the best characters in any of your plays, and that Prerumble is nice – my! I do wish you'd put those speeches by Skerighan and Bernadette in Act II about the fiver and the tenner back in. They're too good to go, and certainly one wouldn't like Bernadette any the less for bilking Skerighan. He deserves it.' O'Casey agreed to the restoration of the episode; it also appears in the printed text. The play was first staged by the Lafayette Little Theatre in Lafayette, Indiana, on April 25, 1959, directed by Robert Hogan. The English première was at the Queen's Theatre, Hornchurch, in November 1960; while the Tavistock Repertory Company introduced the work to London audiences in May 1965. Dublin finally saw the play on June 6, 1966 when it was presented at the Olympia Theatre.

The Drums of Father Ned appeared in print on June 16, 1960. On June 27 the author wrote to T. M. Farmiloe to give his reactions to the published play: 'I do indeed like "the final appearance of the book." It looks very handsome, and I am delighted that you have done so well. The expressionistic (or is it symbolic?) design on the cover is very pleasing to me, and, if I may say so, marks a step forward in the Macmillan book-format. I am very pleased with the whole work, and [think it] justifies its issue in a paper back.' The dust-jacket of the St Martin's Press printing calls it 'An ironic comedy in the true O'Casey tradition, a grand mixture of fantasy, outrageous farce, satire, symbolism, melodrama, expressionism, song and dance. The central theme is a favorite of the older O'Casey: let us choose life and youth and song, and pit their buoyant strength against the forces of death and rusty age and tears; let us love life, not just endure it. Here O'Casey drops for a prolonged dramatic moment his indulgent gentle wit, and lets fly some stinging observations on the contemporary Irish scene, the strangle-hold of Ireland's clergy, and the stultification of the socially entrenched "lace curtain classes."' Writing to Lewis Funke on November 6, 1957, O'Casey explains the change of title: 'I have given the play another name. In the course of writing it, it grew somewhat away from the original, and, in the making of three drafts, many changes were made. The first title – THE NIGHT IS WHISPERING —wasn't bold enough; it had within it a breath of melancholy which is absent (I think) from the play; and so I gave it the new and bolder name.' At the end of this letter the author expressed the hope that 'the beat of the drums of Father Ned find a responsive echo in the hearts of many of my own people, the indomitable Irishry.' O'Casey had considered several other titles for the play: 'Green Geese' and 'The Rainbow Ends' are to be found on early drafts, while 'The Night of Whispering' (and 'The Night is Whispering') and 'The Drums of Father Dowd' were also considered in later stages. The play is dedicated to five priests, Dr Walter McDonald, Dr Morgan Sheedy, Father Yorke, Canon Hayes and Father O'Flanagan. O'Casey describes them as follows in his dedication, 'The Memory be Green': 'Each in his own time was a Drummer for Father Ned, and the echoes of their drumming sound in Ireland still.'

The 'Prerumble', pp. 1–12, was first published in *Esquire* in its issue for December 1959 (C518). The penultimate speech on p. 84 is wrongly ascribed to Mrs Binnington when clearly, from the context, it should be spoken by Mrs McGilligan. *The Drums of Father Ned* was reprinted in *The Sean O'Casey Reader* (A45).

Reviews: *The Drums of Father Ned* was reviewed by Gabriel Fallon in *Evening Press* (Dublin), June 25, 1960; by M. Myson in *Daily Worker* (London), June 27, 1960; by Brett Duffield in *John O'London's*, June 30, 1960; by G. Wilson Knight in *Stand*, summer 1960; in *Irish Times*, Aug 27, 1960; by George Freedley in *Library Journal*, Nov 1, 1960; by Harold Clurman in *Saturday Review*, Nov 5, 1960; in *New Statesman*, Nov 19, 1960; in *Times Literary Supplement*, Nov 25, 1960; by Vivian Mercier in *Hudson Review*, winter 1960–1; by Marketa Goetz in *Canadian Forum*, Jan 1961.

BEHIND THE GREEN CURTAINS 1961

a. *first edition*
BEHIND THE GREEN CURTAINS / FIGURO IN THE NIGHT / THE
MOON SHINES / ON KYLENAMOE / *Three Plays* / BY / SEAN O'CASEY /
LONDON / MACMILLAN & CO LTD / NEW YORK [centered dot] ST
MARTIN'S PRESS / 1961

19.5 × 13cm.

[i], publisher's description of book; [ii], blank; [iii], title-page as above;
[iv], copyright, publisher's imprints, printing; v, Contents; [vi], blank; [1]
introductory note; [2], blank; [3]–157, text; [158], Acknowledgement; [159]–
[164], Music for the Incidental Songs; [165], printer's imprint; [166]–[170],
blank.

Green cloth, front and back covers blank; spine: BEHIND / THE / GREEN /
CURTAINS / *and other* / *plays* / · / SEAN / O'CASEY / MACMILLAN /; lettered
and decorated in gold; white endpapers, all edges trimmed; dust-jacket
in green, white and black with photograph of O'Casey by W. Suschitzky
on back.
A total of 3000 copies was printed by R. & R. Clark, Ltd, Edinburgh: 1000
copies in cloth were published in June 1, 1961 at 18s; 2000 copies in paper
covers in green and black with photograph of O'Casey by W. Suschitzky
on back cover, were issued on June 22, 1961, at 12s 6d.

b. *American (offset) edition*
BEHIND THE GREEN CURTAINS / FIGURO IN THE NIGHT / THE
MOON SHINES / ON KYLENAMOE / *Three Plays* / BY / SEAN O'CASEY /
ST MARTIN'S PRESS / NEW YORK

20 × 13.5cm.

[i], publisher's description of book; [ii], blank; [iii], title-page as above;
[iv], copyright, Library of Congress card number, manufacture, performing
rights; v, Contents; [vi], blank; [1], introductory note; [2], blank; 3–157,
text; [158], Acknowledgment; [159]–[164], Music for the Incidental Songs;
[165]–[170], blank.

Blue paper-covered boards with white cloth spine; front and back covers
blank; spine lettered lengthwise in blue: sean o'casey *Behind the Green Curtains*
ST MARTIN'S /; white endpapers, all edges trimmed; dust-jacket in white,
red and blue with photograph of O'Casey by W. Suschitzky on front.
Published August 17, 1961 at $2.95; 2500 copies printed; reprinted March
16, 1962 (976 copies).

Notes: On April 6, 1959, O'Casey wrote to Ronald Ayling: 'I've just finished
a satiric fantasy—short two-scened—dedicated to "Ireland's ferocious
chastity," called "Figuro in the Night." ' The publisher's contract for *The
Drums of Father Ned* had not been signed at this time. On August 4, 1959
the dramatist told the same correspondent that he had written several essays
for the book that was to become *Under a Colored Cap*, adding, ' "Figuro in

the Night" is finished (I hope) but has to be sent away, too, to be typed. Working on another—"Behind Green Curtains"—but it may not come to a fruit.' The latter was written fairly quickly, in fact, becoming a full-length work in three scenes. The manuscripts of *Behind the Green Curtains* and 'Figuro in the Night' were received at Macmillan and Co. on October 27, 1959. Macmillan decided to delay publication until after *The Drums of Father Ned* was published. O'Casey had thus had time to write 'The Moon Shines on Kylenamoe', a one-act sketch, and add it to his final volume of plays. On February 12, 1960 he had sent a typescript to Jane Rubin, his American agent. The manuscript for publication was received by Macmillan on May 18, 1960 and on June 15 a letter, indicating the company's desire to publish the three plays, was sent to O'Casey. He wrote to Ronald Ayling on July 5: 'Macmillans are ready to start gathering the 3 last plays ready for the printers, and this, too, [is] unexpected so soon.' On August 31, 1960 the publishers received the music for the songs. The music and lyrics of 'Oh, What a Beautiful Mornin'', were included but did not appear in the published version owing to difficulties with the copyright agents.

There were problems in choosing a title for the volume, which were finally resolved by O'Casey's letter of July 26 to T. M. Farmiloe: 'I've thought & thought of a name for the vol., but can't think of a better [one] than BEHIND THE GREEN CURTAINS, a pleasant title; & enclosing all three plays, since all deal with phenomena behind green curtains (understood in one sense) . . .' It was originally intended that the entire edition would be in papercover until Macmillan received O'Casey's permission to publish part of the edition in hardcover to satisfy requests from libraries. In his letter of February 12, 1960 to Jane Rubin, O'Casey made this comment: 'Under another cover, by registered post & surface mail, I have sent you the one-act play, The Moon Shines on Kylenamoe; and also the script of a two-act play called Figuro in the Night . . . It is a much better play, a kinda fantasy & had a humorous origin.' He was hoping as always for a production prior to publication. On March 17, 1963 in a letter to Miss E. Higgins, of the League of Dramatists, he indicates the production problems of 'The Moon Shines on Kylenamoe': 'No; "The Moon Shines on Kylenamoe" is not to be performed by amateurs yet. "The Moon" is a difficult play, needing precise & accurate timing, as do "Time to Go" and "Bedtime Story"; & I do not wish these to be destroyed.' The publishers describe the book: 'The plays are in the true O'Casey tradition, a grand mixture of fantasy, outrageous farce, satire, symbolism, melodrama, expressionism, song, dance – all these dissimilar elements being woven together with the author's peculiar skill.'

Reviews: *Behind the Green Curtains* was reviewed by Alan Brien in *Sunday Telegraph*, June 4, 1961; by M. Myson in *Daily Worker*, June 19, 1961; in *Twentieth Century*, July 1961; by Brooks Atkinson in *New York Times*, July 14, 1961; by Alan Simpson in *Sunday Times*, July 23, 1961; by George Freedley in *Library Journal*, Sep 15, 1961; by Michael Newton in *Kansas City Star*, Sep 23, 1961; by Gabriel Fallon in *Kilkenny Magazine*, winter 1961.

FEATHERS FROM THE GREEN CROW   1962

a. *first edition*
Feathers From the Green Crow/ Sean O'Casey, 1905–1925 / Edited by ROBERT
HOGAN / *University of Missouri Press* [centred dot] *Columbia*

21.5 × 14cm.

[i], half-title: *Feathers From the Green Crow / Sean O'Casey, 1905–1925* /; [ii],
blank; frontispiece, photograph: O'Casey in London /; [iii], title-page as
above; [iv], performance permissions, copyright, Library of Congress card
number, printing and binding; v–vii, Contents; [viii], blank; ix–xv Introduction; [xvi], blank; [xvii], fly title: *Opinions* /; [xviii], blank; 1–335, text; 336–42,
Biographical Notes.

Green cloth; front and back covers blank; spine: FEATHERS / FROM THE /
GREEN / CROW / SEAN O'CASEY / 1905–1925 / Robert Hogan /
[publisher's mark] / MISSOURI /; lettered and decorated in gold; white endpapers, all edges trimmed; dust-jacket in green and white; lettered in black
and green.
Published October 23, 1962 at $6.50; 1500 copies printed.

b. *English (offset) edition*
Feathers from the Green Crow / Sean O'Casey, 1905–1925 / Edited by ROBERT
HOGAN / LONDON / MACMILLAN & CO LTD / 1963

21.6 × 13.5cm.

[i], half-title: *Feathers from the Green Crow / Sean O'Casey, 1905–1925* /; [ii],
blank; frontispiece, photograph: O'CASEY IN LONDON /; [iii], title-page
as above; [iv], copyright, publication, acknowledgement, permissions,
publisher's imprints, printing; v–vii, Contents; ix–xv, Introduction; [xvi],
blank; [xvii], fly title: *Opinions* /; [xviii], blank; 1–335, text; 336–42,
Biographical Notes, printer's imprint at foot of 342.

Green cloth; front and back covers blank; spine: SEAN / O'CASEY /
[ornament] / *FEATHERS / FROM THE / GREEN / CROW* / [ornament] /
MACMILLAN /; lettered and decorated in gold; white endpapers, all edges
trimmed; dust-jacket in green and white, lettered in black and green.
Published August 8, 1963 at 30s; 2905 copies printed by Lowe & Brydone
(Printers) Ltd, London.

Contents:
Introduction by Robert Hogan

[SECTION ONE]   OPINIONS
                    EDUCATION AND CULTURE

The introductory paragraph to this section appeared as the first paragraph
of the Preface to *Windfalls* (A16).
Sound the Loud Trumpet
First appeared in *Peasant and Irish Ireland*, May 25, 1907 (C1).

Room for the Teachers
  First appeared in *Irish Opinion*, Jan 12, 1918 (C76) and not June 12, 1918 as here stated.
Life and Literature
  First appeared in *Irish Statesman*, Dec 22, 1923 (C89).

NATIONALISM

Guth ar an Ngadre
  First appeared in *Irish Freedom*, Mar 1913 (C18). Ngadre is a misprint for nGaoith.
Faithful Forever (poem)
  First appeared in *Irish Worker*, Apr 26, 1913 (C23).
'Irish Freedom' and the 'Irish Nation'
  First appeared in *Irish Worker*, May 10, 1913 (C24).
Tone's Grave
  First appeared in *Irish Worker*, June 21, 1913 (C30).
The Soul of Davis
  First appeared in *Irish Worker*, Mar 7, 1914 (C50).
A Day in Bodenstown
  First appeared in *Irish Worker*, June 27, 1914 (C66).

THE IRISH LANGUAGE

From the Gaelic League in Dublin: How to Make it a Great Power
  First appeared in a fuller version in *Peasant and Irish Ireland*, July 6, 1907 (C2).
Down with the Gaedhilge!
  First appeared in *Irish Opinion*, Mar 9, 1918 (C81).
The Gaelic Movement To-day
  First appeared in *Irish Opinion*, Mar 23, 1918 (C83).

LABOUR

Declenda est Larkinism!
  First appeared in *Irish Worker*, Apr 19, 1913 (C22).
The Gathering
  First appeared in *Irish Worker*, Sep 27, 1913 (C35).
Striking for Liberty
  First appeared in *Irish Worker*, Oct 18, 1913 (C37).
Ecce Nunc
  First appeared in *Irish Worker*, Nov 15, 1913 (C38).
To the Editor of The Irish Worker
  Letter dated November 26, signed jointly with P. Lennon; first appeared under the title, 'Relief Fund Committee' in *Irish Worker*, Nov 29, 1913 (C39).
I Been Workin' on the Railroad
  First appeared under the title 'Great Northern Railway, Ireland: Some of its Works and Pomps', in *Irish Worker*, June 8, 1912 (C7).
Chiefs of the G.N.R.I., I
  First appeared in *Irish Worker*, Jan 25, 1913 (C11).

Chiefs of the G.N.R.I., II
    First appeared in *Irish Worker*, Feb 8, 1913 (C13).
Chiefs of the G.N.R.I., III
    First appeared in *Irish Worker*, Feb 15, 1913 (C15).
Some Slaves of the G.N.R.I. and Others
    First appeared in *Irish Worker*, Mar 1, 1913 (C19).

RELIGION

The Soul of Man (poem)

[SECTION TWO]   CONTROVERSIES
                A NATIONAL CONTROVERSY

To the Editor of *The Irish Worker* (letter)
    First appeared under the title ' "Euchan" and Ireland' in *Irish Worker*,
    Feb 8, 1913 (C12); collected in *The Letters of Sean O'Casey* (A46).
'Euchan' and Ireland, a Challenge to a Verbal Combat
    First appeared in *Irish Worker*, Feb 22, 1913 (C17); collected in *The Letters
    of Sean O'Casey*.
To the Editor of *The Irish Worker* (letter)
    First appeared under the title ' "Euchan" and a Critic' in *Irish Worker*,
    Mar 8, 1913 (C20); collected in *The Letters of Sean O'Casey*.

A LABOUR CONTROVERSY

An Open Letter to Workers in the Volunteers
    First appeared in *Irish Worker*, Jan 24, 1914 (C47); collected in *The Letters
    of Sean O'Casey*.
Volunteers and Workers (letter)
    First appeared in *Irish Worker*, Feb 21, 1914 (C48); collected in *The Letters
    of Sean O'Casey*.
Irish Workers and Irish Volunteers (letter)
    First appeared in *Irish Worker*, Mar 7, 1914 (C49); collected in *The Letters
    of Sean O'Casey*.

A LANGUAGE CONTROVERSY

To the Editor of *The Irish Statesman* (letter)
    First appeared under the title 'The Innocents at Home' in *Irish Statesman*,
    Jan 10, 1925 (C94); collected in *The Letters of Sean O'Casey*.
To the Editor of *The Irish Statesman* (letter)
    First appeared under the title 'Barr Buadh and Piccolo' in *Irish Statesman*,
    Feb 7, 1925 (C95); collected in *The Letters of Sean O'Casey*.

[SECTION THREE]   SONGS

The Grand Oul' Dame Britannia
    First appeared in *Worker's Republic*, Jan 15, 1916 (C68).
The Bonnie Bunch of Roses, O!
    First appeared in *More Wren Songs* (A8).

If the Germans Came to Ireland in the Mornin'
    First appeared in *Songs of the Wren* (A5).
Mary is Faithful to Me
    First appeared in *Songs of the Wren*.
The Demi-Semi Home Rule Bill
    First appeared in *Songs of the Wren*.
As I Wait in the Boreen for Maggie
    First appeared in *Irish Opinion*, Jan 12, 1918 (C77).
We Welcome the Aid of Japan
    First appeared in *More Wren Songs* (A8).
The Girl from the County Kildare
    First appeared in *More Wren Songs*.
We've Captured the Cave of Machpelah
    First appeared in *Songs of the Wren* No. 2 (A6).
Since Maggie Went Away
    First appeared in *Songs of the Wren* No. 2.
The Divil's Recruitin' Campaign
    First appeared in *Songs of the Wren* No. 2.

[SECTION FOUR]   A LAMENT

The Sacrifice of Thomas Ashe (A4b, 1917)
    The four-line quotation from the poem by Eoghan Ruadh O'Súilleabháin,
    as well as the poem 'To Thomas Ashe' by Anna G. Lang, are omitted.

[SECTION FIVE]   A HISTORY

The Story of the Irish Citizen Army (A9, 1919)

[SECTION SIX]   STORIES

The Seamless Coat of Kathleen, A Parable of the Ard Fheis
    First appeared in *Poblacht na h-Eireann*, Mar 29, 1922 (C87).
The Corncrake
    First appeared in two parts in *The Gael*, June 12 and 19, 1922 (C88).
Gulls and Bobbin Testers
    First appeared in *Irish Statesman*, Sep 6, 1924 (C90).
Irish in the Schools
    First appeared in *Irish Statesman*, Nov 29, 1924 (C91).

[SECTION SEVEN]   PLAYS

Kathleen Listens In: A Political Phantasy in One Act
    First appeared in *Tulane Drama Review*, June 1961 (C551).
Nannie's Night Out: A Comedy in One Act

Notes: This selection from O'Casey's early work covers his writing up to the
period just before his departure from Ireland in 1926. Only two pieces are
here published for the first time. The poem 'The Soul of Man' is, according to
Hogan, the earliest work of O'Casey that he had found, and this is its first

appearance in print. It is dated November 1905. The one-act play 'Nannie's Night Out' – here presented to readers for the first time – had its first stage performance in the Abbey Theatre, Dublin, on September 29, 1924, sharing the bill with Shaw's *Arms and the Man*. On July 22, 1924 O'Casey told Lady Gregory that he was 'working at "Penelope's Lovers" ', (the original title for the sketch) while thinking over ideas for, but not yet writing, *The Plough and the Stars*. Three days later Joseph Holloway recorded a meeting with the author in his *Journal*: 'O'Casey told me he has a one-act play nearly finished . . . It is a very long one-act, and he has been cutting it down as much as he can.' The play was finished in the summer of the same year and was submitted to the Abbey Theatre with the title *Irish Nannie Passes*. On September 3, Lady Gregory wrote to the playwright, 'I have just had the real pleasure of reading "Irish Nannie"—a fine and witty piece of ironical comedy—I look forward to seeing it on the stage.' Replying to her in October 1924, O'Casey wrote: 'Nannie's Night Out went well; Mr. Perrin tells me that "houses" were remarkably good: I don't like the play very much myself.' Of the three endings which O'Casey had written for the play, two are printed here. In Hogan's words, 'The third ending does not differ materially from the second, except for the excision of the gunman scene.' Further details about the work's genesis are provided in 'Nannie's Night Out' by Ronald Ayling in *Modern Drama*, v (Sep 1962) 152–63 (C572).

'Kathleen Listens In' was first staged by the Abbey Theatre on October 1, 1923 as 'Cathleen Listens In'; it is almost certainly a reworking of 'The Seamless Coat of Cathleen' which O'Casey submitted to the Abbey on April 10, 1922 as, in his words, 'an allegorical play in one act dealing with the present situation in Ireland—from my point of view.' That version was rejected by the Abbey later in April 1922. The version printed here includes several speeches absent from the text first published in *Tulane Drama Review* in June 1961 (C551). It seems likely that the additional dialogue was written by the playwright for the revival of the work that opened on the Abbey stage on March 3, 1925. In a letter to Lady Gregory dated February 22, 1925, O'Casey states, 'I sent in to the theatre the beginning of the week the Revised Version of "Kathleen Listens In." ' It is this version that appears in *Feathers from the Green Crow*.

The major portion of the writings in this collection comprises polemical articles on political and social subjects originally published between 1907 and 1925. We know the playwright's retrospective thoughts on the massive amount of work and energy that this writing entailed because, though he only included one example of the genre in *Windfalls* (A16), he made the following comment in his preface to that book, dated 1934: 'How I enjoyed the glory that was mine when something I had written first appeared in print! It was an article criticizing the educational policy in Ireland sponsored by Mr. Augustine Birrell.' Of his journalism after his first article appeared in 1907 he wrote: 'Many hot and weary days of activities in various National and Labour Organisations followed. This was the time before the symbol of Irish Republicanism had blossomed out into the now well-known flags of green and white and orange, but was represented by little tiny bows of these colours worn by the stewards in charge of the gatherings held in the Mansion House or in the Rotunda, to celebrate the memories and deeds of Wolfe Tone or of Robert Emmet. Finally came the crash of the guns in the Great War, and England's hurried and agitated recruiting campaign in Ireland calling on Irishmen of goodwill to go out and fight a fight for little Catholic Belgium. Then "The Grand Oul' Dame Britannia" was written, printed as a "nix job" by friendly printers, and circulated among the various National Societies. Many others followed, all of which have gone down into the limbo of forgotten things. But I often wish that they were alive again, for buried in them are a wild joy and a savage bitterness that I shall never know again.' It is not surprising therefore that the playwright received some satisfaction in seeing the 'wild joy' and 'savage bitterness' uncovered once more in Robert Hogan's collection. That his feelings were not wholly nostalgic, however, is shown in his letter of August 12, 1962 to T. M. Farmiloe of Macmillan: 'I am pleased to hear that you will be publishing the English edition of FEATHERS FROM THE GREEN CROW. I amnt enamoured of the contents, for the feathers werent full-grown, being so young, and the colors have faded after so many years; but it may, they may, still be interesting—something like exhibits in a corner of a local rural museum . . . I saw no proofs at all, having warned R. Hogan that damage might be done to him by me if he sent me any. To be honest, I'm glad, however that you think the things worth publishing.'

Reviews: *Feathers from the Green Crow* was reviewed by Will Wharton in *St. Louis Post-Dispatch*, Nov 25, 1962; in *Christian Science Monitor*, Nov 29, 1962; by John R. Willingham in *Kansas City Times*, Jan 25, 1963; by Jean Wells in *St. Louis Review*, Mar 8, 1963; by Desmond Ryan in *Irish Times*, Aug 3, 1963; by Robert Greacen in *Listener*, Aug 8, 1963; by John Wain in *Observer*, Aug 11, 1963; in *Time and Tide*, Aug 22, 1963; in *Times Literary Supplement*, Sept 6, 1963; by Robert Nye in *Scotsman,* Sept 7, 1963; by Valentin Iremonger in *Spectator*, Sep 27, 1963; by Philip Hengist in *Punch*, Oct 30, 1963; by Gabriel Fallon in *Kilkenny Magazine*, autumn-winter 1963; in *The Times*, Oct 3, 1963; by Ronald Ayling in *Dubliner*, spring 1964; by Augustine Martin in *Studies*, autumn 1964.

UNDER A COLORED CAP   1963

first edition
UNDER / A COLORED CAP / Articles Merry and Mournful / with Comments
and a Song / BY / SEAN O'CASEY / (The Green Crow) / 'Tell me to whom
you are addressing / yourself when you say that.' / 'I am addressing myself—I
am / addressing myself to my cap.' / *Molière* / LONDON / MACMILLAN &
CO LTD / NEW YORK [centred dot] ST MARTIN'S PRESS / 1963

19.5 × 13cm.

[i], half-title: UNDER A COLORED CAP /; [ii], list of books by O'Casey;
[iii], title-page as above; [iv], copyright, publisher's imprints, printing; [v],
dedication: For / LITTLE ALISON AND LITTLER OONA / To be read when
the sturdier airs of womanhood / flow around them— / should they then
desire to do so /; vi, Publisher's Note; vii, Contents; [viii], blank; 1–[277],
text, printer's imprint at foot of [277]; [278]–[280], blank.

Red cloth, front and back covers blank; spine: UNDER / A / COLORED /
CAP / [short double rule] / SEAN / O'CASEY / MACMILLAN /; lettered and
decorated in gold; white endpapers, all edges trimmed; dust-jacket has
portrait of O'Casey on front, lettered and decorated in red, white and black.
Published January 3, 1963 at 21s; 5050 copies printed by R. & R. Clark,
Ltd, Edinburgh; reprinted 1964 (1013 copies).

Contents:
Under a Colored Cap, part one, An Army with Banners
Under a Colored Cap, part two
The Green Bushes: A Song [with music]
The Green Crow Caws
Under a Greenwood Tree He Died
The Lark in the Clear Air Still Sings
   First appeared in *New York Times Magazine*, Jan 11, 1959 under the title
   'The Harp in the Air Still Sings' (C505). This is a revised version.
Immanuel
Merrical of Miracles
The People and the Theatre
   First appeared in *Theatre Today*, Mar 1946 (C322).
Culture, Inc.
Out, Damned Spot!
   First appeared in *Theatre Arts*, May 1960 (C531). It is here reprinted with
   slight modifications.
Purple Dust in Their Eyes

Notes: This was the last of O'Casey's books published in his lifetime. Of
the twelve pieces in the book, all except one – 'The People and the Theatre',
originally published in 1946 – were written in the late fifties or early sixties.
All but three are published for the first time in this volume. Only a few
minor changes were made in the text as the author explained to Ronald
Ayling in a letter dated December 7, 1962: 'I had to make a few alterations

in some of the expressions appearing in *Under a Colored Cap*. Macmillan's Solicitors were afraid of a possible libel action, and so these alterations had to be made; another damned chore.' O'Casey's first choice of title for the collection was 'Reveries in the Dusk' but he later decided on the 'less pretentious title'. Both the dust-jacket and the Publisher's Note explain the title: 'Sean O'Casey's collection of colored caps (he prefers the American spelling) has come to him from friends and admirers in many different countries, and has given him a symbol for the gay, free, intrepid life and outlook which he defends in several of the papers included in this volume.'

In the photograph on the dust-jacket he is shown wearing a cap, 'The first I ever wore, made by our daughter, Shivaun, for me', according to a letter of July 28, 1962 to Macmillan and Co. After seeing the dust-jacket he wrote on March 28, 1963 to T. M. Farmiloe of Macmillan: 'I could readily have parted with the old face of the author, but it doesn't look too impressive, rather simple, just a case for an old mind trying to keep young by thought.' The book is dedicated to his two grandchildren, the daughters of his son Breon: 'For little Alison and littler Oona, to be read when the sturdier airs of womanhood flow around them—should they then desire to do so.'

'An Army With Banners' is a story, based on early childhood experience, that has much in common with chapters in *I Knock at the Door* (A19). The essay 'Under a Greenwood Tree He Died' was occasioned by the death of his son Niall from leukemia in 1956. The Publisher's note includes the following in the description of the book: 'Among the other longer papers are some typically combative discussions of orthodox beliefs, and the myths and mysteries behind them, while contemporary "Culture, Inc." and criticisms of a recent production of *Purple Dust* come in for some very candid and pungent comments. Altogether, with a sprightly song and a few verses for good measure, the reader is assured of some rewarding hours in the company of "The Green Crow," a pen-name which the author adds to his title-page because it is so well known in the United States.'

Reviews: *Under a Colored Cap* was reviewed by Tim Enright in *Daily Worker* (London), Apr 11, 1963; in *Time and Tide*, Apr 11, 1963; in *The Times*, Apr 11, 1963; by Robert Robinson in *Sunday Times*, Apr 14, 1963; by Robert Greacen in *Listener*, Apr 18, 1963; by L. E. in *Irish Times*, Apr 20, 1963; by Gerard Fay in *Manchester Guardian*, Apr 26, 1963; by Louis MacNeice in *New Statesman*, May 3, 1963; by T. P. Coogan in *Spectator*, May 3, 1963; in *Times Literary Supplement*, May 3, 1963; by Christopher Hollis in *Punch*, May 5, 1963; by Cahir Healy in *Irish News*, May 11, 1963; by Frank O'Connor in *Sunday Independent*, May 12, 1963; by Brooks Atkinson in *New York Times*, May 17, 1963; by J. F. Moran in *Library Journal*, June 1, 1963; by Anne O'Neill-Barna In *New York Times Book Review*, June 23, 1963; by Sean Callery in *Saturday Review*, June 29, 1963; in *New Yorker*, Aug 3, 1963; by John Wain in *Observer*, Aug 11, 1963; by Hilda Kirkwood in *Canadian Forum*, Sep 1963; by Gabriel Fallon in *Kilkenny Magazine*, autumn–winter 1963; by Augustine Martin in *Studies*, autumn 1964.

THREE MORE PLAYS   1965

first edition
THREE MORE PLAYS / BY / SEAN O'CASEY / THE SILVER TASSIE /
PURPLE DUST / RED ROSES FOR ME / With an introduction by / J. C.
Trewin / LONDON / MACMILLAN & CO LTD / NEW YORK [centred dot]
ST MARTIN'S PRESS / 1965

17 × 11.5cm.

[i], half-title: THREE MORE PLAYS /; [ii], list of titles in St Martin's
Library; [iii], title-page as above; [iv], publisher's imprints, copyright notice,
dates of first editions, copyright of Trewin's introduction, printing; [v],
Contents; [vi], performance permissions and fees, acknowledgement of
permission to reprint *Purple Dust* and *Red Roses for Me*; vii–xvi, Introduction by
J. C. Trewin; [17]–317, text; [318], printer's imprint; [319]–[320], blank.

Stiff paper covers in green and black, lettered in yellow, white and black.
Published January 7, 1965 at 7s 6d and $1.25; 15,077 copies printed by
Richard Clay and Co. Ltd, Bungay, Suffolk; reprinted 1969 in Papermac
series (5000 copies); 1971 (6000 copies).

Notes: Although this collection was not published until after his death,
the plays were selected by O'Casey himself and he had worked on the text
making changes in *Red Roses for Me* and *Purple Dust*. The text of *The Silver
Tassie* is that of the 'Stage Version' first printed in the second volume of
Collected Plays (A29). For the other plays the dramatist chose, not the much
revised acting versions that had been published in 1956 and 1957, but slightly
modified versions of the texts printed in the third volume of *Collected Plays*
(A29).

On October 23, 1963 T. M. Farmiloe of Macmillan and Co. wrote to
O'Casey: 'We are keen to publish another selection from your plays in
St. Martin's Library ... and would be interested to know which plays you
suggest we should include and whether you would be prepared to introduce
this selection.' O'Casey made the selection but declined to write an
introduction suggesting instead that J. C. Trewin should write it. Trewin
accepted the invitation and his essay was approved by O'Casey on April
8, 1964.

The text of *Purple Dust* is, basically, that published in the third volume
of *Collected Plays* with but one alteration in Act II. In a letter to T. M. Farmiloe,
dated March 16, 1964, the dramatist discusses the change: 'The change I desire
in Purple Dust is marked in Collected Plays on pages 74–75, and in the
Stage Version on pages 52–53; it is an alteration in action and dialogue
between Souhan and the 2nd Workman (O'Dempsey) ... the dialogue
previously given as between O'Killigan and Souhan, now, in the amendment,
takes place between Souhan and the 2nd Workman.' The changes may be
found on pp. 180–1 of *Three More Plays*. There are several extra speeches in the
episode as well as the re-allocation of some dialogue from O'Killigan
to O'Dempsey. However, the changes here do not incorporate many others
in the version published by Dramatists Play Service in 1957 (A21b). This

is a surprising decision because as late as September 19, 1961 O'Casey had written to T. M. Farmiloe: 'More important [than the inclusion of *Kathleen Listens In* in *Collected Plays*] is a change I have made in PURPLE DUST, a few amendments and a song, all of which appear in the Amateur booklets of the play, published by THE DRAMATISTS PLAY SERVICE, INC., New York; and which I'd like, if possible, to have included in some future issue of the Collected Plays; also a few alterations to RED ROSES FOR ME.' When the opportunity arose, however, O'Casey decided on a more partial modification of *Purple Dust*, largely ignoring the extensive changes made in 1953 and 1954 and incorporated into the 1957 printed version.

The text of *Red Roses for Me* is, similarly, that printed in the third volume of *Collected Plays* with the addition of a short scene in Act III. In the same letter to Farmiloe of March 16, 1964, O'Casey speaks of the change desired in the work: 'For some time an addition has been used in performances. I enclose this herewith in typescript, and a stage version of the plays that includes this change. You will find it on page 53 of this version to show you how it goes. It is on page 192, Vol. III Collected Plays, when Eeada says to Dympna "That was a long time ago if you ask me." Here the change begins as shown in the typescript. Since the reprinting is a new one, I should like this change to be made if at all possible. The script joins the original when the strikers (1st, 2nd and 3rd men) leave the stage, and Brennan comes in slowly with his melodeon over his shoulder, as shown in the amended typescript.' This scene (pp. 281–2) was first published in the revised edition of the play issued in 1956 by Dramatists Play Service Inc., New York (A23c); it is not found in any other edition published in England. However, Brennan's song (pp. 282–3) follows the text of *Collected Plays* (A29, pp. 192–4) and not the truncated version of the Dramatists Play Service edition (pp. 54–5). In many other respects, too, this version differs from the 1956 Acting Version. As the playwright's letter of March 16, 1964 indicated, the text of *Red Roses for Me* in *Three More Plays* must be regarded as the final 'approved' version of the work.

In an earlier letter to T. M. Farmiloe, dated November 11, 1963, O'Casey states his failure to suggest a title for the collection: 'I have been thinking of a title for the further plays, and haven't succeeded in thinking of any suitable one, rosy or dusky.' In a letter of November 7, 1963, Farmiloe had suggested the title 'Three More Plays'.

O'Casey also gave his ideas for a design for the cover in his letter of November 11, 1963: 'I suggest that the shamrock design should have more of a margin round it, and the design could be stylised a little; that the colour of the shamrock should be blue or red, for I'm heartily sick of the green always paramount on most of the books. Green is a lovely color, but one can get too much of it, as one can of any color used too often. You may exclaim when you see the design Oh, my God! If you do, never mind for I shant care—I shant hear you anyway.' We can sympathise with O'Casey on his aversion to the too frequent use of green on the covers of his works. It was one of long standing. On September 30, 1938 he had written to Harold Macmillan concerning the cover of *I Knock at the Door* (A19): 'Let me say a word about the cover: if possible, don't have it green; & let no shamrocks blossom on the cover; or harp either. The format of the first volumes—"Two Plays," etc., was fine; but, if I remember right, the green cover of "Five Irish Plays" has shamrocks on its edges. The green immortal shamrock! I dread the look of them in book or picture. They represent a dead & sentimental Ireland to me. And I am neither dead nor sentimental.'

His suggestions were not incorporated in the cover design for *Three More Plays*; the front cover featured black and the ubiquitous green, though subsequent reprints in the Papermac series are in black and red.

A43   TWO LETTERS   1966

first edition
Two Letters by / SEAN O'CASEY / Referring to the / Assassination of / PRESI-
DENT KENNEDY / From the Correspondence of / Sean O'Casey and Franklin
D. Murphy / 1963

21.5 × 13cm.

[1], title-page as above; [2]–[3], blank; [4], letter dated November 23, 1963;
[5], letter dated December 2, 1963; [6]–[7], blank; [8], colophon.
Published privately in 1966 for the friends of Franklin and Judy Murphy;
10 copies printed by Andrew H. Horn at the Battledore Press, Glendale,
California.

The Grand Oul' Dame Brittannia.

(Air: Leather away with the Wattle O.)

——:0:——

Ah! Ireland sure I'm proud of you,
  Ses the Grand Oul' Dame Brittannia;
To poor little Belgium, tried and true,
  Ses the Grand Oul' Dame Brittannia.
For ye don't believe the Sinn Fein Lies
And ye know each Gael that for England dies,
Ill enjoy Home Rule in the clear blue skies,
  Ses the Grand Oul' Dame Brittannia.

Sure it often made me proud blood boil,
  Ses the Grand Oul' Dame Brittannia;
When they tried to make out you were still disloyal,
  Ses the Grand Oul' Dame Brittannia;
But Redmond's proved to be good and great,
He's a piller of the English State—
Who fears to speak of Ninety-Eight,
  Ses the Grand Oul' Dame Brittannia.

You want a pound or two from me,
  Ses the Grand Oul' Dame Brittannia;
For your oul' Hibernian Academy,
  Ses the Grand Oul' Dame Brittannia.
But you know we've got the Huns to quell,
And we want the cash for shot and shell,
Your artists (?) let them go to Hell!
  Ses the Grand Oul' Dame Brittannia.

The Castle's now an altered place,
  Ses the Grand Oul' Dame Brittannia—
Its the Drawin' Room o' the Irish Race,
  Ses the Grand Oul' Dame Brittannia.
John Redmond to the Throne is bowed,
'Mid a frantic cheerin' Irish crowd—
Great! —its like the days of Shane the Proud!
  Ses the Grand Oul' Dame Brittania.

Oh! Johnny Redmond you're the Boy,
  Ses the Grand Oul' Dame Brittannia—
You're England s pride an' you're Ireland's joy!
  Ses the Grand Oul' Dame Brittannia.
For he went to France and he faced the Hun,
Then he turned around and he fired a gun—
Faix, you should have seen the Germans run!
  Ses the Grand Oul' Dame Brittannia.

And Redmond now Home Rule has won,
  Ses the Grand Oul' Dame Brittannia;
And he's finished what Wolfe Tone begun,
  Ses the Grand Oul' Dame Brittannia.
Yet Rebels through the Country stalk,
Shouting "Sixty-Seven" and "Bachelor's Walk"—
Did you ever hear such foolish talk,
  Ses the Grand Oul' Dame Brittannia.

Oh! Scholars, Hurlers, Saints, and Bards,
  Ses the Grand Oul' Dame Brittannia;
Come along and list in the Irish Guards,
  Ses the Grand Oul Dame Brittannia.
Each man that treads on a German's feet,
Will be given a parcel tied up neat—
Of a Tombstone Cross and a Winding Sheet!
  Ses the Grand Oul' Dame Brittannia

THE STORY

OF

THOMAS ASHE

By SEAN O CATHASAIGH.

"God must judge the guiltless, leave them as they are
Whichever one's the guiltless, to his glory,
And whichever one the guilt's with to my story."
— *Browning.*

PRICE   -   TWOPENCE.

Published by Fergus O'Connor, Dublin.

THOMAS ASHE.

I.

THE Children of Eireann are listening again
To Death's sullen, sad, sombre beat of the drum;
Oppression has seized on a man amongst men,
And so eloquent life's stricken senseless and dumb,
While we, left behind, wait the life from your death that shall come!

II.

In your fight to unfetter Humanity's soul,
Your body was blazoned with scars,
To oppression you fearlessly tendered the toll,
Removing for progress the Bolts and the Bars,
With your hand to the Plough and your eyes on the stars.

III.

On the cold seat of death now your body's enthroned,
And your warm heart is silent and still,
For our life that is Death, your great life has been stoned,
And we feel in our hearts a swift unswerving thrill,
To take up your work, all hard fallow nature to till.

IV.

Here hope and Endeavour with energy braid
Leaves of honour to garland the Dead,
Here Liberty rests with calm Courage arrayed,
By the side of the Kingly but now passive head,
Anointed with blood that this Hero has shed.

V.

Huge Labour looks down on your battle-scarred face,
Ignoble and noble with sweat on his brow,
Unable to fathom this soul of his race,
Half conscious that soon, when he springs from the Slough,
He shall understand thee, if he can't do it now!

VI.

To your soul, for awhile, we all murmur, Farewell!
And we take the Dear Gift that you gave,
For your great Life stamped out in the cold prison cell
Shall be potent our own slavish nature to save,
Tho' your body we leave in the drear hidden gloom of the grave.

SEAN O CATHASAIGH.

FERGUS O'CONNOR, DUBLIN.

Lament for Thomas Ashe.

By SEAN O CATHASAIGH.

The breasts of the mountains with anger are heaving,
Swift rivers of tears down their rugged cheeks flow;
Their mantle of heather the wild wind is rearing,
And their proud heads are capp'd with a storm cloud of woe
Why gathers the gloom in a manner appalling—
What causes the sunshine in terror to die?
The mountains of Eirinn are plaintively calling—
Thomas Ashe, Thomas Ashe, we are mourning for thee.

The wild mountain glens are now silent and lonely,
And Grief on their bosom has laid Her poor Head,
Here thoughts of new life have no place, for now only
The green woods are wrapped in dear thoughts of the dead!
The leaves from the trees, sadly sighing, are falling
And form a bronze pall for the once flower'd lea,
The winds rustling thro' them, are plaintively calling—
Thomas Ashe, Thomas Ashe, we are mourning for thee.

In the ears of the coast Erin's grey waves are beating
A curse on the Pow'r that his life would nob spare,
And mingle a prayer in their gloomy retreating,
With a caoine for the soul that had courage to dare!
The grey restless waves are all rising and falling—
Oh ! a sorrowful breast is the Breast of the Sea—
And her waters, uneasy, are plaintively calling
Thomas Ashe, Thomas Ashe, we are mourning for thee.

Shall we then to Nature's sad, heart-broken grieving
Our own Gaelic Nature in apathy close?
Ah! No! To our hearts this dear sorrow receiving
We'll send in a shout to our circle of foes!
Your thoughts, Thomas Ashe, now, shall shortly be ours—
As you fought the good fight so we'll fight to be free,
'Gainst all the vain pomp of their princes and powers,
Made strong by the thought of dear vengeance for thee.

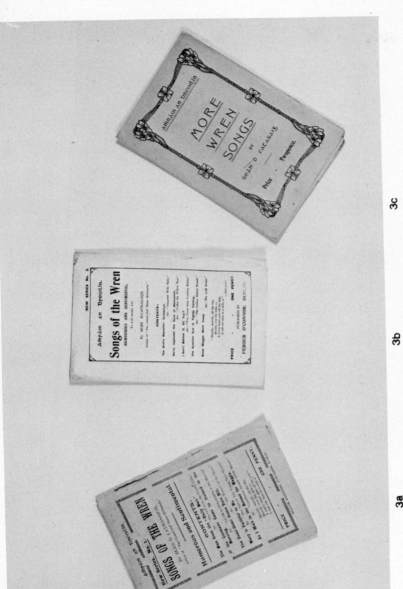

3a

3b

3c

The Harvest Festival
Act 2.

Scene: The Home of the Rocliffes, a tenement in Curzon St. A room which is very poorly furnished. A common deal table stands in the centre of the room. At the left is a tiny fireplace. The window is at back. Under the window is a sofa, on which a number of books are lying. To the right of the sofa is a dresser, but the shelves, instead of holding crockery, are packed with books. To the right of this dresser is a door leading down into the street. A small, single bed is at the extreme right of stage. On the wall over the door at right is a picture of the late Queen Victoria, & over the fireplace is a coloured picture of King Billy crossing the Boyne. A washstand with basin & jug stands near the bed in a corner. A few chairs complete the furnishing of the room. The few necessary articles of delph are in the press beneath the dresser. The basin & jug have been taken from the top of the washstand and placed underneath, to make room on top for a pile of writing paper.

Mrs Rocliffe is discovered at the fireplace on which is a small saucepan, the contents of which she is stirring. The table in centre is laid for tea, & is covered with a newspaper instead of a cloth.

As the curtain ascends, Mrs Rocliffe is humming in a vigorous way, the air, "Haste to the Wedding." She is an old woman of about seventy-six years of age. Although afflicted with the infirmities of age, her movements are surprisingly sharp and active. Her eyes are still shining, & her hair is only beginning to turn grey. She has evidently been in her day a very strong, active woman, & still possesses a wonderful reserve of vital force.

MRS R. (with a wistful sigh) Ah! no; it's the terrible thing to have a sad heart. But I suppose I have had me day, an' I oughtn't to complain. But it was a cold day, an' a bitter day; oftener cold than warm; oftener hungry than full; oftener tired than at ease; oftener sad than merry. But, sure, I ought to be thankful that I was able to stick it all, an', I always had me health, an' that was somethin'. I wish to God this strike was over, for I never easy in me mind, the way Jack does be talkin' about things. He has such a terrible temper, though he was always very gentle with me; an' if he got into any trouble, I suppose they'd take the old-age pension off me; not that it'ud be much loss, though we'd miss it now, with nothin' else comin' into the house. I hope he'll be in soon; he knows I want to go to the Harvest Festival tonight, an' he promised he'd be in time to get his dinner & tea so that I could go.

She begins to sweep the floor.

I don't think it'll be long till Higgins turns turk on us; it's the long, sour face he had on him this mornin' when I went

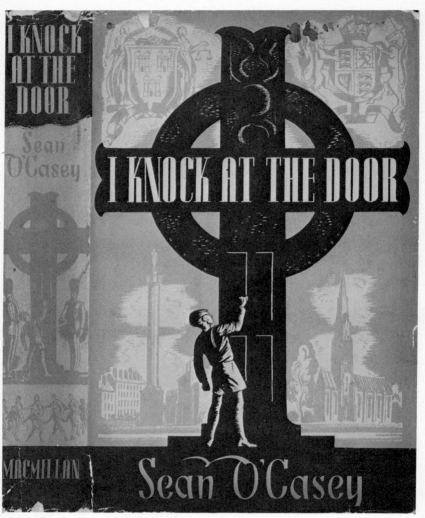

I KNOCK AT THE DOOR

Sean O'Casey

MACMILLAN

6

SUNSET AND EVENING STAR
Sean O'Casey
SUNSET AND EVENING STAR
MACMILLAN
Sean O'Casey

Angela. Oh, that. No, he hasnt. I'd say it was St. Joseph only for th'
        beard floatin' too far out on th' sides.

Lizzie. Wel,, St. Angela here is goin' to float over to th' bench for a
        sit down, an' leave yeh to your studies.   (she does so)

Angela. I wondher now: Yis, it might well be some ould Irish saint,
        (seein' th' green stuff around it,)   banished be time an' dis-
        turbance from th' minds o' mortal men.

Lizzie. Aw, pull yourself together, Anela, an' quit sendin' your
meditations probin' questions inta x another's head; stabbin', stabbin'
        away any quietness that a mind needs on a day like this.
        (she cocks an ear to the solemn music trickling from the church
        (porch) Aw, that music !   As hot as I am, it sends me shiver-
        in'. (to Angela) What kinda stuff is it ?

Angela (not noticing the question - suddenly an' eagerly to Lizzie) Eh,
        remember th' oul' x Irish saint that let a bird nest in his
        beard, an' stood stock till till the eggs had hatched, and
        th' chicks reared, an' got th' power to fly away ? What was
        th' boyo's name, Lizzie ? (Give over before roamin outa
        your right mind, an')

Lizzie (nowsitting down on the bench) I dont know, Lizzie, an' I during
        dont care, Angela. (angrily) Will yeh, for God's sake, leave
        your bearded gent I alone in his green battlement, an' sit down
        or go away, for if yeh go on questionin', questionin', you'll
        question yourself inta a question of whether you are or you arent
        arent.

Angela (in deep reflection) Where, now, did I see that sterun face before
        before ? (standin' them here on a sea board)

Lizzie (with irritation) Aaw, come an' sit down, an' dont stand fizzin'
questions outa with your who is its and where was its, *buzzin' me ear,*
yeh will to ketch your questions refusin' to hear, but forced to
Angela (with certitude) I'm as certain I seen, in walkin' in some road, listen all th' time
        sittin' in some place, or presented in a picture, certain as I
        live that I seen that face before.

(If yeh don't mind, you'll have a nest in your own oul' nut ouls,
ketchin' odd things out 'll set yeh inta throuble one day or another)

8

BLASTS AND BENEDICTIONS 1967

first edition
BLASTS AND / BENEDICTIONS / Articles and Stories / by / SEAN O'CASEY / Selected and Introduced / by / RONALD AYLING / MACMILLAN / *London* [centred dot] *Melbourne* [centred dot] *Toronto* / ST MARTIN'S PRESS / *New York* / 1967

19.5 × 12.8cm.

[i], half-title: BLASTS AND BENEDICTIONS /; [ii], list of O'Casey titles in print; [iii], title-page as above; [iv], copyright, publisher's imprints, library of Congress card number, printer's imprint; v–vii, Contents; [viii], blank; ix–xix, Preface by Ronald Ayling; xx, Acknowledgements; [1]–308, text; [309]–314, Index; [315]–[316], blank.

Red paper-covered boards; front and back covers blank; spine: [rule] / Blasts and / Benedictions / [rule] / Sean O'Casey / [rule] / ST MARTIN'S / PRESS; lettered and decorated in silver; white endpapers, all edges trimmed; dust-jacket in red and white, photograph of O'Casey on front, lettered in black white and red.
Published in London on January 12, 1967 at 30s.; published in New York February 28, 1967 at $6.50; 6682 copies, including 2500 for St Martin's Press, printed by Richard Clay (The Chaucer Press), Ltd., Bungay, Suffolk.

Contents:
Preface by Ronald Ayling.

PART ONE: THE CURTAINED WORLD. O'CASEY ON THE
THEATRE

Playwright and Box Office
First appeared in *Listener* July 7, 1938 (C204); reprinted in *The Sting and the Twinkle* (B72).
Behind the Curtained World
First appeared under title 'The Curtained World' in *Saturday Book* 3, 1943 (B15).
The Theatre and the Politician
First appeared in *Common Wealth Review* Jan 1946 (C320).
The Play of Ideas
First appeared in *New Statesman and Nation* April 8, 1950 (C387).
Melpomene an' Thalia Beggin' for Bread
First appeared as a contribution to a symposium 'Ten Best for a Repertory Theatre' in *New York Times Magazine* Nov 9, 1959 (C515) not 1958 as erroneously recorded here.
Shakespeare Among the Flags
First appeared under the title 'Ode to an Impudent Upstart' in *New York Times Magazine*, Apr 19, 1964 (C593) with a slightly different ending; collected in *The Sean O'Casey Reader* (A45).

John Millington Synge
> First appeared as 'Vyzyvauschie P'esy J. M. Sindje' in *Britansky Soyuznik* June 23, 1946 (C327). This is its first publication in English.

One of the World's Dramatists
> Printed in a shorter version in *Culture and Life* (Moscow) Sep 1966 (C626).

Dramatis Personae Ibsenisensis
> First appeared in *American Spectator* July 1933 (C130); reprinted in *American Spectator Yearbook* 1934 (B6).

Not Waiting for Godot
> First appeared in *Encore*, Easter 1956 (C452); collected in *The Sean O'Casey Reader* (A45).

Mr. Wesker's March Past
The Bald Primaqueera
> First appeared in *Atlantic Monthly*, Sep 1965 (C617); collected in *The Sean O'Casey Reader* (A45).

Art is the Song of Life
> First appeared as 'Iskusstvo–pesn' zhizni', in *Literaturnaya Gazeta*, Apr 5, 1960 (C527). This is its first publication in English.

An Irishman's Plays
> First appeared under the title 'The Drama of the Future' in *Radio Times*, Jan 25, 1957 (C461). The article was written as an introduction to a broadcast season of O'Casey's plays which opened on the BBC Third Programme in January 1957.

O'CASEY ON O'CASEY

A Word Before Curtain-Rise
> First appeared under the title 'Before Curtain-Rise' as a forward to his *Selected Plays*, 1954 (A32).

The Plough and the Stars: A Reply to the Critics
> First appeared in *Irish Times*, Feb 19, 1926 (C101) and in *Irish Independent*, Feb 20, 1926; collected in *The Letters of Sean O'Casey* (A46).

Nationalism and *The Plough and the Stars*
> First appeared under the title 'Mr. O'Casey's Play: Author's Rejoinder' in *Irish Independent,* Feb 26, 1926 (C102); collected in *The Letters of Sean O'Casey*.

The Plough and the Stars in Retrospect
> First appeared under the title 'Memories of a Farewell to Ireland' in *New York Times*, Dec 4, 1960 (C544).

W. B. Yeats and *The Silver Tassie*
> First appeared under the title 'The Abbey Directors and Mr. Sean O'Casey' in *Irish Statesman*, June 9, 1928 (C109); collected in *The Letters of Sean O'Casey*.

The Silver Tassie
> First appeared under the title 'The Plays of Sean O'Casey: A Reply' in *Nineteenth Century*, Sep 1928 (C117); collected in *The Letters of Sean O' Casey*.

Blasphemy and *The Silver Tassie*
> An article sent to Yeats following attacks on *The Silver Tassie* after its first production at the Abbey Theatre. The article entitled 'A Stand on *The Silver Tassie*' was not published until Saros Cowasjee printed in his *Sean O'Casey: The Man Behind the Plays* (B45). The present version is a transcription from a carbon of the article sent by O'Casey to Yeats on November 23, 1935; reprinted in *The Letters of Sean O'Casey*.

From *Within the Gates*
   First appeared in *New York Times*, Oct 21, 1934 (C155).
Within the Gates and Without
The Church Tries to Close the Gates
Badtime Story
O'Casey in Hungarian Costume
   First appeared as 'O'Casey és P. G. Wodehouse Nyilatkozata a Tájékozta-
   tónak', in *Tájékoztató* (Budapest), Dec 1957 (C482), not October 1957 as
   erroneously attributed in the book. This is its first publication in English.
O'Casey's Drama—Bonfire
   First Appeared as 'K Chitatelyam "Zvezdy": O Drame "Koster Episkopa" '
   in *Zvezda* (Leningrad), Jan 1958 (C483).
Cockadoodle Doo
   First appeared in part under the title 'O'Casey's Credo' in *New York Times*,
   Nov 9, 1958 (C503), and later under the title 'Cock-A-Doodle-Dandy' in
   Playwrights on Playwriting (B38).
On the Banks of the Ban
   First appeared under the title 'Behind a Ban' in *New York Times* Jan 5,
   1964 (C589).

PART TWO: ON BOOKS AND WRITERS

What Thou Seest, Write in a Book
Empty Vessels
   First appeared in *Irish Freedom* May 1942 (C272).
Censorship
   First appeared in *Bell* Feb 1945 (C307).
Literature in Ireland
   First appeared as 'Literatura v Irlandii' in *Internatsional'naya Literatura* Dec
   1939 (C227).
Ireland's Silvery Shadow
   Text of a talk broadcast in the BBC Spanish Service. First appeared in *Tribune*,
   Sep 27, 1946 (C332).
Melpomene in Ireland
   Review of *The Irish Theatre* by Peter Kavanagh (1946). First appeared in
   abbreviated form in *Tribune* Jan 31, 1947 (C336).
G.B.S. Speaks out of the Whirlwind
   Review of *Three Plays* by Bernard Shaw (1934). First appeared in *Listener*
   Mar 7, 1934 (C148).
Shaw's Primrose Path
   Review of *Bernard Shaw and Mrs. Patrick Campbell: Their Correspondence* (1952).
   First appeared under the title 'With Love and Kisses from Bernard Shaw'
   in *New York Times Book Review* Nov 9, 1952 (C416).
A Protestant Bridget
   Review of *Lady Gregory's Journals* (1946). First appeared in *Bell*, Feb 1947
   (C339).
A Sprig of Rosemary Among the Laurel
   Originally appeared as foreword to *Lady Gregory: Selected Plays* (B44).
The Gaelic Black-Headed Boy
   Review of *The Midnight Court* by Brian Merriman translated into English

by Frank O'Connor (1945). Originally appeared in *Our Time* Nov 1945 (C314).

A Prophet in the Theatre
Review of *Robert Loraine* by Winifred Loraine (B8). Originally appeared in *Sunday Times* Sep 18, 1938 (C208).

A Miner's Dream of Home
Review of *A Collier's Friday Night* by D. H. Lawrence (1934). Originally appeared in *New Statesman and Nation* July 28, 1934 (C154).

Charles Lever's Stormy Life
Review of *Dr. Quicksilver* by Lionel Stevenson (1939). Originally appeared in *Sunday Times* Feb 5, 1939 (C217).

Great Man, Gorki!
Originally appeared in *Tribune* May 3, 1946 (C326); reprinted in *Tribune 21* (B34).

PART THREE: PEOPLE AND PLACES

London Passes By
Originally appeared under the title 'London Passes By: Impressions of Five Weeks' in *Daily News* (London), May 24, 1926 (C105).

Hyde Park Orator
Originally appeared as preface to *Hyde Park Orator* by Bonar Thompson (B5).

There Go the Irish
Originally appeared as an article in *They Go, The Irish: A Miscellany of War-time Writing* (B17).

Crabbed Age and Youth
Based on the answers to five questions put to O'Casey by Senator Thomas C. Desmond, Chairman of the New York State Joint Legislative Committee on Problems of the Ageing, in December 1957; collected in *The Sean O'Casey Reader* (A45). A shorter version appeared under the title 'The Delicate Art of Growing Old' in *Harper's*, Aug 1959 (C512).

The Day the Worker Blows a Bugle
Originally appeared as 'Den', Kogda Rabochy Trubit v Svoĭ Rog' in *Novoe Vremya* (Moscow), May 1958 (C495). It was also printed in the English-language version of *Novoe Vremia – New Times*, May 1958. It was reprinted in *New World Review*, Nov 1958 and in *Mainstream*, May 1959. An offprint from *Mainstream* was issued in May 1959. The essay was also collected in *The Sean O'Casey Reader* (A45).

Resurgam (1960)

PART FOUR: STORIES

Toreador
Originally appeared in *Time and Tide*, Dec 2, 1933 (C137).

Dum Vivimus Vivamus
Originally appeared in *Time and Tide*, May 5, 1934 (C150).

The Dog
Originally appeared in *Million: New Left Writing* (B16).

Notes: This book of essays and stories covers a large span of O'Casey's life, from 1926 to 1964, as well as a great variety of topics. The dust-jacket, written by the editor, describes the work: 'These personal, often spontaneous writings . . . comprise a fascinating self-portrait, showing the colorful and exuberant writer in many moods and humors. A great variety of subjects are covered, from the playwright's first impressions of London to his reflections on old age and the problems of the elderly, and discussion of censorship as well as politics and religion. There are especially revealing articles on the Irish people and Irish literature; and combative comments on modern trends in the theatre, such as the Theatre of the Absurd and the Theatre of Cruelty, written only a few weeks before O'Casey's death. He discusses his own work with candor and insight and, at times, with characteristic pugnacity . . . The collection is at once a grand celebratory hymn to life and an enduring monument to a lovable man and artist.'

Most of the material had already been published previously. 'Mr. Wesker's March Past' (1963), 'Within the Gates and Without' (1934), 'The Church Tries to Close the Gates' (1935), 'Badtime Story' (*c.* 1955), 'What Thou Seest, Write in a Book' (*c.* 1950) and 'Resurgam' (1960) appear here in print for the first time.

An English language textbook selected from *Blasts and Benedictions*, with annotations in Japanese by K. Yamaguchi and F. Sakata, was published under the title *Toreador* by Kobunsha (Tokyo) in 1968. The following writings were included: 'Toreador', 'Dum Vivimus, Vivamus', 'The Dog', 'Crabbed Age and Youth' and 'The Day the Worker Blows a Bugle'.

Reviews: *Blasts and Benedictions* was reviewed in *Evening Herald* (Dublin), Jan 13, 1967; by J. C. Trewin in *Birmingham Post*, Jan 14, 1967; in *Sunday Times*, Jan 15, 1967; by Elizabeth Coxhead in *Sunday Telegraph*, Jan 15, 1967; by Michael Foot in *Evening Standard*, Jan 17, 1967; in *The Times*, Jan 19, 1967; by John Arden in *Manchester Guardian*, Jan 20, 1967; by Irving Wardle in *Observer*, Jan 22, 1967; in *Times Literary Supplement*, Jan 26, 1967; by Mervyn Wall in *Irish Times*, Jan 28, 1967; by Elizabeth Coxhead in *Lady*, Feb 16, 1967; by John McCann in *Sunday Press* (Dublin), Feb 19, 1967; by Sam Wellbaum in *Independent Shavian*, spring 1967; by Connolly Cole in *Chicago Tribune Books Today*, Apr 16, 1967; in *New York Times Book Review*, Apr 23, 1967; by John O'Riordan in *Tribune*, June 2, 1967; by Gerald Colgan in *Plays and Players*, July 1967; by K. J. Worth in *Shavian III*, July 1967; by Sean Cronin in *Nation*, Oct 2, 1967; in *Choice*, Dec 1967; by M. J. Sidnell in *Canadian Forum*, Mar 1968; by David Krause in *Modern Drama*, Dec 1968; by John Midgley in *News-Letter* (Belfast), Nov 28, 1969.

A45   THE SEAN O'CASEY READER   1968

first edition

THE / SEAN O'CASEY / READER / PLAYS, AUTOBIOGRAPHIES, OPINIONS [all above in Solemnis type] / [ornament] / Edited, *with an Introduction*, by / Brooks Atkinson / 1968 [centred dot] ST. MARTIN'S PRESS [centred dot] *New York* / MACMILLAN [centred dot] *London* [centred dot] *Toronto* [centred dot] *Melbourne*

23.5 × 15.5cm.

[i], half-title: THE SEAN O'CASEY READER [in Solemnis type] /; [ii], frontispiece, photograph of O'Casey by Wolf Suschitzky; [iii], title-page as above; [iv], copyright, rights, Library of Congress card number, manufacture, printing, copyright dates of individual titles, permissions, publisher's imprints; [v]–[vii], Contents; [viii]–[ix], Chronology of the O'Casey works; [x], blank; [xi]–xxiv, Introduction by Brooks Atkinson; [1]–992, text; [993]–999, A Sean O'Casey Bibliography by Charles A. Carpenter; [1000], blank; [1001]–1008, Index.

Green cloth; front and back covers blank; spine: [triple rule] / THE / SEAN O'CASEY / READER [all above in Solemnis type] / [ornament] / Brooks Atkinson / [triple rule] / ST. MARTIN'S /; lettered and decorated in gold; white endpapers, all edges trimmed; .dust-jacket in light grey, lettered in black and orange.

Published October 18, 1968 at $12.50; 10,000 copies printed (including 500 copies imported to London for sale on June 8, 1969 at 147s).

Contents:

Chronology of the O'Casey Works
Introduction by Brooks Atkinson

PLAYS

Juno and the Paycock
    First appeared in *Two Plays*, 1925 (A10).
The Plough and the Stars
    First appeared in 1926 (A13).
The Silver Tassie
    First appeared in 1928 (A14).
Within the Gates
    First appeared in 1933 (A15).
Purple Dust
    First appeared in 1940 (A21).
Red Roses for Me
    First appeared in 1942 (A23).
Cock-a-Doodle Dandy
    First appeared in 1949 (A28).
Bedtime Story
    First appeared in *Collected Plays*, vol. 4, 1951 (A29).

The Drums of Father Ned
    First appeared in 1960 (A38).

AUTOBIOGRAPHIES

From *I Knock at the Door*
    First appeared in 1939 (A19).
From *Drums Under the Window*
    First appeared in 1945 (A24).
From *Inishfallen, Fare Thee Well*
    First appeared in 1949 (A27).
From *Rose and Crown*
    first appeared in 1952 (A30).
From *Sunset and Evening Star*
    First appeared in 1954 (A31).

OPINIONS (ALSO, A SHORT STORY)

Under the Greenwood Tree He Died
    First appeared in *Under a Colored Cap*, 1963 (A41).
Bonfire Under a Black Sun
    First appeared in *The Green Crow*, 1956 (A34).
Shakespeare Among the Flags
    First appeared under the title 'Ode to an Impudent Upstart' in *New York Times Magazine* Apr 19, 1964 (C593). Reprinted in *Blasts and Benedictions*, 1967 (A44).
The Bald Primaqueera
    First appeared in *Atlantic Monthly,* Sep 1965 (C617); reprinted in *Blasts and Benedictions*.
Crabbed Age and Youth
    First appeared in a shorter version under the title 'The Delicate Art of Growing Old' in *Harpers* Aug 1959 (C512). This version first published in *Blasts and Benedictions*.
The Day the Worker Blows a Bugle
    First appeared in *New Times* May 1958 (C495). This version first published in *Blasts and Benedictions*.
Not Waiting for Godot
    First appeared in *Encore* Easter 1956 (C452); reprinted in *Blasts and Benedictions*.
I Wanna Woman
    First appeared in *Windfalls*, 1934 (A16).
Purple Dust in Their Eyes
    First appeared in *Under a Colored Cap*, 1963 (A41).
A Sean O'Casey Bibliography by Charles A. Carpenter
    First appeared in *Modern Drama* May 1967.

Notes: This anthology, the contents of which had all been previously published in book form, was compiled by Brooks Atkinson, the drama critic for the *New York Times* 1922 to 1965. The dust-jacket describes the relationship with O'Casey, 'Sean O'Casey and Brooks Atkinson had been friends for many years . . . Their relationship had started as a purely professional one in the nineteen twenties when O'Casey began to write plays and Atkinson to review them, but gradually developed by correspondence and visits into a warm friendship . . . Mr. Atkinson begins with a long and perceptive introduction, an appreciation of both man and artist, scrupulous in not permitting his feeling for the first to color his judgement of the second . . .' In a letter to Daniel Macmillan, dated December 9, 1945, O'Casey mentions various suggestions made to him for an ' "Omnibus" Edition' of his works. He tells of his dislike of the idea and concludes, 'I imagine a book, in which the plays would be jammed together with the biography, would be terrible. But I may be wrong.'

Reviews: *The Sean O'Casey Reader* was reviewed in *Christian Science Monitor*, Dec 5, 1968; by Anne O'Neill-Barna in *New York Times Book Review*, Dec 15, 1968; by Marguerite McAneny in *Library Journal*, Jan 15, 1969; by William J. Clew in *Hartford Courant Magazine*, Jan 19, 1969; in *Critic*, Feb 1969; in *Choice*, May 1969; by Terence de Vere White in *Irish Times*, May 10, 1969; in *Times Literary Supplement*, July 17, 1969.

a. *first edition*
[Ornamental rule] / THE / LETTERS OF / Sean O'Casey / 1910–41 / [rule] /
VOLUME I / *Edited by* / DAVID KRAUSE / Macmillan Publishing Co., Inc. /
NEW YORK

23 × 15.5cm.

[i], half-title: THE / LETTERS OF / Sean O'Casey / 1910–41 /; [ii], blank;
[iii], title-page as above; [iv], copyright, Library of Congress Cataloging in
Publication Data; v, Contents; [vi], blank; vii–xvi, Introduction, A Self-
Portrait of the Artist as a Man; [xvii]–xxiii, Text and Acknowledgments; xxiv–
xxx, O'Casey Chronology; [1]–921, text; [922], blank; 923–972, indexes;
[973]–[974], blank.

Green cloth; front cover blank, ISBN number on back; spine: [ornamental
rule] / THE / LETTERS OF / Sean O'Casey / 1910–1941 / [rule] / VOLUME I
/ *Edited by* / DAVID KRAUSE / MACMILLAN /; lettered and decorated in
gold; green endpapers, all edges trimmed; white dust jacket, lettered and
decorated in black, green and orange.
Published March 27, 1975 at $35.00; 6000 copies printed. Cassell & Collier
Macmillan, London, imported 2000 bound copies from Macmillan Publishing Co., Inc., New York. They were issued for sale on September 29, 1975 at
£12.50.

Notes: Vol. I contains 653 letters by O'Casey; 124 letters to or about him;
21 news reports and reviews by or about him: a total of 798 entries. It
covers his life from the age of thirty to sixty-one. The dust-jacket describes
the work, 'The letters reveal O'Casey's complex and paradoxical nature—
his tenacious loyalties and broken friendships, his generosity and vindicti-
veness, his pride and compassion . . . A prodigious and eloquent fighter,
idealistic and discontent, words were the only weapons he employed during
his long and stormy life.' The Reader's Subscription book club offered
the volume as the main selection for January 1975 to its membership.

Reviews: Volume I was reviewed in *Library Journal*, Nov 1, 1974; in *Publisher's
Weekly*, Nov 25, 1974; in *Kirkus Reviews*, Dec 1, 1974; by Robert G. Lowery in
Sean O'Casey Review spring 1975; by Richard Gilman in *New York Times Book
Review*, Mar 16, 1975; by Keith S. Fulton in *Los Angeles Times* Mar 23, 1975;
in *Newsweek* Mar 31, 1975; by Ernest Schier in *Evening Bulletin* (Philadelphia),
Apr 8, 1975; by Robert Cormie in *Chicago Tribune Book World*, Apr 20, 1975;
by Denis Donoghue in *New Republic*, Apr 26, 1975; in *New Yorker*, May
5, 1975; in *Booklist*, June 15, 1975; by Kevin Sullivan in *Nation*, July 19,
1975; by Denis Johnston in *Irish University Review* Autumn 1975; in *Best
Sellers*, Sep 1975; in *Evening Standard*, Sep 5, 1975; by Tom Nugent in *Detroit
Free Press*, Sep 14, 1975; by Sean Day-Lewis in *Daily Telegraph*, Sep 25, 1975;
by Jack Sutherland in *Morning Star*, Sep 25, 1975; in *Economist*, Sep 27, 1975;
by Denis Johnston in *Irish Times*, Sep 27, 1975; by Bernard Levin in *Observer*,
Sep 28, 1975; by Gabriel Fallon in *Irish Independent*, Sep 29, 1975; by J.

C. Trewin in *The Times* (London), Sep 29, 1975; by Tomás MacAnna in *Hibernia*, Oct 3, 1975; by J. C. Trewin in *Birmingham Post*, Oct 4, 1975; by John O'Riordon in *Irish Press*, Oct 4, 1975; by Hugh Leonard in *Sunday Independant*, Oct 5, 1975; by Nigel Dennis in *Sunday Telegraph*, Oct 5, 1975; by Jack Sutherland in *Morning Star*, Oct 6, 1975; by W. T. in *Oxford Times*, Oct 14, 1975; by Martin Esslin in *Drama,* winter 1975; in *Sunday Times,* Oct 12, 1975; by Ian Stewart in *Country Life*, Oct 1975; by Julian Moynihan in *Times Literary Supplement*, Jan 2, 1976; by Robert Hogan in *The Journal of Irish Literature*, May 1976; in *Theatre Research International*, autumn 1976; by William A. Armstrong in *Theatre Notebook*, [spring] 1977; by B. K. Clarke in *Educational Theatre Journal*, Mar 1977.

SECTION B

Contributions to Books

Items here are restricted to first appearance in book form. This means that O'Casey's many contributions to drama anthologies are omitted from the list. The arrangement is by date of publication. Usually, only the first edition is described, with subsequent reprintings ignored unless some particular significance attaches to them.

APPEAL FOR ST LAURENCE O'TOOLE'S PIPERS' CLUB 1910

first edition
[LETTER APPEALING FOR FUNDS FOR ST LAURENCE O'TOOLE'S PIPERS' CLUB]

26 × 20cm; 1 leaf.

Letter, mimeographed.
Published summer/autumn 1910; number of copies undetermined.

Notes: O'Casey was secretary of the club, which was formed to organise a pipers' band for the St Laurence O'Toole parish, and to encourage the study of Irish history and the Irish language. A copy of the letter is in the National Library of Ireland. Collected in *The Letters of Sean O'Casey* (A46).

REASONS WHY YOU SHOULD JOIN THE IRISH CITIZEN ARMY 1914

first edition
REASONS WHY / YOU SHOULD JOIN / The Irish Citizen Army.

20 × 13.5cm; broadside.

Published March-April 1914; number of copies unknown; printed by City Printing Works, 13 Stafford Street, Dublin.

Notes: At a meeting held in the Concert Room, Liberty Hall, Dublin, on March 22, 1914, a Constitution was adopted for the Irish Citizen Army and an Army Council elected. The honorary secretary of the Army Council was Sean O'Cathasaigh. The broadside directs anyone wishing further information to apply to: Secretary, Citizen Army, Liberty Hall, Dublin. Reproduced in *Fifty Years of Liberty Hall: The Golden Jubilee of the Irish Transport and General Workers' Union 1909–1959*, Dublin, 1959.

It is almost certain that the text was drafted by O'Casey, as was the text for other leaflets and posters issued for the period March–July 1914, during which he served as secretary for the Irish Citizen Army: *Manifesto to Irish Trades Bodies*; *Why Irish Workers should not Join the National Volunteers*; *Reasons Why the Workers should Join the Irish Citizen Army*; *Constitution of the Irish Citizen Army*; Membership Card; Citizen Army Council Posters, etc. These pieces were printed in the appendix to *The Story of the Irish Citizen Army* (A9); reprinted in *The Letters of Sean O'Casey* (A46).

Another poster addressed 'To the People of Ireland', is reproduced in the *Sean O'Casey Review* for spring 1976.

B3   LITIR CHUMAINN SHEUMAS UI LORCAIN   1921

first edition
LITIR CHUMAINN SHEUMAS UI LORCAIN. / [line followed by broken line] / (THE JIM LARKIN CORRESPONDENCE COMMITTEE). / [line]
26 × 20cm; 1 leaf.

Letter, mimeographed; published by the Committee, Banba Hall, Parnell Square, Dublin.
Published November 1921; number of copies undetermined.

Notes: O'Casey was secretary of the Committee. A copy of the letter signed Sean O'Cathasaigh, Hon. Sec., is among the O'Brien Papers in the National Library of Ireland. The letter was also published in *The Gael*, Nov 7, 1921 (C86); collected in *The Letters of Sean O'Casey* (A46).
   On November 8, 1919, the day following the second anniversary of the Bolshevik Revolution, some seventy-three radical centres in New York were raided and a number of arrests were made. James Larkin was among those arrested and charged with violating the New York State statute on criminal anarchy. Larkin's trial opened on April 16, 1920 and on May 3 he received a sentence of five to ten years to be served in Sing Sing. Larkin's association with the Irish Labour movement, particularly during the 1913 Lock Out, had made of him an international figure. The Jim Larkin Correspondence Committee was organised by his Dublin colleagues who sought to interest people in mailing greeting cards to Larkin during his internment.

B4   JUNO OCH PÅFÅGELN   1926

first edition
JUNO OCH PÅFÅGELN / EN TRAGEDI I TRE AKTER / AV / *SEAN O'CASEY* / [short rule] / BEMYNDIGAD ÖVERSÄTTNING AV / *EBBA LOW OCH GUSTAF LINDEN* / [publisher's mark] / *STOCKHOLM* / HUGO GEBERS FÖRLAG

19 × 12cm; pp. 134.

Issued in stiff paper covers, lettered and decorated in black and yellow.
Published December 1926 at kr. 3.50; 2000 copies printed.

Contains: 'Min Hälsning till Sverige', pp. 3–6. This preface, written for the first published translation of one of his plays, is dated 1926.

B5   HYDE PARK ORATOR   1934

first edition
HYDE PARK ORATOR / By / BONAR THOMPSON / *With Preface by* / SEAN O'CASEY / JARROLDS *Publishers* LONDON / *Limited 34 Paternoster Row E.C. 4* / MCMXXXIV

21.5 × 13.5cm; pp. xv, [3], 19–287.

Issued in dark blue cloth; lettered and decorated in gold on spine; white endpapers, all edges trimmed.

Published March 9, 1934 at 10s 6d; number of copies unknown; a cheaper edition (so noted on the title-page) was issued in 1936. Though the British Museum has no record of it and the National Union Catalog has no location for it, the *English Catalogue* records that it was published in February 1936 at 3s 6d. The publishers have no record of the 1936 printing but concede that this may be because much of their records perished in the London blitz during the Second World War.

Contains: 'Preface', pp. ix–xiii. The American edition (New York, 1934) did not include O'Casey's preface. Collected in *Blasts and Benedictions* (A44).

AMERICAN SPECTATOR YEARBOOK   1934

first edition

The / AMERICAN SPECTATOR / YEAR BOOK / *Edited by* / GEORGE JEAN NATHAN SHERWOOD ANDERSON / ERNEST BOYD JAMES BRANCH CABELL / THEODORE DREISER EUGENE O'NEILL / [publisher's device] / FREDERICK A. STOKES COMPANY / NEW YORK MCXXXIV

22 × 14.5cm; pp. xii, 359.

Issued in black cloth; lettered and decorated in gold and orange on the spine; white endpapers, top and bottom edges trimmed.

Published March 23, 1934 at $2.75; number of copies undetermined.

Contains: 'Dramatis Personae Ibsenisensis', pp. 251–6; first appeared in *American Spectator*, July 1933 (C130). Collected in *Blasts and Benedictions* (A44).

87 SEAN O'CASEY ALS DRAMATIKER   1937

first edition

Sean O'Casey als Dramatiker / Ein Beitrag zum Nachkriegsdrama Irlands / [three short rules, the middle rule being slightly longer than the other two] / INAUGURAL – DISSERTATION / zur / Erlangung der Doktorwürde / der / Hohen Philosophischen Fakultät / der / Martin Luther-Universität Halle – Wittenberg / vorgelegt von / Kurt Wittig / aus Eisenach / Halle 1937 / [double rule] / Fritz Scharf – Leipzig

20.5 × 13.5cm; pp. 91.

Issued in grey-green boards with green cloth spine.

Published November 13, 1937; number of copies undetermined.

Contains: Letters from O'Casey to the author dated March 3 and May 22, 1937, quoted on pp. 10, 13, 18.

B8   ROBERT LORAINE   1938

first edition

ROBERT LORAINE / *Soldier* [centred dot] *Actor* [centred dot] *Airman* / [short
swelled rule] / *by* / WINIFRED LORAINE / [publisher's mark] / COLLINS
[centred dot] PUBLISHERS / FORTY-EIGHT [centred dot] PALL MALL
[centred dot] LONDON / 1938

22 × 14.5cm; pp. 390.

Issued in navy cloth; spine lettered in silver; white endpapers, top edge
stained dark blue, all edges trimmed.
Published September 12, 1938 at 10s 6d; number of copies unknown; a
cheap reprint was issued in March 1940 at 5s. An American edition was
published in 1939 by William Morrow & Co. Inc. at $3.50, under the title
Head Wind: The Story of Robert Loraine.

Contains: Letter, pp. 333–4; reprinted in *The Strange Life of August Strindberg*
by Elizabeth Sprigge (1949); collected in a fuller version in *The Letters
of Sean O'Casey* (A46); *Robert Loraine* was reviewed by O'Casey in *Sunday Times*,
Sep 18, 1938, under the title 'A Prophet in the Theatre' (C208); the review
was reprinted in *Blasts and Benedictions* (A44).

B9   HANDS OFF THE DAILY WORKER   1940

first edition

HANDS OFF [in red] / THE [in red] / DAILY WORKER / 1^D [in red, within
border of red rules] / [all above incorporated in design depicting a worker
backed by a newspaper facing a well-dressed audience]

18.5 × 12.5cm; pp. 15, [1].

Issued in paper covers, front cover serves as title-page; lettered and decorated
in black and red; all edges trimmed.
Published July/August 1940 at 1d; between sixty and eighty thousand copies
were printed.

Contains: 'The Golden Boys', pp. 13–15; first appeared in *Daily Worker*, July
17, 1940 (C245).

B10   THE CASE FOR THE DAILY WORKER   1941

first edition

The Case / for the / Daily Worker / *By* / The Members of the former / Editorial
Board: / J. B. S. Haldane (*Chairman*); Sean O'Casey; / Councillor J. Owen;
R. Page Arnot / PRICE ONE PENNY / [all above enclosed within border
of rules]

18 × 12cm; pp. 20.

Issued in paper covers, front cover serves as title-page; lettered and decorated in black; all edges trimmed.
Published February 1941 at 1d; number of copies unknown.

CURTAIN UP   1942

first edition
LENNOX ROBINSON / [swelled rule] / *Curtain Up* / *an* / *autobiography* / [publisher's mark] / MICHAEL JOSEPH LTD. / *26 Bloomsbury Street, London,* *W.C. 1*

22 × 14cm; pp. 224.

Issued in cream cloth; lettered and decorated in silver on spine; white end-papers, all edges trimmed.
Published February 1942 at 10s 6d; number of copies undetermined.

Contains: Letter to Lennox Robinson dated October 9, 1922, quoted pp. 138–9; the complete letter was subsequently published in *A Self-portrait of the Artist as a Man* (B58); collected in *The Letters of Sean O'Casey* (A46).
Letter to Lennox Robinson undated [November 17, 1922], quoted p. 139; the complete letter subsequently published in *The Letters of Sean O'Casey* (A46). Inscription in Yeats's copy of *Juno and the Paycock*, p. 139.

THE SATURDAY BOOK 1943   1942

first edition
THE / 1943 / SATURDAY / BOOK / EDITED BY / Leonard Russell / HUTCHINSON / [title lines enclosed in decorative swelled rules]

22.5 × 15cm; pp. 270.

Issued in orange cloth; front and back covers blank; lettered and decorated in gold on spine; white endpapers, all edges trimmed.
Published October 1942 at 12s 6d; 10,000 copies printed.

Contains: 'The Lady of Coole', pp. 96–115; this includes a good deal of the material which was subsequently used in Chapters 10 ('Blessed Bridget of Coole') and 11 ('Where Wild Swans Nest') of *Inishfallen, Fare Thee Well* (A27). Much is added in *Inishfallen*, but some human details and a good anecdote, in this account, are omitted.

3 TWENTIETH CENTURY AUTHORS   1942

first edition
TWENTIETH CENTURY / AUTHORS / A Biographical Dictionary of Modern Literature / *Edited by* / STANLEY J. KUNITZ / *and* / HOWARD HAYCRAFT / COMPLETE IN ONE VOLUME WITH / 1850 BIOGRAPHIES AND / 1700

PORTRAITS / [publisher's device] / NEW YORK / THE H. W. WILSON COMPANY / NINETEEN HUNDRED FORTY-TWO

25.5 × 17cm; pp. vii, 1577.

Issued in green cloth; lettered and decorated in gold on spine; white end-papers, all edges trimmed.
Published December 1, 1942 at $8.50; number of copies undisclosed.

Contains: 'Autobiographical Sketch', p. 1039.

B14   THE RIBBON IN HER HAIR   1943

first edition
BLAND [in white] / The [in green] / Ribbon [in green] / in her [in green] / hair [in green] / WORDS BY / SEAN O'CASEY [in outline letters] / MUSIC BY / ELIZABETH MACONCHY / PRICE / 6 [in outline] / PENCE / PUBLISHED BY / THE WORKERS' MUSIC ASSOCIATION, 9 GREAT NEWPORT ST. LONDON W.C. 2 [all above incorporated in design depicting a girl in green tying a green ribbon round her hair, factory building to the right, with black smoke belching from the smokestacks, trees to the left in green, green foreground]

Sheet music; 28 × 11.5cm; pp. 5, [1].
Published January–February? 1943 at 6d; number of copies undetermined.

The text was originally published without the music in *Irish Freedom*, Jan 1943 (C286), where it was advertised as 'appearing soon in a separate publication by the Workers' Music Association.'

B15   THE SATURDAY BOOK 3   1943

first edition
THE [in outline letters] / SATURDAY [in outline letters] / BOOK [in outline letters] / 3 [in outline letters] / *edited by* / *Leonard Russell* / *with decorations by* / *Laurence Scarfe* / HUTCHINSON / [all above within decorative border signed: Laurence Scarfe]

22.5 × 15cm; pp. 280.

Issued in orange cloth; lettered in gold on spine; white endpapers, all edges trimmed.
Published October 1943 at 12s 6d; number of copies unknown.

Contains: 'The Curtained World', pp. 139–48; reprinted in *Blasts and Benedictions* (A44) under the title 'Behind the Curtained World'.

MILLION NEW LEFT WRITING 1943

first edition
MILLION / NEW LEFT WRITING / *Edited by JOHN SINGER* / FIRST
COLLECTION / [rule] / Contents / [Table of Contents, 32 lines, follows]

22 × 14cm; pp. 64.

Issued in brown paper covers; lettered and decorated in black and purple.
Published in December 1943 at 2s by William Maclellan, 240 Hope Street,
Glasgow; number of copies undisclosed.

Contains: 'The Dog', pp. 3–7; short story reprinted in *Blasts and Benedictions*
(A44). It is almost certain that this autobiographical episode was originally
part of O'Casey's life-story, probably written at the time the chapters that
comprise *Pictures in the Hallway* (A22) were drafted; it was eventually excluded
from the volume, possibly because (as several of O'Casey's letters record)
the length of the narrative had outstripped the publisher's original estimates.
Another chapter, 'He Paints His First Picture', was omitted from *Pictures in
the Hallway* for the same reason.

THEY GO, THE IRISH 1944

first edition
THEY GO, THE IRISH / A Miscellany of / War-time Writing / *Compiled by* /
LESLIE DAIKEN / LONDON NICHOLSON & WATSON

18 × 12cm; pp. 123.

Issued in paper wrappers; lettered and decorated in green, black, red and
white; all edges trimmed.
Published December 1944 at 1s.; printed by The Kerryman Ltd, Tralee,
Ireland; number of copies undetermined.

Contains: 'There Go the Irish', pp. 7–25; collected in *Blasts and Benedictions*
(A44).

Notes: This essay was completed in December 1943. On June 9, 1944 O'Casey,
writing to Daniel Macmillan, tells him: 'Some time ago, I wrote a six
or seven thousand word article for an Irish book a friend of mine roared
about having published. But I haven't heard from him for a long time,
and presume he has had to give it up ... It is called *Here Come the Irish*,
and deals generally with them in relation to England and the world.'

8 THE MINT 1946

first edition
THE / MINT / *A Miscellany / of / Literature, Art / and Criticism* / EDITED BY
GEOFFREY GRIGSON / [swelled rule] / ROUTLEDGE AND SONS LTD

21.5 × 13.7cm.; pp. xii, 220.

Issued in dark brown cloth; spine lettered and decorated in orange and gold; white endpapers, all edges trimmed.
Published July 14, 1946 at 8s 6d; number of copies undisclosed.

Contains: 'The Raid, An Autobiographical Sketch', pp. 24–39; reprinted with minor changes as 'The Raid' in *Inishfallen, Fare Thee Well* (A27).

B19   LADY GREGORY'S JOURNALS   1946

first edition
LADY GREGORY'S / JOURNALS / 1916–1930 / *Edited by* / Lennox Robinson / PUTNAM & COMPANY LTD. / 42 GREAT RUSSELL STREET

20.5 × 14cm.; pp. 343, [1].

Issued in dark blue cloth; lettered in gold on spine; white endpapers, all edges trimmed.
Published September 1946 at 18s; number of copies unknown. An American (offset) edition was published in March 1947 by the Macmillan Company, New York.

Contains: O'Casey letter to Lady Gregory, quoted on pp. 320–1.

Notes: This book was reviewed by O'Casey, whose review appeared in *The Bell*, Feb 1947 under the title 'A Protestant Bridget' (C339).

B20   THE HOLIDAY BOOK   1946

first edition
The Holiday Book [in red] / EDITED BY / JOHN SINGER / [publisher's mark] / WILLIAM MACLELLAN

24.5 × 18cm.; pp. 333, [9].

Issued in pale blue cloth; lettered and decorated in purple on covers and on spine; white endpapers, all edges trimmed.
Published December 1946 at 21s; number of copies undetermined.

Contains: 'How to Succeed as a Playwright', pp. 275–7.
A 'Holiday Book Gallery' pp. [335]–[342] contains photographs and short biographies of contributors to the book. The paragraph on O'Casey, p. [341], though in the third person, was clearly written by the playwright himself.

B21   THE POPE, THE PEOPLE, AND POLITICS   1948

THE POPE, / THE PEOPLE, / AND POLITICS / THREE ARTICLES ON / THE CATHOLIC CHURCH / ITS POLICY, ITS POLITICS / AND ITS PROPAGANDA / CAN CATHOLICS WORK FOR SOCIALISM? / *by Harry*

McShane / STUDY COURSE FOR A VATICAN RECRUIT / *by Sean O'Casey* / A GIRL WITH NO NERVOUS SYSTEM / *by Professor J. B. S. Haldane, F. R. S.* / TWOPENCE

21.5 × 14.5cm.; pp. [8].

Issued in paper covers, front cover serves as title-page; lettered in black; all edges trimmed.
Published May/June 1948 at twopence, by the People's Press Printing Society, Ltd, London; printed by Illustrated Periodicals, Ltd.; number of copies unknown.

Notes: O'Casey's essay, pp. [4]–[5], first appeared in *Daily Worker*, May 4, 1948 (C362).

WEST COUNTRY BOOK   1949

first edition
WEST COUNTRY BOOK / NUMBER ONE / [swelled rule] / *Edited by* / J. C. TREWIN / *Introduction by* / WAVENEY GIRVAN / *Line Illustrations by* / R. M. LANDER / LONDON / WESTAWAY BOOKS

21.5 × 13.5cm.; pp. 180.

Issued in brown cloth; lettered and decorated in gold on front cover and on spine; white endpapers, all edges trimmed, top edge stained brown.
Published October 1949 at 10s 6d; number of copies undetermined.

Contains: 'Totnes of Gentle Mien', pp. [106]–110. First appeared in *West Country Magazine*, Dec 1946 (C334).

SEAN O'CASEY AND THE ELECTIONS   1951

first edition
SEAN O'CASEY AND THE ELECTIONS [hand lettered]

25 × 20cm.; 1 leaf.

Election address, mimeographed; published by Sean Nolan, Election Agent, 'Hinchoge', Carrickmines, Co. Dublin on behalf of Michael O'Riordan.
Published May 1951; number of copies undetermined.

Contains: Extracts from an O'Casey letter in support of Mr O'Riordan.

Notes: Mr O'Riordan stood as a candidate for the Irish Workers' League in Dublin South West constituency, in the Irish general election of May 1951. Voting took place on Wednesday, May 30, 1951.

B24   APPROACH PATTERN   1951

first edition
APPROACH PATTERN / *by* / HILDA E. ALLBERRY / "An honest tale
speeds best, plainly told." / —Shakespeare. / [ornament] / An Irish
Traveller's Impressions of the Soviet Union / —Autumn, 1950 / Preface by
SEAN O'CASEY

18 × 12cm.; pp. 55.

Issued in paper covers; illustration on front cover by Harry Kernoff; lettered
and decorated in black; all edges trimmed.
Published 1951 at sixpence by the Irish-U.S.S.R. Society, Dublin.

Contains: 'Preface. Look at the Soviet Union', p. [5].

B25   WE PLEDGE PEACE   1953

first edition
WE PLEDGE Peace [the word 'peace', taller than the other two words, is
reproduced from hand-lettered copy] / A FRIENDSHIP BOOK

21.5 × 28cm.; pp. 99.

Issued in stiff blue paper covers, front cover serves as title-page; lettered in
dark blue, all edges trimmed.
Published 1953 at $1.00 by the American Russian Institute, San Francisco;
exact date of publication unknown; 5000 copies printed.

Contains: 'Come Let Us Reason Together', p. 75. Excerpts had been published
under the title 'Sean O'Casey, Irish Playwright, Sends a Message for Peace'
in *Daily Worker* (New York), July 29, 1952 (C413); the complete text appeared
under the title 'Sean O'Casey Puts Plea to Americans' in *Daily Worker*,
Aug 1, 1952.

B26   7 ARTS NUMBER TWO   1954

first edition
7 ARTS / # Two / Selected and edited by / FERNANDO PUMA / [reproduction
of Horse and Rider by Marino Marini] / PERMABOOKS / a division of /
Doubleday & Company, Inc., Garden City, N.Y.

18 × 10.5cm.; pp. 196.

Issued in paper covers lettered and decorated in black, white, red and blue.
Published January 1954 at $0.50.

Contains: 'The Arts Among the Multitude', pp. [13]–19; reprinted in *The Green
Crow* (A34).

HIGHLIGHTS OF MODERN LITERATURE 1954

first edition
Highlights of / MODERN LITERATURE / *A Permanent Collection of Memorable
Essays from* / The New York Times Book Review [in Gothic type] / *Edited by
Francis Brown* / [publisher's mark] / A MENTOR BOOK / Published by THE
NEW AMERICAN LIBRARY

18 × 11cm.; pp. 240.

Issued in stiff paper covers; lettering decorated with areas of black, white,
purple, gold and maroon; all edges trimmed.
Published March 1954 at 35 cents; 146,054 copies printed.

Contains: 'Always the Plow and the Stars', pp. 25–9; originally appeared in *New
York Times Book Review*, Jan 25, 1953 (C417); reprinted in *The Green Crow* (A34).
'Bernard Shaw: An Appreciation of a Fighting Idealist', pp. 229–33;
originally appeared in *New York Times Book Review*, Nov 12, 1950 (C399);
reprinted in *The Green Crow* (A34).

A.E.: AN IRISH PROMETHEAN 1954

first edition
A.E.: AN IRISH PROMETHEAN / A Study of the Contribution of / George
William Russell to World Culture / *By* / FRANCIS MERCHANT / *Head, Division
of the Humanities* / *Benedict College* / BENEDICT COLLEGE PRESS / Columbia, South
Carolina / 1954

22.5 × 14cm.; pp. 242.
Published June 15, 1954 at $4.50.

Contains: Letters, quoted extensively pp. 238–9. Excerpts from the letters,
dated November 20, 1949 and February 11, 1950, are repeated on pp. 205–6.

SHAKESPEARE AND THE YOUNG ACTOR 1955

first edition
SHAKESPEARE / AND THE / YOUNG ACTOR / *A Guide to Production* / *by*
/ GUY BOAS / HEADMASTER, SLOANE SCHOOL, CHELSEA / *"Do the
boys carry it away?* / *They do, my lord."* / HAMLET / [publisher's mark] /
SALISBURY SQUARE / LONDON

21.5 × 13.5cm.; pp. 126.

Issued in purple boards; lettered in gold on spine; white endpapers, all
edges trimmed.
Published February 25, 1955 at 16s; Messrs Rockliff, the original publishers,
were subsequently absorbed by Barrie & Jenkins Ltd, who estimate that about

2500 copies were printed. Another edition was published by Barrie and Rockliff on December 11, 1961, at 21s; 1500 copies were printed.

Contains: Letter, quoted extensively pp. 47–8; the letter, dated October 9, 1938, was subsequently published in full in *The Letters of Sean O'Casey* (A46). Brief excerpt from a programme note (C187), p. 53. The contributions to the 1961 edition are as in the first edition, with the addition of a short excerpt from a letter quoted on the dust-jacket.

B30 JUNO AND THE PAYCOCK   1956

first edition
SEAN O'CASEY [in white on bottom left corner of photograph of O'Casey] / *photo by Suschitzky, 1955* / JUNO AND THE PAYCOCK / *starring*: SIOBHÁN McKENNA [centred dot] CYRIL CUSACK [centred dot] MAIRE KEAN [centred dot] SEAMUS KAVANAGH / CYRIL CUSACK PRODUCTIONS, IRELAND

28 × 22cm.; pp. 11, [1].

Pamphlet issued with album for the Angel recording of *Juno and the Paycock*. Published February 27, 1956.

Contains: 'Preamble, Spoken by the Author', p. 9. This is the text of the introduction to the recording, composed by O'Casey, and spoken on the recording by him.

B31 DAS NEUE NATIONALTHEATER   1957

first edition
DAS NEUE NATIONALTHEATER / Festschrift zur Eröffnung des neuen Mannheimer Nationaltheaters / am 175. Jahrestag der Uraufführung der "Räuber"

23.5 × 21cm.; pp. 256.

Issued in white cloth mottled with gold; lettered in gold on front cover and on spine.
Published January 1957; number of copies unknown.

Contains: [Greetings], pp. 19–20. The greetings were sent on the occasion of the one hundred and seventy-fifth anniversary of the first production of Schiller's *Die Räuber* at Mannheim, January 13, 1782.

B32 JAMES JOYCE'S WORLD   1957

first edition
JAMES JOYCE'S WORLD / *by* / PATRICIA HUTCHINS / METHUEN AND CO. LTD / 36 ESSEX STREET [centered dot] STRAND [centred dot] LONDON W.C. 2

21 × 15.5cm.; pp. 256.

Issued in green cloth; lettered and decorated in gold on spine; white end-papers, all edges trimmed, top edge stained green.
Published March 21, 1957 at 30s; 3310 copies printed.

Contains: Letter to James Joyce, dated May 30, 1939, pp. 235–6; reprinted in *Letters of James Joyce*, vol. III (B55); collected in *The Letters of Sean O'Casey* (A46).

WISDOM 1958

first edition
WISDOM / CONVERSATIONS WITH THE / ELDER WISE MEN OF OUR DAY / *Edited and with an introduction by* / JAMES NELSON / [swelled rule] / [publisher's mark] / W [centred dot] W [centred dot] NORTON & COMPANY [centred dot] INC [centred dot] *New York*

21 × 13.5cm.; pp. xii, 273.

Issued in black cloth; lettered and decorated in gold on spine; white end-papers; all edges trimmed.
Published November 1958 at $3.95; number of copies printed unknown.

Contains: 'Sean O'Casey', pp. 25–33. The text of a conversation between O'Casey and Robert Emmett Ginna, Jr, at the playwright's home in Torquay in 1955. The text of the interview was prepared and written by O'Casey beforehand. The filmed interview was broadcast by NBC on January 22, 1956 in its Wisdom series. A tape recording of the interview was issued in 1970 by The Center for Cassette Studies under the title *Sean O'Casey's World*. A shortened version of the conversation was printed in *The Sting and the Twinkle* (B72).

TRIBUNE 21 1958

first edition
Tribune 21 / [rule] / *Edited by Elizabeth Thomas* / London / MACGIBBON & KEE / 1958

20 × 13cm.; pp. 312.

Issued in black boards; lettered in gold on spine; white endpapers; all edges trimmed.
Published December 1958 at 18s; number of copies undetermined.

Contains: 'Great Man, Gorki', pp. 128–30; first appeared in *Tribune*, May 3, 1946 (C326).

B35   GLAZAMI DRUZEĬ   1959

first edition
Глазами / *Друзей* / [large dot] / *Лениздат* / *1959* / [all above surrounded by facsimile signatures of contributors]

22 × 17cm.; pp. 359.

Issued in white vinyl cloth; lettered and decorated in gold and red on front cover and on spine; white endpapers, all edges trimmed.
Published 1959.

Contains: 'Voskhodyashchaya zvezda', pp. [305]–309; originally appeared in *Literaturnaya Gazeta*, Nov 5, 1957 (C481).

B36   COLLEGE ENGLISH: THE FIRST YEAR   1960

Third edition (the first to include the O'Casey contribution)
THIRD EDITION / [ornamental rule] / College English: / the first year / J. HOOPER WISE [centered dot] ALTON C. MORRIS / *University of Florida* / JOHN C. HODGES / *University of Tennessee* / HARCOURT, BRACE AND COMPANY / *New York* [publisher's mark] *Burlingame*

24 × 18cm.; pp. x, 982.

Issued in tan-grey cloth; lettered and decorated in red and brown; black endpapers at front, back endpapers lettered and decorated in orange and black, all edges trimmed.
Published March 23, 1960 at $6.50; number of copies undisclosed.

Contains: 'The Harp in the Air Still Sings', pp. 251–4. Originally appeared in *New York Times Magazine*, Jan 11, 1959 (C505); reprinted under the title 'The Lark in the Clear Air Still Sings' in *Under a Colored Cap* (A41). The essay was also reprinted under the title 'The Harp Still Sings' in *Background and Foreground, An Anthology of Articles from the New York Times Magazine* (Channel Press, November 15, 1960). The O'Casey contribution did not appear in editions previous to the third edition of *College English*. Further editions with the O'Casey contribution were published in 1964 (4th ed.) and 1968 (5th ed.). A flyer to promote this edition of *College English* printed an O'Casey letter in facsimile. The letter dated July 25, 1959 was addressed to Alton C. Morris, one of the compilers, granting permission for the use of the essay 'The Harp in the Air Still Sings'.

B37   SEAN O'CASEY THE MAN AND HIS WORK   1960

first edition
DAVID KRAUSE / [ornamental line] / Sean O'Casey / THE MAN AND HIS WORK / LONDON / MACGIBBON & KEE / 1960

21.5 × 13.5cm.; pp. 340.

Issued in black boards; lettered in gold on spine; white endpapers, all edges trimmed.

Published March 28, 1960 at 30s; number of copies undetermined. An American offset edition was published by the Macmillan Company on August 8, 1960 at $4.50; 5000 copies printed. A paperback edition was published in July 1962 at $1.50 by Collier Books, New York. An 'enlarged edition' was published in 1975 under the joint imprint of Macmillan Publishing Co., Inc. (New York) and Collier Macmillan Publishers (London).

Contains: Letter to David Krause, undated, quoted p. 36.

Letter to Lennox Robinson, quoted p. 100; originally appeared in *Irish Statesman*, June 9, 1928 (C109); reprinted in *The Experiments of Sean O'Casey* (B39); collected in *Letters of Sean O'Casey* (A46).

Letter to W. B. Yeats, quoted pp. 101–4; remainder of letter is printed on pp. 307–8; originally appeared in *Irish Statesman*, June 9, 1928 (C109); reprinted in full in *The Experiments of Sean O'Casey* (B39); collected in *Letters of Sean O'Casey* (A46).

'O'Casey's Credo' (essay), quoted pp. 201–2; originally appeared in *New York Times*, Nov 9, 1958 (C503); reprinted under the title 'Cock-A-Doodle Dandy' in *Playwrights on Playwriting* (B38), later published in a fuller version under the title 'Cockadoodle Doo' in *Blasts and Benedictions* (A44).

Notes: In the paperback edition, O'Casey's contributions appear on pp. 57–8, 135–9, 257–8, 381–2.

PLAYWRIGHTS ON PLAYWRITING   1960

first edition
Playwrights on Playwriting / THE MEANING AND MAKING OF MODERN / DRAMA FROM IBSEN TO IONESCO / *Edited by* TOBY COLE / *Introduction by* JOHN GASSNER / [publisher's mark] HILL AND WANG [centred dot] NEW YORK

18.5 × 11.2cm.; pp. 299.

Issued in blue cloth; lettered and decorated in black on spine; white endpapers, all edges trimmed.

Published April 18, 1960 at $3.95; number of copies undetermined.

Contains: 'Cock-A-Doodle Dandy', pp. [247]–249. A reprint of an article which originally appeared in the *New York Times*, Nov 9, 1958 (C503) under the title 'O'Casey's Credo'; an excerpt was published in *Sean O'Casey, the Man and His Work* (B37); it was later published in a fuller version under the title 'Cockadoodle Doo' in *Blasts and Benedictions* (A44).

B39   THE EXPERIMENTS OF SEAN O'CASEY   1960

first edition

THE EXPERIMENTS OF SEAN O'CASEY [across facing pages] / *Robert Hogan*
[on right-hand page] / ST MARTIN'S PRESS, NEW YORK [on left-hand page]

21 × 14cm.; pp. 215.

Issued in black boards with red cloth spine, lettered in red on front cover,
lettered in white and red on spine; black and red endpapers, all edges
trimmed, top edges stained black.
Published September 1960 at $5.00; number of copies undisclosed.

Contains: 'From Within the Gates' (essay), quoted pp. 71–3, 174–5; first
appeared in *New York Times*, Oct 21, 1934 (C155), reprinted in full in *Blasts
and Benedictions* (A44).
'O'Casey's Credo' (essay), quoted pp. 121–2, 174–5; first appeared in *New
York Times*, Nov 9, 1958 (C503); reprinted in full in *Playwrights on Playwriting*
(B38) under the title 'Cock-a-Doodle Dandy'; collected in a fuller version
in *Blasts and Benedictions* (A44) under the title 'Cockadoodle Doo'.
'Letter' to *Irish Times*, undated, pp. 130–3; the letter was never sent to the *Irish
Times*; first appeared in *Enquiry* (Nottingham) June 1958 (C496).
'Letters' to David Krause, undated, quoted pp. 133–4, 158.
'Letters' to Robert Hogan, quoted pp. 135, 141, 173–4, 179, 183.
'Letter', quoted pp. 177–8; first appeared in 'Letters from Sean O'Casey to
a Randolph Macon Senior' in the *Randolph-Macon Bulletin*, Sep 1954 (C428);
the quotation is further reprinted in *Drama: the Major Genres* by Robert Hogan
and Sven Eric Molin (New York, Dodd, Mead & Co., 1962).
'The Abbey Directors and Mr. Sean O'Casey' (letters), quoted pp. 192–6;
first appeared in *Irish Statesman*, June 9, 1928 (C109).
'Y.O. and the Silver Tassie' (letter), quoted p. 203; first appeared in *Irish
Statesman*, Aug 4, 1928 (C116).
'Mr. O'Casey Dissents' (letter), quoted p. 206; first appeared in *New York
Times*, Aug 11, 1935 (C165).
The letters of June 9 and August 4, 1928, and the letter of August 11,
1935 are collected in *The Letters of Sean O'Casey* (A46).

B40   NASLEDIE ANGLIĬSKOGO ROMANTIZMA I SOVREMENNOST'   1960

first edition

А. А. ЕЛИСТРАТОВА / [decorative rule] / *Наследие* / АНГЛИЙСКОГО /
РОМАНТИЗМА / *и* / *современность* / [ornament] / издательство /
АКАДЕМИИ НАУК СССР / *Москва* [centred dot] *1960*

19 × 13cm; pp. 504, [3].

Issued in grey cloth; lettered and decorated in gold with some blind stamping
on covers and on spine; white endpapers, all edges trimmed.
Published September 1960 at 15r.; 3000 copies printed.

Contains: Letter of March 19, 1958, quoted pp. 39–41.

O'NEILL AND HIS PLAYS   1961

first edition
O'NEILL / AND HIS PLAYS / *FOUR DECADES OF CRITICISM* / EDITED
BY / Oscar Cargill / N. Bryllion Fagin / William J. Fisher / *NEW YORK
UNIVERSITY PRESS 1961* / [publisher's mark]

23.5 × 15cm.; pp. 528.

Issued in grey and purple cloth; spine lettered and decorated in green and
red; white endpapers, all edges trimmed.
Published December 15, 1961 at $7.50; 5824 copies printed; reprinted August
1962 and August 1967. Of this edition, 425 sets of sheets were imported by
Peter Owen and issued in London in April 1962, with cancel title-leaf,
at 50s; reprinted 1964. The London issue had the title *O'Neill and His Plays*:
A Survey of His Life and Works. The book was reissued by New York University
Press in paper covers, in its Gotham Library series in March 1963 at $2.95;
6565 copies printed, reprinted August 1964 and August 1967. This edition
contains a quotation from a letter from O'Casey to Oscar Cargill on the
back cover.

Contains: 'Tribute to O'Neill', p. 96; first appeared as letter to Lester
Osterman under the title 'Name of O'Neill Adorns Theater' in *New York
Times*, Nov 19, 1959 (C516); reprinted in *O'Neill* by Arthur and Barbara
Gelb (New York, Harper, 1962).

DIE ALTE DAME SAGT: NEIN!   1962

first edition
SCHWEIZER ANGLISTISCHE ARBEITEN / SWISS STUDIES IN ENGLISH /
Gegründet von B. FEHR+ / Herausgegeben von E. DIETH+, Zürich; O.
FUNKE, Bern; / H. STRAUMANN, Zürich / [between rules] 52. BAND /
KASPAR SPINNER / DIE ALTE DAME SAGT: NEIN! / DREI IRISCHE
DRAMATIKER / LENNOX   ROBINSON   SEAN   O'CASEY / DENIS
JOHNSTON / [rule] / FRANCKE VERLAG BERN

23 × 15cm.; pp. vi,210.

Issued in paper covers.
Published May 1962 at 15fr.; number of copies undisclosed.

Contains: Letter dated November 16, 1958, quoted p. 50.
Letter dated January 17, 1959 quoted pp. 122, 124, 131.

B43   TOLSZTOJ EMLÉKKÖNYV   1962

first edition

TOLSZTOJ / EMLÉKKÖNYV / FÓVÁROSI SZABÓ ERVIN KÖNYVTÁR /
BUDAPEST, 1962.

24 × 17cm.; pp. 501.

Issued in silver-grey cloth, lettered in gold on front cover and on spine;
yellow endpapers, all edges trimmed.
Published June 1962 at 50z.; 2500 copies printed.

Contains: Letter to Ferenc Révész, dated October 19, 1960; a photocopy of
the letter is printed with others between pp. 336 and 337; a Hungarian translation of the letter is included on p. 406.
'Halhatatlan Csillagok', pp. 403–5; according to O'Casey's letter this article
on Tolstoy had been written '. . . at their request, for THE LITERARY GAZETTE,
Moscow; and I enclose a copy of it in the faint hope that it may be of
use to you, or that portion of it may be suitable for use in the work you
are doing . . .' The essay had previously been published in a Russian translation in *Literaturnaya Gazeta*, Sep 15, 1960 (C536).

B44   SELECTED PLAYS BY LADY GREGORY   1962

first edition

LADY GREGORY / SELECTED PLAYS / *Chosen and Introduced / by / Elizabeth
Coxhead / Foreword by Sean O'Casey* / [publisher's mark] / PUTNAM / 42 GREAT
RUSSELL STREET / LONDON

21.5 × 14cm.; pp. 269.

Issued in maroon boards, lettered and decorated in gold on spine.
Published October 1, 1962 at 25s; 3000 copies printed. In May 1969 Colin
Smythe Ltd took over the distribution of the remaining 318 copies of the
Putnam edition.

Contains: 'Foreword, a Sprig of Rosemary Among the Laurel', pp. 7–9;
reprinted in *Blasts and Benedictions* (A44).

B45   SEAN O'CASEY: THE MAN BEHIND THE PLAYS   1963

first edition

SAROS COWASJEE / [ornamental line in green] / *SEAN O'CASEY / The Man
Behind the Plays* / [ornamental line in green] / OLIVER & BOYD /
EDINBURGH AND LONDON / 1963

21.5 × 14cm.; pp. 266.

Issued in navy cloth; spine lettered and decorated in gold; white endpapers,
all edges trimmed.

Published October 1963 at 30s; 3000 copies printed; reissued April 1965 in the O. & B. Paperbacks series at 15s; 3000 copies printed.

Contains: Facsimile of letter to W. B. Yeats dated May 11, 1928, between pp. 112 and 113.

Letter to W. B. Yeats dated November 23, 1935, pp. 130–1; collected in *The Letters of Sean O'Casey* (A46).

'A Stand on the *Silver Tassie*', pp. 131–4; collected under the title 'Blasphemy and the Silver Tassie' in *Blasts and Benedictions* (A44); the version in *Blasts and Benedictions* is a transcription from a carbon copy of the article sent by O'Casey to Yeats on November 23, 1935; reprinted in *The Letters of Sean O'Casey* (A46). The latter corrects inaccuracies in Cowasjee's text.

'O'Casey's Letter on His Affinities with George Bernard Shaw', pp. 253–4. Letters of O'Casey are quoted on pp. xi, 1, 10, 24–5, 56, 82–3, 90, 95, 99–100, 120, 130–1, 167, 171, 178, 205, 211, 216, 220–5, 229–31, 234–5, 242–52.

The ballad 'A Son of Granuaile', printed on p. 255, is not by O'Casey and is omitted from 1965 paper edition.

FOUR DAYS 1964

first edition
FOUR DAYS / THE HISTORICAL RECORD / OF THE DEATH / OF PRESIDENT KENNEDY / compiled by / UNITED PRESS INTERNA-TIONAL / [UPI mark] / and / AMERICAN HERITAGE MAGAZINE / [American Heritage mark] / Published by AMERICAN HERITAGE PUBLISHING CO., INC. / ©1964 by American Heritage Publishing Co., Inc., and United Press International. / All rights reserved under Berne and Pan-American Copyright Conventions. / Reproduction in whole or in part without permission is prohibited.

27.5 × 21cm.; pp. 143.

Issued in ivory paper-covered boards; colour portrait of President Kennedy on front cover, presidential seal in colour on back cover, lettered in black on front cover, and on spine; white endpapers, all edges trimmed.
Published January 1, 1964 at $2.95; number of copies undetermined.

Contains: Facsimile of letter to Miss Rose Russell, dated November 20, 1963, p. 46; originally appeared in *New York Times*, Nov 27, 1963 (C586).

THE SOCIALIST REGISTER 1965 1965

first edition
THE / SOCIALIST REGISTER / 1965 / EDITED BY / RALPH MILIBAND / and / JOHN SAVILLE / THE MERLIN PRESS / LONDON

21.5 × 13.5cm.; pp. 362.

Issued in green boards, lettered and decorated in gold on spine; white endpapers, all edges trimmed.

Published May 1, 1965 at 35s; 3500 copies printed; an American edition was published by the Monthly Review Press July 15, 1965 at $6.00; 1500 copies in cloth, 500 copies in paper at $3.45.

Contains: 'Two Letters of Sean O'Casey', pp. 237–40; the letters, to Ken Coates, are dated July 1 and 17, 1955.

B48   SEAN O'CASEY THE MAN I KNEW   1965

first edition
SEAN O'CASEY / The Man I Knew / by / GABRIEL FALLON / [publisher's mark] / LONDON / ROUTLEDGE & KEGAN PAUL

21.5 × 14cm.; pp. [x], 213.

Issued in brown cloth; lettered in gold on spine; white endpapers, all edges trimmed; dust-jacket in navy and white with portrait of O'Casey on cover, lettered and decorated in blue, white and olive.
Published June 10, 1965 at 30s; number of copies undisclosed; an American offset edition was published by Little, Brown and Company, Boston, on September 21, 1965 at $5.00; 5000 copies printed.

Contains: 'Letter' to Gabriel Fallon dated September 2, 1924, quoted p. 1; subsequently published in full in *The Letters of Sean O'Casey* (A46).
'Specimens of Autographed Title-pages', reproduced in facsimile, facing p. 55.
'Sean's Skill as a Caricaturist', sketch reproduced in facsimile, facing p. 87; this sketch first appeared in *Feature Magazine*, Feb 1948 (C356).
'Letter', quoted p. 155; first appeared in *Standard*, Aug 9, 1946 (C330).
'Programme Note for the World Première of the *Bishop's Bonfire*', pp. 171–2; first appeared February 28, 1955 (C433).
'Letter', pp. 177–8; first appeared in *Irish Press*, Mar 15, 1955 (C434).
'Letter', quoted pp. 178–9; first appeared in *Irish Times*, Mar 23, 1955 and in *Irish Press*, Mar 24, 1955 (C436).
'Letter', p. 180; first appeared in *Irish Press*, Apr 5, 1955 (C437).
'Letter to Ernest Blythe', dated September 1, 1964, p. 209.

Notes: Many letters to Mr Fallon are paraphrased in the work. The originals are now in the library of the University of Texas at Austin.

B49   IRISH RENAISSANCE   1966

first edition
IRISH RENAISSANCE [in red] / *A Gathering of Essays, Memoirs, and Letters* / *from The Massachusetts Review* / EDITED BY / ROBIN SKELTON & DAVID R. CLARK / MR [publisher's monogram in red] / THE DOLMEN PRESS

23.5 × 15.5cm.; pp. 167.

Issued in tan paper boards; lettered and decorated in gold and black; pale brown endpapers, all edges trimmed, top edge stained brown.

Published February 2, 1966 at 35s; 1000 copies printed by the Vermont Printing Company, Brattleboro, Vermont.

Contains: 'Sean O'Casey concerning James Joyce', pp. 128–9; three letters to Joseph Prescott dated November 1, 1949, May 10, 1954 and August 4, 1958 which first appeared in the *Massachusetts Review*, winter 1964 (C610). 'Playwright to Critic: Sean O'Casey's Letters to George Jean Nathan' by Seymour Rudin, pp. 130–8; in this essay letters to Nathan are quoted throughout; the essay first appeared in the *Massachusetts Review*, winter 1964 (C609). A conversation with O'Casey is recorded by David Krause in 'Sean O'Casey: 1880–1964', pp. 139–57; the essay first appeared in the *Massachusetts Review*, winter / spring 1965; it was reprinted in *The World of Sean O'Casey* (B53) and in *The Sting and the Twinkle* (B72).

POUSSIÈRE POURPRE [1966]

first edition
POUSSIÈRE POURPRE / de / SEAN O'CASEY / [double rule] / Texte français / de Jacqueline AUTRUSSEAU et Maurice GOLDRING / Musique de Georges Delerue / Décor et costumes de Jacques LE MARQUET / Mise en scène de Georges WILSON / [double rule]

13.5 × 10.5cm.; pp. [16].

Caption title as above. Pamphlet issued for distribution with programme for Théâtre National Populaire production of *Purple Dust*.
Published March 1966.

Contains: [Autobiographical Note], pp. [2]–[3].

PEOPLE'S THEATRE ARTS GROUP 1966

first edition
PEOPLE'S / THEATRE / ARTS / GROUP / [all above in brown] / the story of a centre / for the North East / its origins / its growth and / its current activities / [table of contents in the lower left-hand corner]

24.5 × 22.5cm.; pp. [40].

Issued in stiff paper covers; front cover lettered and decorated in gold, tan, black and white; all edges trimmed.
Published April 28, 1966 at 5s; 3000 copies printed.

Contains: Tribute by O'Casey quoted in 'what they've said', p. 12.

ABBEY THEATRE—DUBLIN 1904–1966 1966

first edition
"ireland, in proportion to her human resources, / has enriched the art of the stage and the / screen in the twentieth century more than has / any other section of the English-

speaking / world". / The Early Irish Stage / By William Smith Clark, University of Cincinnati. / Abbey Theatre—Dublin 1904–1966 [lettered in white] / [all above on blue background]

18 × 24cm.; pp. [36].

Pamphlet issued on the occasion of the dedication of the new Abbey Theatre, July 18, 1966.
Published July 18, 1966; number of copies unavailable.

Contains: Three-line telegram dated July 18, 1951 in editor's (Gabriel Fallon) message, 'A New Abbey for a New Age', p. [35].

B53   THE WORLD OF SEAN O'CASEY   1966

first edition
The World of / Sean O'Casey / edited by / SEAN McCANN / Drawings by John Cullen Murphy / [publisher's mark] / A FOUR SQUARE BOOK

18 × 11cm.; pp. 252.

Issued in paper covers, portraits of O'Casey on front and back covers, lettered and decorated in black, white, red and grey.
Published September 2, 1966 at 5s; 25,000 copies printed.

Contains: 'The Call of the Tribe' (poem), pp. 36–7.
'Thoughts of Thee' pp. 37–8; this poem had already appeared with a different fifth stanza in *Windfalls* (A16).
'The Summer Sun is Tightly Folding', p. 39; this poem had already appeared in *Songs of the Wren Humourous and Sentimental* (A6) – the version published here has four additional lines in each stanza.
'To Maire' (poem), p. 40; this poem had appeared in a revised version in *Windfalls* (A16) as 'The Garland'.
Letters from O'Casey are quoted on pp. 30, 38–9, 41–2, 69–71, 182–3, 240–50.

B54   LADY GREGORY   1966

second edition (the first to include the O'Casey letters)
ELIZABETH   COXHEAD / Lady   Gregory / A   LITERARY   PORTRAIT / SECOND EDITION / REVISED AND ENLARGED / LONDON / Secker & Warburg

21.5 × 13cm.; pp. xii, 226, [1].

Issued in maroon boards, lettered in gold; white endpapers, all edges trimmed.
Published September 5, 1966 at 35s; 2000 copies printed; in September 1969, 1018 copies were remaindered to Colin Smythe Ltd, Publishers, for sale to the public at £1.05.

Contains: Letter, quoted p. 192; the letter was written after the first edition of the work appeared in 1961.
Letter, quoted p. 210; the letter originally appeared in the *Irish Times*, Mar 6, 1942 (C268); reprinted in *Joseph Holloway's Irish Theatre 1938–1944 (B64)*.

LETTERS OF JAMES JOYCE   1966

first edition
LETTERS / OF / JAMES   JOYCE / VOLUME   III / *edited*   *by* / RICHARD ELLMANN / FABER AND FABER / 24 Russell Square / London

23.5 × 15cm.; pp. xxxi, 584.

Issued in grey cloth; spine lettered in gold; light grey endpapers, all edges trimmed, top edge stained blue.
Published December 1, 1966 at £12.12 for vols 2–3; 2000 copies printed. American edition published simultaneously by Viking at $25.00 for vols 2–3; 6000 copies printed, reprinted January 1967 (3500 copies).

Contains: 'Statement Regarding the Piracy of Ulysses', February 2, 1927, pp. 151–3; O'Casey's name appears among the 163 signatures.
'Letter to James Joyce', dated May 30, 1939, pp. 442–3; previously appeared in *James Joyce's World* by Patricia Hutchins (B32); collected in *The Letters of Sean O'Casey* (A46).

THE EASTER LILY   1967

second edition (the first with the O'Casey contribution)
THE EASTER LILY / The Story of the I.R.A. / SEAN O'CALLAGHAN / With a review by Sean O'Casey / [publisher's mark] / A FOUR SQUARE BOOK

18 × 11cm.; pp. 191.

Issued in paper covers; decorative front cover; lettering in black, white and green on front cover, on spine and on back cover; all edges trimmed.
Published February 2, 1967 at 6s; 20,000 copies printed.

Contains: 'Poor Puzzled Ireland', pp. 7–10; first appeared in *Tribune*, Feb 22, 1957 (C466) as a review of the book on its original publication by Allan Wingate (Publishers) Ltd in 1956.

LETTERS TO MACMILLAN   1967

first edition
LETTERS TO / MACMILLAN / SELECTED AND EDITED BY / SIMON NOWELL–SMITH / Our guiding principle ... is that publishers / exist to satisfy their authors. / HAROLD MACMILLAN / MACMILLAN / LONDON/ [centred dot] MELBOURNE [centred dot] TORONTO / ST MARTIN'S PRESS/ NEW YORK / 1967

22 × 14cm.; pp. 384.

Issued in maroon cloth; lettered and decorated in gold on spine; black endpapers decorated with facsimile signatures in white; all edges trimmed, top edge stained maroon:
Published November 9, 1967 at 55s; 4000 copies printed, including 1000 for St Martin's Press. Published by St Martin's, March 20, 1968 at $10.95.

Contains: Letters to Harold Macmillan dated September 25, 1936, pp. 361–3; April 28, 1938, p. [364]; September 29, 1951, pp. 365–7; the letter of April 28, 1938 is reproduced in facsimile, and had already appeared in facsimile in *Sunday Telegraph*, Oct 22, 1967 (C630); the letters of September 25, 1936 and April 28, 1938 are collected in *The Letters of Sean O'Casey* (A46).
Letter to Daniel Macmillan dated March 7, 1951, pp. 363, 365.
Letters to Thomas Mark dated April 12, 1954, pp. 367–8; April 20, 1954, p. 368.
Letter to Macmillan and Co. dated March 28, 1960, p. 369.

B58   A SELF-PORTRAIT OF THE ARTIST AS A MAN   1968

first edition
DAVID KRAUSE / A SELF–PORTRAIT / OF THE ARTIST AS A MAN / *Sean O'Casey's Letters* / THE DOLMEN PRESS

20 × 14cm.; pp. 37.

Issued in paper wrappers as no. 6 of the New Dolmen Chapbooks; lettered and decorated in grey-blue and rust; all edges trimmed.
Published April 18, 1968 at 10s 6d; 1250 copies printed.

Contains: Self-caricature by O'Casey, 'characteristically "armed" with pen and ink' (1926), reproduced on front cover.
'Letters', quoted pp. 7–27, 29–37.

Notes: Most of these extracts are from unpublished correspondence; the earliest letter is dated 1911 and the latest 1962. An extract from a letter to Lennox Robinson dated October 9, 1922 was first published in the latter's autobiography, *Curtain Up* (B11); another letter to Robinson quoted here was first printed in the *Irish Statesman*, June 9, 1928 (C109). Lady Gregory included an extract from O'Casey's letter of February 1928 in her *Journals* (B19). David Krause also includes excerpts from a letter that first appeared in the *New York Times*, Aug 11, 1935 (C165), and from a letter in the *New York Herald Tribune*, May 20, 1962 (C569); the letters were subsequently collected in *The Letters of Sean O'Casey* (A46).

B59   JOSEPH HOLLOWAY'S IRISH THEATRE VOLUME ONE   1968
       1926–1931

first edition
JOSEPH HOLLOWAY'S / IRISH THEATRE / VOLUME ONE—1926–1931 / *Edited by Robert Hogan aud* [sic] *Michael J. O'Neill* / [publisher's mark] / PROS-CENIUM PRESS / P.O. Box 561 / Dixon, California 95620

21.5 × 14cm.; pp. 88.

Issued in white paper wrappers; portrait of Holloway on front wrapper; lettered and decorated in black; all edges trimmed.
Published December 16, 1968 at $2.00; 1000 copies printed.

Contains: 'Letter', quoted p. 35; first appeared in *Irish Independent*, June 9, 1928 (C110).
'Letter', quoted p. 57; first appeared in *An Poblacht*, Jan 18, 1930 (C122); the letters of June 9, 1928 and January 18, 1930 were collected in *The Letters of Sean O'Casey* (A46).
O'Casey is quoted on pp. 14–15, 22, 24, 34–5, 50.

Notes: An earlier selection from the Holloway diaries, *Joseph Holloway's Abbey Theatre*, covering the years 1899–1926, was edited by Robert Hogan and Michael J. O'Neill and published by Southern Illinois University Press in March 1967. It included O'Casey letters which had originally appeared in the *Irish Times*, Feb 19, 1926 (C101) and in the *Irish Independent*, Feb 26, 1926 (C102). The letters were subsequently reprinted in *Blasts and Benedictions* (A44); collected in *The Letters of Sean O'Casey* (A46).

THE MOVIES MR. GRIFFITH AND ME   1969

first edition
[ornaments] / LILIAN GISH / The Movies / Mr. Griffith / and Me / *By* / *Lillian Gish* / *with Ann Pinchot* / PRENTICE-HALL, INC., ENGLEWOOD CLIFFS, N.J. / [ornaments]

23 × 15cm.; pp. xii, 388.

Issued in light tan cloth with light blue spine; spine lettered and decorated in gold; light tan endpapers, all edges trimmed.
Published February 24, 1969 at $7.95; 15,000 copies printed; reprinted April 18, 1969.

Contains: 'Letter', pp. 322–3. Inscription on Miss Gish's copy of *Within the Gates* is also quoted on p. 323. Reprinted in *Sean* by Eileen O'Casey (B68), and in *The Sting and the Twinkle* (B72). The letter is quoted in *Dorothy and Lillian Gish* by Lillian Gish (1973). The letter, written on April 8, 1935 towards the end of the New York production of *Within the Gates* (A15), is published in full in *The Letters of Sean O'Casey* (A46).

JOSEPH HOLLOWAY'S IRISH THEATRE VOLUME TWO   1969
  1932–1937

first edition
JOSEPH HOLLOWAY'S / IRISH THEATRE / VOLUME TWO—1932–1937 / *Edited by Robert Hogan aud* [sic] *Michael J. O'Neill* / [publisher's mark] / PROSCENIUM PRESS / P.O. BOX 561 / Dixon, California 95620

21.5 × 14cm.; pp. 85.

Issued in paper wrappers; portrait of Holloway on front cover; lettered and decorated in black; all edges trimmed.
Published June 16, 1969 at $2.00; 1000 copies printed.

Contains: 'Letter', quoted pp. 18–19; first appeared in *Irish Times*, Oct 11, 1932 (C128).
'Letter', quoted p. 46; first appeared in *Irish Press*, Aug 20, 1935 (C166).
'Letter', quoted p. 47; first appeared in *Irish Press*, Sep 11, 1935 (C167).
'Letter', p. 66; first appeared in *Irish Times*, Feb 23, 1937 (C186).
The letters are published in full in *The Letters of Sean O' Casey* (A46). O'Casey is quoted on pp. 19, 70.

B62 PEN AND BRUSH   1969

first edition
LOLA L. SZLADITS AND / HARVEY SIMMONDS / [the following five lines enclosed within pen and ink sketch depicting artists, writers, quill pen and artist's brush] PEN & BRUSH [in red] / The Author as Artist / AN EXHIBITION IN THE / BERG COLLECTION OF ENGLISH / AND AMERICAN LITERATURE / THE NEW YORK PUBLIC LIBRARY / Astor, Lenox and Tilden Foundations

25.5 × 20cm.; pp. 59.

Issued in paper covers; lettered and decorated in black, yellow and grey.
Published October 1, 1969 at $3.00; 2000 copies printed.

Contains: Part of page of a manuscript draft of *Pictures in the Hallway* with pen and ink portrait in margin, p. 50. The editors assume that this small sketch is a self-portrait but there is no evidence in the manuscript that this is necessarily so; O'Casey often drew characters that he was writing about and this may be one. The editors also credit the playwright with the drawing of 'St. Donat's Castle, Glamorgan. Great Hall', that is to be found in another of his notebooks in the Berg Collection. Our opinion is that this meticulous and carefully documented pencil sketch is not by O'Casey but by one of his children, probably Breon.

B63 THE PLAYS OF SEAN O'CASEY   1969

first edition
The Plays / of Sean O'Casey / *Maureen Malone* / WITH A PREFACE BY / *Harry T. Moore* / SOUTHERN ILLINOIS UNIVERSITY PRESS / *Carbondale and Edwardsville* / FEFFER & SIMONS, INC. / *London and Amsterdam*

20 × 12cm.; pp. [xiv], 169.

Issued in orange-red cloth; lettered and decorated in gold on spine; white endpapers, all edges trimmed, top edge stained red.
Published October 20, 1969 at $4.95; 2000 copies printed.

Contains: Letter to author dated January 1959, quoted p. 37. Letter to author, undated, quoted p. 132.

JOSEPH HOLLOWAY'S IRISH THEATRE VOLUME THREE 1970
1938–1944

first edition
JOSEPH HOLLOWAY'S / IRISH THEATRE / VOLUME THREE—1938–1944 / *Edited by Robert Hogan and Michael J. O'Neill* / [publisher's mark] / PROSCENIUM PRESS / P.O. Box 561 / Dixon, California 95620

21.5 × 14cm.; pp. 110.

Issued in paper wrappers; portrait of Holloway on front cover; lettered and decorated in black; all edges trimmed.
Published March 2, 1970 at $2.50; 1000 copies printed.

Contains: Letter in answer to T. C. Murray's review of *Purple Dust* in *Irish Press*, Dec 20, 1940, pp. 54–5; the letter originally appeared under the title 'O'Casey's Advice to Dramatists' in *Irish Press*, Jan 17, 1941 (C254).
Letter to *Irish Times* columnist Quidnunc, p. 71; originally appeared under the title 'Coole House' in *Irish Times*, Mar 6, 1942 (C268); part of letter quoted in *Lady Gregory* by Elizabeth Coxhead (B54).
The letters are collected in *The Letters of Sean O'Casey* (A46).

IN PRAISE OF COMEDY 1970

paperback edition (the first with the O'Casey contribution)
JAMES K. FEIBLEMAN / IN PRAISE OF / COMEDY / A Study in Its / Theory and Practice / HORIZON PRESS   NEW YORK

20.5 × 14cm.; pp. 284.

Issued in stiff paper covers; lettered and decorated in orange, black and white.
Published June 9, 1970 at $2.95; 3000 copies printed.

Contains: Quotation from O'Casey's review of the original edition on back cover; the review was published under the title 'Laughter Down the Years: the Role of Comedy' in *Sunday Times*, Aug 20, 1939 (C223).

NEW IN THE BERG COLLECTION: 1965–1969 1971

first edition
New in the Berg Collection: 1965–1969 / [dotted rule] / An Exhibition from the Henry W. and Albert A. / Berg Collection of English and American / Literature in The New York Public Library / [reproduction of dust-jacket designed by Sean O'Casey for *Sunset and Evening Star*]

27 × 11cm.; pp. [43].

Cover title; issued in brick-red paper covers, lettered and decorated in black and white. The catalogue was compiled and annotated by Lola L. Szladits. A preprint of the text appeared in the *Bulletin of the New York Public Library*, Jan 1971; published January 18, 1971 at $2.00; 2000 copies printed.

Contains: Quotations from O'Casey manuscripts in the Berg Collection, pp. [29]–[32].

B67   THE EARLY LIFE OF SEAN O'CASEY   1971

first edition

MARTIN B. MARGULIES / THE EARLY LIFE OF / SEAN O'CASEY / THE DOLMEN PRESS

22 × 14cm.; pp. 87.

Issued in brown paper boards; lettered in gold on spine; chocolate endpapers, all edges trimmed.
Published February 25, 1971 at £1.40.

Contains: Letter to Secretary G.N.R., quoted pp. 53–4; the letter, dated December 18, 1911, was published in full in *Irish Worker*, Mar 9, 1912 (C5); collected in *The Letters of Sean O'Casey* (A46).
Letter to James Shiels, quoted pp. 70–1; the letter, dated July 17, 1916, is published in full in *The Letters of Sean O'Casey* (A46).
Letters to his brother Michael, quoted p. 87; one of the letters, dated December 18, 1938, is published in full in *The Letters of Sean O'Casey* (A46).

B68   SEAN   1971

first edition

SEAN / EILEEN O'CASEY / [swelled rule] / *EDITED WITH AN INTRO-DUCTION BY* / J. C. TREWIN / MACMILLAN / GILL AND MACMILLAN

21.5 × 13.5cm.; pp. 318.

Issued in olive cloth; spine lettered and decorated in gold and green; green endpapers, all edges trimmed; dust-jacket in yellow and white with wedding photograph on front, lettered in black and green.
Published September 23, 1971 at £3.25; 6000 copies printed. An offset edition was published in the United States by Coward, McCann & Geoghegan, Inc., New York, on February 25, 1972 at $6.95; 7500 copies printed. A paper edition was published by Pan Books, London, on March 9, 1973 at 50p; 25,000 copies printed.

Contains: (letters are to Eileen O'Casey unless noted otherwise) Letter dated sometime in May 1926, p. 50; collected in *The Letters of Sean O'Casey* (A46).
Letter, undated, quoted p. 51.
Letter dated August 4, 1927, pp. 56–7.
Letter, undated, quoted p. 57.
Letter dated September 10, 1927, p. 58.
Letter to David Krause dated sometime in 1963, pp. 75–6.
Letter to George Bernard Shaw dated June 29, 1928, quoted pp. 86–7; published in full in *The Letters of Sean O'Casey* (A46).
Dedication on flyleaf of copy of *The Silver Tassie* dated September 23, 1928, p. 88.

Two letters dated September 1928, pp. 91–3.

Letter dated July 2, 1929, pp. 98–9.

Dedication and first verse of the prose poem 'Gold and Silver Will Not Do' which was subsequently published with alterations in *Windfalls* (A16), p. 99.

Letter to Lady Gregory dated October 15, 1929, quoted p. 103; published in full in *The Letters of Sean O'Casey* (A46).

Letter to a correspondent, undated, quoted p. 111.

Letter to the Tax Collector (J. R. Storey) dated July 1932, p. 118; published in full in *The Letters of Sean O'Casey* (A46).

Letter dated September 23, 1933, pp. 127–8.

Letter to C. B. Cochran dated August 7, 1933, pp. 129–30; collected in *The Letters of Sean O'Casey* (A46).

Letters dated September–November 1934, quoted pp. 136–40.

Letter of April 8, 1935 and inscription to Lillian Gish, pp. 140–41, first published in *The Movies Mr. Griffith and Me* (B60).

Letter dated 1935? quoted p. 148.

Letter to Charlotte Shaw dated October 1938, p. 162.

Letter to Barrows Dunham dated July 14, 1949, pp. 203–4.

Letter to Daniel Macmillan dated March 7, 1951, p. 211.

Letter to Harold Macmillan dated sometime in 1951, pp. 211–2.

Letter to Sam Wanamaker dated April 5, 1953, quoted p. 214.

Letter to Sam Wanamaker dated May 26, 1953, pp. 216–17.

Letter to R. A. Butler, Chancellor of the Exchequer, dated sometime in 1953, p. 218.

Comment on letter of his son Niall sometime in 1956, pp. 250–1.

Letter to Brendan Smith dated October 1957, p. 262; published in full in *A Paler Shade of Green* (B70).

Letter to *Irish Times* dated February 17, 1958 and published in the issue for March 11, 1958 (C493), quoted pp. 263–4.

Notes in response to enquiries concerning *Rose and Crown* (A30), pp. 278–80.

Last will of Sean O'Casey dated September 15, 1962.

Letter dated August 12, 1964, pp. 289–92.

Letter to Editor, *New York Times Magazine*, dated September 12, 1964 (not published in this journal), p. 293.

THE GEMS SHE WORE 1972

first edition

JAMES PLUNKETT / The / Gems She / Wore / A Book of Irish Places / HUTCHINSON OF LONDON [all above within ornamental border]

23.5 × 15.5cm.; pp. 208.

Issued in green cloth; decoration blind stamped on front cover, lettered and decorated in green and gold on spine; map of Ireland on green endpapers; all edges trimmed, top edge stained green.

Published May 15, 1972 at £2.80; 10,000 copies printed by the Print Division of Jefferson Smurfit Group, Dublin.

Contains: 'A letter from Sean O'Casey to the author', p. [43]. The letter, dated July 20, 1964, is reproduced in photocopy.

B70   A PALER SHADE OF GREEN   1972

first edition
A PALER SHADE OF / GREEN / *by* / Des Hickey and Ġus Smith / [ornament]
/ LESLIE FREWIN of LONDON

22.5 × 14.5cm.; pp. 253.

Issued in green paper-covered boards; lettered and decorated in gold on
spine.
Published July 24, 1972 at £3.30. An offset edition was published in the
United States by the Bobbs-Merrill Company, Inc., New York, in March
1973 at $7.95 under the title *Flight from the Celtic Twilight*.

Contains: 'The Drums of Father Ned: O'Casey and the Archbishop', pp. 134–51.
Seven previously unpublished letters of O'Casey are included; the letters
to Brendan Smith are dated July 19, 1957, September 9, 1957, October 11,
1957, October, 1957, December 16, 1957, January 29, 1958 and February 5,
1958; the letter dated October 1957 had been previously published in part
in *Sean* (B68).

B71   STÜCKE   1973

first edition
Sean O'Casey / Stücke / 1920–1940 / [rule] / Das Erntefest / Der Schatten eines
Rebellen / Juno und der Pfau / Der Pflug und die Sterne / Kathleen hört
zu / Nannie geht aus / Der Preispokal / Der Park / Ein Pfund abheben / Das
Ende vom Anfang / Purpurstaub / [rule] / *Herausgegeben* / *und mit einem Vorwort*
/ *von Wolfgang Schuch* / [publisher's mark] / *Henschelverlag Berlin 1973*

21.5 × 12.5cm.; pp. 599, [1].

Issued in off-white cloth; lettered and decorated in black on front cover and on
spine; white endpapers, all edges trimmed.
Published autumn 1973 at 16,50 M.

Contains: 'Das Erntefest' (The Harvest Festival), pp. [15]–62. This constitutes
the first publication of 'The Harvest Festival' which was completed by O'Casey
late in 1919, rejected by the Abbey Theatre in January 1920 and partially
revised in 1920. The translation by Konrad Zschiedrich is based on a typescript transcription of O'Casey's manuscript (E5) prepared by Ronald Ayling.

B72   THE STING AND THE TWINKLE   1974

first edition
THE / STING / AND THE / TWINKLE / Conversations with Sean O'Casey /
Edited by / E. H. MIKHAIL / and / JOHN O'RIORDAN / Macmillan

21.5 × 14cm.; pp. xii, 184.

Issued in light grey cloth; lettered and decorated in gold on spine; dark
brown endpapers, all edges trimmed, top edge stained dark brown.
Published May 30, 1974 at £4.95; 1750 copies printed; 750 extra copies
printed with the Barnes & Noble imprint, for sale in the United States at
$16.00.
Contains: 'Letter', undated, quoted p. 6.

'Letter' to Susan Brown, undated, quoted pp. 7–8.
'Letter' to Judy Goldberg, undated, quoted pp. 8–9.
'Letter' to Leslie Rees, undated, quoted p. 46; first appeared in *Meanjin Quarterly* (Melbourne), Dec 1964 (C615).
Letter to Saros Cowasjee dated July 5, 1959, quoted pp. 102–103.
'Letter' to David Phethean, undated but probably written in November 1960, pp. 114–15.

AUGUSTUS JOHN: THE YEARS OF EXPERIENCE 1975

first edition
AUGUSTUS JOHN / [swelled rule] / A BIOGRAPHY / by / MICHAEL HOLROYD / [swelled rule] / VOLUME II / The Years of Experience / '*Moral sentiment corrupts the young. Children are the first / to lose their innocence, artists the second: idiots never*'. / (Augustus John. *Chiaroscuro*, p. 279) / [printer's mark] / HEINEMANN: LONDON

23.3 × 15.3cm; pp. xiii, [v], 263.

Issued in brown cloth; spine lettered in gold; illustrated endpapers; all edges trimmed, top edge stained brown.
Published March 24, 1975 at £5.25; 17,500 copies printed, of which 7,500 were for the Book Club Associates. An American edition in one volume was published on August 21, 1975, by Holt, Rinehart and Winston at $17.95; 12,500 copies printed.

Contains: Letter dated Jan 15, 1929, quoted p. 143.

CONTINUITY AND INNOVATION IN SEAN O'CASEY'S DRAMA 1976

first edition
SALZBURG STUDIES IN ENGLISH LITERATURE / UNDER THE DIRECTION OF PROFESSOR / ERWIN A. STÜRZL / POETIC DRAMA & POETIC THEORY / EDITOR: DR. JAMES HOGG / 23 / CONTINUITY AND INNOVATION / IN / SEAN O'CASEY'S DRAMA / A CRITICAL MONOGRAPH / BY / RONALD AYLING / 1976 / INSTITUT FÜR SPRACHE / UND LITERATUR / UNIVERSITÄT SALZBURG / A-5020 SALZBURG / AUSTRIA

21 × 15cm.; pp. xi, 187.

Issued in stiff buff-coloured paper boards; front cover and spine lettered in black; all edges trimmed.
Published June 28, 1976 at $11.00; 200 copies printed.

Contains: Letter to George Jean Nathan dated December 2, 1947, quoted p. 18.
Letter to Ronald Ayling dated March 21, 1958, quoted pp. 99–100.
Letter to Harry M. Ritchie dated November 26, 1957, quoted pp. 106–7.
Letter to Herbert Coston dated October 30, 1958, quoted pp. 107–8, 109.
Letter to Ivor Brown dated June 24, 1928, quoted p. 109.
Letter to Ronald Ayling dated September 23, 1957, quoted pp. 154, 155, 168.
Letter to Douglas Jacobs dated January 30, 1955, quoted p. 180. Quotations

from material which had originally been published elsewhere but which
are here published in book form for the first time are printed on pp. 52,
119, 173–4, 180.

B75   SEAN O'CASEY AND HIS WORLD   1976
first edition
DAVID   KRAUSE / SEAN   O'CASEY / and   his   world / [publisher's   mark] /
THAMES AND HUDSON / LONDON

23.5 × 18cm.; pp. 128.

Issued in rust paper boards; front cover and spine lettered and decorated
in gold; white endpapers, all edges trimmed.
Published August 9, 1976 at £3.50; number of copies printed unavailable;
3500 copies were imported by Charles Scribner's Sons, New York, and offered
for sale on November 30, 1976 at $8.95.

Contains: Letter to George Jean Nathan dated February 8, 1944, quoted p. 80.
Letter to William Rust dated September 11, 1944, quoted p. 80.
Letter to an official of the Irish Civil Liberties Organization, undated, quoted
p. 80.
Letter to Desmond MacCarthy dated February 7, 1949, quoted p. 81.

B76   EILEEN   1976
first edition
EILEEN / EILEEN O'CASEY / [swelled rule] / *EDITED WITH AN
INTRODUCTION BY* / J. C. TREWIN / M

21.5 × 13.5cm.; pp. 224.

Issued in dark brown paper boards; spine lettered and decorated in gold;
white endpapers, all edges trimmed.
Published September 30, 1976 at £4.50; 3000 copies printed; released for sale
in the United States in February 1977 at $8.95 by St. Martin's Press.

Contains: Letter to J. P. Mitchell, Registrar, Trinity College, Dublin dated
February 4, 1961, pp. 189–90.
Previously published letters are quoted on pp. 86, 87, 94–5, 106–7, 113–14,
117, 144, 150–1, 162 and 182.

B77   ARRIVALS IN THE BERG COLLECTION   1976
first edition
Arrivals in the / ABC [in red] / Berg Collection / 1973–1975 / [all above on
off-white lozenge-shaped mounted label within double border of black
and red rules]

25.5 × 23cm.; 20 leaves.

Cover title. Issued in red, stiff paper portfolio.
Published October 1976 at $4.00 by the New York Public Library & Readex
Books; 400 copies printed.

Contains: Reproduction of pen-and-ink drawing and text by O'Casey in which
'a chorus formed by Yeats, Lady Gregory, and Lennox Robinson rejects
O'Casey's play *The Silver Tassie* for the Abbey Theatre'.

SECTION C

Contributions to Periodicals

Materials by O'Casey first published in periodicals are arranged chronologically by date of publication. As a rule, only first periodical appearances have been listed, of contributions not already printed in book form. Later first periodical publication in, say, the United States of a contribution first printed in an Irish or an English periodical (and vice versa) has normally been noted only under the first entry. All contributions to periodicals later reprinted in books are noted in both Section C and Section B. Under the heading of periodicals we include newspapers and occasional publications such as theatre programmes. Interviews are excluded.

SOUND THE LOUD TRUMPET

The Peasant and Irish Ireland, May 25, 1907
Published under the pseudonym 'An Gall Fada'. Collected in *Feathers from the Green Crow* (A40).

In the preface to *Windfalls* (A16) O'Casey wrote: 'How I enjoyed the glory that was mine when something I had written first appeared in print! It was an article criticizing the educational policy in Ireland sponsored by Mr. Augustine Birrell, and the article appeared in a paper called The Nation [*sic*] ... I remember sending the paper in which the article appeared to a Protestant pastor for whom I had a deep fondness, and from whom I expected great praise and many words of encouragement, but the comment he made was a dead silence. Venturing, some weeks later, to ask him what he thought of it, he placed a hand gently on my shoulder and shocked me, saying, "The man who wrote that article, John, is a traitor, and ought to be in jail." '

THE GAELIC LEAGUE IN DUBLIN: HOW TO MAKE IT A GREAT POWER

The Peasant and Irish Ireland, July 6, 1907
Published under the pseudonym 'An Gall Fada'. Collected in abbreviated form in *Feathers from the Green Crow*.

OUR READERS' OPINIONS : THE EMMET COMMEMORATION CONCERT (letter)

Sinn Féin, March 19, 1910
Published under the pseudonym 'An Gall Fada'. Collected in *The Letters of Sean O'Casey* (A46).

OUR READERS' OPINIONS: THE EMMET COMMEMORATION CONCERT (letter)

Sinn Féin, April 2, 1910
Signed 'S.Ua Cathasaigh, nó "An Gall Fada" '. Collected in *The Letters of Sean O'Casey*.

TO THE EDITOR THE IRISH WORKER

Irish Worker, March 9, 1912
Open letter dated February 4, 1912 signed 'J. O'Casey', including correspondence between himself and the Great Northern Railway covering the

period from December 7, 1911 to January 5, 1912; two letters from the author are dated December 7 and 18, 1911. The complete correspondence is collected in *The Letters of Sean O'Casey* (A46).

C6   THE DUBLIN FEIS AND THE PIPERS

Sinn Féin, May 11, 1912
Editorial page paraphrases letter from 'S. O. Cathasaigh, hon. secretary of the St Lorcan O'Toole Pipers' Band'.

C7   GREAT NORTHERN RAILWAY, IRELAND: SOME OF ITS WORKS AND POMPS

Irish Worker, June 8, 1912
Collected in *Feathers from the Green Crow* (A40).

C8   PÍOBAIRÍ NAOIMH LORCHÁIN UÍ TUATHAIL: THE O'TOOLE PIPERS

Irish Worker, August 10, 1912
Unsigned contribution.

C9   THE O'TOOLE PIPERS' AERIDHEACHT

Irish Worker, August 17, 1912
Unsigned contribution.

C10   THE BONNIE BUNCH OF ROSES, O ! (poem)

Irish Worker, January 11, 1913
This pro-Labour ballad should not be confused with the author's Irish nationalist poem with the same title that is to be found in *More Wren Songs* (A8) and *Feathers from the Green Crow* (A40).

C11   CHIEFS OF THE G.N.R.I.

Irish Worker, January 25, 1913
Collected in *Feathers from the Green Crow* as 'Chiefs of the G.N.R.I., I'.

'EUCHAN' AND IRELAND (letter)

CHIEFS OF THE G.N.R.

Irish Worker, February 8, 1913
Both reprinted in *Feathers from the Green Crow*, the latter as 'Chiefs of the G.N.R.I., II'. The letter is also collected in *The Letters of Sean O'Casey* (A46).

ST LAURENCE O'TOOLE'S PIPERS' CLUB

Irish Worker, February 8, 1913
Notes signed S.O'C.

CHIEFS OF THE G.N.R.I.

Irish Worker, February 15, 1913
Collected in *Feathers from the Green Crow* (A40) as 'Chiefs of the G.N.R.I., III'.

THE PERIL OF THE STREETS

Irish Worker, February 15, 1913
Translation of an article in Irish by the Rev. P. Dinneen, originally printed in *The Leader*, February 1, 1913; the translation is signed 'S. O'Catasaig'.

'EUCHAN' AND IRELAND: A CHALLENGE TO A VERBAL
   COMBAT (letter)

Irish Worker, February 22, 1913
Collected in *Feathers from the Green Crow* (A40) and in *The Letters of Sean O'Casey* (A46).

GUTH AR AN NGADRE [*recte GUTH AR AN NGAOITH*]

Irish Freedom, March 1913
Collected in *Feathers from the Green Crow*. The title, misprinted in the journal, means A Voice on the Wind.

SOME SLAVES OF THE G.N.R.I. AND OTHERS

Irish Worker, March 1, 1913
Collected in *Feathers from the Green Crow*.

C20   'EUCHAN' AND A CRITIC (letter)

>   *Irish Worker*, March 8, 1913
>   Collected in *Feathers from the Green Crow* and in *The Letters of Sean O'Casey* (A46).

C21   CONSUMPTION AND A LIVING WAGE

>   *Irish Worker*, March 15, 1913
>   Translation of an article in Irish by the Rev. P. Dinneen, originally printed in *The Leader*, Mar 1, 1913.

C22   DECLENDA EST LARKINISM !

>   *Irish Worker*, April 19, 1913
>   Signed 'Craob nan Dealg' [*sic*], a misprint for Craobh na nDealg. Collected in *Feathers from the Green Crow* (A40).

C23   FAITHFUL FOREVER (poem)

>   *Irish Worker*, April 26, 1913
>   Signed 'Craobh na nDealg'. Collected in *Feathers from the Green Crow*.

C24   'IRISH FREEDOM' AND THE 'IRISH NATION'

>   *Irish Worker*, May 10, 1913
>   Signed 'Craobh na nDealg'. Collected in *Feathers from the Green Crow*.

C25   THE WOLFE TONE MEMORIAL COMMITTEE
C26   THE O'TOOLE PIPERS

>   *Irish Worker*, May 24, 1913
>   Both unsigned notes.

C27   A GREAT ENTERTAINMENT AND FRESH AIR FOR THE WORKERS

>   *Irish Worker*, May 31, 1913
>   Unsigned note.

THE IRISH FETE IN JONES ROAD

Irish Worker, June 7, 1913
Contribution signed 'Craobh na nDealg'. Reprinted in *The Letters of Sean O'Casey*
(A46).

THE BATTLE OF THE FORD

Irish Worker, June 14, 1913
Unsigned contribution.

TONE'S GRAVE

Irish Worker, June 21, 1913
Signed 'Craobh na nDealg'. Collected in *Feathers from the Green Crow* (A40).

THE WOLFE TONE MEMORIAL COMMITTEE

Irish Worker, July 5, 1913
Unsigned contribution.

THE RECENT TRAGEDY ON THE G.N.R.I.

Irish Worker, July 12, 1913

WOLFE TONE COMMITTEE

Irish Worker, July 19, 1913
Unsigned contribution reprinted in *The Letters of Sean O'Casey* (A46).

THE WOLFE TONE MEMORIAL COMMITTEE

Irish Worker, August 2, 1913
Unsigned contribution.

C35   THE GATHERING

> *Irish Worker*, September 27, 1913
> Signed 'Craobh na nDealg'. Collected in *Feathers from the Green Crow* (A40);
> reprinted in *1913 Jim Larkin and the Dublin Lock-out*, ed. Donal Nevin (1964).

C36   CORRESPONDENCE. CUMANN TOMANA NAOMH
       LORCHAIN UI THUATHAIL

> *Irish Worker*, October 18, 1913
> Unsigned contribution.

C37   STRIKING FOR LIBERTY: 'SAY, ARE YE FRIENDS TO
       FREEDOM?'

> *Irish Worker*, October 18, 1913
> Collected in *Feathers from the Green Crow* (A40); reprinted in *1913 Jim Larkin
> and the Dublin Lock-out*, ed. Donal Nevin (1964).

C38   ECCE NUNC

> *Irish Worker*, November 15, 1913
> Signed 'Craobh na nDeal' [*sic*]. Collected in *Feathers from the Green Crow*.

C39   RELIEF FUND COMMITTEE (letter)

C40   WOMEN AND CHILDREN'S RELIEF FUND: THE WOMEN
       AND CHILDREN FIRST!

> *Irish Worker*, November 29, 1913
> The letter is signed by Patrick Lennon and Sean O Cathasaigh, honorary
> secretaries of the Women and Children (of Locked-Out Workers) Relief Fund;
> it is collected in *Feathers from the Green Crow* and in *The Letters of Sean O'Casey*
> (A46), where the date of publication is given as November 26 as well as
> being (as it was) the date on which the letter was written.

C41   WOMEN AND CHILDREN (OF LOCKED-OUT WORKERS)
       RELIEF FUND

> *Irish Worker*, December 13, 1913
> Letter signed by Lennon and O Cathasaigh.

WOMEN AND CHILDREN (OF LOCKED-OUT WORKERS) RELIEF FUND

Irish Worker, December 20, 1913
Letter signed by Lennon and O Cathasaigh.

DOWZARD : THE HECTOR OF THE QUAYS

Irish Worker, December 20, 1913
The subject of this article reappears as a character with the same name in the play *Red Roses for Me* (A23).

WOMEN AND CHILDREN (OF LOCKED-OUT WORKERS) RELIEF FUND

Irish Worker, January 3, 1914
Letter signed by Lennon and O Cathasaigh.

WOMEN AND CHILDREN (OF LOCKED-OUT WORKERS) RELIEF FUND

Irish Worker, January 10, 1914
Letter signed by Lennon and O Cathasaigh, collected in *The Letters of Sean O'Casey* (A46).

WOMEN AND CHILDREN (OF LOCKED-OUT WORKERS) RELIEF FUND

Irish Worker, January 24, 1914
Letter signed by Lennon and O Cathasaigh.

AN OPEN LETTER TO WORKERS IN THE VOLUNTEERS

Irish Worker, Janaury 24, 1914
Collected in *Feathers from the Green Crow* (A40) and in *The Letters of Sean O'Casey* (A46). .

C48   VOLUNTEERS AND WORKERS (letter)

Irish Worker, February 21, 1914
Collected in *Feathers from the Green Crow* and in *The Letters of Sean O'Casey*.

C49   IRISH WORKERS AND IRISH VOLUNTEERS (letter)
C50   THE SOUL OF DAVIS

Irish Worker, March 7, 1914
Both contributions collected in *Feathers from the Green Crow*; the letter is collected in *The Letters of Sean O'Casey*.

C51   CITIZEN ARMY

Irish Worker, March 28, 1914
Unsigned article almost certainly written by O'Casey (at this time newly elected honorary secretary of the Irish Citizen Army), quoting the principle clauses of the army's new constitution drawn up by him. This constitution was reprinted in his Appendix to *The Story of the Irish Citizen Army* (A9) and in *The Letters of Sean O'Casey*.

C52   BY THE CAMP FIRE

Irish Worker, April 4, 1914
Unsigned Irish Citizen Army notes almost certainly written by O'Casey, including a manifesto 'To the People of Ireland' which is undoubtedly his work. The manifesto was reprinted in the Appendix to *The Story of the Irish Citizen Army* and in *The Letters of Sean O'Casey*.

C53   BY THE CAMP FIRE

Irish Worker, April 11, 1914
Irish Citizen Army notes signed S.O'C.

C54   THE IRISH CITIZEN ARMY : SPECIAL PARADE
C55   WORKERS' RALLY IN BRAY

Irish Worker, April 18, 1914
The first of these contributions is unsigned; the second is signed S.O'C.

BY THE CAMP FIRE : CITIZEN ARMY NOTES

Irish Worker, April 25, 1914
Unsigned contribution.

BY THE CAMP FIRE. SPLENDID MEETING IN FINGLAS.
COMPANY OF THE IRISH CITIZEN ARMY FORMED

Irish Worker, May 2, 1914
Contribution signed S.O'C.

RIVAL ARMIES : CHALLENGE TO NATIONALIST VOLUNTEERS

Irish Times, May 4, 1914
Unsigned statement, drafted by O'Casey and issued by Irish Citizen Army
Council. An identical letter, signed 'S. O Cathasaigh, Hon. Sec. Irish Citizen
Army', was printed in *Dublin Evening Mail*, May 6, 1914 under the title 'The
"Citizen" Army and Nationalist Volunteers'.

RIGHT ABOUT TURN : WAGE SLAVES IN THE VOLUNTEERS

BY THE CAMP FIRE : LABOUR CHALLENGE TO THE IRISH
VOLUNTEERS

Irish Worker, May 9, 1914
The first contribution is signed S. O'Cathasaigh; 'By the Camp Fire' is signed
S. O'C. and reprinted in *The Letters of Sean O'Casey* (A46).

BY THE CAMP FIRE

Irish Worker, May 16, 1914
Unsigned notes.

SUNDAY, MAY 24th, IN CROYDON PARK

Irish Worker, May 23, 1914
Unsigned notes.

C63   BY THE CAMP FIRE

Irish Worker, May 30, 1914
Unsigned contribution.

C64   THE CITIZEN ARMY AND NATIONAL VOLUNTEERS (letter)

Irish Worker, June 13, 1914
Contribution signed 'Hon. Sec. Irish Citizen Army'; collected in *The Letters of Sean O'Casey* (A46).

C65   BY THE CAMP FIRE

Irish Worker, June 20, 1914
Unsigned notes.

C66   A DAY IN BODENSTOWN

Irish Worker, June 27, 1914
Collected in *Feathers from the Green Crow* (A40).

C67   RECRUITING! (poem)

Workers' Republic, January 8, 1916
Signed 'An Gall Fadd' [*sic*], a misprint for An Gall Fada.

C68   THE GRAND OUL' DAME BRITANNIA (poem)

Workers' Republic, January 15, 1916
Signed 'An Gall Fadd' [*sic*]. Also printed separately as a broadsheet ballad (A1). Reprinted in *The Kiltartan History Book* (1926 and 1971 editions). Collected in *Windfalls* (A16) and in *Feathers from the Green Crow* (A40). A phonograph recording of the ballad was made by Tommy Makem and the Clancy Brothers for the C.B.S. Legacy Collection, *The Irish Uprising: 1916–1922*.

IRISH PROTESTANTS AND REAL HOME RULE

Irish Opinion, July 1, 1916
This article, and the following two (C70 and C71), are signed 'S.O'C.' and
are attributed to Sean O'Casey in *The Letters of Sean O'Casey* (A46), though
they are not reprinted in that volume. The present compilers doubt O'Casey's
authorship of all three essays. There is no stylistic evidence within them
and a good deal in the content of each to dispute the attribution.

CORK UNIVERSITY AND SOCIALISM

Irish Opinion, July 8, 1916
See note to C69.

EXPERIMENTS IN COMMUNISM

Irish Opinion, January 13, 1917
See note to C69.

LABOUR AND SINN FEIN (letter)

Dublin Saturday Post, September 22, 1917
Collected in *The Letters of Sean O'Casey* (A46).

THOMAS ASHE: REPUBLICAN AND INTERNATIONALIST

Dublin Saturday Post, October 6, 1917
Obituary tribute signed S. O. Cathasaigh; reprinted in *The Letters of Sean
O'Casey*.

THOMAS ASHE

Bottom Dog (Dublin), November 3, 1917
This poem of two stanzas, each of five lines, is not to be confused with
the poem of the same title that had earlier been issued as a broadside of
six stanzas (A3). Signed Sean O'Cathasaigh.

C75 FOOD AND WAGES

Dublin Saturday Post, November 17, 1917

C76 ROOM FOR THE TEACHERS

Irish Opinion, January 12, 1918
Collected in *Feathers from the Green Crow* (A40), where the date of first publication is wrongly given as June 12, 1918. Whereas three earlier articles in *Irish Opinion* were signed 'S. O'C.' (C69, C70, C71) and O'Casey's authorship seems extremely doubtful, there is no disputing the present article, signed 'Sean O'Cathasaigh'.

C77 AS I WAIT IN THE BOREEN FOR MAGGIE (poem)

Irish Opinion, January 12, 1918
Collected in *Songs of the Wren: First Series* (A5) and in *Feathers from the Green Crow* (A40).

C78 IRELAND'S FUTURE

Dublin Saturday Post, January 19, 1918

C79 CASE OF PATRICK HIGGINS (letter)

Evening Telegraph (Dublin), February 11, 1918
Collected in *The Letters of Sean O'Casey* (A46).

C80 MR P. T. DALY AND RUMOURS: RELATIONS WITH TOM CLARKE AND SEAN MACDERMOTT (letter)

Evening Telegraph, March 7, 1918
Reprinted in *Dublin Saturday Post*, Mar 16, 1918 under the author's title 'P. T. Daly and the Hibernian Nights Entertainments'. Collected in *The Letters of Sean O'Casey*.

C81 DOWN WITH THE GAEDHILGE!

Irish Opinion, March 9, 1918
Collected in *Feathers from the Green Crow* (A40).

MRS T. CLARKE, P. T. DALY, AND SEAN O'CATHASAIGH (letter)

Evening Telegraph, March 14, 1918
Letter dated March 13; a slightly expanded version of this letter, dated March 17, 1918, was printed under the same title in *Dublin Saturday Post*, Mar 23, 1918. The text of the letter in the *Evening Telegraph* is reprinted in *The Letters of Sean O'Casey* (A46).

THE GAELIC MOVEMENT TODAY

Irish Opinion, March 23, 1918
Collected in *Feathers from the Green Crow* (A40).

JIM LARKIN AND HIS WORK

The Gael, October 31, 1921
This article is attributed to R. M. Fox, who later wrote of it *(Irish Times*, Dec 1, 1964): 'I had almost forgotten about this when I saw it announced on the poster of *The Gael*, a Dublin journal. Though my article appeared it was about twice as long as I had written it. Delia [Larkin] explained that she had handed it over to Sean O'Casey who said he might get it published. He did so and left my name to it, though he filled it out with attacks on . . . groups about which I knew nothing.'

FOR CHRISTMAS GREETINGS TO JIM LARKIN (letter)

The Gael, October 31, 1921
Reprinted in the *Worker's Republic*, Nov 12 and 19, 1921.

LITIR CUMANN SHEMMAIS UI LORCAIN (THE JIM LARKIN CORRESPONDENCE COMMITTEE)

The Gael, November 7, 1921
Unsigned letter. Also issued separately in mimeographed form (B3); reprinted in *The Letters of Sean O'Casey* (A46).

THE SEAMLESS COAT OF KATHLEEN: A PARABLE OF THE ARD FHEIS

Poblacht Na h-Eireann, March 29, 1922
Collected in *Feathers from the Green Crow* (A40).

C88   THE CORNCRAKE

The Gael, June 12 and June 19, 1922
Short story, in two parts, translated from the Irish; collected in *Feathers from the Green Crow* (A40).

C89   LIFE AND LITERATURE

Irish Statesman, December 22, 1923
Collected in *Feathers from the Green Crow*.

* * *   THE GAELICISATION OF IRISH EDUCATION was a letter signed 'Sean O'Cathasaigh' and printed in the *Irish Statesman* for July 5, 1924. It is included in *The Letters of Sean O'Casey* (A46) but the playwright denied writing it, in conversation with one of the compilers of this bibliography, and it bears no marks of his style.

C90   GULLS AND BOBBIN TESTERS

Irish Statesman, September 6, 1924
Short story collected in *Feathers from the Green Crow* (A40).

C91   IRISH IN THE SCHOOLS

Irish Statesman, November 29, 1924
Collected in *Feathers from the Green Crow*.

C92   [LETTER]

Svenska Dagsbladet (Stockholm), December 19, 1924
An anonymous translation of a written contribution to a symposium of dramatis

C93   [O'CASEY AND THE IRISH LANGUAGE]

The Leader, December 20, 1924
Collected in *The Letters of Sean O'Casey* (A46).

THE INNOCENTS AT HOME (letter)

Irish Statesman, January 10, 1925
Collected in *Feathers from the Green Crow* (A40) and in *The Letters of Sean O'Casey*.

BARR BUADH AND PICCOLO (letter)

Irish Statesman, February 7, 1925
Collected in *Feathers from the Green Crow* and in *The Letters of Sean O'Casey*.

MOLLSER

Irish Statesman, April 25, 1925
Short story reprinted in a slightly revised form in *Life and Letters*, Dec 1933 (C136) as 'A Fall in a Gentle Wind'; collected in *Windfalls* (A16) and in *The Green Crow* (A34).

THE BLINDMAN PRIZE (letter)

Irish Statesman, July 4, 1925

A PLAYWRIGHT FROM THE SLUMS (letter)

The Star (London), November 11, 1925

LETTER FROM O'CASEY

New York Times, December 27, 1925
Letter dated December 8, 1925; reprinted in part in 'Nannie's Night Out' by Ronald Ayling, *Modern Drama*, Sep 1962. Collected in *The Letters of Sean O'Casey* (A46).

ST PATRICK'S DAY IN LONDON

Irish Times, February 12, 1926
A paraphrase of a letter to the editor.

C101   THE PLOUGH AND THE STARS: A REPLY TO CRITICS (letter)

Irish Times, February 19, 1926
A longer version of this letter was printed in the *Irish Independent* for February 20, 1926 under the title 'The Plough and the Stars: Letter from the Author'. Reprinted in *Blasts and Benedictions* (A44) and in *Joseph Holloway's Abbey Theatre*, ed. R. Hogan and M. J. O'Neill (1967); quoted in *The World of Sean O'Casey* (B53). Collected in *The Letters of Sean O'Casey* (A46).

C102   Mr O'CASEY'S PLAY: AUTHOR'S REJOINDER (letter)

Irish Independent, February 26, 1926
Collected in *Blasts and Benedictions* as 'Nationalism and *The Plough and the Stars*'; reprinted in *Joseph Holloway's Abbey Theatre*, ed. R. Hogan and M. J. O'Neill (1967); quoted in *The World of Sean O'Casey*. Collected in *The Letters of Sean O'Casey*.

C103   O'CASEY AND "THE VOICE"

Voice of Labour (Dublin), February 27, 1926
Collected in *The Letters of Sean O'Casey*.

C104   MR SEAN O'CASEY AND ST. PATRICK'S NIGHT (letter)

An Phoblacht (Dublin), April 2, 1926
Collected in *The Letters of Sean O'Casey*.

C105   LONDON PASSES BY: IMPRESSIONS OF FIVE WEEKS

Daily News (London), May 24, 1926
Collected in *Blasts and Benedictions* (A44) as 'London Passes By'.

C106   PLAYWRIGHT'S PLEA FOR MINERS' CHILDREN

Liverpool Post and Mercury, June 2, 1926
Extract from a letter to the Women's Committee for the Relief of Miners' Wives and Children.

MR O'CASEY'S NEW PLAY

Observer, June 3, 1928
Extracts from letters between the playwright, W. B. Yeats and Lennox
Robinson on the subject of *The Silver Tassie*. Reprinted in the *Irish Times*,
June 4, 1928 and, in part, in the *Irish Independent*, June 5, 1928. The full
text of O'Casey's letter to W. B. Yeats was printed in *Blasts and Benedictions*
(A44) as 'W. B. Yeats and *The Silver Tassie*'. The full text of each letter
is published in *The Letters of Sean O'Casey* (A46).

ABBEY PLAY CONTROVERSY: STATEMENT BY MR O'CASEY

Irish Times, June 5, 1928
A fuller account of the correspondence than that printed in the *Observer*
on June 3, 1928 and in the *Irish Times* on June 4, 1928. Collected in full
in *The Letters of Sean O'Casey*.

THE ABBEY DIRECTORS AND MR SEAN O'CASEY

Irish Statesman, June 9, 1928
A further and more comprehensive selection of letters. Reprinted in part
in the *Literary Digest* (New York), Aug 4, 1928 and as an appendix to *The
Experiments of Sean O'Casey* (B39); also reprinted in *Sunday Independent*
(Dublin), June 10, 1928, with an additional quotation from a letter by
O'Casey. The full correspondence is collected in *The Letters of Sean O'Casey*.

O'CASEY AND THE BIG FOUR (letter)

Irish Times and *Irish Independent*, June 9, 1928
Collected in *The Letters of Sean O'Casey*.

PLOUGHING THE STAR (letter)

Manchester Guardian, June 12, 1928
Collected in *The Letters of Sean O'Casey*.

[The entry originally attributed to O'Casey here is, at a late stage in publication, now found not to have been written by him. It is, however, too late
to alter the sequence of numbers in Section C.]

C113 MR SEAN O'CASEY'S 'LAST WORD': CROSSING THE BRIDGE (letter)

Irish Times and *Irish Independent*, June 21, 1928
The author's title, used as a sub-title in the *Irish Times*, was 'Tying Things Together'. Collected in *The Letters of Sean O'Casey* (A46).

C114 O'CASEY AND THE ABBEY THEATRE (letter)

The Nation, June 23, 1928
Collected in *The Letters of Sean O'Casey*.

C115 SIR BARRY JACKSON (letter)

Observer, June 24, 1928
Collected in *The Letters of Sean O'Casey*.

C116 Y.O. AND THE SILVER TASSIE (letter)

Irish Statesman, August 4, 1928
Y.O. was one of the pseudonyms of George Russell (A.E.), editor of the *Irish Statesman*. Collected in *The Letters of Sean O'Casey*.

C117 THE PLAYS OF SEAN O'CASEY : A REPLY

Nineteenth Century, September 1928
Collected in *Blasts and Benedictions* (A44) as 'The Silver Tassie' and in *The Letters of Sean O'Casey* under the original title.

C118 [LETTER]

Saturday Review, September 22, 1928
Extract from a letter to Ivor Brown quoted in his article 'Roscius Unbound'.

C119 [PORGY]

The Stage, May 9, 1929
Review of stage production printed in 'Chit Chat' gossip column.

CONTRADICTIONS (letter)

Irish Statesman, November 30, 1929
Collected in *The Letters of Sean O'Casey* (A46).

CONTRADICTIONS (letter)

Irish Statesman, December 14, 1929
Collected in *The Letters of Sean O'Casey*.

APOSTLE OF ART (letter)

An Poblacht, January 18, 1930
A continuation of the controversy printed in the *Irish Statesman* under the title 'Contradictions' in November and December 1929. Extracts reprinted in *Joseph Holloway's Irish Theatre, 1, 1926–1931* (B59). Collected in *The Letters of Sean O'Casey*.

MR O'CASEY EXCEPTS (letter)

New York Times, March 20, 1930
Collected in *The Letters of Sean O'Casey*.

[LETTER]

The Star (Dublin), March 29, 1930
Collected in *The Letters of Sean O'Casey*.

[LETTER]

International Forum (Berlin), February 1931

LETTER FROM SEAN O'CASEY

Irish Worker, September 26, 1931
A fuller version of this letter is collected in *The Letters of Sean O'Casey* (A46).

BRITAIN WITH HER BACK TO THE SCREEN (letter)

Listener, July 27, 1932

C128   THE ACADEMY OF LETTERS (letter)

Irish Times, October 11, 1932
Reprinted in part in *Joseph Holloway's Irish Theatre, 2, 1932–1937* (B61). A fuller version is collected in *The Letters of Sean O'Casey* (A46).

C129   LAUREL LEAVES AND SILVER TRUMPETS

American Spectator, December 1932

C130   DRAMATIS PERSONAE IBSENISENSIS

American Spectator, July 1933
Reprinted in *The American Spectator Yearbook* (B6) and collected in *Blasts and Benedictions* (A44).

C131   HORACE PLUNKETT'S THOUSAND YEAR PLAN

Time and Tide, July 29, 1933
Review of *England and Sir Horace Plunkett* by Rupert Metcalf.

C132   WHY NOT A CHURCH FOR SHAKESPEARE?

The Era, August 16, 1933

C133   O'CASEY'S HATRED OF THE MIDDLE CLASS: A REPLY TO PAUL
       BANKS

New English Weekly, September 14, 1933

C134   O'CASEY AND THE MIDDLE CLASS (letter)

New English Weekly, October 12, 1933

C135   NONINTRUSION OF OFFICERS IN 'THE SILVER TASSIE'

Festival Theatre (Cambridge) New Lease Programme, November 13, 1933

A FALL IN A GENTLE WIND

Life and Letters, December 1933
Slightly revised version of the short story, 'Mollser', originally printed in the *Irish Statesman* (C96). Collected in *Windfalls* (A16) and in *The Green Crow* (A34).

TOREADOR

Time and Tide, December 2, 1933
Short story collected in *Blasts and Benedictions* (A44).

MR ST. JOHN ERVINE (letter)

Time and Tide, December 16, 1933
Collected in *The Letters of Sean O'Casey* (A46).

PICKING PLAYS FOR POSTERITY: WHAT WILL SURVIVE IN 1984?

The Era, January 3, 1934
Brief contribution to a symposium.

NOTES ON THE WAY

Time and Tide, February 3, 1934

NOTES ON THE WAY

Time and Tide, February 10, 1934

SEAN O'CASEY AND GORDON BECKLES AT LOGGERHEADS (letter)

Daily Express, February 12, 1934
Collected in *The Letters of Sean O'Casey* (A46).

C143   NOTES ON THE WAY

C144   STAGE AND SCREEN (letter)

Time and Tide, February 17, 1934
The letter is collected in *The Letters of Sean O'Casey* (A46).

C145   [WITHIN THE GATES]

Sunday Times, February 18, 1934
Extracts from a letter which was subsequently expanded into the article 'Cutting an Agate' printed in *The Flying Wasp* (A18). The full text of the letter to the *Sunday Times* is printed in *The Letters of Sean O'Casey* under O'Casey's own title 'The Shaping of an Agate'.

C146   NOTES ON THE WAY

Time and Tide, February 24, 1934

C147   STAGE AND SCREEN (letter)

Time and Tide, March 3, 1934
Collected in *The Letters of Sean O'Casey* (A46).

C148   G.B.S. SPEAKS OUT OF THE WHIRLWIND

Listener (Supplement), March 7, 1934
Review of *Three Plays: Too True to be Good, A Village Wooing, and On the Rocks* by G. Bernard Shaw. Collected in *Blasts and Benedictions* (A44).

C149   WITHIN THE GATES (letter)

Motley: Journal of the Gate Theatre, May 1934

C150   DUM VIVIMUS VIVAMUS

Time and Tide, May 5, 1934
Short story collected in *Blasts and Benedictions* (A44).

WISDOM AND LIFE (poem)

Time and Tide, June 23, 1934
Collected in *Windfalls* (A16).

A PROTESTANT KID THINKS OF THE REFORMATION

American Spectator, July 1934
Printed in a considerably expanded version in *I Knock at the Door* (A19).

SHE WILL GIVE ME REST

Time and Tide, July 7, 1934
Poem collected in *Windfalls* (A16).

A MINER'S DREAM OF HOME

New Statesman and Nation, July 28, 1934
Review of *A Collier's Friday Night* by D. H. Lawrence. Collected in *Blasts and Benedictions* (A44).

FROM WITHIN THE GATES

New York Times, October 21, 1934
Collected in *Blasts and Benedictions* (A44).

WHY I DON'T WEAR EVENING DRESS

American Spectator, November 1934

AUTHOR INTERPRETS 'WITHIN THE GATES'

Daily Princetonian, January 10, 1935

THE THING THAT COUNTS

New Statesman and Nation, February 9, 1935
Review of *Seven Plays* by Ernst Toller and *Love on the Dole* by R. Gow and W. Greenwood. Reprinted in *The Letters of Sean O'Casey* (A46).

C159   NOTES ON THE WAY

Time and Tide, April 13, 1935
Reprinted in *The Letters of Sean O'Casey* (A46).

C160   LOVE ON THE DOLE (letter)

Time and Tide, May 4, 1935
Collected in *The Letters of Sean O'Casey*.

C161   LOVE ON THE DOLE (letter)

Time and Tide, May 11, 1935
Collected in *The Letters of Sean O'Casey*.

C162   NURSING-HOME SNOBBERY (letter)

Time and Tide, July 6, 1935
Part of the chapter 'Childermess' in *Sunset and Evening Star* (A31) was based on this letter, which is collected in *The Letters of Sean O'Casey* under the title 'A Letter of Thanks'.

C163   THE PUBLIC DEATH OF SHAKESPEARE

Time and Tide, July 13, 1935
Reprinted in *Irish Digest*, July 1939. Collected in *The Flying Wasp* (A18) and in *The Green Crow* (A34).

C164   THREE CHEERS FOR NOAH

Time and Tide, August 10, 1935
Collected in *The Flying Wasp*.

C165   MR O'CASEY DISSENTS (letter)

New York Times, August 11, 1935
Reprinted in *The Experiments of Sean O'Casey* (B39). Collected in *The Letters of Sean O'Casey* (A46).

THE SILVER TASSIE (letter)

Irish Press, August 20, 1935
Reprinted in part in *Joseph Holloway's Irish Theatre, 2, 1932–1937* (B61).
Collected in full in *The Letters of Sean O'Casey* (A46).

THE SILVER TASSIE (letter)

Irish Times, September 11, 1935
A shortened version, with the title 'Mr O'Casey and the Abbey Theatre: "Defensive Words" on *The Silver Tassie*', was printed in the *Irish Press* on the same date. Reprinted in part in *Joseph Holloway's Irish Theatre, 2, 1932–1937* (B61). Collected in full in *The Letters of Sean O'Casey*.

NATIONAL THEATRE BUNKUM I

Time and Tide, October 12, 1935
Collected in *The Flying Wasp* (A18) and in *The Green Crow* (A34).

NATIONAL THEATRE BUNKUM II

Time and Tide, November 9, 1935
Collected in *The Flying Wasp* and in *The Green Crow*.

NATIONAL THEATRE BUNKUM III: A FEW BOOS

Time and Tide, December 7, 1935

STORM OVER ASIA (letter)

Time and Tide, December 14, 1935
Collected in *The Letters of Sean O'Casey* (A46).

HIS FATHER'S DUBLIN FUNERAL

English: Magazine of the English Association, vol. 1, no. 1, 1936
Expanded version printed in *I Knock at the Door* (A19) as 'His Father's Wake'.

C173   COWARD CODOLOGY

Time and Tide, January 11, 1936
Collected in an expanded version in *The Flying Wasp* (A18) and in *The Green Crow* (A34). A second article on Noel Coward, 'Worms in a Winecup', was refused publication in *Time and Tide* at this time; it was eventually included in *The Flying Wasp* as 'Coward Codology: II, Design for Living'.

C174   LET THE WHEEL TURN

Time and Tide, February 1, 1936
Collected in *The Flying Wasp*.

C175   AGATE, O'CASEY, AND COWARD (letter)

Sunday Times, March 1, 1936
Reprinted as the opening to 'Sainte-Beuve, Patron of Poor Playwriters, Pray for Us!' in *The Flying Wasp*. The full text of the letter is collected in *The Letters of Sean O'Casey* (A46).

C176   MURDER IN THE CATHEDRAL (letter)

Irish Press, March 3, 1936
Collected in *The Letters of Sean O'Casey*.

C177   SHAKESPEARE LIVES IN LONDON LADS

Time and Tide, April 18, 1936
Collected in *The Flying Wasp* (A18) and in *The Green Crow* (A34).

C178   PERSONAL VIEW

Manchester Evening News, April 24, 1936

C179   SAINTE BEUVE, PATRON OF POOR PLAYWRITERS, PRAY FOR US!

Time and Tide, May 9, 1936
Collected in *The Flying Wasp* (A18).

WORSE THAN MUSTARD GAS (letter)

Time and Tide, May 23, 1936
Collected in *The Letters of Sean O'Casey* (A46).

RED FLAG OR WHITE (letter)

Time and Tide, June 6, 1936
Collected in *The Letters of Sean O'Casey*.

HAIL, COLUMBIA !

Time and Tide, August 1, 1936
Collected in *The Flying Wasp* (A18).

PONTIFFS OF THE THEATRE
[SELF PORTRAIT]

Fortnightly Review, October 1936
'Pontiffs of the Theatre' was collected in *The Flying Wasp* as 'Critici Infallibili-bombast' and reprinted in part in *The Green Crow* (A34) in 'Critica Silentio Luna'; the autobiographical sketch is included in 'Our Contributors' column.

MURDHER IN THE THEATRE

Time and Tide, October 10, 1936
Collected in *The Flying Wasp* and in *The Green Crow*.

THE END OF THE BEGINNING (letter)

Irish Times, February 23, 1937
Reprinted in *Joseph Holloway's Irish Theatre, 2, 1932–1937* (B61). Collected in *The Letters of Sean O'Casey* (A46).

[MACBETH]

Sloane School (London) Programme, March 18, 1937
Brief programme note for production of *Macbeth*, staged according to O'Casey's ideas. Quoted in *The Times*, Mar 19, 1937 and in *Shakespeare and the Young Actor* (B29).

C188   MR SEAN O'CASEY REPLIES TO MR AGATE (letter)

Sunday Times, March 28, 1937

C189   MORTALS AND MEN

Listener, April 7, 1937
Review of *Palace Scenes* by Laurence Housman, *These Mortals* by H. M.
Harwood, *Last Plays of Maxim Gorki*, and of *The Cathedral* by Hugh Walpole.

C190   MY REJOINDER TO MR AGATE (letter)

John O'London's Weekly, April 9, 1937
Collected in *The Letters of Sean O'Casey* (A46).

C191   BUZZ, BUZZ (letter)

Country Life, April 10, 1937
Collected in *The Letters of Sean O'Casey*.

C192   THE DREAM SCHOOL: A STORY

Yale Review, June 1937
Collected in a slightly expanded version in *I Knock at the Door* (A19) as
'The Dream School'.

C193   SIGMA'S NOTES ON THE WAY (letter)

Time and Tide, March 5, 1938
Collected in *The Letters of Sean O'Casey* (A46).

C194   SIGMA'S NOTES ON THE WAY (letter)

Time and Tide, March 19, 1938
Collected in *The Letters of Sean O'Casey*.

C195   THE SWORD OF THE SOVIET

Daily Worker, March 25, 1938

SEAN O'CASEY DEFENDS 'THE SWORD OF THE SOVIET' (letter)

Forward (Glasgow), April 16, 1938
Collected in *The Letters of Sean O'Casey* (A46).

SEAN O'CASEY SAYS (letter)

Daily Worker, April 27, 1938

SWORD OF THE SOVIET (letter)

Forward, April 30, 1938
Collected in *The Letters of Sean O'Casey* (A46).

MAY DAY GREETINGS

Left Review, May 1938

THE RUSSIAN TRIALS (letter)

Time and Tide, May 7, 1938
Collected in *The Letters Of Sean O'Casey* (A46).

SUPPRESSED BY THE 'DAILY WORKER' (letter)

Forward, May 14, 1938
Collected in *The Letters of Sean O'Casey*.

PRESS CENSORSHIP? (letter)

Time and Tide, May 28, 1938
Collected in *The Letters of Sean O'Casey*.

PRESS CENSORSHIP? (letter)

Time and Tide, June 11, 1938
Collected in *The Letters of Sean O'Casey*.

C204   PLAYWRIGHT AND BOX OFFICE

Listener, July 7, 1938
BBC discussion between Maurice Browne and O'Casey, written by the play-
wright. Collected in *Blasts and Benedictions* (A44); further reprinted in *The
Sting and the Twinkle* (B72).

C205   O'CASEY QUESTIONS MAURICE LEAHY (letter)

Irish Times, August 29, 1938
Collected in *The Letters of Sean O'Casey* (A46).

C206   WALT WHITMAN (letter)

Time and Tide, September 3, 1938
Collected in *The Letters of Sean O'Casey*.

C207   ATHEISM A LA MODE (letter)

Irish Times, September 6, 1938
Collected in *The Letters of Sean O'Casey*.

C208   A PROPHET IN THE THEATRE

Sunday Times, September 18, 1938
Review of *Robert Loraine* by Winifred Loraine (B8). Collected in *Blasts and
Benedictions* (A44).

C209   INVITATION TO MR SEAN O'CASEY (letter)

Irish Press, October 17, 1938
Collected in *The Letters of Sean O'Casey* (A46).

C210   PORTRAIT OF JACK LONDON: A LIGHT THAT FAILED

Sunday Times, October 30, 1938
Review of *Sailor on Horseback* by Irving Stone.

PISATELI MIRA PROTIV FASHISTSKOĬ AGRESSII, ZA DEMOKRATIYU, MIR I SSSR.

Internatsional'naya Literatura, [November] 1938

THE LIGHT OF THE WORLD (letter)

Time and Tide, November 5, 1938
Collected in *The Letters of Sean O'Casey* (A46).

FROM PRISON CELL: A SMUGGLER'S JOURNAL

Sunday Times, November 20, 1938
Review of *Lover of the Great Bear* by Sergiusz Piasetski.

[LETTER]

Forward, December 10, 1938
Collected in *The Letters of Sean O'Casey* (A46).

5 WHEN THE IRISH WILL FIGHT: ULSTER FOR IRELAND

Forward, January 7, 1939
Reprinted in *Irish Freedom*, May 1939, as 'Ulster for Ireland: Home Truths for Irishmen'.

6 SEAN O'CASEY SAYS

Irish Freedom, February 1939

7 CHARLES LEVER'S STORMY LIFE

Sunday Times, February 5, 1939
Review of *Dr Quicksilver* by Lionel Stevenson. Collected in *Blasts and Benedictions* (A44).

18 IRELAND'S TONGUE OF FIRE

Irish Freedom, March 1939
Review of *Irish Mitchel* by Seamus McCall. This review, commissioned by the *Sunday Times*, was refused publication by that newspaper.

C219　IRELAND HURRIES PAST: THE PATTERN OF HER HISTORY

Sunday Times, March 26, 1939
Review of *Irish Cavalcade* by M. J. MacManus.

C220　PIS'MA V REDAKTSIYU (letters)

Internatsional'naya Literatura [May–June] 1939

C221　THE VALUE OF VIOLENCE

Picture Post, July 5, 1939

C222　ENGLAND HAS IRELAND BY THE THROAT: IRELAND MUST
　　　BE UNITED!

Irish Freedom, August 1939
Review of *Bombs! and their Reverberations* by Joseph H. Fowler.

C223　LAUGHTER DOWN THE YEARS: THE ROLE OF COMEDY

Sunday Times, August 20, 1939
Review of *In Praise of Comedy: A Study in its Theory and Practice* by
James Feibleman (B65).

C224　SOVIET MOVE (letter)

Reynolds News, October 1, 1939

C225　EPIC OF THE AIR

Sunday Times, October 8, 1939
Review of *Wind, Sand, and Stars* by Antoine de Saint-Exupéry.

C226　WHAT ARE OUR WAR AIMS? (letter)

Picture Post, November 11, 1939
Collected in *The Letters of Sean O'Casey* (A46).

LITERATURA V IRLANDII

Internatsional'naya Literatura [December] 1939
A fuller text was printed in *Blasts and Benedictions* (A44) as 'Literature in Ireland'.

SEAN O'CASEY'S MESSAGE : IRELAND SHOULD BE AGAINST THE WAR (letter)

Irish Freedom, January 1940
Collected in *The Letters of Sean O'Casey* (A46).

ROYAL RISIDENCE

Virginia Quarterly Review, January 1940
Collected in expanded version in *Pictures in the Hallway* (A22).

SHON O'KEĬSI O POLITIKE SSSR.

Internatsional'naya Literatura [January] 1940

MOST INDISPENSABLE POWER OF ALL FOR WORKERS

Daily Worker, January 12, 1940
Review of anonymous pamphlet *The Inside Story of the Daily Worker*. Reprinted in *Internatsional'naya Literatura* [Mar–Apr] 1940 and in *Literatura Obozrenie*, [May] 1940.

DRAMATIST ON FINLAND

Daily Worker, January 12, 1940

WHY IRELAND IS RESTLESS

Tribune, January 26, 1940
Review of *Ireland, Whose Ireland?* by Desmond Ryan.

HOPES FOR SPEEDY END FOR MANNERHEIM

Daily People's World (San Francisco), January 31, 1940

C235   FOR MANY WAR IS STUPID, FOR FEW PROFITABLE

Daily People's World, February 13, 1940

C236   IRELAND—A DRAMATIST'S VIEW (letter)

Picture Post, February 24, 1940
Collected in a fuller text in *The Letters of Sean O'Casey* (A46).

C237   LANCASHIRE IN FLASHES

Sunday Times, March 3, 1940
Review of *Lancashire for Me: T. Thompson's Little Biography*.

C238   THE STAR TURNS RED (letter)

New Statesman and Nation, March 30, 1940

C239   DRAMATIST O'CASEY REPLIES (letter)

Picture Post, March 30, 1940
Collected in *The Letters of Sean O'Casey* (A46).

C240   SEAN O'CASEY TO IRISH EXILES (letter)

Irish Freedom, April 1940
Collected in *The Letters of Sean O'Casey*.

C241   [SEAN O'CASEY REPORTS]

Books Abroad, xiv, spring 1940
Collected in *The Letters of Sean O'Casey* as a letter to R. T. House dated August
15, 1939.

C242   SERVING WITH THE COLOURS

Labour Monthly, May 1940
Review of *Serving My Time* by Harry Pollitt.

THE DAILY WORKER (letter)

Daily Worker, June 10, 1940
Collected in *The Letters of Sean O'Casey* (A46).

CAT 'N' CAGE

Virginia Quarterly Review, July 1940
Collected in *Pictures in the Hallway* (A22).

THE GOLDEN BOYS

Daily Worker, July 17, 1940
Printed separately in pamphlet entitled *Hands off the Daily Worker* (B9). Reprinted in *Literatura Obozrenie*, no. 21, 1940.

SEAN O'CASEY ON THE BAN (letter)

Picture Post, August 10, 1940

WHY I JOINED THE EDITORIAL BOARD

Daily Worker, September 11, 1940
Letter to *New Masses* (New York), printed in that journal on October 1, 1940; further reprinted in *Internatsional' naya Literatura*, [Nov–Dec] 1940.

DEFENDER OF HIS FAITH (letter)

Picture Post, September 28, 1940

SEAN O'CASEY ANSWERS G. R. STRAUSS M.P.

Daily Worker, October 3 and 4, 1940
Also printed in *Tribune*, Oct 4, 1940, under the title 'The *Daily Worker* and the War'.

[SEAN O'CASEY AND THE TRIBUNE]

Daily Worker, October 25, 1940
Includes short quotation from a letter by O'Casey.

C251   [EXTRACT FROM LETTER]

Tribune, November 1, 1940
Editorial, entitled 'From the Editor's Chair', quotes brief extracts from a letter
suppressed by the journal; reprinted in *The Letters of Sean O'Casey* (A46).

C252   GREETINGS!

Daily Worker, November 9, 1940
Editorial signed by O'Casey and three other members of the editorial board.

C253   THE PORTS CONTROVERSY (letter)

Irish Freedom, January 1941
Reprinted in *Daily Worker*, January 16, 1941 as 'O'Casey on Eire and War'
Collected in *The Letters of Sean O'Casey* (A46).

C254   O'CASEY'S ADVICE TO DRAMATISTS (letter)

Irish Press, January 17, 1941
Reprinted in *Joseph Holloway's Irish Theatre, 3, 1938–1944* (B64). A fuller text is
collected in *The Letters of Sean of O'Casey*.

C255   PLAN FOR BRITAIN (letter)

Picture Post, January 18, 1941

C256   SEAN O'CASEY APPEALS FOR FRANK RYAN

Daily Worker, January 18, 1941

C257   CONNOLLY SPEAKS AGAIN

Labour Monthly, May 1941
Review of *James Connolly—A Socialist and War* by P. J. Musgrove.

C258   SHEKSPIR V ANGLII I V SSSR. (letter)

Internatsional'naya Literatura, [May] 1941

WODEHOUSE IN BERLIN (letter)

Daily Telegraph and Morning Post, July 8, 1941
Collected in *The Letters of Sean O'Casey* (A46).

WORTHLESS LEADERSHIP IN ART (letter)

Totnes Times, July 12, 1941
Collected in *The Letters of Sean O'Casey*.

WORTHLESS LEADERSHIP IN ART (letter)

Totnes Times, July 26, 1941
Collected in *The Letters of Sean O'Casey*.

THE DAILY WORKER (letter)

New Statesman and Nation, August 2, 1941
Collected in *The Letters of Sean O'Casey*.

BE BOLD (letter)

Picture Post, August 9, 1941

AN IRISH INSTITUTION (letter)

Irish Times, November 25, 1941
Collected in a fuller version in *The Letters of Sean O'Casey* (A46).

AN IRISH INSTITUTION (letter)

Irish Times, December 15, 1941
Collected in *The Letters of Sean O'Casey*.

A SOVIET PLAY

Labour Monthly, January 1942
Review of *Distant Point* by A. N. Afinogenov.

C267   [LETTER]

   Plebs, March 1942
   Collected in *The Letters of Sean O'Casey* (A46).

C268   COOLE HOUSE (letter)

   Irish Times, March 6, 1942
   Reprinted in *Joseph Holloway's Irish Theatre, 3, 1938–1944* (B64). Collected
   in *The Letters of Sean O'Casey*.

C269   IRISH EMBLEMS (letter)

   Irish Freedom, April 1942

C270   PICTURES IN THE HALLWAY (letter)

   Time and Tide, April 11, 1942

C271   A NEW CHALLENGE (letter)

   Sunday Times, April 26, 1942
   Collected in *The Letters of Sean O'Casey* (A46).

C272   EMPTY VESSELS

   Irish Freedom, May 1942
   Collected in *Blasts and Benedictions* (A44).

C273   CORRESPONDENCE: I.R.B. AND THE FLAG

   Irish Freedom, May 1942
   Collected in *The Letters of Sean O'Casey* (A46).

C274   'STILL MORE IDEALS . . .' (letter)

   Puck's Fare (Dublin), May 1942
   Collected in *The Letters of Sean O'Casey*.

[COMMENT ON THE TRADES UNION BILL]

Workers Action, May Day edition, 1942*

* Not examined by compilers, but photocopy seen.

MR AGATE: A CURT REPLY (letter)

Sunday Times, May 10, 1942
Collected in *The Letters of Sean O'Casey* (A46).

FURTHER THEY GO, NEARER THEY COME

Daily Worker, September 24, 1942

A FLAME IN OVERALLS : MAYAKOVSKY AND HIS POETRY

Anglo-Soviet Journal, October–December 1942
Review of *Mayakovsky and his Poetry* by Herbert Marshall.

MR SEAN O'CASEY AND LT-COL. RAYNER'S SPEECH (letter)

Western Guardian (Totnes), October 29, 1942
Also printed in *Totnes Times and Devon News*, Oct 31, 1942. Collected in
The Letters of Sean O'Casey (A46).

TWENTY-FIVE YEARS AGO

Daily Worker, November 9, 1942

MR SEAN O'CASEY REPLIES TO LIEUT-COL. R. RAYNER, M.P. (letter)

Western Guardian, November 12, 1942
Reprinted in *Totnes Times and Devon News*, Nov 14, 1942. Collected in *The
Letters of Sean O'Casey* (A46).

A PEOPLE'S ARMY (letter)

Totnes Times and Devon News, November 28, 1942
Collected in *The Letters of Sean O'Casey*.

C283   REAL DUBLINERS (letter)

Reynolds News, December 6, 1942

C284   LT.-COL. RAYNER'S THREE THINGS (letter)

Western Guardian, December 31, 1942
Reprinted in *Totnes Times and Devon News*, Jan 2, 1943. Collected in
The Letters of Sean O'Casey (A46).

C285   THE IRISH BUSY-BODIES

Irish Freedom, January 1943

C286   THE RIBBON IN HER HAIR (poem)

Irish Freedom, January 1943
Also printed separately as a broadsheet ballad (B14).

C287   WHAT SEAN O'CASEY SAYS (letter)

Picture Post, January 9, 1943

C288   PIS'MO IZ ANGLII (letter)

Novy Mir, [April] 1943

C289   FALSE WITNESS AGAINST THE SOVIET UNION

Daily Worker, April 3, 1943

C290   THE IRISH

Daily Worker, August 12, 1943

C291   THE IRISH ARE EVERYWHERE

Irish Freedom, September 1943

IRISH BADGES (letter)

Daily Worker, October 4, 1943

AS IT WILL BE WITH US SO SHALL IT BE WITH OUR THEATRE

Irish Freedom, December 1943
Also printed in *Saturday Book 3* (B15) where it appeared as 'The Curtained World'. Collected in *Blasts and Benedictions* (A44) as 'Behind the Curtained World'.

THE SONG OF LIFE

Daily Worker, December 30, 1943

FUTURE OF THE DAILY WORKER

Daily Worker, January 1, 1944
Statement signed by thirteen members of the editorial board including O'Casey.

MOSKOVSKIM DRUZ'YAM

Znamya, [March] 1944

THE INTERNATIONALE (letter)

Irish Independent, March 7, 1944

STOP THIS CELTIC TWILIGHT

Daily Worker, March 17, 1944
Reprinted in *Daily People's World*, Apr 29, 1944.

SHADOW OF THE VATICAN

Daily Worker, March 23, 1944.

C300   THE VATICAN DICTATES: SEAN O'CASEY REPLIES TO HIS CRITICS

       Daily Worker, April 10, 1944

C301   EIRE'S NEUTRALITY (letter)

       Time and Tide, April 22, 1944
       Collected in *The Letters of Sean O'Casey* (A46).

C302   THE PLOUGH AND THE STARS (letter)

       Irish Times, April 25, 1944
       Collected in *The Letters of Sean O'Casey*.

C303   EIRE'S NEUTRALITY (letter)

       Time and Tide, May 20, 1944
       Collected in *The Letters of Sean O'Casey* in a fuller version.

C304   RED GRAVE IN BURMA

       Daily Worker, October 21, 1944
       Review of *British Soldier in India* by Clive Branson.

C305   DON'T TALK NONSENSE, LADY GIBBS!

       Daily Worker, October 31, 1944

C306   SEAN O'CASEY'S FINGAL DAYS (letter)

       Irish Press, January 10, 1945

C307   THE CENSORSHIP

       The Bell, February 1945
       Collected in *Blasts and Benedictions* (A44) and in *The Letters of Sean O'Casey* (A46).

CLERICALISM GONE LOONY

Daily Worker, March 20, 1945
O'Casey was very angry when he saw the title given to this article by the journal's editor.

THE FUTURE OF THE DAILY WORKER

Daily Worker, March 26, 1945
Report of editorial board whose thirteen members included O'Casey.

SOBOLEZNOVANIE PO POVODU SMERTI A.N. TOLSTOGO

Literaturnaya Gazeta, April 3, 1945

IN THOUSANDS THEY RALLIED FOR THE ALLIES BUT NOT ONE FIRED A SHOT FOR THE NAZIS

Irish Democrat, June 1945

WE MUST BE BORN AGAIN

Daily Worker, June 28, 1945

BERTRAND RUSSELL AND RUSSIA

Forward, October 13, 1945

THE GAELIC BLACK-HEADED BOY

Our Time, November 1945
Review of *The Midnight Court* by Brian Merriman, translated into English by Frank O'Connor. Collected in *Blasts and Benedictions* (A44).

SEAN O'CASEY REPLIES (letter)

Forward, November 17, 1945

C316   MR O'CASEY REPLIES (letter)

    Spectator, November 23, 1945
    Collected in *The Letters of Sean O'Casey* (A46).

C317   O'CASEY V. ERVINE (letter)

    Spectator, December 7, 1945
    Collected in *The Letters of Sean O'Casey*.

C318   SEAN O'CASEY AND RUSSIA (letter)

    Forward, December 15, 1945

C319   SPIRITS IN PRISON

    Spectator, December 28, 1945
    Review of *I Did Penal Servitude* by D. 83222.

C320   THE THEATRE AND THE POLITICIAN

    Common Wealth Review, January 1946
    Collected in *Blasts and Benedictions* (A44).

C321   LARKIN VERSUS CONNOLLY (letter)

    Irish Democrat, February 1946
    Collected in *The Letters of Sean O'Casey* (A46).

C322   THE PEOPLE AND THE THEATRE

    Theatre Today, March 1946
    Reprinted in *Théâtre Populaire*, no. 48, 1962 (D43). Collected in *Under a Colored Cap* (A41).

C323   SCIENTIFIC SOCIALIST (letter)

    Irish Democrat, April 1946
    Collected in *The Letters of Sean O'Casey* (A46).

RISE O' THE RED STAR

Anglo-Soviet Journal, spring 1946
Reprinted in *Indo-Soviet Journal* (Bombay), Nov 1946.

MAYAKOVSKY IMMORTAL

Anglo-Soviet Journal, spring 1946

GREAT MAN, GORKI

Tribune, May 3, 1946
Reprinted in *Tribune 21* (B34). Collected in *Blasts and Benedictions* (A44).

'VYZYVAYUSHCHIE' P'ESY Dzh. M. Sindzha

Britansky Soyuznik (Moscow) June 23, 1946
Possibly printed also in a Polish translation in Warsaw in 1946. First printed in English in *Blasts and Benedictions* (A44) as 'John Millington Synge'.

VPOLGOLOSA O BERNARDE SHOU

Britansky Soyuznik July 21, 1946
Possibly printed also in a Polish translation in Warsaw in 1946. First printed in a full version in English in *The Green Crow* (A34) as 'A Whisper about Bernard Shaw'.

RED ROSES FOR ME (letter)

Standard (Dublin) July 26, 1946
Collected in *The Letters of Sean O'Casey* (A46).

AND SEAN O'CASEY WROTE (letter)

Standard, August 9, 1946
Quoted in *Sean O'Casey, the Man I Knew* by Gabriel Fallon (B48). Collected in *The Letters of Sean O'Casey*.

C331 [CORRESPONDENCE]

Feature Magazine (Dublin), September 1946
Three letters dated September 2, 1924, February 27, 1928 and July 17, 1941 with two postcards of June 1926 and July 13, 1926 quoted in 'Dublin's Sean O'Casey' by Gabriel Fallon. An extract from the letter of September 2, 1924 is also quoted in the journal's editorial. The correspondence is collected in *The Letters of Sean O'Casey* (A46).

C332 IRELAND'S SILVERY SHADOW

Tribune, September 27, 1946
Text of a talk about W. B. Yeats commissioned by the BBC and broadcast in the BBC Spanish Service (in a translation by J. L. Plaza) in 1946. Collected in *Blasts and Benedictions* (A44).

C333 DON'T BE AFRAID OF BOOKS

Irish Democrat, October 1946

C334 TOTNES OF GENTLE MIEN

West Country Magazine, winter [December] 1946
Reprinted in *West Country Book* (B22); reprinted in *Sean O'Casey Review*, spring 1976 (C655). Collected in *The Letters of Sean O'Casey* (A46).

C335 VATICAN AND RED STAR IN YUGOSLAVIA

Daily Worker, December 12, 1946

C336 MELPOMENE IN IRELAND

Tribune, January 31, 1947
Review of *The Irish Theatre* by Peter Kavanagh. Complete text collected in *Blasts and Benedictions* (A44).

C337 JIM LARKIN DIES: SEAN O'CASEY TRIBUTE

Irish Times, January 31, 1947
Reprinted in *Sean O'Casey Review*, fall 1976.

LARKIN DEAD: SEAN O'CASEY WRITES

Daily Worker, January 31, 1947
Collected in *The Letters of Sean O'Casey* (A46).

A PROTESTANT BRIDGET

The Bell, February 1947
Review of *Lady Gregory's Journals* edited by Lennox Robinson. Collected in *Blasts and Benedictions* (A44).

SEAN O'CASEY'S TRIBUTE (letter)

Irish People (Dublin), February 8, 1947
Collected in *The Letters of Sean O'Casey* (A46).

JAMES LARKIN, LION OF IRISH LABOUR

Irish Democrat, March 1947
Reprinted in *The Sean O'Casey Review*, spring 1975 and, in part, in the *Irish Democrat* for February 1976.

A MESSAGE FROM SEAN O'CASEY

The Tyneside Phoenix, spring 1947

TENDER TEARS FOR POOR O'CASEY

Irish Writing (Cork), June 1947
Collected in a slightly revised version in *The Green Crow* (A34).

O'CASEY APPEALS FOR I.R.A. IN BRITISH PRISONS

Irish Times, October 13, 1947
Extracts from a letter to Eoin O'Mahoney; this is not the same letter as either of the subsequent ones to O'Mahoney quoted in the *Irish Times* on December 2, 1947 or in *Irish Press* on December 16, 1947. The full text of the letter quoted on October 13 is given in *The Letters of Sean O'Casey* (A46).

C345   POSER FOR A PLAYWRIGHT (letter)

Chronicle and Echo (Northampton), October 21, 1947

C346   ACTING MORE IMPORTANT THAN ACCENT (letter)

Independent (Northampton), October 31, 1947

C347   O'CASEY'S CALL FOR AMNESTY (letter)

Irish Democrat, November 1947

C348   TOLSTOY'S STORIES

Tribune, November 28, 1947
Review of Folio Society edition of *Tales by Tolstoy*.

C349   SEAN O'CASEY URGES RELEASE OF REPUBLICAN PRISONERS

Irish Times, December 2, 1947
Extract from a letter to Eoin O'Mahony; this is not the same letter that
was published in the *Irish Times* on October 13 or in the *Irish Press* on
December 16, 1947

C350   I.R.A. PRISONERS (letter)

Tribune, December 5, 1947

C351   PARKHURST PRISONERS, O'CASEY'S PLEA

Irish Press, December 16, 1947
Extracts from a letter to Eoin O'Mahoney; this is neither the letter that
was quoted in the *Irish Times* on October 13 nor that cited in that journal
on December 2, 1947.

C352   OPEN THE PRISON GATES!

Daily Worker, December 22, 1947

[DUBLIN CONTRIBUTES]

Irish Democrat, January 1948
Letter quoted in column entitled 'How *Not* To Free the Prisoners'.

A PROTEST TO TRUMAN

Our Time, January–February 1948
Text of a telegram to President Truman signed by O'Casey and thirty-three leading British writers, artists and musicians.

ODD MAN OUT (letter)

Tribune, January 9, 1948

[SELF-PORTRAIT]

Feature Magazine, February 1948
Sketch drawn in ink by O'Casey here reproduced in 'Lover's Quarrels at the Abbey' by Gabriel Fallon. Subsequently reproduced in his book *Sean O'Casey, the Man I Knew* (B48).

[FOR ALL PRISONERS]

Our Time, March 1948
Extracts from a letter by O'Casey quoted in 'Notes and Comments' column by T. A. Jackson.

THE LANE PICTURES (letter)

Manchester Guardian, March 30, 1948
Collected in *The Letters of Sean O'Casey* (A46).

SEAN O'CASEY WRITES

Irish Democrat, April 1948
Letter to P. J. Clancy.

C360   O WOMEN, BE BRAVER NOW

        Daily Worker, April 3, 1948
        Reprinted in *Sunday Worker* (New York), May 30, 1948.

C361   THE LANE PICTURES (letter)

        Manchester Guardian, April 12, 1948
        Collected in *The Letters of Sean O'Casey* (A46).

C362   STUDY COURSE FOR A VATICAN RECRUIT

        Daily Worker, May 4, 1948
        Reprinted in *The Pope, the People and Politics* (B21).

C363   PIS'MO SHONA O'KEĬSI (letter)

        Literaturnaya Gazeta, May 12, 1948

C364   SEAN O'CASEY'S REPLY TO BRIG. R. RAYNER, M.P. (letter)

        Totnes Times and Devon News, May 12, 1948
        Collected in *The Letters of Sean O'Casey* (A46).

C365   O'CASEY'S REPLY TO BRIGADIER RAYNER (letter)

        Totnes Times and Devon News, May 29, 1948
        Collected in *The Letters of Sean O'Casey*.

C366   SEAN O'CASEY TAKES UP SYNGE CUDGELS (letter)

        Chronicle and Echo (Northampton), November 18, 1948

C367   RUSSELL'S RAGE

        Daily Worker, November 27, 1948

[LETTER]

New York Times Magazine, December 26, 1948
Extracts from letter by O'Casey quoted in article 'In and Out of Books' by
Ralph Thompson, who introduces the passages as though they were obtained
in an interview with the playwright. The full text of the letter is printed in *The
Letters of Sean O'Casey* (A46).

THE RICH TAPESTRY OF LIFE

Book Find News (New York), no. 79, 1949

NORTHERN STAR

New Theatre, February 1949
Review of *The Strange Life of August Strindberg* by Elizabeth Sprigge.

ARTHUR GRIFFITH AND PADRAIC COLUM (letter)

Irish Writing, February 1949

INISHFALLEN, FARE THEE WELL (letter)

Irish Times, February 5, 1949
Collected in *The Letters of Sean O'Casey* (A46).

MR O'CASEY (letter)

Manchester Guardian, February 14, 1949

NO FLOWERS FOR FILMS

Leader Magazine, February 19, 1949
Collected in *The Green Crow* (A34).

AN ARGUMENT FOR PEACE

Daily People's World (Our Times Supplement) February 25, 1949

C376 PAGEANT OF POPES AND PEOPLE

Forward March 19, 1949
Review of *Church and People in Britain* by Archibald Robertson and of *The Popes and Social Problems* by J. W. Poynter.

C377 A MESSAGE FROM SEAN O'CASEY

Daily Worker, March 26, 1949

C378 THE ABBEY THEATRE (letter)

Drama, May 1949

C379 THE POLITICAL SITUATION (letter)

Totnes Times and Devon News, October 22, 1949
Collected in *The Letters of Sean O'Casey* (A46).

C380 THE POLITICAL SITUATION (letter)

Totnes Times and Devon News, November 5, 1949
Collected in a fuller version in *The Letters of Sean O'Casey*.

C381 THE SIMCOX CASE (letter)

English Churchman, November 25, 1949
Collected in *The Letters of Sean O'Casey*.

C382 A MESSAGE FROM THE AUTHOR

People's Theatre (Newcastle upon Tyne) Programme, December 10, 1949
Note for the world première of *Cock-a-Doodle Dandy*, reprinted in *Daily Worker*, Dec 12, 1949.

C383 COCK-A-DOODLE DANDY (letter)

Irish Times, December 30, 1949
Collected in *The Letters of Sean O'Casey* (A46).

COCK-A-DOODLE DANDY (letter)

Irish Times, January 13, 1950
Collected in *The Letters of Sean O'Casey* (A46).

O'CASEY REPORTS (letter)

New York Times, March 12, 1950
Reprinted in *Daily Worker* (New York), Mar 23, 1950 and in *Sean O'Casey Review*, spring 1976.

COUNTER ATTACK (letter)

Tyneside Phoenix, spring 1950

THE PLAY OF IDEAS

New Statesman and Nation, April 8, 1950
Collection in *Blasts and Benedictions* (A44).

SEAN O'CASEY GREETS NEW YORK CONNOLLY RALLY (letter)

Daily Worker (New York), May 4, 1950

A NEW APPROACH

New Statesman and Nation, May 6, 1950
Letter signed by O'Casey and nine other writers.

SHOULD WE HAVE A NATIONAL ORDER?

Irish Times Weekly Pictorial, June 7, 1950
Contribution to a symposium.

LET IT ROT WHERE IT LIES

Daily Worker, June 17, 1950
Collected in *The Letters of Sean O'Casey* (A46).

C392 DOLOĬ ATOMNUYU BOMBU!

    Literaturnaya Gazeta, June 24, 1950

C393 O'CASEY ANSWERS CHURCHILL: 'WAR IS A DAMNED BAD THING'

    Daily Worker, July 20, 1950

C394 PIS'MO SHONA O'KEĬSI (letter)

    Literaturnaya Gazeta, July 25, 1950

C395 [NO BELFAST HALL FOR PEACE CONFERENCE]

    Irish Times, September 8, 1950
    O'Casey letter quoted.

C396 CAUSE FOR WHICH ORANGE AND GREEN CAN UNITE: SEAN
      O'CASEY WARNS CHURCHILL (letter)

    Irish Democrat, October 1950

C397 WE ARE TOO BUSY WITH LIFE

    Irish Democrat, October 1950
    Extracts reprinted in *Daily People's World*, Oct 23, 1950.

C398 THE TUMULT AND PATHOS

    New York Times Book Review, October 15, 1950
    Review of *The Story of the Abbey Theatre* by Peter Kavanagh.

C399 BERNARD SHAW: AN APPRECIATION OF A FIGHTING IDEALIST

    New York Times Book Review, November 12, 1950
    Reprinted in *Highlights of Modern Literature* (B27). Collected in *The Green Crow*
    (A34).

C400 A GATE CLANGS SHUT

    Irish Writing, December 1950
    Collected in *Rose and Crown* (A30).

SAINTLY SINNER, SING FOR US (poem)

New Statesman and Nation, December 16, 1950
Reprinted in *Meanjin Quarterly*, winter 1951, and in *Masses and Mainstream*, Dec 1951. Collected in *Sunset and Evening Star* (A31).

THERE ARE OTHER, MORE DANGEROUS CENSORSHIPS (letter)

Picture Post, February 3, 1951
Collected in *The Letters of Sean O'Casey* (A46).

THE HOLLYWOOD TEN (letter)

Author, spring 1951
Collected in *The Letters of Sean O'Casey*.

TWELVE FAMOUS WRITERS IN PEACE CALL

Daily Worker, April 25, 1951
Letter signed by O'Casey and eleven other writers; also printed in the *Irish Times*, Apr 26, 1951 and in *Pravda*, Apr 26, 1951. Collected in *The Letters of Sean O'Casey*.

THE RED TICKET (letter)

Irish Times, December 28, 1951
Reprinted in part in *Sunset and Evening Star* (A31) and in *The Plays of Sean O'Casey* by M. Malone (B63). Collected in *The Letters of Sean O'Casey*.

THE RED TICKET (letter)

Irish Times, January 24, 1952
Collected in *The Letters of Sean O'Casey*.

FRANK RYAN (letter)

Irish Times, April 5, 1952
Collected in *The Letters of Sean O'Casey*.

C408 LET'S WRITE A PLAY

The Writer, May 1952

C409 FRANK RYAN (letter)

Irish Times, May 10, 1952
Collected in *The Letters of Sean O'Casey* (A46).

C410 FRANK RYAN (letter)

Irish Times, May 21, 1952
Collected in *The Letters of Sean O'Casey*.

C411 STOP THE DRIFT TO WAR

Irish Democrat, June 1952
Letter signed by O'Casey and seventeen other Irish writers. Collected in *The Letters of Sean O'Casey*.

C412 SEAN O'CASEY TO ALFRED A. KNOPF

New York Times Book Review, June 8, 1952
Letter to A. A. Knopf, commending the publication of *The World of George Jean Nathan*, here used as an advertisement for the book.

C413 SEAN O'CASEY IRISH PLAYWRIGHT SENDS A MESSAGE FOR PEACE (letter)

Daily Worker (New York), July 29, 1952
Message for *We Pledge Peace, A Friendship Book* (B25), extracts printed here in advance of the book's publication; reprinted in fuller text in London *Daily Worker*, Aug 1, 1952.

C414 SEAN O'CASEY: FORMERLY OF DUBLIN (letter)

New York Herald Tribune, October 12, 1952

C415 THE SONG OF THE SOVIETS

New World Review (New York), November 1952

WITH LOVE AND KISSES FROM BERNARD SHAW

New York Times Book Review, November 9, 1952
Review of *Bernard Shaw and Mrs Patrick Campbell : Their Correspondence*, ed. Alan Dent. Collected in *Blasts and Benedictions* (A44) as 'Shaw's Primrose Path'.

ALWAYS THE PLOW AND THE STARS

New York Times Book Review, January 25, 1953
Reprinted in *Highlights of Modern Literature* (B27). Collected in *The Green Crow* (A34).

ST. PATHRICK'S DAY

New York Times Magazine, March 15, 1953
Collected in a fuller version in *The Green Crow* as 'St Pathrick's Day in the Morning'.

DAS EXPERIMENTELLE THEATER

Schiller-Theater (Berlin) Programme, June 20, 1953
Programme note for production of *The Silver Tassie*.

JEEPS, BE JEEPERS!

New Statesman and Nation, July 18, 1953
Collected in *Sunset and Evening Star* (A31).

THE POWER OF LAUGHTER : WEAPON AGAINST EVIL

Saturday Night (Toronto), October 3, 1953
Collected in *The Green Crow* (A34).

[JUNO AND THE PAYCOCK]

West Cumberland Times (Cockermouth), October 3, 1953
Quotes letter from O'Casey, also printed in the *Cockermouth Players Theatre Programme*, Oct 14, 1953.

C423   [THE PLOUGH AND THE STARS]

Smith College (Massachusetts) Department of Theatre Programme, December 9, 1953
Extract from O'Casey letter to George Brendan Dowell quoted.

C424   SIR THOMAS MORE (letter)

New Statesman and Nation, December 26, 1953
Collected in *The Letters of Sean O'Casey* (A46).

C425   MY FRIEND, CHEKHOV

Voks Bulletin (Moscow), [March] 1954
Reprinted in *National Affairs* (Toronto), Oct 1954 under the title 'On Chekhov'.

C426   THE FLUTTER OF FLAGS—A HEALTHY PRIDE

Saturday Night, July 24, 1954
Collected in *The Green Crow* (A34).

C427   SEAN O'CASEY'S WORLD (letter)

Life, August 16, 1954

C428   LETTERS FROM SEAN O'CASEY TO A RANDOLPH-MACON
         SENIOR

Randolph-Macon Bulletin, September 1954
Eight letters to Anthony Harvey written between March and August 1954.
Extracts from this correspondence were reprinted in *The Experiments of Sean
O'Casey* (B39) and in *Drama: the Major Genres* by Robert Hogan and Sven
Eric Milin (1962).

C429   SEAN O'CASEY AND MR WORSLEY (letter)

New Statesman and Nation, November 6, 1954
Collected in *The Letters of Sean O'Casey* (A46).

PHILOSOPHY OF DESPAIR—A MODERN SICKNESS

Saturday Night, December 25, 1954
Collected in *The Green Crow* (A34) as 'Come to the Fair'.

CORRESPONDENCE

Act: The Drama Magazine (Leeds), January 1955
Two letters dated September 3, 1954 and November 19, 1954; extracts
reprinted in *The Times*, Feb 4, 1955.

A LETTER FROM SEAN O'CASEY

Times Pictorial (Dublin), February 26, 1955
Letter dated February 11, 1955.

[THE BISHOP'S BONFIRE]

Gaiety Theatre (Dublin) Programme, February 28, 1955
Note for the world première of the play, also printed in the *Irish Press*,
Feb 28, 1955. Reprinted in *Sean O'Casey, the Man I Knew* by Gabriel Fallon
(B48).

BISHOP'S BONFIRE (letter)

Irish Press, March 15, 1955
Reprinted in *Sean O'Casey, the Man I Knew*.

SEAN O'CASEY AND DUBLIN (letter)

Sunday Times, March 20, 1955

THE BISHOP'S BONFIRE (letter)

Irish Times, March 23, 1955
Also printed in *Irish Press*, Mar 24, 1955.
Quoted in *Sean O'Casey, the Man I Knew*.

B437   THE BISHOP'S BONFIRE (letter)

Irish Press, April 5, 1955
Reprinted in *Sean O'Casey, the Man I Knew* (B48).

C438   THE BONFIRE (letter)

Irish Press, April 12, 1955

C439   PERILOUS SEAS (letter)

Irish Times, April 27, 1955

C440   SEAN O'CASEY COMPLAINS (letter)

Plays and Players, May 1955

C441   SEAN O'CASEY'S LETTER ABOUT ARTISTS WHO 'FACE
       FRONT AND FEAR LITTLE'

Daily Worker (New York), May 25, 1955
Letter to the Bronx American Labour Party dated May 19, 1955, quoted
in column by David Platt.
Reprinted in *Daily People's World*, June 14, 1955.

C442   SEAN O'CASEY LAUDS 'THE SEARCHING LIGHT' (letter)

Daily Worker (New York), July 13, 1955
Comment on *The Searching Light* by Martha Dodd; reprinted in *Daily People's
World*, July 19, 1955.

C443   RICHES OF THE DEEP BLUE SEA (letter)

Irish Press, August 13, 1955
Letter dated August 11, 1955.

C444   SEAN O'CASEY GREETS GURLEY FLYNN (letter)

Daily Worker (New York), October 30, 1955

FROM SEAN O'CASEY, KEEP THE FLAG OF FRIENDSHIP
   FLYING (letter)

New World Review, November 1955
Reprinted in part in the same journal in October 1964.

LETTER FROM ENGLAND

Cleveland Playhouse Programme, November 16, 1955
Letter to Frederic McConnell, director of *The Plough and the Stars* production.

SEAN O'CASEY IS AN GHAEILGE (letter)

Inniu (Dublin), December 2, 1955

END THE TRAMP, TRAMP, TRAMP, THE BOYS ARE MARCHING

Challenge (London), December 10, 1955 *

* Not examined by the compilers, but photocopy seen.

O'CASEY: PLAYWRIGHT IN EXILE

New York Times, December 25, 1955
Collected in the English edition of *The Green Crow* (A34b) as 'Playwright
in Exile'.

) TRIBUTE TO BERNARD SHAW

   Icarus (Dublin), January 1956

1   SEAN O'CASEY'S MESSAGE ON WORKERS' DEBT TO
        LARKIN (letter)

   Dublin Evening Mail, January 31, 1956

C452   NOT WAITING FOR GODOT

Encore, Easter [March] 1956
Collected in *Blasts and Benedictions* (A44).

C453   SEAN O'CASEY'S MESSAGE TO TEACHER'S UNION (letter)

Daily Worker (New York), March 27, 1956
Reprinted in *Canadian Tribune* (Toronto), Apr 16, 1956 under the title 'All
Tapsallteerie O!'

C454   THANKS FROM SEAN O'CASEY (letter)

New York Times, April 20, 1956
Letter dated April 16, 1956.

C455   THE RUINED ROWAN TREE (poem)

Chanticleer (Totnes), summer 1956
Song written for the 1953 revival of *Purple Dust*; printed in the 1957 stage
version of the play (A21b).

C456   G. B. SHAW: THE LORD OF A CENTURY

New York Times, July 22, 1956
Centenary tribute collected in the English edition of *The Green Crow* (A34b)
as 'Shaw—Lord of a Century'.

C457   [LETTER]

Theatre World, August 1956
Extracts from a letter by O'Casey used as an advertisement for *Shakespeare
and the Young Actor* by Guy Boas (B29).

C458   SIDELIGHTING ON SOME 'PICTURES'

New York Times, September 16, 1956

C459   SYMBOL, PROPHECY, SLAPSTICK

New York Herald Tribune, December 23, 1956
Printed in part in *Continuity and Innovation in Sean O'Casey's Drama* (B74).

GLOBAL GREETINGS (letter)

Sing Out! winter 1956

THE DRAMA OF THE FUTURE

Radio Times, January 25, 1957
Collected in *Blasts and Benedictions* (A44) as 'An Irishman's Plays'.

VY POSTROITE NOVUYU BOL'SHUYU ZHIZN' (letters)

Invstrannaya Literatura, [February] 1957

HAVE YOU READ? (letter)

News Chronicle, February 14, 1957

EIN IRISCHES DRAMA

Schlosspark-Theater (Berlin) Programme, February 15, 1957
Note for production of *Red Roses for Me*.

[PURPLE DUST]

National Guardian, February 18, 1957
Three extracts (possibly from a letter) quoted in a review by James Aronson
of the New York production of *Purple Dust*.

POOR PUZZLED IRELAND

Tribune, February 22, 1957
Review of *The Easter Lily: the Story of the I.R.A.* by Sean O'Callaghan. Reprinted
as a preface to the subsequent paperbound edition of the book (B56).

[SEASONABLE GREETINGS]

Irish Times, March 19, 1957
Letter printed in 'An Irishman's Diary' column; reprinted in *Irish Times*, July
4, 1972.

C468　OTVET SHONA O'KEISI MAKKARTISTAM

Inostrannaya Literatura, [April] 1957

C469　IRISH WRITERS (letter)

Irish Times, May 18, 1957
Letter dated May 14, 1957.

C470　IRISH WRITERS (letter)

Irish Times, May 30, 1957
Letter dated May 27, 1957.

C471　ROSE TATTOO FUND

New Statesman and Nation, June 1, 1957
Letter signed by O'Casey and seven other figures prominent in the theatre.

C472　IRISH WRITERS (letter)

Irish Times, June 8, 1957

C473　ROZA YUNOSTI

Novy Mir, [July] 1957

C474　REDAKTORU ZHURNALA 'TEATR'

Teatr (Leningrad), [July] 1957
Answers to a questionnaire entitled 'In Your Opinion'.

C475　NUCLEAR TESTS

Manchester Guardian, July 31, 1957
Letter signed by O'Casey, H. K. Handoo, David Pitt and Tefkros Anthias.

C476　IRISH FAMILIES (letter)

Irish Times, October 15, 1957

PŘED VYTAŽENÍM OPONY

Realistické Divadlo Zdeňka Nejedlého (Prague) Programme, October 27, 1957
Note for production of *Red Roses for Me*.

[GOOD WISHES FROM O'CASEY]

The Plough (Dublin), November 1957
Untitled letter.

KOGDA VEST' PRISHLA V DUBLIN

Inostrannaya Literatura, [November] 1957

DIE OKTOBERREVOLUTION (letter)

Sonntag (Berlin), November 3, 1957

VOSKHODYASHCHAYA ZVEZDA

Literaturnaya Gazeta, November 5, 1957
Reprinted in *Glazami Druzei*, ed. V. V. Ustinov and I. K. Kirik (B35).

O'CASEY ÉS P. G. WODEHOUSE NYILATKOZATA A
TÁJÉKOZTATÓNAK

Tájékoztató (Budapest), December 1957
Translation of article introducing *Juno and the Paycock* to Hungarian readers.
First printed in English in *Blasts and Benedictions* (A44) as 'O'Casey in
Hungarian Costume'.

K CHITATELYAM 'ZVEZDY': O DRAME 'KOSTER EPISKOPA'

Zvezda (Leningrad), [January] 1958
First printed in English in *Blasts and Benedictions* as 'O'Casey's Drama-Bonfire'.

CHRISTIANITY AND COMMUNISM (letter)

Irish Times, January 6, 1958

C485   THERE MUST BE NO MORE WAR (letter)

Jugopress Information Bulletin, January 7, 1958
Answers to a questionnaire.

C486   IRLANDII NE NADO VOENNYKH BAZ

Literaturnaya Gazeta, January 25, 1958

C487   DRUMS OF FATHER NED (letter)

Irish Times, February 17, 1958

C488   DEYATELI KUL'TURY O SOVESHCHANII NA VYSSHEM UROVNE

Inostrannaya Literatura, [March] 1958
Reply to the journal's questionnaire.

C489   [LETTER]

Enquiry, March 1958
Extract from a letter dated November 3, 1957 to Ronald Ayling quoted
in his article 'Rowdelum Randy: A Postscript on O'Casey and his Critics'.

C490   TORKUEĬ—PERM' (letter)

Ural (Sverdlovsk), [March] 1958

C491   O'CASEY MAKES A CHALLENGE (letter)

Irish Press, March 1, 1958
Letter dated February 26, 1958.

C492   O'CASEY REPLIES

The Plough, March 5, 1958
Extracts from a letter to the editor.

THE THEATRE FESTIVAL (letter)

Irish Times, March 11, 1958
Extracts reprinted in *Sean* by Eileen O'Casey (B68) and in *A Paler Shade of Green* (B70).

O'CASEY PLAY (letter)

Irish Press, March 12, 1958
Letter dated March 5, 1958.

DEN', KOGDA RABOCHY TRUBIT V SVOĬ ROG

Novoe Vremya, [May] 1958
This article, entitled 'The Day the Worker Blows a Bugle', was also printed in the English-language edition of *Novoe Vremya—New Times*, May 1958. Reprinted in *New World Review*, Nov 1958, and in *Mainstream*, May 1959. Collected in a fuller version in *Blasts and Benedictions* (A44).

THE DRUMS OF FATHER NED (letter)

Enquiry (Nottingham), June 1958
Also printed in part in *The Experiments of Sean O'Casey* (B39).

POSLANETS MIRA V KOSMOSE

Literaturnaya Gazeta, June 3, 1958

YA S VAMI, KOMSOMOL'TSY, I ETO ZNACHIT—YA ZA BUDUSHCHEE! (letter)

Komsomol'skaya Pravda, June 5, 1958.

MEZHDUNARODNAIA ANKETA

Inostrannaya Literatura [July] 1958
Answers to the journal's questionnaire.

O'CASEY RECORDS (letter)

Irish Times, August 7, 1958
Letter dated August 1, 1958.

C501 LENTY NA SHAPKE MOLODOSTI

   Komsomol'skaya Pravda, August 8, 1958

C502 V NOGU S NARODOM

   Literaturnaya Gazeta, October 4, 1958

C503 O'CASEY'S CREDO

   New York Times, November 9, 1958
   An excerpt was reprinted in *Sean O'Casey, the Man and his Work* (B37); reprinted
   under the title 'Cock-A-Doodle Dandy' in *Playwrights on Playwriting* (B38);
   published in a fuller version under the title 'Cockadoodle Doo' in *Blasts
   and Benedictions* (A44).

C504 VDOKHNOVENNOE DERZANIE

   Literaturnaya Gazeta, January 8, 1959

C505 THE HARP IN THE AIR STILL SINGS

   New York Times Magazine, January 11, 1959
   Reprinted in part in *New World Review*, Feb 1959 and in *Komsomol'skaya Pravda*,
   May 15, 1959; reprinted in *College English: The First Year* (B36); also reprinted
   under the title 'The Harp Still Sings' in *Background and Foreground, an Anthology
   of Articles from The New York Times Magazine* (Channel Press, Nov 15, 1960).
   Collected under the title 'The Lark in the Clear Air Still Sings' in *Under
   A Colored Cap* (A41).

C506 EXCERPTS FROM A LETTER TO FREDERICK MCCONNELL

   Cleveland Play House Programme, February 11, 1959
   Note for production of *Purple Dust*.

C507 PRIVETSTVIE TRET'EMU S"EZDU PISATELEĬ SSSR.

   Inostrannaya Literatura, [March] 1959

LOOK TO THE STARS (letter)

New York Times, March 1, 1959

THE LASS ON THE STAMP (letter)

Irish Times, April 16, 1959
Letter dated April 11, 1959.

TSVETY

Komsomol'skaya Pravda, April 26, 1959

GORNISTY CHELOVECHESTVA

Literaturnaya Gazeta, May 18, 1959

THE DELICATE ART OF GROWING OLD

Harper's (New York), August 1959
Excerpts from a letter written in 1957 to Senator Thomas C. Desmond, chairman of the New York State Joint Legislative Committee on Problems of the Ageing. Collected in a slightly fuller version in *Blasts and Benedictions* (A44) as 'Crabbed Age and Youth'.

SEAN O'CASEY ON PEACE AND FRIENDSHIP

New World Review, September 1959
Message for the Stockholm meeting of the World Council of Peace, May 1959.

O'CASEY'S LIKING FOR LIFE

Royal Court Theatre (London) Programme, September 17, 1959
Note for production of *Cock-a-Doodle Dandy*.

TEN BEST FOR A REPERTORY THEATRE

New York Times Magazine, November 9, 1959
Collected under the title 'Melpomene an' Thalia Beggin' for Bread' in *Blasts and Benedictions* (A44), where the date is erroneously given as November 9, 1958.

C516   NAME OF O'NEILL ADORNS THEATER (letter)

     New York Times, November 9, 1959
     Letter to Lester Osterman reprinted in *O'Neill and his Plays: A Survey of his Life and Work* (B41) as 'Tribute to O'Neill'.

C517   THE LANE PICTURES (letter)

     Irish Times, November 30, 1959

C518   PRERUMBLE

     Esquire (New York), December 1959
     Prologue to *The Drums of Father Ned* (A38).

C519   KAK BYSTRO LETIT VREMYA

     Literaturnaya Gazeta, January 1, 1960

C520   CHELOVECHESTVO IDET VPERED

     Izvestiya, January 24, 1960

C521   VELIKY PISATEL', VELIKY CHELOVEK

     Literaturnaya Gazeta, January 28, 1960

C522   [LETTER]

     Theatre Arts, February 1960

C523   SEAN O'CASEY'S GREETINGS

     Daily Worker, February 11, 1960

C524   SEAN O'CASEY GREETS VETS' RALLY (letter)

     The Worker (New York), March 13, 1960

A MESSAGE FROM O'CASEY

Daily Worker, March 31, 1960

YA GORYACHO POLYUBIL EGO

Inostrannaya Literatura, [April] 1960

ISKUSSTVO—PESN' ZHIZNI

Literaturnaya Gazeta, April 5, 1960
First printed in English in *Blasts and Benedictions* (A44) as 'Art is the Song of Life'.

THANKS ON HIS EIGHTIETH BIRTHDAY (letter)

New York Times, April 10, 1960

OGNENNY PODSOLNECHNIK

Izvestiya, April 21, 1960

SVETOCH ROSSII

Literaturnaya Gazeta, April 23, 1960
Reprinted in part in *Irish Times*, May 13, 1960 as 'The Torch of Russia' in 'An Eye on Russia' column by Séamus O Coigligh.

OUT, DAMNED SPOT!

Theatre Arts, May 1960
Reprinted in *Encore: the Voice of Vital Theatre*, May–June 1963, and collected in *Under a Colored Cap* (A41).

THE DRUMS OF FATHER NED

Theatre Arts, May 1960
Complete text of three-act play subsequently published in book form (A38).

C533   PASTERNAK AND JOYCE (letter)

Irish Times, July 19, 1960
Letter dated July 16, 1960.

C534   PASTERNAK AND JOYCE (letter)

Irish Times, July 26, 1960
Letter dated July 23, 1960.

C535   O'CASEY AGUS COISTE NA bPÁISTÍ (letter)

Feasta (Dublin), August 1960

C536   VECHNYE ZVEZDY

Literaturnaya Gazeta, September 15, 1960
A Hungarian translation was published under title 'Halhatatlan Csillagok'
in *Tolsztoj Emlékkönyv* (B43).

C537   NOTIZ ZU 'GOCKEL, DER GECK'

Wuppertaler Bühnen Programmblätter für die Spielzeit 1960/61
Comment written for the production of *Cock-a-Doodle Dandy* which opened
on September 28, 1960.

C538   MOLODYM DANO MECHTAT'

Inostrannaya Literatura, [October] 1960
Reprinted in *Komsomol'skaya Pravda* (Supplement), November 25, 1960.

C539   A BELIEVER? SEAN O'CASEY ANSWERS THE QUESTION
        (letter)

National Guardian, October 10, 1960

C540   [LETTER]

MD: Medical Newsmagazine (New York), November 1960
Message to the journal included in 'Unrepentant Rebel', an anonymous
article; letter dated June 4, 1960.

SENTENCED TO DEATH

The Times, November 5, 1960
Letter signed by about one hundred signatories.

LETTER FROM O'CASEY

Icarus (Dublin), December 1960
Letter addressed to Victor Blease.

FIFTY LEADING CITIZENS WIRE BROOKEBOROUGH

Irish Democrat, December 1960
Text of a telegram signed by fifty-seven prominent men and women.

MEMORIES OF A FAREWELL TO IRELAND

New York Times, December 4, 1960
Reprinted in part in *Evening Press* (Dublin), Dec 5, 1960. Collected in *Blasts and Benedictions* (A44) as '*The Plough and the Stars* in Retrospect.'

[BEDTIME STORY]

University of Hawaii Theatre Group Programme, December 9, 1960
Extract from letter to the director of *Bedtime Story* production.

SHON O'KEĬSI O SEBE

Literaturnaya Gazeta, December 15, 1960

ROSES ROUGES POUR MOI (letter)

Bref: Journal Mensuel du Théâtre National Populaire, February 1961
Letter to Jean Vilar dated January 18, 1961 translated by Michel Habart; reprinted in part in *TNP Chaillot Programme* for the play dated November 10, 1962.

C548 A LETTER FROM SEAN O'CASEY 'LEATHER AWAY WITH THE WATTLE O!'

New World Review, April 1961

C549 TVORCHESKIE PLANY ZARUBEZHNYKH PISATELEI

Inostrannaya Literatura, [May] 1961
Replies to an international questionnaire.

C550 PORA SIRENI

Literaturnaya Gazeta, May 1, 1961

C55'1 KATHLEEN LISTENS IN

Tulane Drama Review, June 1961
Complete text of one-act play first staged by Abbey Theatre, Dublin, on October 1, 1923 as *Cathleen Listens In*; there is also a short introductory note by the author. The play was collected in *Feathers from the Green Crow* (A40) in a slightly revised version.

C552 [LETTER]

Irish Times, July 11, 1961
English translation of a letter by O'Casey, written in Irish, quoted in 'An Irishman's Diary' column.

C553 THE BISHOP'S BONFIRE

Mermaid Theatre (London) Programme, July 26, 1961
Programme note for the London première, reprinted in part in 'An Irishman's Diary' in *Irish Times*, July 27, 1961.

C554 VERYU S 1917 GODA!

Literaturnaya Gazeta, August 17, 1961

NO O'CASEY PLAYS FOR IRELAND

Irish Times, August 24, 1961
Extracts from two letters to Frank O'Neill.

[LETTERS]

English Studies in Africa, September 1961
Extracts from two letters to Ronald Ayling dated March 21 and December 12, 1958, quoted in his article 'That Laurelled Head: A Literary Portrait of Lady Gregory'; also printed in *Shaw Review*, Sep 1961.

SLAVA KRASNOÏ ZVEZDE!

Literaturnaya Gazeta, October 17, 1961

GREETINGS FROM O'CASEY (letter)

Peace Campaign (London), November–December, 1961*

* Not examined by compilers

SEAN O'CASEY APPEALS TO BRITAIN TO SAVE WORLD DON'T MAKE THE EARTH A GREAT GRAVE (letter)

Daily Worker, November 11, 1961

THE BIG BOMBS (letter)

Irish Times, November 13, 1961

THE BIG BOMB (letter)

Irish Times, November 23, 1961

[LETTERS]

Arizona Quarterly, winter 1961
Brief extracts from five letters (written in 1959 and 1960) to Ronald Rollins quoted in his article 'Sean O'Casey's Mental Pilgrimage'.

C563   [LETTERS]

West Virginia University Philological Papers, December 1961
Extracts from three letters to Ronald Rollins quoted in his article 'O'Casey,
O'Neill and the Expressionism in *Within the Gates*'.

C564   SEAN O'CASEY'S VISION OF WORLD TO COME

Daily People's World, January 13, 1962
Printed in fuller version in *Look*, Jan 16, 1962 as 'I Predict'; and reprinted
in *Inostrannaya Literatura*, [June] 1962.

C565   O'CASEY AND THE ABBEY (letter)

Irish Times, March 21, 1962

C566   [LETTER]

The Explicator, April 1962
Extract from undated letter to Ronald Rollins quoted in his 'O'Casey's *The
Silver Tassie*'.

C567   TWO MARXISTS (letter)

Irish Times, April 13, 1962

C568   [LETTERS]

Bucknell Review, May 1962
Extracts from three letters (written in 1959 and 1960) to Ronald Rollins
quoted in his article 'O'Casey, O'Neill and Expressionism in *The Silver Tassie*'.

C569   A BIBFUL OF THANKS FROM O'CASEY (letter)

New York Herald Tribune, May 20, 1962
Reprinted in part in *Sunday Press* (Dublin), June 3, 1962 and in *A Self-Portrait
of the Artist as a Man* by David Krause (B58).

O'CASEY BY CASEY

Mermaid Theatre (London) Programme, August 15, 1962
Note written for the Mermaid 'Sean O'Casey Festival'; reprinted in *Aldwych Theatre (London) Programme*, Sep 10, 1969 for the Royal Shakespeare Company's production of *The Silver Tassie*.

POETY KOSMOSA

Literaturnaya Gazeta, August 16, 1962

[NANNIE'S NIGHT OUT]

Modern Drama, September 1962
Article entitled 'Nannies's Night Out' by Ronald Ayling gives substantial extracts from the manuscript text of the one-act play subsequently first printed in full in *Feathers from the Green Crow* (A40); also quotes letter published in *New York Times*, Dec 27, 1925 (C99) and an extract from a letter to Ayling dated May 1, 1962.

[LETTERS]

Modern Drama, September 1962
Excerpts from two letters (dated November 26, 1957 and July 18, 1958) to Harry M. Ritchie quoted in his essay 'The Influence of Melodrama on the Early Plays of Sean O'Casey'.

[LETTER]

New York Times, September 4, 1962
Letter to Brooks Atkinson quoted in his column 'Critic at Large'.

THE SILVER TASSIE (letter)

Observer, September 16, 1962

[LETTER]

Bulletin of the New York Public Library, November 1962
Letter dated March 16, 1961 quoted in part in 'Patterns of Greek Tragedy in O'Casey's *Purple Dust*' by Walter C. Daniel.

C577   ICH GLAUBE SEIT 1917

Deutsches Theater (Berlin) Spielzeit 1962–1963
Programme note for production of *Red Roses for Me*; brochure also includes
extract from a letter by O'Casey.

C578   ALL THINGS DELIGHTFUL DEPEND ON WAGES

Irish Times, February 1, 1963
Letter to William Blease reproduced; this letter is also printed in *Irish Press*
for the same date under the title 'O'Casey Sends "Blessing" '

C579   [LETTERS]

Mississippi Quarterly, spring 1963
Extracts from three letters to Ronald Rollins (dated 1959 and 1961) quoted
in his article 'Sean O'Casey's *The Star Turns Red*: A Political Prophecy'.

C580   SEAN O'CASEY GREETS GURLEY FLYNN EVENT (letter)

Worker (New York), March 26, 1963
Reprinted in *National Guardian*, Mar 28, 1963.

C581   [GREETINGS]

Württembergische Staatstheater (Stuttgart) Programme, April 11, 1963
Short extract from letter quoted in programme for *Purple Dust* production.

C582   [LETTER]

Irish Echo (New York), May 3, 1963
Letter quoted in 'Forever Green' column.

C583   [LETTER]

New York Post, July 30, 1963
Letter quoted in 'The Lyons Den' column.

PENTRU MINE VIAŢA RĂMÎNE MINUTATĂ

Tribuna (Bucharest), October 17, 1963
Written replies to a questionnaire.

THE ONE JOURNAL A WORKER CAN TRUST

Daily Worker Supplement, November 26, 1963

LETTER TO MISS ROSE RUSSELL ON THE DEATH OF PRESIDENT KENNEDY

New York Times, November 27, 1963
Letter dated November 20, 1963. Reprinted in *Worker* (New York), December 3, 1963; in *Sing Out!* Feb–Mar 1964; and in *Four Days* (B46). Written after the assassination, the letter is erroneously dated.

WHAT DOES MUSIC MEAN TO ME? (letter)

Portland Symphony Journal, December 2, 1963

A ZHAVORONOK V YASNOM NEBE POET, KAK PEL VSEGDA

Literaturnaya Gazeta, January 1, 1964

BEHIND A BAN

New York Times, January 5, 1964
Collected in *Blasts and Benedictions* (A44) as 'On the Banks of the Ban'.

IN DEN BURGERKRIEG

Schlosspark-Theater (Berlin) Programme, January 7, 1964
Note for production of *Juno and the Paycock*.

[LETTERS]

Kilkenny Magazine, spring–summer 1964
Extract from an unpublished essay by O'Casey entitled 'O'Casey Versus the Abbey' and quotations from two letters dated December 28 and December 30, 1963 to Ronald Ayling quoted in his 'Sean O'Casey: The Writer Behind his Critics'; reprinted in *Drama Survey*, spring – fall 1964.

C592   SEAN O'CASEY TILTS AT CULTURAL IRELAND: EXTRACTS
        FROM SOME LETTERS TO HIS NIECE, LORRAINE [BEAVER]

Irish Independent, April 7, 1964
Passages from four letters dated August 11, November 2 and December 6,
1962 and May 11, 1963.

C593   ODE TO AN 'IMPUDENT UPSTART'

New York Times Magazine, April 19, 1964
Reprinted in part in *New World Review*, June 1964 and in *Literaturnaya Gazeta*,
Sep 22, 1964. Collected in fuller version in *Blasts and Benedictions* (A44) as
'Shakespeare Among the Flags'.

C594   JUNO AND THE PAYCOCK

Aldwych Theatre (London) Programme, April 20, 1964
Extract from a letter to Derek Bowman.

C595   THE PLOUGH AND THE STARS

Aldwych Theatre (London) Programme, April 27, 1964

C596   THE OKAY AND THE ONE WHO WROTE IT

UCLA Playhouse Programme, May 15, 1964
Note for production of *Red Roses for Me*.

C597   [RED ROSES FOR ME]

Teatr Dramatyczny m.st. Warszawy (Warsaw) Programme, May 16, 1964
Note for Polish production of *Red Roses for Me*.

C598   SEAN O'CASEY GREETS WSP MISSION TO THE HAGUE

New World Review, July 1964

C599   O'CASEY'S TELEGRAM TO ABBEY [THEATRE]

Evening Herald (Dublin), August 18, 1964

[LETTERS]

The Explicator, September 1964
Extracts from three letters to Ronald Rollins (dated October 2, 1959, March 11, 1963 and October 28, 1963) quoted in his article 'O'Casey's *Cock-a-Doodle Dandy*'.

[LETTERS]

Vértice (Coimbra), September–October 1964
A translation of two letters to M. de Oliveira Vilaça.

IRISH EYES STILL SMILE ON THE PEOPLE'S

Newcastle Evening Chronicle, September 7, 1964
Letter to the People's Theatre, Newcastle upon Tyne.

A MESSAGE FROM SEAN O'CASEY (letter)

People's Theatre (Newcastle upon Tyne) Programme, September 19, 1964

WHEN THE 'SWALLAS' CAME FLYING OVER

Irish Times and *Irish Independent*, September 21, 1964
Letter to Garry McEligot, similar to that quoted in *New York Times*, Sep 4, 1962 (C574).

WHEN O'CASEY TOLD THE PEOPLE'S THEATRE, 'YOU ARE A NUISANCE'

The Journal (Newcastle upon Tyne), September 21, 1964
Extracts from letters to the People's Theatre over the years.

[LETTER]

Irish Times, September 22, 1964
Extract from an undated letter quoted in 'An Irishman's Diary' column under the title 'O'Casey on Connolly'.

C607   [LETTER]

Sunday Press (Dublin), September 27, 1964
Extracts from a letter written in Irish by O'Casey quoted in 'Tuairimî faoi
Sheán O'Casey' by Seosamh O'Duibhginn.

C608   [LETTERS]

Irish Times, September 28, 1964
Extracts from letters in an article 'The Culinary O'Casey'.

C609   PLAYWRIGHT TO CRITIC: SEAN O'CASEY'S LETTERS TO
       GEORGE JEAN NATHAN
C610   SEAN O'CASEY CONCERNING JAMES JOYCE

Massachusetts Review, winter 1964
Extracts from letters to Nathan edited by Seymour Rudin and three letters
(on Joyce) to Joseph Prescott dated November 1, 1949, May 10, 1954 and
August 4, 1958. Both contributions were reprinted in *Irish Renaissance*, ed.
Robin Skelton and David R. Clark (B49). These letters were collected, several
in fuller versions, in the second and third volumes of *The Letters of Sean
O'Casey* (A46).

C611   LETTERS FROM O'CASEY

Irish Echo, October 3, 1964
Three letters dated April 14, May 27 and November 25, 1963.

C612   BLACK TOP BOOTS AND SPURS

E. Vilde nim. Rahvateater (Tartu, Estonia) Programme, October 3, 1964
Includes sketch by O'Casey of costumes for stage production of *Red Roses
for Me*, reproduced from a letter to Ott Ojamaa, translator of the play into
Estonian.

C613   [LETTERS]

Irish Democrat, November 1964
Extracts from four letters to Jim Kavanagh quoted in his 'My Friend O'Casey';
two of them were reprinted in *Sean O'Casey Review*, spring 1976.

SÚIL RÚISEACH AR O'CASEY

Comhar (Dublin), November 1964.
Includes letter submitting 'Shakespeare Among the Flags' for publication in
Literaturnaya Gazeta; the essay was published in the issue for September 22,
1964. It had previously appeared in *New York Times Magazine*, Apr 19, 1964
under the title 'Ode to an "Impudent Upstart"' (C593); collected in *Blasts
and Benedictions* (A44). The essay is here published in part with brief commentary by Séamus O'Coigligh.

[LETTER]

Meanjin Quarterly (Melbourne), December 1964
Short extract from an undated letter to Leslie Rees quoted in his article
'Remembrance of Things Past: On Meeting Sean O'Casey'. Reprinted in *The
Sting and the Twinkle* (B72).

[LETTER]

Inostrannaya Literatura, [March] 1965
Text of a letter to A. Elistratova dated March 19, 1959, extracts from which
were originally printed in her book, *Nasledie angliiskogo romantizma i
sovremennost'* (B40).

THE BALD PRIMAQUEERA

Atlantic Monthly, September 1965
O'Casey's last article completed August 21, 1964. Reprinted in part in
Inostrannaya Literatura, [Jan] 1966. Collected in *Blasts and Benedictions* (A44).

[LETTERS]

Keel ja Kirjandus, September 1965
Photographic facsimiles of two pages from letters to Ott Ojamaa and of
three sketches by O'Casey of costumes for *Red Roses for Me* – together with
Estonian translations of two letters dated February 26 and March 24, 1964 –
reproduced in 'Ühest maailmakirjanduslikust kontaktist' by Ojamaa.

LAST LETTER FROM O'CASEY

Irish Times, September 25, 1965
Letter to Peader Mac Maghnais quoted in an article by him.

C620   NOTE FROM SEAN O'CASEY TO A YOUNG POET

Nimrod, fall 1965
Letter to Patti Merrell dated June 23, 1964.

C621   O'CASEY LETTERS THROW LIGHT ON HIS BREACH WITH THE
        ABBEY [THEATRE]

The Times, October 6, 1965
Two letters to Mary O'Malley dated November 9, 1959 and November 23,
1959. Reprinted in *Sunday Independent* (Dublin), Dec 5, 1965.

C622   [LETTERS]

Modern Drama, February 1966
Extracts from four letters dated March 29 and March 31, 1959, July 25,
1959 and July 19, 1963 to Ronald Rollins, quoted in his article 'Form
and Content in Sean O'Casey's Dublin Trilogy'.

C623   JUNO AND THE PAYCOCK

National Theatre (London) Programme, April 25, 1966
Extract from letter written in 1955.

C624   [LETTERS]

West Virginia University Philological Papers, June 1966
Extracts from two letters dated March 30, 1959 and December 4, 1960 to
Ronald Rollins, quoted in his article 'Dramatic Symbolism in Sean O'Casey's
Dublin Trilogy'.

C625   [LETTER]

Arizona Quarterly, autumn 1966
Extract from letter dated March 30, 1959 to Ronald Rollins, quoted in
his article 'O'Casey and Synge: the Irish Hero as Playboy and Gunman'.

FROM SEAN O'CASEY'S LETTERS

Culture and Life (Moscow), September 1966
Excerpts from seven letters to Soviet literary officials, 1942–5, edited by Ludmila Ioffe.
A tribute to Chekhov, entitled 'One of the World's Dramatists' (1944), is also included; it was subsequently published in a fuller version in *Blasts and Benedictions* (A44). The extracts from letters were printed in an anonymous translation in the German edition, *Kulter und Leben*, in September 1966.

[EXTRACTS]

New World Review, November 1966
First publication in English of excerpts from three essays written for Russian readers (1959–60) quoted in 'Sean O'Casey's Words Live On' by Ronald Ayling.

[EXTRACT FROM LETTER TO MACMILLAN COMPANY]

Bulletin of the New York Public Library, January 1967
Letter to O'Casey's American publisher.

[LETTER]

Shaw Review, May 1967
Extract from letter dated August 14, 1962 to Ronald Rollins, quoted in his article 'Shaw and O'Casey: John Bull and His Other Island'.

[LETTER]

Sunday Telegraph, October 22, 1967
Facsimile of letter to Harold Macmillan dated April 28, 1938 reproduced in article entitled 'Top Authors Get Down to Business'. The letter was subsequently published in *Letters to Macmillan*, ed. S. Nowell-Smith (B57).

[LETTER]

West Virginia University Philological Papers, November 1967
Extract from letter to Ronald Rollins dated July 25, 1959, quoted in 'Mythical Dimensions in O'Casey's *Within the Gates*' by B. J. Harman and R. G. Rollins.

C632 [QUOTATION]

Sotheby Sale Catalogue, March 11–12, 1968
Extracts from an undated letter to Tom Kealy (*c.* 1925) and an inscription, with a facsimile photograph, from a presentation copy of *The Plough and the Stars* dated April 13, 1926; these items together with a presentation copy of *Two Plays* were sold in a Sotheby sale of 'Modern First Editions, Presentation Copies, Autograph Letters and Literary Manuscripts' on March 12, 1968.

C633 [ANSWERS TO QUESTIONS]

Dublin Magazine, spring 1968
Excerpts from letters to Saros Cowasjee.

C634 [O'CASEY AND 'THE BODY ELECTRIC']

Irish Press, March 19, 1969
Letter dated 1954, quoted by W. A. Newman in his 'Talking Points' column.

C635 [LETTER]

Bulletin of the New York Public Library, June 1969
Extract from letter to Douglas M. Jacobs dated January 30, 1955, quoted in 'A Note on Sean O'Casey's Manuscripts and His Working Methods' by Ronald Ayling.

C636 [LETTER]

Irish Times, August 2, 1969
Letter to Myles M. Sudbury dated April 20, 1956 quoted in 'An Irishman's Diary'.

C637 [LETTER]

Library Review (Glasgow), spring 1970.
Extract from letter dated April 2, 1963 to John O'Riordan, quoted in his 'Sean O'Casey: Colourful Quixote of the Drama'.

[LETTER]

Opera News, March 14, 1970
Letter to Elie Siegmeister dated April 8, 1960, included in Siegmeister's essay, 'A Long, Long Road', on the making of the opera *The Plough and the Stars*. The essay together with a facsimile of O'Casey's letter was reprinted in *The Sean O'Casey Review*, fall 1974 (C616).

[LETTERS]

Irish Independent, May 29, 1970
Eleven extracts from letters to various individuals quoted in 'Tatler's Parade' column by Desmond Rushe.

[LETTERS]

New York Times, July 13, 1970
Extracts from eleven letters (nine of which appeared earlier in *Irish Independent*, May 29, 1970) quoted in 'Dublin: Epistles of a Saintly O'Casey' by Desmond Rushe.

FOUR LETTERS: SEAN O'CASEY TO OLIVER ST. JOHN
    GOGARTY

James Joyce Quarterly (O'Casey Issue), fall 1970
Letters dated May 20, 1928; February 5 and 16, 1929 and April 14, 1930, together with the facsimile reproduction of a page from the last letter which contains a sketch by O'Casey. These letters are collected in *The Letters of Sean O'Casey* (A46), whose editor claims that the copies in this journal are 'imperfect' ones. Two extracts from letters to Roland Rollins, dated October 2, 1959 and October 28, 1963, are also quoted in Rollins's article 'Clerical Blackness in the Green Garden: Heroine as Scapegoat in *Cock-a-Doodle Dandy*'.

[LETTER]

The Explicator, September 1970
Brief extract from letter dated July 25, 1959 to Ronald Rollins, quoted in his 'O'Casey's *Within the Gates*'.

C643   [LETTERS]

Irish University Review, spring 1971
Extracts from two letters dated July 14, 1959 and March 24, 1960 to Ronald
Rollins in his article 'Portraits of Four Irishmen as Artists: Verisimilitude
and Vision'.

C644   UNPUBLISHED LETTERS OF SEÁN O'CASEY

Eire–Ireland, summer 1971
Two letters to Ronald Rollins dated July 25, 1959 and September 17, 1961
with facsimiles of the originals. Extracts were subsequently printed in *Eire–
Ireland*, winter 1971 in 'Pervasive Patterns in *The Silver Tassie*' by Ronald
Rollins.

C645   [LETTER]

Irish Times, June 2, 1971
Extract from undated letter to Proinsias Mac an Bheatha printed in 'An
Irishman's Diary' column.

C646   [MESSAGE]

Theatre Quarterly, October–December 1971
Extract from letter to Unity Theatre, London, quoted in 'The Early Years
at Unity' by Malcolm Page.

C647   [LETTERS]

Dalhousie Review, spring 1972
Extracts from nine letters quoted in 'Sean O'Casey and the Abbey Theatre,
Dublin' by Ronald Ayling. Three are letters to Lady Gregory dated February
22, September 11 and November 1, 1925; four are to Sara Allgood dated
November 7, December 7, December 21 and December 28, 1925, and
February 10, 1926; one is to Lennox Robinson dated October 9, 1922, and
another is to Ivor Brown dated June 24, 1928. Reprinted in *Irish University
Review*, spring 1973.

[LETTERS]

Colby Library Quarterly, June 1972
Four letters to Irma S. Lustig quoted in full in her article 'American and Apollonian Temples: Conversations and Correspondence with Sean O'Casey'; the letters are dated November 28 and December 11, 1950, November 29, 1951, and May 30, 1964. In 'Two O'Casey Letters' Richard Cary quotes in full letters, now in Colby College library, to Eric Capon (dated December 9, 1945) and to John Anthony O'Brien (March 8, 1954); there are also brief extracts from a letter of 1964 to Albert Tentor and one to Huntley Carter dated March 20, 1926.

[LETTERS]

Lyric Players Theatre (Belfast) Programme, March 28 1973
Extracts from seven letters, written between January 1940 and November 1954, quoted in '*Purple Dust* at the Lyric' by Ronald Ayling.

[LETTERS]

Modern Drama, February 1974
Extracts from three letters to Ronald Rollins (dated July 25 and October 2, 1959, and October 28, 1963) quoted in his article 'From Ritual to Romance in *Within the Gates* and *Cock-a-Doodle Dandy*'.

[LETTERS]

Sean O'Casey Review, fall 1974
Three letters printed in full. One to Ruth C. France dated March 1, 1963, and one to George B. Murphy dated April 11, 1963, are included as 'Two Unpublished Letters'. The third, dated April 8, 1960, is addressed to Elie Siegmeister and is quoted (with a facsimile) in his article entitled 'A Long, Long Road'.

[LETTER]

Irish Times, February 25, 1975
Letter signed by Ernest Blythe, Sean O'Casey, George Irvine and Seamus Deakin quoted in obituary tribute to Ernest Blythe. This appears to be the first publication of the letter which is dated April 22, 1907.

C653   [LETTERS]

Sean O'Casey Review, spring 1975
Five letters are reproduced in full. One to Edith Segal is dated August 15, 1957. Four to Jack Lindsay are dated April 28 and May 1, 1945; March 27 and April 6, 1955. O'Casey's article, 'James Larkin: The Lion of Irish Labour', is also printed in this issue; it originally appeared in the *Irish Democrat* for March 1947 and was reprinted, in part, in the same journal in February 1976.

C654   [QUOTATION]

Irish Times, July 24, 1975
Letter from Michael McInerney, in 'An Irishman's Diary', quotes from a letter to him from O'Casey (April 1939).

C655   WOMEN'S REVEILLE (poem)

Sean O'Casey Review, fall 1975
First publication in English of a poem written during the Second World War, transcribed from a typescript among the playwright's papers. O'Casey's essay, 'Totnes of Gentle Mien', is also reprinted in this issue; it was originally published in *West Country Magazine*, winter 1946 (C334). Two letters from O'Casey to Jim Kavanagh are also reprinted here; they originally appeared in the *Irish Democrat* in November 1964 (C613).

C656   [EXTRACTS]

Éire-Ireland, autumn 1975
' "To Bring Harmony": Recurrent Patterns in O'Casey's Drama' by Ronald Ayling quotes extracts from several letters and from manuscript material. There is a short passage from one of the playwright's holograph notebooks, two longer extracts from the holograph text of 'The Harvest Festival' and a quotation from an unpublished letter to George Jean Nathan dated December 2, 1947.

C657   [LETTERS]

Sean O'Casey Review, spring 1976
Two letters reproduced; one to Ronald Rollins dated March 30, 1959 and one to Edward H. Mabley dated November 15, 1961. In the same issue there is a letter to the Hudson Guild Players of New York; it originally appeared in

the *New York Times* for March 12, 1950 (C385). An essay, 'The Plough and the Stars in Retrospect', is also reprinted; it was first published in the *New York Times* for December 4, 1960 under the title 'Memories of a Farewell to Ireland' (C544). An Irish Citizen Army poster (*c.* 1914), designed by O'Casey, is reproduced here as well.

[JUNO AND THE PAYCOCK]

Modernist Studies [spring] 1976
Extracts from hitherto unpublished drafts of the play quoted in 'Juno and the Paycock: A Textual Study' by Ronald Ayling.

O'CASEY'S LETTERS

Sean O'Casey Review, fall 1976
Four letters to Helen Kiok, dated August 3, 1955, June 4 and October 31, 1956 and November 6, 1958 are here published for the first time. The issue also reprints O'Casey's obituary tribute to James Larkin, originally published in the *Irish Times* for January 31, 1947 (C337).

[QUOTATION]

Etudes irlandaises, December 1976
Brief extract from *The Harvest Festival* quoted by Emile-Jean Dumay in an article entitled 'Enter O'Cathasaigh'.

[LETTERS]

Sean O'Casey Review, spring 1977
Seven letters to William J. Maroldo are printed in full: they are dated December 31, 1960; May 12 and October 18, 1961; April 9 and August 10, 1962; February 26, 1963 and May 20, 1964. A long extract from a letter to Ronald Ayling (dated January 26, 1960) is quoted in an article entitled 'Sean O'Casey and Jim Larkin After 1923'.

SECTION D

Translations

Arranged alphabetically by language and, within language groups, chronologically under the headings of Books and Periodicals. Entries marked by an asterisk have not been examined by the compilers.

AFRIKAANS

BOOK

1 TWEE RAND TREK
Johannesburg: Dalro, 1969. [iv] 18 pp. A translation by Nerina Ferreira of
A Pound on Demand.

ARABIC

BOOKS

2 JUNU WA-AL-TA'US
Cairo: Al-Sharikah al Qawmiyah lil-Tiba'ah wa-al-Nashr, 1961. 216 pp.
A translation by Ali Jamal al-Din 'Izat of *Juno and the Paycock*.*

3 AL-MIHRATH WA-AL-NUJUM
Cairo: Al-Dar al-Misriyah lil-Ta'lif wa-al-Tarjumah, 1965. 222 pp. A translation by Faauzi al-'Antil of *The Plough and the Stars*.*

PERIODICAL

4 AL-TURAB AL-URJUWANI
al-Masrah (Cairo), September 1964. A short extract from *Purple Dust* included
in a critical article on O'Casey by Louis Murcus.*

BULGARIAN

BOOKS

D5 AZ ČUKAM NA VRATATA
Sofia: Narodna Kultura, 1962. 224 pp. A translation by Atanas Slavov of
I Knock at the Door, with an introduction by the translator (pp. 5–7).

D6 ČERVENI ROZI ZA MEN
Sofia: Komitet po Kulturata i Izkustvoto, 1965. 57 pp. A translation by Ilija
Ljuckanov of *Red Roses for Me*.*

D7 POD CVETNATA ŠAPKA: RAZKAZI
Sofia: Profizdat, 1967. 80 pp. A translation by Ivan Belčev of extracts from
Under a Colored Cap.*

D8 ČERVENI ROZI ZA MEN
Sofia: Narodna Kultura, 1972. 136 pp. A further translation by Ilija Ljuckanov
of *Red Roses for Me*, with a critical epilogue by Sevelina Gjorova (pp. 128–36).

CHINESE

In March 1945 O'Casey received a request from the Sino-British Cultural Association for permission to translate and publish *Juno and the Paycock*. The author and his publisher agreed to this, a small fee was paid, and a limited edition may well have been printed. The compilers have been unable to check this or any other possible Chinese publication prior to the establishment of the People's Republic in 1949.

BOOKS

D9   WO GIAO MEN
Peking: People's Literature Publishing House, 1958. 327 pp. A translation by Chung Sung-fan of *I Knock at the Door* (pp. 1–317), with an epilogue by the translator (318–27).

D10   OU-KAI-XI XI-JU XUAN-JI
Taipei: Ching Cheng Publishing Company, 1970. 234 pp. An anonymous translation of *Juno and the Paycock* and of *Purple Dust*, sponsored by the Tamkang College of Arts and Sciences.*

PERIODICALS

D11   XING-XING BIAN HONG LIAO
Shi-jie wen-xue (Peking), February and March 1959. A translation by Chu Yen and Ying Jo-ch'eng of *The Star Turns Red*.*

D12   KAI-XI-DI TAI-TAI XIU-JIA QU LIAO
Shi-jie wen-xue, March 1962. A translation by Chao Lo-jui of 'Mrs Casside Takes a Holiday' from *Inishfallen, Fare Thee Well*.* The journal has been issued as *World Literature* from 1962 onwards.

CZECH

BOOKS

D13   BUBNY OTCE NEDA
Praha: Dilia, 1964. 97 pp. A translation by František Vrba of *The Drums of Father Ned*.*

D14   KAMARADI
A translation by Aloys Skoumal of Chapter 8, 'Comrades', from *Inishfallen, Fare Thee Well*, included in an anthology of Irish prose writings, selected by the translator, entitled *Ni králi, ni císarí*, Praha: Naše vojsko, 1965. pp. 176–83.

TLUČU NA DVEŘE
Praha: Odeon, 1966. 616 pp. A translation by František Vrba of substantial selections (made by Eva Masnerová) from the first four autobiographical books: *I Knock at the Door* (twelve chapters), 19–127; *Pictures in the Hallway* (eleven chapters), 128–260; *Drums under the Windows* (twelve chapters), 261–472; *Inishfallen, Fare Thee Well* (ten chapters), 473–613. With a frontispiece photograph and an introduction by František Vrba.

5 PURPUROVÝ PRACH
Praha: Dilia, 1970. 105 pp.
A translation by Břetislav Hodek of *Purple Dust.* *

DANISH

BOOKS

7 RØDE ROSER TIL MIG
København: Danmarks Radio, Hørespilarkivet, [1966]. 75 pp. A translation by Tom Kristensen of *Red Roses for Me*, adapted for radio by Molly Greenhalgh. *

18 JUNO OG PÅFUGLEN
København: Danmarks Radio, Fjernsynsteatret, [1967]. 117 pp. An anonymous translation of *Juno and the Paycock.* *

19 MÅNESKIN OVER KYLENAMOE
København: Danmarks Radio, Hørespilarkivet, [1968]. 39 pp. A translation by Jens Louis Petersen of *The Moon Shines On Kylenamoe.**

DUTCH

BOOKS

20 JUNO EN DE PAUW
Amsterdam: P. N. Van Kampen & Zoon N.V., [1949]. 95 pp. A translation by C. van Polen of *Juno and the Paycock*, with an introduction by L. P. J. Braat.

21 DE DUIVELSHAAN
Amsterdam: De Bezige Bij, 1962. 127 pp. A translation by Cees Nooteboom of *Cock-a-Doodle Dandy*.

ESTONIAN

BOOK

D22   PUNASEID ROOSE MULLE TOOB
Tallinn: Kirjastus Eesti Raamat, 1965. 127 pp. A translation by Ott Ojamaa
of *Red Roses for Me*, with an essay by the translator. The songs were translated by Ain Kaalep.

PERIODICALS

D23   ROHELINE VARES
Sirp ja Vasar (Tallinn), January 19, 1968.
A pseudonymous translation of extracts from two articles—'The Power of
Laughter' and 'Always the Plow and the Stars'—in *The Green Crow*.

D24   ÖINE LUGU
Kultuur ja Elu (Tallinn), September 1971.
A slightly abridged translation by Ilmar Sepp of *Bedtime Story*.

FINNISH

BOOK

D25   MINÄ KOLKUTAN
Helsinki: Kansankulttuuri, 1961. 248 pp.
A translation by Elvi Sinervo of *I Knock at the Door*. *

FRENCH

BOOKS

D26   [EXCERPTS]
In *Théâtre d'Hier et d'Aujourd'hui*, Paris: Editions du Pavois, 1945. Excerpts
from *The Shadow of a Gunman* and *The Plough and the Stars* in anonymous
translations.

D27   THÉÂTRE I
JUNON ET LE PAON; ROSES ROUGES POUR MOI; HISTOIRE DE
NUIT. Paris: L'Arche, 1959. 189 pp. Translations by Michel Habart of
Juno and the Paycock, 5–73; *Red Roses for Me*, 75–160; and *Bedtime Story*, 161–87.

D28   THÉÂTRE II
LA CHARRUE ET LES ÉTOILES; ON ATTEND UN ÉVÊQUE; PAIEMENT
À VUE. Paris: L'Arche, 1960. 189 pp. *The Plough and the Stars*, translated

by Robert Soulat, 7–89; *The Bishop's Bonfire*, trans. Madeleine Steinberg, 91–166; *A Pound on Demand*, trans. Michel Habart, 167–87.

ROSES ROUGES POUR MOI
Paris: L'Arche, 1961. 79 pp.
A translation by Michel Habart of *Red Roses for Me*, originally printed in *Théâtre I* in 1959. This separate edition was published as no. 48 in the Collection du Répertoire series of plays produced by the Théâtre National Populaire.

THÉÂTRE III
L'OMBRE D'UN FRANC-TIREUR; LES TAMBOURS DU PÈRE NED; LE DISPENSAIRE. Paris: L'Arche, 1961. 175 pp. *The Shadow of a Gunman*, trans. Philippe Kellerson, 7–60; *The Drums of Father Ned*, trans. Céline Zins, 61–140; *Hall of Healing*, trans. Michel Habart, 141–73.

THÉÂTRE IV
COQUIN DE COQ; L'ÉTOILE DEVIENT ROUGE; LA FIN DU COMMENCEMENT. Paris: L'Arche, 1961. 199 pp. *Cock-a-Doodle Dandy,* trans. Michel Habart, 7–87; *The Star Turns Red*, trans. Céline Zins, 89–174; *The End of the Beginning*, trans. François Rongier, 175–97.

PRO-PER PROSCENIUM
In *L'Art du Théâtre* by Odette Aslan, Paris: Editions Seghers, 1963. pp. 313–15. A translation by Michel Habart of the essay 'Pro-Per Proscenium', first published in *The Flying Wasp* (A18).

THÉÂTRE V
POUSSIÈRE POURPRE; DERRIÈRE LES RIDEAUX VERTS; IL EST TEMPS DE PARTIR. Paris: L'Arche, 1963, 203 pp. Translations by Jacqueline Autrusseau and Maurice Goldring of *Purple Dust*, 7–101, *Behind the Green Curtains*, 103–71, and *Time To Go*, 173–201.

L'OMBRE D'UN FRANC-TIREUR
Paris: L'Arche, and Lausanne: La Cité, 1963. 117 pp. A translation by Philippe Kellerson of *The Shadow of a Gunman*, originally printed in *Théâtre III* in 1961. This separate edition was published as one of the Collection du Répertoire series of plays produced by the Théâtre National Populaire and (in this case) by the Théâtre Populaire Romand. The preface, 'Sean O'Casey Parle' (pp. 20–4), is a selection from his essay 'The People and the Theatre' (C322) translated by Maurice Goldring.

THÉÂTRE VI
LA COUPE D'ARGENT; LAVANDE ET FEUILLES DE CHÊNE; NANNIE SORT CE SOIR. Paris: L'Arche, 1966. 203 pp. Translations by Jacqueline Autrusseau and Maurice Goldring of *The Silver Tassie*, 7–84; *Oak Leaves and Lavender*, 85–171; and *Nannie's Night Out* (with alternative ending, as printed in *Feathers from the Green Crow*), 173–202.

D36   POUSSIERE POURPRE
       Paris: L'Arche, 1966. 117 pp. A translation by Jacqueline Autrusseau and
       Maurice Goldring of *Purple Dust*, originally printed in *Théâtre V* in 1963.
       This separate edition was published as no. 27 in the Collection du Répertoire
       series of plays produced by the Théâtre National Populaire.

D37   JUNON ET LE PAON
       La Revue de Paris (Paris), September 1927. A translation by Comtesse Jean de
       Pange of *Juno and the Paycock*; Act 1 was printed in the issue for September 1,
       and Acts 2 and 3 in the issue dated September 15, 1927.

D38   CE N'EST PAS DIEU QUI A CRÉÉ FALSTAFF, C'EST SHAKESPEARE
       Théâtre Populaire (Paris), 34, 2e trimestre, 1959. A translation by Michel Habart
       of extracts from various articles – including 'Pro-per Proscenium' and 'The
       Green Goddess of Realism' – in *The Green Crow*.

D39   LE DISPENSAIRE
       Théâtre Populaire, 35, 3e trimestre, 1959. A translation by Michel Habart of
       Hall of Healing.

D40   HISTOIRE DE NUIT
       A translation by Michel Habart of *Bedtime Story*, published in *l'Avant Scène,
       Fémina Théâtre* (Paris), no. 230, [November 1960].

D41   ROSES ROUGES POUR MOI
       Bref: Journal Mensuel du Théâtre National Populaire, February 1961. A translation
       by Michel Habart of a letter from O'Casey to Jean Vilar, dated January 18,
       1961. Reprinted in *Mercure de France*, November 1964.

D42   LES PÂQUES ROUGES DE DUBLIN
       Les Lettres Françaises, February 16–22, 1961. A translation by Céline Zins of
       an extract from the final chapter of *Drums Under the Windows*.

D43   LE PEUPLE ET LE THÉÂTRE
       Théâtre Populaire, 48, 4e trimestre, 1962. A translation by Maurice Goldring
       of 'The People and the Theatre', first published in *Theatre Today* in March
       1946 (C322).

D44   DERRIÈRE LES RIDEAUX VERTS
       Théâtre Populaire, 48, 1962. A translation by Jacqueline Autrusseau and Maurice
       Goldring of *Behind the Green Curtains*, later included in *Théâtre V* (1963).

D45   LA CULTURE, SOCIÉTÉ ANONYME
       La Nouvelle Critique: Revue du Marxisme Militant, no. 153, February–March 1964.
       A translation by Annette Lanoix of 'Culture Inc.', originally published in
       Under a Colored Cap.

GERMAN

BOOKS

DER BISCHOFS FREUDENFEUER
Emsdetten (Westf.): Lechte, [1956]. 173 pp. A translation by Elisabeth Freundlich and Günther Anders of *The Bishop's Bonfire*.

ICH KLOPFE AN
Leipzig: Paul List Verlag, 1957 (repr. 1959 and 1965). 240 pp. A translation by Georg Goyert of *I Knock at the Door*, with an essay by Otto Brandstädter.

ICH KLOPFE AN
Leipzig: Verlag Philipp Reclam, 1957 (repr. 1962). 333 pp. A translation by Georg Goyert of *I Knock at the Door*.

ER HATTE AN DIE TÜR GEKLOPFT
A translation by Georg Goyert of part of the final chapter from *I Knock at the Door*, included in *Almanach des Paul List Verlags auf das Jahr 1959*, Leipzig: Paul List Verlag, 1959, pp. 306–10.

BILDER IN DER VORHALLE
Leipzig: Paul List Verlag, 1959 (repr. 1964). 364 pp. A translation by Georg Goyert of *Pictures in the Hallway*, with an essay by Otto Brandstädter.

IRISCHE TROMMELN
Leipzig: Paul List Verlag, 1961 (repr. 1969). 560 pp. A translation by Werner Beyer of thirteen chapters from *Drums under the Windows*, 7–266, and fourteen chapters from *Inishfallen, Fare Thee Well*, 267–518, with an essay by Otto Brandstädter.

ROSE UND KRONE
Leipzig: Paul List Verlag, 1962 (repr. 1968). 404 pp. A translation by Werner Beyer of *Rose and Crown*, with an essay by Otto Brandstädter.

DER PFLUG UND DIE STERNE
A translation by Georg Goyert of *The Plough and the Stars*, included in *Spectaculum VI: Sieben moderne Theaterstücke*, Frankfurt: Suhrkamp Verlag, 1963, pp. [209]–263.

DER PFLUG UND DIE STERNE
A translation by Georg Goyert of an extract from Act III of *The Plough and the Stars*, included in *Ein Almanach der Autoren des Verlages Kurt Desch 1963*, Wien, München, Basel: Verlag Kurt Desch, 1963, pp. 233–7.

DÄMMERUNG UND ABENDSTERN
Leipzig: Paul List Verlag, 1963 (repr. 1972). 424 pp. A translation by Werner Beyer of *Sunset and Evening Star*, with an essay by Otto Brandstädter.

D56 ICH KLOPFE AN. AUTOBIOGRAPHIE BAND 1
Zürich: Diogenes Verlag, [1965]. 214 pp. A translation by Georg Goyert of *I Knock at the Door* (identical to that published by Paul List in 1957), with an introduction by Kaspar Spinner and a frontispiece photograph.

D57 UNTER EINER BUNTEN KAPPE
Leipzig: Paul List Verlag, 1966. 332 pp. A translation (with introductory essay) by Werner Beyer of prose writings from four books by O'Casey. Although it bears the collective title of *Under a Colored Cap*, there are in fact only three pieces from that particular book, together with six articles and four stories from *The Green Crow*; two articles and two stories from *Feathers from the Green Crow*; and one article from *The Flying Wasp* (though the four stories in *The Green Crow* were originally printed in *The Flying Wasp*).

D58 BILDER IN DER VORHALLE. AUTOBIOGRAPHIE BAND II
Zürich: Diogenes Verlag, [1966]. 301 pp. A translation by Georg Goyert of *Pictures in the Hallway* (identical to that published by Paul List in 1959), with a frontispiece photograph.

D59 ROTE ROSEN FÜR MICH. AUSGEWÄHLTE DRAMEN
Berlin, Weimar: Aufbau-Verlag, 1966. xxxi, 853 pp. A translation by Irmhild and Otto Brandstädter of eleven plays, with music and explanatory notes and an introduction by Otto Brandstädter. Contents: *The Shadow of a Gunman*, 1–56, *Juno and the Paycock*, 57–131, *The Silver Tassie* (revised ed.), 133–221, *The End of the Beginning*, 223–47, *The Star Turns Red*, 249–352, *Red Roses for Me*, 353–447, *Cock-a-Doodle Dandy*, 449–544, *Hall of Healing*, 545–82, *Bedtime Story*, 583–611, *The Bishop's Bonfire*, 613–727, *Behind the Green Curtains*, 729–804.

D60 REBELL ZUM SCHEIN. AUSGEWÄHLTE STÜCKE
Zürich: Diogenes Verlag, [1967]. 875 pp. A translation by Irmhild and Otto Brandstädter of eleven plays: texts, music and notes identical to those published in 1966 by Aufbau-Verlag under the title *Rote Rosen Für Mich*.
An essay by Heinz Dietrich Kenter replaces Otto Brandstädter's introduction, however, and another additional feature is a checklist of German stage premières of O'Casey's plays.

D61 TROMMELN UNTER DEN FENSTERN. AUTOBIOGRAPHIE
BAND III
Zürich: Diogenes Verlag, [1967]. 288 pp. A translation by Werner Beyer of fifteen chapters from *Drums under the Windows*, identical to that published by Paul List in 1961 under the title *Irische Trommeln* – though with two additional chapters, for *Irische Trommeln* included only thirteen chapters from *Drums under the Windows*. With frontispiece photograph.

D62 IRLAND, LEB WOHL! AUTOBIOGRAPHIE BAND IV
Zürich: Diogenes Verlag, [1968]. 276 pp. A translation by Werner Beyer of fifteen chapters from *Inishfallen, Fare Thee Well*, identical to that published by

Paul List in 1961 under the title *Irische Trommeln* – though with one additional chapter, for *Irische Trommeln* included only fourteen chapters from *Inishfallen, Fare Thee Well*. With frontispiece photograph.

ROSE UND KRONE. AUTOBIOGRAPHIE BAND V

Zürich: Diogenes Verlag, [1968]. 311 pp. A translation by Werner Beyer of *Rose and Crown*, identical to that published by Paul List in 1962, with frontispiece photograph.

HALLE DER HEILUNG. EIN PFUND ABHEBEN. DER MOND SCHEINT AUF KYLENAMOE: DREI KLEINE STÜCKE

Berlin: Henschelverlag, [1968]. 118 pp. Translations by Maik Hamburger and Adolf Dresen of *Hall of Healing*, 1–46, *A Pound on Demand*, 1–23, and *The Moon Shines on Kylenamoe*, 1–36, with eight pages of music as an appendix.

KIKERIKI

Berlin: Henschelverlag, [1968]. vi, 117 pp. A translation by Helmut Baierl and Georg Simmgen of *Cock-a-Doodle Dandy*.

PURPURSTAUB

Berlin: Henschelverlag, and Frankfurt: Suhrkamp, [1968]. iii, 141 pp. A translation by Helmut Baierl and Georg Simmgen of *Purple Dust*.

DÄMMERUNG UND ABENDSTERN. AUTOBIOGRAPHIE BAND VI

Zürich: Diogenes Verlag, [1969]. 315 pp. A translation by Werner Beyer of *Sunset and Evening Star*, identical to that published by Paul List in 1963; with frontispiece photograph.

DER SCHATTEN EINES REBELLEN

Berlin: Henschelverlag, [1969]. iii, 69 pp. A translation by Maik Hamburger of *The Shadow of a Gunman*.

DER STERN WIRD ROT

Berlin: Henschelverlag, [1969]. iv, 124 pp. A translation by Helmut Baierl of *The Star Turns Red*.

EIN FREUDENFEUER FÜR DEN BISCHOF

Berlin: Henschelverlag, and Frankfurt: Suhrkamp, [1969]. ii, 96 pp. A translation by Kurt Heinrich Hansen and Dieter Hildebrandt of *The Bishop's Bonfire*.

GUTNACHTGESCHICHTE

Berlin: Henschelverlag, [1969]. iii, 35 pp. A translation by Maik Hamburger and Adolf Dresen of *Bedtime Story*.

JUNO UND DER PFAU

Berlin: Henschelverlag, [1969]. iii, 28 pp. A translation by Maik Hamburger and Adolf Dresen of *Juno and the Paycock*.

DAS ENDE VOM ANFANG

Berlin: Henschelverlag, [1969]. iii, 28 pp. A translation by Maik Hamburger and Adolf Dresen of *The End of the Beginning*, with one page of music as an appendix.

D74 DER PREISPOKAL
Berlin: Henschelverlag, and Frankfurt: Suhrkamp, [1969]. 69 pp. A translation by Tankred Dorst of *The Silver Tassie*, with songs translated by Karl Wesseler.

D75 DER PFLUG UND DIE STERNE
Berlin: Henschelverlag, and Frankfurt: Suhrkamp, [1970]. 80 pp. A translation by Volker Canaris and Dieter Hildebrandt of *The Plough and the Stars*.

D76 ICH KLOPFE AN. EINE KINDHEIT IN IRLAND
München: Deutscher Taschenbuch Verlag, 1970. 209 pp. A translation by Georg Goyert of *I Knock at the Door* (identical to that published by Paul List in 1957 and by Diogenes in 1965), with an introduction by Kaspar Spinner.

D77 WÜNSCHE UND VERWÜNSCHUNGEN: EINE KRITISCHE NACHLESE AUS VIER JAHRZEHNTEN
Leipzig: Paul List Verlag, [1970]. 430 pp. A translation by Werner Beyer of thirty-seven of the fifty-three prose pieces published under the title *Blasts and Benedictions* (A44), with a new introduction by Ronald Ayling.

D78 EINE AUSWAHL AUS DEN STÜCKEN, DER AUTOBIOGRAPHIES UND DEN AUFSÄTZEN
Zürich: Diogenes, [1970]. 346 pp. A collection, edited by Urs Widmer, which includes translations by Maik Hamburger and Adolf Dresen of *Juno and the Paycock* and *The End of the Beginning*; and by Helmut Baierl and Georg Simmgen of *Cock-a-Doodle Dandy*. There are also translations by Werner Beyer of extensive extracts from five of the autobiographical volumes (only *Rose and Crown* is excluded); two essays, 'Always the Plow and the Stars' (from *The Green Crow*, A34) and 'Room for the Teachers' (from *Feathers from the Green Crow*, A40); and passages from the preface to *Windfalls* (A16) and from 'The Power of Laughter' (*The Green Crow*, A34). The anthology also contains introductory essays by Heinrich Böll and Klaus Volker.

D79 PURPURSTAUB
Zürich: Diogenes, and Wels: Welsermühl, 1971. 120 pp. A translation by Helmut Baierl and Georg Simmgen of *Purple Dust*.

D80 DUBLINER TRILOGIE: DER SCHATTEN EINES REBELLEN, JUNO UND DER PFAU, DER PFLUG UND DIE STERNE
Zürich: Diogenes, [1972]. 244 pp. A translation by Maik Hamburger of *The Shadow of a Gunman*, 9–68, by Maik Hamburger and Adolf Dresen of *Juno and the Paycock*, 69–144, and by Volker Canaris and Dieter Hildebrandt of *The Plough and the Stars*, 145–241. With a short preface by Volker Canaris and Dieter Hildebrandt.

D81 SEAN O'CASEY STÜCKE, 1920–1940
Berlin: Henschelverlag, 1973. 553 pp. A translation by Konrad Zschiedrich

of *The Harvest Festival*, 15–62, by Maik Hamburger of *The Shadow of a Gunman*, 63–106, translations by Maik Hamburger and Adolf Dresen of *Juno and the Paycock*, 107–64, *Nannie's Night Out*, 257–81, *A Pound on Demand*, 431–46, and *The End of the Beginning*, 447–65, by Volker Canaris and Dieter Hildebrandt of *The Plough and the Stars*, 165–238, by Eva Walch of *Kathleen Listens In*, 239–56, by Tankred Dorst of *The Silver Tassie*, 283–347, by Eva Walch and Klaus Tews of *Within the Gates*, 349–430, and by Helmut Baierl and Georg Simmgen of *Purple Dust*, 449–553. First volume of O'Casey's *Collected Works* in German edited by Wolfgang Schuch. English text of *The Harvest Festival* transcribed from the author's MS. by Ronald Ayling (B71).

Note: Three further books in German first quote writings by O'Casey and are thus recorded in Section B of this bibliography: see B7, B31 and B42.

PERIODICALS

DER PFLUG UND DIE STERNE
Der Querschnitt (Berlin), December 1926. A translation by Grete Scherk of part of Act II of *The Plough and the Stars*.

DIE OKTOBERREVOLUTION
Sonntag (Berlin), November 3, 1957. Translation of a letter (C480).

BILDER IN DER VORHALLE
Sinn und Form: Beiträge zur Literatur (Berlin), vol. XI, nos. 5–6, 1959. A translation by Georg Goyert of the last chapter in *Pictures in the Hallway*.

FRAU CASSIDE MACHT FERIEN
Sinn und Form: Beiträge Zur Literatur, vol. XIII, no. 2, 1961. A translation by Werner Beyer of 'Mrs. Casside Takes a Holiday' from *Inishfallen, Fare Thee Well*.

DER REBELL, DER KEINER WAR
Theater Heute (Hannover), April 1961. A translation by Hagan Mueller–Stahl of *The Shadow of a Gunman*.

BEI W. B. YEATS
Sinn und Form: Beiträge Zur Literatur, XIV, nos. 5–6, 1962. A translation by Werner Beyer of part of 'Black Oxen Passing By', chapter 6 of *Rose and Crown*.

PURPURSTAUB
Theater Heute, August 1963. A translation by Jörg Wehmeier and Werner Wolff of *Purple Dust*.

DÄMMERUNG UND ABENDSTERN
Theater Heute, December 1964. A translation by Werner Beyer of the final part of the last chapter of *Sunset and Evening Star*.

D90   AUS DEN BRIEFEN VON SEAN O'CASEY
      Kultur und Leben (Berlin), September 1966. An anonymous translation of
      passages from the dramatist's letters (C626).

D91   DER POTT
      Sonderheft der Wuppertaler Bühnen (Wuppertal), 1967.
      A translation by Tankred Dorst and Karl Wesseler of *The Silver Tassie* in
      the stage version prepared by Peter Zadek. *

D92   JUNO UND DER PFAU
      Theater der Zeit (Berlin), June 1970.
      A translation by Maik Hamburger and Adolf Dresen of *Juno and the Paycock*.

                              HUNGARIAN

                                 BOOKS

D93   JUNO ÉS A PÁVA
      Budapest: Európa Könyvkiadó, 1957. 87 pp.
      A translation by Péter Nagy of *Juno and The Paycock* (1932 acting edition,
      A11c), with an essay by the translator.

D94   VÖRÖSBE FORDUL A CSILLAG
      Budapest: Európa Könyvkiadó, 1959. 137 pp. A translation by Péter Nagy
      of *The Star Turns Red*, with an essay by the translator.

D95   HAJNALI KOMÉDIA
      In *Egyfelvonásosok*, Budapest: Táncsics, 1960. pp. 49-75. A translation by István
      Takács of *Bedtime Story*. *

D96   HALHATATLAN CSILLAGOK
      In *Tolsztoj Emlékkönyv*, Budapest: Fövárosi Szabó Ervin Könyvtár, 1962. pp.
      403–6. Translation of an essay on Tolstoy commissioned for a commemorative
      volume edited by Tóbiás Áron (B43).

D97   JUNO ÉS A PÁVA
      A translation by József Füsi of passages from *Juno and the Paycock*, included
      in *Világirodalmi Antológia*, VI, no. 1, Budapest: Tankönyvkiadó, 1962. pp.
      287–9. *

D98   BÍBOR POR
      Budapest: Szinháztudományi Intézet, 1963. 141 pp.
      A translation by György Székely of *Purple Dust*.*

D99   ZÖRGETTEM AZ AJTÓN
      Budapest: Magvetö, 1963. 283 pp.
      A translation by György Déri of *I Knock at the Door* (poems by József Tornai),
      with an introduction by Tamas Ungvári.

CSILLAG-JAZZ
A translation by János Elbert of 'The Star-Jazzer', included in *Nagyvilág*, no. 5, 1963. pp. 725–9. Also printed in *Antológia*, Budapest: Magvetö, 1968. pp. 5–13.*

AZ EZÜST KUPA
A translation of five songs and chants from the second act of *The Silver Tassie*, included in *Nagy László: Darázskirály*, Budapest: Magvetö, 1968. pp. 125–8.*

PERIODICAL

O'CASEY ÉS P.G. WODEHOUSE NYILATKOZATA A TÁJÉKOZTATÓNAK
Tájékoztató (Budapest), December 1957. Reprinted in English in *Blasts and Benedictions* (A44) as 'O'Casey in Hungarian Costume'.*

IRISH

BOOK

PUNT AR ÉILEAMH
Dublin: An Chomhairle Náisiunta Drámaiochta, n.d. A translation by Aodh MacDhubhain of 'A Pound on Demand'.*

PERIODICALS

Several of O'Casey's letters in Irish have been printed in Dublin journals: see C447, C535, C607 and C614.

ITALIAN

BOOKS

4 IL FALSO REPUBBLICANO
Milano: Rosa e Ballo Editori, 1944. viii, 99 pp. A translation by Carlo Linati of *The Shadow of a Gunman*.*

5 GIUNONE E IL PAVONE
Milano: Editrice La Fiaccola, 1956. ix, 147 pp. A translation by Carlo Linati of *Juno and the Paycock*.*

6 IL FALÒ DEL VESCOVO
A translation by Gigi Lunari of *The Bishop's Bonfire* included in an anthology of six Irish plays, entitled *Teatro irlandese*, ed. and trans. Gigi Lunari, Milano: Nuova Accademia Editrice, 1961. pp. 173–272.

D107   TEATRO. GIUNONE E IL PAVONE; LA PARVENZA DI UN
        RIBELLE; L'ARATRO E LE STELLE; LA TAZZA D'ARGENTO;
        POLVERE DI PORPORA; ROSE ROSSE PER ME; CHICCHIRIBEL; I
        TAMBURI DI PADRE NED
        Torino: Giulio Einaudi Editore, 1966. 591 pp. *Juno and the Paycock*, translated
        by Antonio Meo, 7–69; *The Shadow of a Gunman*, trans. Nicoletta Neri and
        Bruno Fonzi, 71–116; *The Plough and the Stars*, trans. Franca Cancogni, 117–88;
        The Silver Tassie, trans. Floriana Bossi and Bruno Fonzi, 189–262; *Purple Dust*,
        trans. F. Bossi and B. Fonzi, 263–347; *Red Roses for Me*, trans. Antonio Meo,
        349–429; *Cock-a-Doodle Dandy*, trans. F. Bossi, 431–506; *The Drums of Father
        Ned*, trans. B. Fonzi, 507–87.

D108   ROSE ROSSE PER ME
        Torino: Giulio Einaudi Editore, 1967. 111 pp. A translation by Antonio
        Meo of *Red Roses for Me*; the text is that earlier published in Einaudi's *Teatro*
        [*Selected Plays*].

PERIODICALS

D109   IL FALSO REPUBBLICANO
        Il Convegno (Milano), October 29, 1936. A translation by Carlo Linati and
        Nina Porcelly of *The Shadow of a Gunman*.*

D110   LA SPIA
        Il Dramma (Torino), March 1–15, 1943. A translation by Alessandra Scalero
        of *Juno and the Paycock*.*

D111   L'ARATRO E LE STELLE
        Il Dramma, March 1, 1948. A translation by Giancarlo Galassi-Beria and
        O. Olivet of *The Plough and the Stars*.*

JAPANESE

BOOKS

D112   JUSHI NO KAGE
        A translation by Ken'ichi Yarita of *The Shadow of a Gunman* included in
        the anthology, *Shinko Bungaku Zenshu*, vol. 11, Tokyo: Heibon-sha, 1928.
        pp. 363–431.*

D113   JUNO TO KUJAKU
        A translation by Takaoki Katsuta and Michio Miura of *Juno and the Paycock*
        included in the anthology, *Sekai Gikyoku Zenshu*, vol. 9, Tokyo: Sekai Gikyoku
        Zenshu Kankokai, 1928. pp. 523–92.*

NIWATORI
A translation by Takashi Sugawara of *Cock-a-Doodle Dandy* included in the anthology, *Konnichi no Eibei Engeki*, vol. 1, Tokyo: Hakusui-sha, 1968. pp. 245–326.*

SOGEKIHEI NO KAGE
A translation by Yushi Odashima of *The Shadow of a Gunman* included in the anthology, *Gendai Sekai Engeki*, vol. 12, Tokyo: Hakusui-sha, 1971. pp. 7–58.*

PERIODICALS

KOJIN
Shingeki (Tokyo), February 1968, pp. 78–143. A translation by Yushi Odashima of *Purple Dust*.*

SUKI TO HOSHI
Teatro (Tokyo), November 1969. A translation by Hiroko Watanabe of *The Plough and the Stars*.*

KOREAN

At least two articles by O'Casey have appeared in a Korean translation: these are 'Always the Plow and the Stars' (C417) and 'Bernard Shaw: Appreciation of a Fighting Idealist' (C399). They were included in the anthology, *Highlights of Modern Literature* edited by Francis Brown (B27), which was published in Seoul in a Korean version in the 1950s. No further details have yet been obtained by the compilers of this bibliography.

LATVIAN

BOOK

ES KLAUDZINU PIE DURVĪM
Riga: Liesma, 1971. 280 pp. A translation by Helga Ģintere of *I Knock at the Door*.*

PERSIAN

BOOKS

DAR PUST-E SHIR
Teheran: Zar, 1971. 90 pp. A translation by Ismā'il Khoi of *The Shadow of a Gunman*.*

D120 MĀJARĀ-YE NIMEHSHAB
Teheran: Zar, 1971. 48 pp. A translation by M. Amin Mo'ayyed of 'Bedtime Story'.*

D121 MĀH DAR KAILANAMO MIDERAKHSHAD VA KHAZĀNI DAR BAHĀR
Teheran: Puya, 1972. 70 pp. A translation by Behruz Tabrizi (Dehqāni) of 'The Moon Shines on Kylenamoe' and 'A Fall in a Gentle Wind'.*

D122 GHOBĀR-E ARGHAVĀNI
Teheran: Bābak, 1973. 140 pp. a translation by Hasan Bairāmi of *Purple Dust*.*

D123 GOLHĀ-YE SORKHI BARĀ-YE MAN
Teheran: Payam, 1973. 100 pp. A translation by Manizheh Kāmyāb of *Red Roses for Me*.*

D124 PĀYĀN-E ĀGHAZ
Teheran: Bābak, 1973. 50 pp. A translation by Mohammad Taqi'Alishāhi of 'The End of the Beginning'.*

POLISH

BOOKS

D125 CIEŃ BOHATERA
Warszawa: Centralny Dom Twórczósci Lodowej, 1956. 90 pp. An anonymous translation of *The Shadow of a Gunman*.*

D126 PUKAM DO DRZWI
Kraków: Wydawnictwo Literackie, 1963. 268 pp. A translation by Maria Traczewska of *I Knock at the Door*.

PERIODICALS

D127 KUKURYKU
Dialog (Warszawa), May 1960. A translation by Cecylia Wojewoda of *Cock-a-Doodle Dandy*.

D128 CZERWONE RÓŻE DLA MNIE
Dialog, October 1961. A translation by Cecylia Wojewoda of *Red Roses for Me*.

D129 OPOWIADANIE NA DOBRANOC
Dialog, October 1969. A translation by Cecylia Wojewoda of *Bedtime Story*.

PORTUGUESE

BOOK

JUNO E O PAVÃO
São Paulo: Ed. Brasiliense, [1965]. 94 pp. A translation by Manuel Bandeira of *Juno and the Paycock*, with a preface by Augusto Boal.*

PERIODICAL

[LETTERS.]
Vértice (Coimbra), September–October 1964. A translation of two letters to M. de Oliveira Vilaça (C601).

ROUMANIAN

BOOK

TEATRU
Bucureşti: Editura Pentru Literaturâ Universalâ, 1967. 421 pp. An anthology of six plays, with a preface (pp. 5–14) by Andrei Bâleanu. *The Plough and the Stars*, 15–96, and *The Shadow of a Gunman*, 97–149, are translated by Florian Nicolau; *The End of the Beginning*, 151–73, and *Red Roses for Me*, 175–262, by Andrei Bantaş; *Juno and the Paycock*, 263–332, by Edith Rösler and Mircea Alexandrescu; and *Cock-a-Doodle Dandy*, 333–420, is translated by Radu Nichita.

RUSSIAN

BOOKS

TEN' STRELKA. YUNONA I PAVLIN
Moskva: Goslitizdat, 1935. pp. 149. A translation by N. Treneva and G. Konyushkov of *The Shadow of a Gunman* and by N. Volzhina of *Juno and the Paycock*. Introduction and notes by A. Startsev.

TOVARISHCHI, VSE V BOÎ!
In *Inostrannaya antifashistskaya poeziya*, Moskva: OGIZ, GIKhL, 1943. p. 5. Translation by M. Zenkevich of poems for an anthology. Reprinted in two subsequent collections: *Khrestomatiya po zarubezhnoi literature XX. v. (1917–1945)*, Moskva; Uchpedgiz., 1955. pp. 192–3; and in *V serdtsakh narodov*, Moskva: Izd. inostr. lit., 1957. pp. 368–9.

YA STUCHUS' V DVER'. NA POROGE
Moskva: Goslitizdat, 1946. pp. 392. A translation by V. Toper, N. Daruzes,

M. Lorie, O. Kholmskaya, N. Volzhina, E. Kalashnikova and I. Kashkin of *I Knock at the Door*, pp. 3–175, and by N. Volzhina, O. Kholmskaya, N. Daruzes, V. Toper, E. Kalashnikova and M. Lorie of *Pictures in the Hallway*, 176–390. Chapters from this translation of *I Knock at the Door* were also printed in *Internatsional'naya Literatura* May–June 1940 and in *Literaturnaya Gazeta*, May 1. 1940; chapters from *Pictures in the Hallway* were also printed in *Imushchemu daetsya*, 1946.

D136 IMUSHCHEMU DAETSYA
Moskva: Pravda, 1946. 62 pp. A translation by N. Daruzes, E. Kalashnikova, M. Lorie and N. Volzhina of chapters from *Pictures in the Hallway*. Also printed in *Ogonek*, nos. 34–5.

D137 ZA KRAĬ RODIMY MOĬ. TOVARISHCHI, VSE V BOĬ!
In *Khrestomatiya po zarubezhnoy literature xx v. (1917–1945)*, Moskva: Uchpedgiz.,1955. pp. 185–92 and 192–3. The first passage, translated by N. Volzhina, is a fragment from *I Knock at the Door;* the second contribution comprises poems, translated by M. Zenkevich, originally printed in 1943.

D138 TEN' STRELKA
Moskva: Izd. inostr. lit., 1956. 63 pp. A translation by N. Treneva of *The Shadow of a Gunman*, with notes by A. Startseva.

D139 YUNONA I PAVLIN
Moskva: Izd. inostr. lit., 1956. 87 pp. A translation by N. Volzhina of *Juno and the Paycock*.

D140 YA STUCHUS' V DVER'. NA POROGE
Moskva: Izd. inostr. lit., 1957. 391 pp. Translation by N. Volzhina, N. Daruzes, E. Kalashnikova, I. Kashkin, M. Lorie, V. Toper and O. Kholmskaya of *I Knock at the Door* and of *Pictures in the Hallway*, with an introduction by P. Balashov.

D141 VOSKHODYASHCHAYA ZVEZDA
Essay included in the anthology, *Glazami Druzeĭ*, Leningrad: Lenizdat, 1959. pp. 305–9; originally published in *Literaturnaya Gazeta*, November 5, 1957.

D142 PYAT' ODNOAKTNYKH P'ES
Moskva: Izd. inostr. lit., 1960. 170 pp. A translation of *Five One-Act Plays*, containing 'The End of the Beginning' and 'Time to Go' trans. I. Boronos, and 'A Pound on Demand', 'Hall of Healing' and 'Bedtime Story' trans. N. Loseva.

D143 [LETTER.]
In *Nasledie angliĭskogo romantizma i sovremennost'* by A. Elistratova, Moskva, Izd. Akad. Nauk SSSR, 1960. Extract from a letter to the authoress dated March 19, 1958, pp. 39–41.

P'ESY

Moskva: Iskusstvo, 1961. 608 pp. Contains a translation by N. Volzhina of *Juno and the Paycock*, 29–94, of *the Plough and the Stars* by N. Loseva and I. Boronos, 95–166, of *The Star Turns Red* by V. Lifshits, 167–253, of *Purple Dust* by R. Oblonskaya, 255–342, of *Red Roses for Me* by L. Bol'shintsova, 343–422, of *The Bishop's Bonfire* by M. Druzina, 423–510, and of *The Drums of Father Ned* by N. Loseva, 511–92. With notes by E. Glukhareva-Glumova.

NA SON GRYADUSHCH

Moskva: Iskusstvo, 1961. 24 pp.
A translation by V. V. Rogov of *Bedtime Story*.

KONETS NACHALA

In *Irlandskie teatral'nye miniatyury* (compiled by L. Khvostenko), Moskva, Leningrad: Iskusstvo, 1961. pp. 56–74. A translation by I. Komarova of *The End of the Beginning*.

O VREMENI I O SEBE

In *Den' mira 27 sentyabrya 1960 g.*, Moskva: Izvestiya, 1961. p. 777.

POD TSVETNOĬ SHAPKOĬ

Moskva: Pravda, 1964. 40 pp. A translation by S. Mitina of extracts from *Under a Colored Cap*. Part of this translation, consisting of the story 'An Army with Banners', is reprinted in *Sovremennaya irlandskaya novella*, Moskva, Progress, 1975. pp. 19–42.

ZA TEATRAL'NYM ZANAVESOM: SBORNIK STATEĬ

Moskva: Progress, 1971. 288 pp. A collection of essays on the theatre selected by G. Zlobina with a preface and commentary by the editor. The contents include twenty-six items from *Blasts and Benedictions*, seven from *The Flying Wasp*, four from *Under a Colored Cap* and two articles from *The Green Crow*, translated by R. Oblonskaya, M. Bogoslovskaya and U. Gurova.

PERIODICALS

Many writings by O'Casey first appeared in print in Russian periodicals: see C211, C220, C227, C230, C258, C288, C296, C310, C327, C328, C363, C392, C394, C462, C468, C473, C474, C479, C481, C483, C486, C488, C490, C495, C497, C498, C499, C501, C502, C504, C507, C510, C511, C519, C520, C521, C526, C527, C529, C530, C536, C538, C546, C549, C550, C554, C557, C571, C588.

YA STUCHUS' V DVER'

Internatsional'naya Literatura, [May–June] 1940.
Chapters from *I Knock at the Door* (A19).

YA STUCHUS' V DVER'

Literaturnaya Gazeta, May 1, 1940. Fragment from *I Knock at the Door*, trans. D. Zhantieva.

D152   O BERNARDE SHOU
       Inostrannaya Literatura, [July] 1956. Translation by M. Lorie of a fragment
       from *Sunset and Evening Star* (A31).

D153   PRESTUPLENIE I NAKAZANIE
       Molodezh' mira, [April] 1957. Extract from *I Knock at the Door*.

D154   KOSTER EPISKOPA
       Zvezda (Leningrad), [January] 1958. A translation by M. Druzina of *The Bishop's
       Bonfire* subsequently printed in *P'esy* (D144).

D155   RABOTA
       Teatr, [May] 1958. A translation by D. Solov'ev of 'The Job', short story first
       published in *Windfalls* (A16).

D156   VESNA
       Znamya, [March] 1961. A translation by D. Solov'ev of 'A Fall in a Gentle
       Wind', short story first published in *Windfalls* (A16).

D157   SHEKSPIR SREDI FLAGOV
       Literaturnaya Gazeta, September 22, 1964. A translation of 'Shakespeare Among
       the Flags' (C593).

D158   VECHNO YUNAYA BOGINYA REALIZMA
       Teatr, [November] 1967.

                                    SLOVAK

                                     BOOKS

D159   KOHÜT
       Bratislava: Diliza, 1960. 89 pp. A translation by Eugen S. Rosian of *Cock-a
       Doodle Dandy*.*

D160   STRIEBORNÝ POHÁR
       Bratislava: Diliza, 1962. 83 pp. A translation by Eugen S. Rosian of *The
       Silver Tassie*.*

                                    SPANISH

                                     BOOKS

D161   JUNO Y EL PAVO REAL
       Buenos Aires: Ediciones Ariadna, [1956]. vii, 78 pp. A translation by Floreal
       Mazia of *Juno and the Paycock*.*

EL ARADO Y LAS ESTRELLAS. EL FIN DEL COMIENZO.
CUENTO DE LA HORA DE ACOSTARSE. REEMBOLSO DE UNA
LIBRA.
Buenos Aires: Ediciones Nueva Visión, 1961. 159 pp. A translation
by Manuel Barberá of *The Plough and the Stars*, 7–87; and translations by
Dora Martínez de Vivar of *The End of the Beginning*, 89–111, *Bedtime Story*,
113–39, and *A Pound on Demand*, 141–58.

JUNO Y EL PAVO REAL
A translation by Juan Martín Ruiz–Werner of *Juno and the Paycock*, included
in the anthology *Teatro Irlandés Contemporáneo*, Madrid: Aguilar, 1963. pp.
209–85.

JUNO Y EL PAVO REAL
A translation of *Juno and the Paycock*, included in the anthology *Teatro Irlandés:
Yeats / Lady Gregory / O'Casey / Synge / Carroll / Behan*, ed. Rine Leal, La Habana:
Consejo Nacional de Cultura, 1966. pp. 61–152.

ROSAS ROJAS PARA MI
Madrid: Escelier, 1969. 112 pp. A translation by Alfonso Sastre of *Red Roses
for Me*.*

HOJAS DE ROBLE Y ESPLIEGO. CANTA, GALLO PERSEGUIDO
Madrid: Editorial Cuadernos para el Diálogo, 1972. 275 pp. A translation
by Ana Anton-Pacheco of *Oak Leaves and Lavender*, 37–162, and of *Cock-a-Doodle
Dandy*, 163–274. With a preface by the translator, 5–11, and an introduction
by Alvaro del Amo, 15–36.

EL PUEBLO Y EL TEATRO. CUENTO DE LA HORA DE ACOSTARSE
A translation by Yolanda Aguirre of 'The People and the Theatre' (C322)
and an anonymous translation of 'Bedtime Story' included in a booklet
entitled *Sean O'Casey* (no. 1 in the Cuban 'serie teatro contemporáneo'), La
Habana: Casa del Teatro, [c. 1966]. pp. 43–50 and 51–73.

PERIODICALS

8 CUENTO PARA LA HORA DE ACOSTARSE
Primer Acto (Madrid), 1966. A translation by Renzo Casali of *Bedtime Story*.

9 ROSAS ROJAS PARA MI
Primer Acto, November 1969. A translation by Alfonso Sastre of *Red Roses
for Me*.

SWEDISH

BOOK

D170 JUNO OCH PÅFÅGELN
      Stockholm: Hogo Gebers Förlag, 134 pp. A translation by Ebba Low and
      Gustaf Linden of *Juno and the Paycock*, with a four-page preface by the
      playwright (B4).

PERIODICAL

D171 [LETTER]
      Svenska Dagsbladet (Christmas number), December 19, 1924. An anonymous
      translation of a written contribution to a symposium of dramatists (C92).

TURKISH

BOOKS

D172 SAĞLIK YURDU: OYUN
      Istanbul, De Yayinevi, [1962]. 48 pp. A translation by Cevat Çapan of 'Hall
      of Healing'.*

D173 DÜNYANIN DÜZENI
      Istanbul, Millî Eğitim Basimevi, 1965. 86 pp. A translation by İrfan Şahinba
      of *Juno and the Paycock*.*

SECTION E

Manuscript, Typescript and Proof Material

Arranged in order of, first, holograph material listed chrono-logically – the chronology of each exercise book or notebook being assessed by the date of the earliest ascertain-able item of writing in it – and, secondly, typescript material listed chronologically in order of publication in book form. There are three exceptions within the typescript material: 'Kathleen Listens In' and 'Nannie's Night Out' are listed in order of the date of their composition, which accords with that of their first stage production at the Abbey Theatre, while individual typescripts of articles, stories, and poems that were not printed in O'Casey's books during his lifetime appear in a sequence entitled Miscellaneous Typescripts at the end of the section of typescript material. The section closes with a short checklist of proof material, listed chronologically in order of publication. All the material in Section E is now in libraries or public collections; these sources are named under the individual entries unless the item is in the Berg Collection of the New York Public Library. The latter collection, having acquired both the Sean O'Casey and Fergus O'Connor Papers, has by far the largest collection of O'Casey material in existence. Readers wishing to trace entries by title are requested to use the index to the *Bibliography*. MS represents holograph material and TS represents typescript material.

I HOLOGRAPH MATERIAL

(MS) LOOSE HOLOGRAPH MATERIAL FROM THE F. D. MURPHY COLLECTION

This material was gathered by Franklin D. Murphy, chancellor of the University of California, Los Angeles, and presented to the UCLA Library in July 1970. Some material was purchased by him, other items (typescript as well as holograph, the former listed later in Section E) were presented to him by Sean O'Casey and Robert Hogan. The holograph material appears to be the earliest extant, but the dating is only approximate though the playwright thought it as accurate as could be assessed.

Contents:
(1) 'The Sweet Little Town of Kilwirra'. Poem of four stanzas of eight lines each, 1 p. holograph; on the reverse are pasted some newspaper clippings dated April 11, 1924. Murphy dated this item as *circa* 1900, probably on the basis of the author's guesswork.
(2) 'The Soul of Man'. Poem of six stanzas first printed in *Feathers from the Green Crow* (A40). Two page holograph; on the reverse are pasted some undated newspaper cuttings. 'November 1905' was added in O'Casey's later handwriting near the title.
(3) 'Subjects to be written', 14 pp. holograph torn from a notebook. The first page gives a list of songs and the following pages contain verses intended for Christmas cards written probably 1916 – 18. O'Casey wrote various Christmas card greetings for Fergus O'Connor, as it was a steady if small source of income for him. He hated the task, however, as he told O'Connor in a letter dated March 9, 1918: 'I must confess I am tired of writing Christmas Greetings—it is most difficult to write to order. However, I have ten good ones done, and I want you to send me on the price you are prepared to give for thirty of them before I do any more, for I don't care a lot for the job.' Six such verses are printed in *The Letters of Sean O'Casey* (A46).

(MS) HOLOGRAPH EXERCISE BOOK

Christian Brothers' Exercise Book (20.4×16.2cm) signed 'Sean O'Cathasaigh' in ink on the cover. Title-page reads 'Amhráin an Dreólin. Songs of the Wren. By An Gall Fada.' This pseudonym, meaning the Tall Stranger, was one used by O'Casey on various occasions from 1907 to 1918. The writings in the book are on alternate pages with blank versos; some pages are loose.

Contents:
(1) 'If the Germans Came to Ireland in the Morning' (eight Stanzas), 2 pp. Printed in *Songs of the Wren No. 1* (A5) and in *Feathers from the Green Crow* (A40).
(2) 'Private Cassidy, V.C.' (seven stanzas), 2 pp. Unpublished; another version of this song, entitled 'Private Stephen Gwynn,

M.P.', appears among the loose holograph material in the Fergus
O'Connor Papers (E3).

(3) 'I Don't Believe It, Do You?' (four stanzas with four different choruses),
3 pp.
Printed in *Songs of the Wren No. 2* (A6).

(4) 'How Do You Doodle Do' (three stanzas with three different choruses),
3 pp.
Unpublished; the song appears in a different version among the loose
holograph material in the Fergus O'Connor Papers (E3).

(5) 'The Grand Oul' Dame Brittannia' (eight stanzas), 3 pp.
Printed as a separate broadsheet (A1), in *Windfalls* (A16) and in *Feathers from*
the Green Crow (A40); see also C68; different published versions contain,
variously, six, seven and eight stanzas.

(6) 'Marching Through Germany' (five stanzas), 4 pp.
Unpublished; another version of this song appears among the loose
holograph material in the Fergus O'Connor Papers (E3).

(7) 'The Demi-Semi Home Rule Bill' (six stanzas), 2 pp.
Printed in *Songs of the Wren No. 1* (A5) and in *Feathers from the Green Crow*
(A40).

(8) 'Josephine Ruagh' (seven stanzas), 2 pp.
Unpublished; another version of this song appears among the loose
holograph material in the Fergus O'Connor Papers (E3).

(9) 'As I Wait in the Boreen for Maggie' (four stanzas), 2 pp.
Printed in *Songs of the Wren No. 1* (A5) and *Feathers from the Green Crow* (A40);
see also C77.

(10) 'John Bull's Love Song' (five stanzas), 2 pp.
Unpublished; another version of this song appears among the loose
holograph material in the Fergus O'Connor Papers (E3).

This exercise book, totalling 26 pages of holograph material, was originally
in the possession of Fergus O'Connor, O'Casey's first publisher in Dublin;
it is now in the Berg Collection of the New York Public Library. Other
loose holograph material from the O'Connor Papers is listed in E3.

E3   (MS) LOOSE HOLOGRAPH MATERIAL FROM THE FERGUS
O'CONNOR ARCHIVE

This material, like that in E2, was catalogued before its acquisition by the
Berg Collection of the New York Public Library. It was then haphazardly
gathered together but the following list is in alphabetical order of the titles
of songs and poems that may collectively be entitled Amhráin an Dreóilín
or Songs of the Wren – the author's description which is interpreted in
our Notes to *Songs of the Wren* (A5).

Contents:

(1) One holograph page lists twenty titles of songs and ballads which,
as O'Casey says in a handwritten note, were 'Published by Fergus O'Connor
& Co. 1918'. There seems little doubt that some of the following titles
('O Brothers Lift Your Faces', for instance) were never printed by O'Connor
or any other publisher. These are the titles in the order in which the author

listed them: 'Since Mary Went Away', 'The Divil's Recruitin' Campaign', 'We've Captured the Cave of Machpelah', 'I Don't Believe It, Do You?', 'The Summer Sun is Tightly Folding', 'Marching Through Germany', 'John Bull's Love Song', 'Private Stephen Gwynn, M.P.', 'Life's Blossoms', 'My Modest Brown-haired Mary', 'How Do You Doodle Do?', 'Home Rule for Ireland, Ri tooral li Ay', 'Strolling with Mary', 'The Grand Oul' Dame Brittannia', 'When Night's Deep Shadows Darkly Fall', 'O Brothers Lift Your Faces', 'To Mary', 'Labour's Awakening', 'Lament for Thomas Ashe', 'Thomas Ashe'.

(2) 'The Awakening of Labour'. Poem of four stanzas 'by Sean O'Casey', an unusual attribution at this period of the author's life when he usually used the Gaelic form of his name. One and one-half (torn) page holograph.

(3) 'John Bull in A Hot Corner' and 'Ireland at the Peace Conference'. Two short pieces of four lines apiece, holograph, together with some comments on 'Ashe's Oration at Casement's Fort'. One page of note-paper headed 'O'Toole Pipers and Athletic Club'.

(4) 'John Redmond. Dead. 1918'. Poem of six stanzas. One page holograph signed 'Sean O'Cathasaigh'.
Printed in *The Letters of Sean O'Casey* (A46).

(5) 'Lament for Thomas Ashe'. Poem of four stanzas. One page holograph, unsigned.
Published as a broadside (A2) and incorporated into the prose pamphlet *The Sacrifice of Thomas Ashe* (A4b); reprinted in *Feathers from the Green Crow* (A40).

(6) 'Life's Blossoms': poem of four stanzas. One page holograph signed Sean O'Cathasaigh, torn at bottom of page. Another version, entitled 'Songs Part 3 Life's Blossoms', appears in a one page holograph, unsigned.

(7) 'My Gentle, Brown-haired Mairin'. Poem of four stanzas. One page and one-quarter of a page holograph, unsigned.

(8) 'Sinn Fein Election Ballad'. Poem of four stanzas with a chorus. One page holograph with a note to Fergus O'Connor signed 'Sean O'Cathasaigh'.
Printed in *The Letters of Sean O'Casey* (A46).

(9) 'Sinn Fein Election Song'. Poem of five stanzas with a chorus. Two page holograph, unsigned.
Printed in *The Letters of Sean O'Casey*.

(10) 'Since Mary Went Away'. Poem of five stanzas. One page holograph signed 'S. O. Cathasaigh'. Song variously entitled 'Since Maggie Went Away' and 'Since Maura Went Away'.
Printed in *Songs of the Wren No. 2* (A6) and in *Feathers from the Green Crow* (A40).

(11) 'Songs of the Wren. Home Rule for Ireland. Ri Tooral li Ay'. Poem of five stanzas. One page holograph, unsigned. Another version, entitled 'Home Rule for Ireland, Ri Tooral li Ay', has six stanzas and appears in a two page holograph draft signed 'Sean O'Cathasaigh'.

(12) 'Songs of the Wren. How Do You Doodle Do?' Poem of three stanzas. Two page holograph, unsigned. A different version is found in an exercise book (E2).

(13) 'Songs of the Wren III. John Bull's Love Song'. Poem of five stanzas. One page holograph, unsigned. A different version is found in an exercise book (E2).

(14) 'Songs. Josephine Ruadh'. Poem of seven stanzas. One page holograph,

unsigned. Another version with slight variations is found in an exercise book (E2).

(15) 'Songs of the Wren Part III. Marching Through Germany'. Poem of five stanzas. One page holograph, unsigned. A slightly different version is found in an exercise book (E2).

(16) 'Songs of the Wren Part III. My Modest Brown-haired Mary'. Poem of four stanzas. One page holograph, unsigned.

(17) 'Songs of the Wren Part III. Private Stephen Gwynn, M.P.' Poem of seven stanzas. One page holograph, unsigned. A variation of this song, entitled 'Private Cassidy, V.C.', is found in an exercise book (E2).

(18) 'Songs of the Wren. When Night's Deep Shadows Darkly Fall'. Poem of four stanzas. One page holograph unsigned. Another version with slight variations but the same length is signed 'S. O'Cathasaigh', one page holograph.

(19) 'Songs. Oh! Brothers Lift Your Faces'. Poem of six stanzas. One page holograph unsigned.

(20) 'Songs. Strolling with Mary'. Poem of three stanzas. One page holograph, unsigned.

(21) 'Songs. To Mary'. Poem of four stanzas. One page holograph signed 'S. O'Cathasaigh'.
Unpublished in this version, but a similar poem of seven stanzas, entitled 'To Maire', was printed in *The World of Sean O'Casey* (B53).
A revised version of eight stanzas, entitled 'The Garland', was first printed in *Windfalls* (A16).

(22) 'Thomas Ashe'. Poem of six stanzas signed 'Sean O'Cathasaigh'. One page holograph.
Printed as a broadside (A3) but not to be confused with the poem of two stanzas, with the same title, printed in *Bottom Dog* on November 3, 1917 (C74).

(23) 'The Summer Sun is Tightly Folding'. Poem of three stanzas with a refrain. Two page holograph signed 'Craobh na nDealg.'
First printed in *Songs of the Wren No. 2* (A6) and reprinted with four additional lines in *The World of Sean O'Casey* (B53).

E4 (MS) HOLOGRAPH NOTEBOOK

Dark blue notebook (front cover missing) with worn black leather spine. Size: 18.4 × 11.4cm. On the first page is written 'The Crimson Cornkrakes'; on another page is written, in pencil, 'Sean O'Cathasaigh. 18 Abercorn Road, North Wall, Dublin, March 1918'. The notebook is badly damaged and many pages are loose.

Contents: 'The Crimson Cornkrakes': an incomplete discussion about Bernard Shaw written in the form of dialogue (in pencil), 1 p. Shorthand exercises, 6 pp. Financial Accounts (dated 1948–54), 81 pp. Dialogue entitled 'The Orange Lily', 1 p. Notes, 4 pp. (pages loose). Outline of 'The Harvest Festival: Play' (written 1918–19), 4 pp. Notes for 'The Hill of Healing', 1 p.

(MS) HOLOGRAPH MANUSCRIPT

'The Harvest Festival. A Play in Three Acts'. Written in ink in closely written legible handwriting on separate sheets of ruled exercise paper (27.9 × 21.6cm), 56 pp. On the title-page is signed the Gaelic form of his name that O'Casey used for all his early publications: 'S. O'Cathasaigh. 18 Abercorn Road, Dublin'.

This play, the second by O'Casey and the earliest we now possess or are likely to possess, was written approximately 1918–19. It was rejected by the Abbey Theatre in January 1920 and has not been staged or printed in English though a German translation appeared in 1973 (B71).

The manuscript is divided by acts, each stapled in the top left-hand corner; each act is paginated separately. It is almost certain that this is the only copy of this manuscript as the author had no typewriter at the time that it was written.

Contents: Act I, pp. 1–16, plus title-page which includes list of the *dramatis personae* etc.
Page 1 is torn but none of the dialogue seems to be missing.
Act II, pp. 1–14. The bottom left-hand corner of p. 2 is slightly torn.
Act III, pp. 1–12.

In addition, there is also an unfinished draft of Act I, pp. 1–13, which is a revised and expanded version. Page 3 is crossed out in ink.

(MS) HOLOGRAPH EXERCISE BOOK

'Exercise Book' printed on red cover; spine broken. Size: 20.3 × 15.8cm. Leaf torn out.

Contents: Notes and jottings (dated 1927–9), 7 pp. Draft of opening of Act I of *Shadow of a Gunman*, 25 pp. Notes, 2 pp. The fragmentary draft of *Shadow of a Gunman* (written in 1922) seems to be in its final form. There are very few differences from the printed text and, indeed, this draft contains nothing that is not in the published version. The draft starts at the beginning of the play and ends with Davoren quoting the 'Golden Celandine' poem to Minnie Powell.

(MS) HOLOGRAPH EXERCISE BOOK

Dark red cover (20.3×15.2cm) with note in O'Casey's hand pasted on to front cover: 'Penelope's Lovers. A Walk with Eros'. Some pages loose, one torn, others probably torn out. There are several pages which contain Dublin press cuttings (dated 1923–4) pasted over writings.

Contents: Draft of part of poem, 'Walk with Eros', written in indelible pencil, 2 pp.; notes written in ink and pencil, 4 pp. (all 6 pp. obscured by news cuttings pasted into the book). Dialogue for 'Kathleen Listens In' (1923

approximately), in pencil and ink, 8 pp. Fragmentary dialogue used later
in *Juno and the Paycock*, 3 pp. Notes entitled 'A Free State Sphinx', 2 pp.
Draft entitled 'Penelope's Lovers. Scenario' (later entitled 'Irish Nannie'
in this book; eventually staged and published as 'Nannie's Night Out': written
approximately 1923–4), 27 pp. Draft of 'A Stroll with Venus and her Boy'
('A Walk with Venus'), written probably 1922–4, 22 pp. One page of notes
and another one of interesting caricatures drawn by O'Casey. Draft of play,
'Kathleen Listens In' (1923), written in ink and pencil, 5 pp. Draft of short
story, 'Mollser' (C96), 11 pp. Draft of letter, 1 p. Note for *The Plough and
the Stars*, 1 p. Notes, 2 pp. Draft of two songs: 'Bonnie Winsome Mary',
3 pp.; and 'Grand Oul' Dame Britannia', 1 p. (in later handwriting). Note
concerning controversy over *The Plough and the Stars* (1926), 13 pp. Draft
for biographical chapter published as 'The Dream Review' in *I Knock at
the Door*, 8 pp. Draft of poem, 'Waiting for Maggie', in later handwriting,
4 pp. Notes, 2 pp. Draft of poem, 'Chosen Things', 3 pp.

Several of these poems, written before his first play was staged in 1923,
were eventually published in *Windfalls* (A16). 'Kathleen Listens In' and
'Nannie's Night Out' were published in *Feathers from the Green Crow* (A40).

E8   (MS) HOLOGRAPH NOTEBOOK

Small green notebook (15.8×9.6cm) with dark green, torn spine. 'S. O'Casey'
written in ink on inside cover. Several pages loose.

Contents: Notes, jottings and list of addresses written in ink and pencil. Earlier
ones (written 1923–4 approximately) include note on 'Nannie's Night Out',
1923; one entry in Gaelic. Several press cuttings, one dated December 27,
1924, and others 1928 and 1936, 42 pp. Accounts and statement of income,
August 1934–January 1948, 69 pp. List of names and addresses, 12 pp.

E9   (MS) HOLOGRAPH EXERCISE BOOK

Red cover with broken spine (20.3×15.8cm); 'Exercise Book' printed on the
cover, which is stained and faded.

Contents: Several pages of press cuttings, with notes and fragmentary dialogue
for *The Silver Tassie* and *Within the Gates* (1926–9 approximately), 15 pp.
Complete draft of one-act play, 'House God' (later entitled 'End of the
Beginning'), with many differences from text first printed in *Windfalls* (A16)
and one additional character, 27 pp. Unfinished draft of short story,
'Toreador' or 'Bull of Bashan' (C137), 8 pp. Draft of song for 'End of
Beginning' (in pencil) and dialogue for *Within the Gates*, 2 pp. Notes dated
1926 and 1927, 6 pp.

E10   (MS) HOLOGRAPH EXERCISE BOOK

Pink cover with brown spine (20.3×15.8cm); on front cover is pasted a piece
of paper with the following words typed on it: 'Plough and the Stars' and

'The Red Lily. Rough Copy and Notes'. These notes have been crossed out in ink, and 'The Silver Tassie' has been substituted for them.

Contents: Jottings and snatches of dialogue for *The Silver Tassie*, and short outline of 'The Red Lily', 12 pp. Draft of Act I of *The Silver Tassie*, showing many changes from printed text; there is much dialogue which was omitted from the version published in 1928, 38 pp. Draft of Act II of *The Silver Tassie*, containing less unpublished material than Act I but with many interesting changes, including the rough draft of a song which is not found in the published text, 25 pp. Draft of Act III containing a number of minor changes from the printed text; the blinded Teddy Foran does not appear in this draft, 35 pp. Rough fragmentary draft of setting and opening of Act IV, 3 pp. Drafts of two chapters of *Inishfallen, Fare Thee Well*: 'Pax' and 'Drifting', 12 pp. Notes for review of book on Irish prison system (post-1922), entitled by O'Casey 'Spirits in Prison', 4 pp. Further draft of 'Drifting' (here entitled 'Truce and Treaty'), 11 pp. Notes and ideas for *Inishfallen, Fare Thee Well*, 3 pp. Jottings and Notes, 7 pp.

The main interest here is the long draft of three acts of *The Silver Tassie*. It is likely that the jottings and dialogue at the beginning of the book are the earliest ideas for the play, but the 45 pages of further notes and sketches described in holograph manuscript E11 would seem to contain material written before the drafts of the three acts were written in this exercise book.

(MS) HOLOGRAPH MANUSCRIPT

Contents:
(1) Fragmentary draft of *The Silver Tassie*, written in ink and pencil on the backs of letters and on odd scraps of quarto paper. Some fragments have been crossed out by the author and some snatches of dialogue are written on pages that had already been used for correspondence. These unnumbered pages, fastened together by a steel pin, contain what are probably the earliest notes and dialogue for the play (1926–8), 11 pp.
(2) Further notes and snatches of dialogue for *The Silver Tassie* written on loose double-page sheets of headed note-paper; printed on each sheet is '7 St. Andrew's Mansions, Dorset Street, London, W.1.' It is probable that these rough writings comprise an expanded draft written after the fragment (1) above, and yet earlier than the the more extensive drafts of Acts I-III which are to be found in one of O'Casey's exercise books (E10). Among the notes are six interesting sketches of scenes from Act II and Act IV of the play. Total (including sketches), 34 pp.

(MS) HOLOGRAPH EXERCISE BOOK

Faded red covered exercise book (20.3 × 15.2cm) with dark red spine. Pasted on to the front cover is a label inscribed: 'Red Roses For Me. O'Casey. Tingrith, Totnes, Devon, England'. The book contains fragmentary notes and ideas (in ink, with occasional entries in pencil) for articles and early autobiographical chapters, and the first long-hand draft of *Red Roses For Me*.

Contents: Notes and ideas, press cuttings (two dated 1941); several diary entries dated, variously, from June 27, 1928 until March 8, 1929; list of books wanted (1928–9); draft of a letter. Total, 10 pp. Description entitled 'The Holy Image', 1 p. Scenario notes for *Red Roses For Me*, 1 p. Diary entries dated November 4, 1936 and July 26, 1941; notes for *Red Roses For Me*; extract of sham-battle from the last chapter of *Pictures in the Hallway*, 3 pp. Then follows draft of play entitled 'Astray in a Gold Canoe' (later entitled *Red Roses For Me*), beginning with draft of 'Scene I' and part of 'Act II', with list of characters, 41 pp. Fragment of fantasy—description of Salvation Army; paragraph describing Johnny at School *(I Knock at the Door)* and further list of characters for *Red Roses*, 4 pp. Fragmentary draft of and notes for article entitled 'State and Church' (published as 'England, Say When' in *The Flying Wasp*), 3 pp. Further draft of *Red Roses* (Acts 3 and 4 in published text), 49 pp. Notes for and draft of article entitled 'The Amazing Mr. Coward', 7 pp. Draft of letter entitled 'London Nursing Home', 2 pp. Diary entries (dated from August 1927 to November 1927 and from January 1929 until August 1929); list of books and Income Tax calculations, 7 pp.

This draft of *Red Roses For Me* is a complete one; it differs considerably from the text first printed in 1942 (A23) and contains much unpublished dialogue.

E13   (MS) HOLOGRAPH EXERCISE BOOK

Black cover with red spine (20.3×15.8cm). 'Rich and Rare' written on paper pasted onto cover by O'Casey, and crossed out by him. Pages cut out at both ends of the book.

Contents: Two press cuttings pasted on to inside cover of book. Notes and jottings (some used in *The Silver Tassie*) entitled 'Half Gods Go', 1 p. Speeches from *The Plough and the Stars* (probably revisions), 1 p. Ideas for Scene I of *The Red Star* (subsequently entitled *The Star Turns Red*), 1 p. Then follow rough early drafts of three chapters printed in *Pictures in the Hallway*: draft of biographical chapter entitled 'Room 15' (opening of 'A Coffin Comes to Ireland' in *Pictures in the Hallway*; this short account is very different from the the printed version), 3 pp.; draft of opening of 'Cat 'n Cage', with some material omitted in the published text—this incident, entitled 'Boxer', describes how Archie and Johnny drown a dog in the canal, 9 pp. (subsequently published separately (B16)); draft entitled 'Dung-dodgers over the border' (published as 'The Hawthorn Tree'), 6 pp.; draft of part of the pub scene in 'Cat 'n Cage', with several changes from the printed narrative, 6 pp. Rough fragmentary draft of opening scene of play entitled 'Far From the Madding Crowd', used later as idea for opening to *Purple Dust* ('Mr Eiderdown' here is evidently prototype of 'Poges'), 2 pp. Notes, list of *Dramatis personae*, and draft of one-act play, entitled 'R and R' ('Time to Go'); it includes material omitted from the published play, 27 pp. Draft of one-act play, 'Bedtime Story' (written 1950), 24 pp. Draft of a letter, 1 p. Draft of further part of 'Cat 'n Cage' (*Pictures in the Hallway*), 4 pp. Notes (one entry dated July 6, 1936), 2 pp. Draft of letter to the author's London Solicitors (1939), 2 pp.

(MS) HOLOGRAPH EXERCISE BOOK

20.3×15.8cm. Red cover badly scratched; spine of book damaged. 'No. 2' written in ink on cover. At least 15 leaves cut out of book.

Contents: Notes (dated 1928–30) and several press cuttings, 3 pp. (including inside cover). Ideas, Outline Scenarios, and draft of biographical sketches (some of which were used in *I Knock at the Door*), 123 pp. Fragmentary dialogue for *Within the Gates*, 5 pp. Notes (including one entry in pencil) and press cuttings, dated 1928–31, including short draft of an article on Ibsen, 15 pp. (including inside cover).

It is almost certain that the autobiographical writings in this exercise book are the earliest written by O'Casey; indeed, the fact that the playwright had begun to write the earliest draft of *I Knock at the Door* as early as 1929 or 1930 will surprise many scholars of his work, for the book was published as late as 1939. In these sketches, which comprise a continuous narrative without chapter division, events in Johnny's life are telescoped, and there are many details here which were omitted in the final published form. There is, for instance, a fight between Jimmy (Johnny) and Bella (Ella); and a visit to Bray by Johnny and his sister and her husband. The narrative is written in the first person.

(MS) HOLOGRAPH EXERCISE BOOK

Black cover (20.3×15.8cm) with red spine. Note in O'Casey's hand on cover: 'I Knock at the Door'. Several pages loose; some appear to be missing.

Contents: Notes and news cuttings (1928–30) and diary entries dated 1941–2, 13 pp. General notes and ideas for *Drums Under the Windows*, 5 pp. Draft entitled 'I Go to Coole', 16 pp. This contains material used in the two Coole chapters in *Inishfallen, Fare Thee Well*: there are many differences from the printed text, and the narrative is written in the first person. It is probably the draft for a long article entitled 'The Lady of Coole', published in *The Saturday Book* in 1943 (B12), and later partially used in *Inishfallen*. This item is followed by drafts of seven chapters published in *Drums Under the Windows*, with many differences from printed text, and much material that does not appear in the final form (the date of composition is 1942): these are a draft of 'At the Sign of the Pick and Shovel', 17 pp.; notes and draft entitled 'Ella' ('House of the Dead' in printed version), 4 pp.; notes and draft of first part of 'The Song of a Shift', 4 pp.; further draft of 'House of the Dead', 12 pp. Notes (dated August 27, 1942), 1 p. Draft entitled 'Tom Passes Out' (part of chapter eventually published as 'Poor Tom's A-Cold'), 21 pp.; draft of chapter entitled 'On the Railway' (incomplete biographical sketch not included in any of the autobiographical volumes) 6 pp.; notes and draft of part of chapter entitled 'Drums Under the Windows', 18 pp.; draft of 'Ella' (published as 'Behold My Family is Poor'), 15 pp.; draft of 'Heaven is my Home' (published as 'Home of the Living'), 14 pp. Notes, 1 p.

Contents (from the other end of the book): Notes and press cuttings (one entry dated 'Christmas 1929' and another 'August 10, 1942'), 7 pp. (including inside cover). Notes entitled 'Penmaenmawr', 2 pp. Notes entitled 'The Common Reader: Elizabethan Drama', 3 pp.

The most important writings in this book are the early drafts for chapters in *Drums Under the Windows* and *Inishfallen, Fare Thee Well*, but some of the diary entries are of great interest too. Although O'Casey's note on cover says 'I Knock at the Door', there is none of the material for that volume in this notebook. We assume that the author used this title as a generic one for each of the six autobiographical books until he found individual titles for them.

E16 (MS) HOLOGRAPH EXERCISE BOOK

'Exercise Book' printed on red cover, front leaf of which is sellotaped (scotch taped) on to red spine. 'Danger Don'ts' printed on back cover. Size: 20.3×15.8cm.

Notes and dialogue for *Within the Gates* and other (unwritten) plays; ideas for book of short stories, some of which were later used in the autobiographical volumes (one entry dated October 1, 1930), 9 pp. Rough draft of opening of a play; it appears to be the earliest crude form of what was eventually to become *The Drums of Father Ned*, 3 pp. Notes, 1 p.

E17 (MS) HOLOGRAPH MANUSCRIPT

Early draft of *Within the Gates* (1930–1 approximately), written on loose unnumbered pages torn from a notebook (21.6×14cm). Writing on one side of the paper only; one page torn in half. These notes and drafts of dialogue and scenes for the play were found in no recognisable state of order; they have now been assembled by one of the compilers of this catalogue in what would appear to be a rough working order. This draft was evidently written with film possibilities in mind, as were the earlier typescripts of the play (see E34). Certain scenes in the printed version are clearly recognisable in this draft, but there is a good deal of unpublished material here too. Total, 88 pp.

E18 (MS) HOLOGRAPH NOTEBOOK

Brown notebook (19.7×12.7cm) with faded red spine; hinged at top; ink-stained cover with typed note, 'Ideas for Plays and Stories', pasted on to cover. 'Sean O'Casey' and his Chalfont address are written inside back cover of the pad. Many pages are creased and many others torn out.

Contents: Notes and ideas (one entry dated 1932; another dated September 7, 1950), 7 pp. Snatches of dialogue for *Cock-a-Doodle Dandy*, 2 pp. Notes, including ideas for *Cock-a-Doodle Dandy*, 1 p. Draft of a letter, 1 p. Domestic notes, shopping lists etc., of which 3 pp. are in Sean O'Casey's hand, the others in his wife's.

(MS) HOLOGRAPH EXERCISE BOOK

Grey hard-covered exercise book (22.9×17.8cm) with damaged blue spine. The cover is badly scratched. Some pages have been torn out; there is writing at both ends of the book.

Contents: Notes (including one in pencil) and news cuttings; remarks on the Irish Academy of Letters and its founders (1932), 18 pp. Dialogue for *Within the Gates*, 1 p. Drafts of several private and public letters (1933–6), 4 pp. Draft of play, 'Pound on Demand', including some material not to be found in printed version (A16), 13 pp. Drafts of several letters to the press, and a short story published in *Time and Tide*, 19 pp. Diary entries for 1938 and 1939, and draft of article, 'The Value of Violence', 6 pp. Draft of part of chapter, 'Coming of Age' (*Pictures in the Hallway*), 2 pp. Fragmentary draft of part of play entitled 'Stay in Country' (later to become *Purple Dust*), 9 pp. Diary entries dated September 1946, 3 pp. Draft of part of chapter for *Rose and Crown*, entitled 'The Show-Off' (published as 'London Apprentice'), 6 pp. Outline of play in four scenes entitled 'It's Gonna Rain No-more', 2 pp.

Contents (from the other end of the book): Notes on cast for *Within the Gates* (1933–4), 3 pp. Draft of article on Shakespeare, National Theatre and films (1933–4), 3 pp. Draft of book review on John Mitchel and article on Partition (1938–9), 7 pp. Draft of part of chapter, 'TP and His Invitation', used in *Rose and Crown*, 3 pp. Notes for and drafts of parts of eleven chapters of *Drums Under the Windows*, 124 pp. Notes for and draft of first chapter of *Inishfallen, Fare Thee Well*, here entitled 'Clock Strikes 12', 17 pp. Drafts of several private letters, 5 pp. Notes (dated 1946), 1 p.

The writings in this book were written mostly in two periods: 1932–9 and 1943–6 approximately. The long draft of *Drums Under the Windows*, showing many differences from the printed text, is of especial interest.

(MS) HOLOGRAPH EXERCISE BOOK

Black cover (20.3×15.8cm) with red spine. Two pieces of paper pasted on to cover, on which O'Casey wrote in ink: 'Life. Volume 6. An Cogaidh' (Gaelic for 'the War') and 'America. June 11, 1949. Review of I. Fare Thee Well'. Two leaves cut out. Press cuttings pasted on both inside covers of the book.

Contents: Notes (one entry dated September 18, 1934), 2 pp. Outline, notes and early draft of *The Star Turns Red*, here given the title 'The Red Star' in Gaelic, 31 pp. Notes and draft entitled 'Life. The Chalfonts' (part of 'A Gate Clangs Shut' in *Rose and Crown*), 14 pp. Notes and drafts of parts of 'A Friar by the Fireside' and 'A Long Ash Wednesday', 16 pp. Draft of opening of 'Star of the County Down', 3 pp. Notes and drafts of 'Ship in Full Sail' and 'Stars and Stripes' (published as 'In New York Now'), 8 pp. All the above chapters appear in *Rose and Crown* in expanded form.

Note on a review by Ivor Brown (dated October 8, 1950), 1 p. Fragmentary draft of dialogue for *Within the Gates*, 5 pp. Notes and incomplete drafts of three further chapters in *Rose and Crown*: 'Pennsylvanian Visit', 1 p.; 'Hearts and Clubs', 4 pp.; 'Only 5 minutes More', 6 pp. Ideas and outline for *Sunset and Evening Star*, 3 pp. Then follow drafts and notes for ten chapters published in the sixth volume of autobiography: 'A Drive of Snobs', 12 pp.; 'Shaw's Corner' (first part of chapter), 12 pp.; Notes, 3 pp.; fragmentary ideas for 'Cambridge' and 'Deep in Devon', 3 pp.; 'Orwell Pulls the Green Flag Down' (published as chapter entitled 'Rebel Orwell'), 4 pp.; Notes, 3 pp.; 'Heavily Hangs the Broad Sunflower', 8 pp.; 'Drink at the Door' (published as 'And Evening Star'), 5 pp.; 'Orphans of the storm', 6 pp.; 'In Cellar Cool', 5 pp.; fragmentary draft of chapter entitled 'Sunset', 2 pp. These drafts were written 1951–2. Draft of article entitled, 'Let's Make a Play' (1952), 2 pp. Notes and jottings, 4 pp.

This exercise book is of interest for containing what is probably the earliest draft of *The Star Turns Red* (1937–8 approximately) and long drafts of *Rose and Crown* (nine chapters) and *Sunset and Evening Star* (ten chapters), written 1950–2.

E21 (MS) HOLOGRAPH NOTEBOOK

Red notebook hinged at the top by two steel rings; embossed on the front cover is the brand name, 'The Circus: Reporter's Note Book'.

Contents: Pasted on to inside front cover is a snatch of dialogue in the later handwriting of the playwright entitled 'Joxer and Boyle'; this is the 'What is the Stars?' colloquy from *Juno and the Paycock* (perhaps written for the phonograph recording made by the author for Caedmon); there are several changes from the printed version, 3 pp. Dialogue and scenes entitled 'Red Star' (later Act III of *The Star Turns Red*), 5 pp. (including several torn pages pinned into book). Draft of scenes in the same play, entitled 'Second Act. The R.S.', 17 pp. Fragmentary note explaining his article, 'Sword of the Soviet', 1 p. Further draft of scenes in *The Star Turns Red*: 'Act I', 8 pp.; 'Act III', where the scene is 'the Mansion House' (Act IV in the published version), 6 pp. (pages badly stained and faded). Draft of biographical chapter entitled 'Plans gang agley', published as 'R.I.P.' in *I Knock at the Door*, 10 pp. (pages faded and torn). Drawing of the Great Hall of a Welsh Castle, 1 p. Notes, including fragmentary draft of a review entitled 'Murder in the Cathedral', and notes which, according to a later entry by the playwright, were 'taken for *The Flying Wasp*', 8 pp.

There is, in the draft of *The Star Turns Red*, material omitted from the printed version of the play; and in the chapter, 'Plans gang agley', there is a little more background to Ella and Johnny than is given in *I Knock at the Door*.

E22 (MS) HOLOGRAPH WRITING PAD

Tear-off foolscap pad with the cover missing. Many pages are torn out, others badly creased and stained, and some are difficult to read. Narratives run concurrently on each side of the page.

Contents: Notes and rough incomplete draft of a biographical sketch entitled 'Accident' (not published), 2 pp. Then follow drafts of ten chapters published in *Pictures in the Hallway* (written approximately 1941–2): 'Alice, Where Art Thou', 'Pictures in the Hallway', 'To Him that Hath Shall be Given', 'Touched by the Theatre', 'Death on the Doorstep', 'Work While it is not yet Day', 'The Cap in the Counting House', 'The Sword of Light', 'I Strike a Blow for You, Dear Land' and 'All Heaven and Harmsworth Too'. Although these rough drafts usually comprise only part of the published version of each chapter, there is yet a good deal of unpublished material here, including an account of 'Johnny in the Police Court'. Total, 65 pp. Fragmentary notes, 5 pp.

23 (MS) HOLOGRAPH NOTEBOOK

Autograph book, with blue and yellow coloured pages, a mottled green-blue cover and grey spine. Size: 14 × 10.8cm. Inscribed 'To Dad from Shivaun'.

Contents: Notes, press cuttings, and outline and ideas for *Rose and Crown* and *Sunset and Evening Star*, written 1948–54 approximately, 45 pp. (including both inside covers; 2 pp. torn). Note for *The Drums of Father Ned*, 1 p.

24 (MS) HOLOGRAPH NOTEBOOK

Writing pad with front cover missing (20.3 × 16.5cm), several pages torn out; pages stapled at the top.

Contents: Draft of part of chapter, 'Feathering his Nest' (*Rose and Crown*), including unpublished material, interpolated with draft of a letter on Strindberg, 4 pp. Draft of biographical sketch, some of the material of which was used in 'Outside an Irish Window' (*Sunset and Evening Star*), but a good deal of satirical writing, concerned with the stock exchange, the cinema, the Irish sweep-stake, and Irish sanctity, written in the form of a 'Complaint to the Creator' remains unpublished, 14 pp. Draft of dedication (of *Cock-a-Doodle Dandy*) to James Stephens, 1 p. and general ideas for *Rose and Crown*, 1 p.; both interpolated into the 'Complaint to the Creator'. Fragmentary notes used in 'London Apprentice' and 'Feathering his Nest' (*Rose and Crown*), 2 pp. Jottings, 1 p.

E25 (MS) HOLOGRAPH EXERCISE BOOK

Khaki paper-covered Army book (24.1 × 18.4cm) originally belonging to D. Nichols, with his writing on the first page, and arithmetic and notes by Breon O'Casey. Printed on the cover is the inscription: 'G.R. S.O. Book 135. Supplied for the Public Service'. Some pages torn.

Contents (in Sean O'Casey's handwriting): Notes and ideas entitled 'Life' (this includes material used in *Sunset and Evening Star* and notes on Pinero, used in 'London Apprentice' (*Rose and Crown*), 2 pp. Notes and draft of one-act play, 'Hall of Healing' (1949), 21 pp. Then follow notes for and drafts of three chapters published in *Rose and Crown*: 'Feathering his Nest', 7 pp.; 'Garrick Club' (part of 'London Apprentice', with some dialogue for 'Hall of Healing' interpolated), 8 pp. 'Rose and Crown' (this draft, in particular, contains material omitted in the printed version, including some unpublished comments on Winston Churchill), 26 pp. Draft of chapter entitled 'The Dree Dames' (*Sunset and Evening Star*), with draft of letter to *Totnes Times* interpolated, 13 pp. Notes for review article on book on history of Abbey Theatre (Peter Kavanagh's *Story of the Abbey Theatre*), 6 pp. Note on the 'Collected Plays of O'Casey', 1 p. Fragmentary dialogue for *Purple Dust* (probably revisions to printed text), 2 pp. Ideas for biography and fragment of dialogue for 'Hall of Healing', 2 pp.

E26 (MS) HOLOGRAPH EXERCISE BOOK

Dark green cover (20.3 × 16.5cm) with a black spine. 'Words, Idle Words' is written in O'Casey's hand on paper which is pasted on the cover. This was evidently a school book of Niall O'Casey and contains history notes written by him.

Contents (written by Sean O'Casey): Notes, entitled 'Cambridge' (for chapter in *Sunset and Evening Star*), 2 pp. Notes for articles entitled 'Profile of Ireland' and 'Artist's Place in Life' (published in *The Green Crow*), 8 pp. Draft of poem, 2 pp. Quotations from Bernard Shaw and page references to Dickens's *Bleak House*, 2 pp. Fragmentary draft of chapter entitled 'We're Lost, We're All Lost' (later printed as 'Rebel Orwell' in *Sunset and Evening Star*), 3 pp. Draft of 'Overture, Prologue' to 'Red in the Rainbow': this is a crude early draft of what was to become the 'Prerumble' to *The Drums of Father Ned*, 1 p.

The material in this book, written most probably from 1952 to 1954 or so, comprises rough early drafts, with many differences from the writings in their printed form.

E27 (MS) HOLOGRAPH EXERCISE BOOK

Turquoise cover (20.3 × 15.8cm) with olive green spine. Pages torn out and spine damaged. Book originally belonged to Niall O'Casey and there are notes in his hand in it; on the first page is the signature 'Sean O'Casey. June 1955'.

Contents: Notes written in hospital (1956), 3 pp. Draft of article entitled 'Shaw' (published in *The Green Crow* as 'Lord of a Century: Shaw'), 6 pp. Notes and fragmentary dialogue for *The Drums of Father Ned*, 3 pp. Notes, 2 pp.

8 (MS) HOLOGRAPH NOTEBOOK

Grey covered notebook (15.8×10.2cm) with red spine; writing at both ends.

Contents: Notes and financial accounts (dated December 1959–February 1963), 12 pp.

29 (MS) HOLOGRAPH NOTEBOOK

Wine-red notebook (15.8×10.2cm) containing writings in several hands, including Sean and Eileen O'Casey's. Some pages torn out.

Contents (in Sean O'Casey's handwriting): Notes and Financial accounts (dated 1961–2), 23 pp.

30 (MS) HOLOGRAPH EXERCISE BOOK

Fawn paper-covered book, with 'Tudor Exercise Book' printed on cover, together with 'Eileen O'Casey. French' in Mrs O'Casey's handwriting. Size: 20.3×15.8cm.

Contents (in Sean O'Casey's hand): Notes, 1 p. Draft of poem entitled 'Sob Stuff' (used in article in *Under a Colored Cap*), 3 pp. Notes and rough draft of article here entitled 'Sob Stuff' (later published as 'The Green Crow Caws'), 7 pp. Incomplete draft of letter, 1 p. Further draft of verses written for 'The Green Crow Caws', including some unpublished material, 3 pp. Unfinished rough draft of article entitled 'Shakespeare'; it is *not* the article written by O'Casey to celebrate the former's anniversary in 1964 and reprinted in *Blasts and Benedictions* under the title 'Shakespeare Among the Flags', 7 pp. Note on 'The Mermaid Theatre and the Critics', 1 p. 'Snips of Song from *I Knock at the Door*', 1 p.

Note: Several loose holograph pages among the O'Casey papers seem most usefully listed with typescript rather than manuscript material. See one page of 'characters' for *Within the Gates*, E34(TS)1; one holograph page of 'dramatis personae' for *The Bishop's Bonfire*, E50(TS)1; one page holograph 'contents' for *The Green Crow*, E51(TS)1; nine pages of holograph notes and dialogue for *The Drums of Father Ned*, E52(TS)1; and four pages of notes and dialogue for *Behind the Green Curtains*, E54(TS)1 and E54(TS)2.

II TYPESCRIPT MATERIAL

E31 (TS) KATHLEEN LISTENS IN

Robert Hogan wrote that the text of the play that he assembled for publication in *Feathers from the Green Crow* (A40) was 'based on O'Casey's original typescript, which contains many later marginal and interlinear changes, some evidently added after the play's production [in 1923] . . . I have collated this version with a copy of a slightly different version lent me by Ronald Ayling'. Of the five typescripts recorded below, the first two are among the F. D. Murphy Collection in the library of the University of California, Los Angeles, and were those that Hogan had access to when preparing the play for publication (the burnt set of parts is almost certainly a typescript from the library of the Abbey Theatre, damaged by the fire at the Theatre). Items 3–5 are typescripts that were among the playwright's papers at his death and are now in the Berg Collection. The typescript lent to Hogan by Ayling was a copy made from collating the playwright's three typescripts when Ayling was given access to them by the author in 1960.

(1) 'Kathleen Listens In. A Phantasy in One Act', 14 pp. Typescript with holograph corrections and additions in ink. 'Revised version 3/3/25' appears in pencil on the first page. (F. D. Murphy Collection, UCLA Library.)

(2) Typescript of 'Kathleen Listens In. One Act', 86 pp. with holograph corrections and additions This copy is a complete set of parts rather than a prompt copy. It is described as 'Revised version 3/3/25' and is burned at the edges. (F. D. Murphy Collection, UCLA Library.)

(3) Typescript (carbon copy), entitled 'Kathleen Listens In: A Phantasy in One Act'; this was almost certainly the original draft probably typed in 1923, 18 pp. with several minor additions and corrections in ink by the author.

(4) Typescript on foolscap paper, with corrections in a hand other than O'Casey's, 14 pp. This version is sub-titled 'A Political Fantasy in One Act' and bears the words 'Revised Version 3/3/25. Performed at Abbey, Oct. 1, '23'.

(5) Typescript, typed by Ethel Christian Ltd (London), pp. 1–22 (plus 2 pp.). Minor corrections in author's hand. Plus one complete carbon copy of this typescript, 24 pp.

E32 (TS) NANNIE'S NIGHT OUT

Of the text of this 'Comedy in One Act' published in *Feathers from the Green Crow* (A40), Robert Hogan has said it was 'a recension of four varying and incomplete versions – the original typescript and three Abbey typescripts – and two pages of added material. I have printed only two of the three endings to the play, for the third ending does not differ materially from the second, except for the excision of the gunman scene'. Hogan used the first two typescripts (with additional cue material) described below; they are now among the F. D. Murphy Collection in the library of the University of California, Los Angeles. Typescripts 3 and 4 were among the playwright's own papers and are now in the Berg Collection.

(1) Typescript entitled 'Irish Nannie Passes', 36 pp. with some holograph corrections in pencil and O'Casey's corrections in ink on pp. 22 and 30. With this typescript there are also two alternative endings to the play,

pp. 30–3 and pp. 34–8 in typescript. There are also 2 pp. typescript of cue sheets for Oul Joe's part (probably typed by Gabriel Fallon when learning the part), together with 2 pp. typescript of extra lines for the same character made by O'Casey for Fallon while the play was in rehearsal; one page contains notations for music. (F. D. Murphy Collection, UCLA Library.)

(2) Typescript entitled 'Irish Nannie Passes', 25 pp. with holograph corrections and additions in ink, plus notes in another hand in pencil. (F. D. Murphy Collection, UCLA Library.)

(3) Carbon copy of typescript entitled 'Irish Nannie Passes', with minor alterations and additions in ink in O'Casey's handwriting. There are several minor differences from the text printed in *Feathers from the Green Crow* (A40). Although the first page is numbered 1, the beginning of the opening stage direction is missing; the title-page is also missing. Original version of play, pp. 1–25; plus two alternative endings to the play: pp. 21–3 and pp. 23–6.

(4) Typescript entitled 'Irish Nannie Passes', pp. 1–38. Although the first page is numbered 1, the opening stage direction of the play is missing. This version is almost certainly a later copy of typescript (3) listed above.

(TS) THE SILVER TASSIE

Of the six typescript versions described below, the first four were among the playwright's papers and are now in the Berg Collection. Typescript 5 was typed by O'Casey and sent to Gabriel Fallon in 1928; it is now in the Humanities Research Center at the University of Texas at Austin. The sixth typescript was found among the papers of Lady Gregory and is now in the Berg Collection; it is probably a copy made of the typescript O'Casey submitted to the Abbey Theatre in 1928.

(1) Notes, 2 pp.; typescript pages entitled 'Rough Copy', pp. 6, 7, 9. Typescript entitled 'Rough Copy': Act III, pp. 2–15; Act IV, pp. 6–8, 10–14. This incomplete draft differs considerably from the printed version of 1928.

(2) Incomplete early draft typescript: Act II, 2 pp.; Act IV, 15 pp. (unnumbered). This draft also differs considerably from the printed version of the play.

(3) Typescript with minor changes in author's hand. Text is virtually that of the published version of 1928. Act I, 37 pp. (plus title-page and *dramatis personae*, 2 pp.); Act II, pp. 38–63; III, pp. 64–93; IV, pp. 1–26.

(4) Typescript with minor changes in author's hand. Text as typescript (3) above. Act I, pp. 1–33; II, pp. 1–22; III, pp. 1–27; IV, pp. 1–29.

(5) Typescript comprises original and carbon copy material, largely unpaginated: total, 84 pp. The pages of Act I are numbered 1–24, but hardly any of the other pages are numbered at all. There are some holograph revisions by the author. (Humanities Research Center, University of Texas.)

(6) Typescript of the first three acts of *The Silver Tassie* (probably typed by Lady Gregory), 89 pp. with a copy of the fourth act in her handwriting, 31 pp. Contents: Act I, pp. 1–35; II, pp. 1–26; III, pp. 1–26; IV, pp. 1–31. (Berg Collection, Lady Gregory Papers.)

E34   (TS) WITHIN THE GATES

Of the following thirteen typescripts, the first eleven were found among
the playwright's papers and are now in the Berg Collection. The twelfth
and thirteenth items are in the Theatre Collection of the New York Public
Library.

(1) Holograph notes: 'Characters', 1 p.; Chant of Down and Outs, 2 pp.
Typescript note entitled 'Hyde Park', 1 p. Draft of dialogue and notes
entitled 'The Park', 12 pp. (some pages numbered, others unnumbered).
This draft is written as a film scenario, and differs considerably from both
printed versions of the play. Corrections in ink by the author are found in
notes and draft.

(2) Typescript, headed 'Rough Draft' by O'Casey: early draft of the opening
scene of the play, pp. 1–20 (with one carbon copy, 20 pp.).

(3) Typescript, headed 'Rough Copy': incomplete early draft, 47 pp.

(4) Draft of an early typescript version of Scene I of the play, with occasional
corrections in ink, pp. 1–37.

(5) Draft of an early typescript version of Scene III of the play (incomplete);
only pp. 12–20 extant. The texts of all the above typescripts differ in many
details from the printed versions of the play. They contain corrections in
ink by the author.

(6) Draft of later typescript version: Scene I, 26 pp.; II, pp. 1–17 (with carbon
copy, 17 pp.); III, pp. 1–24 (with carbon copy, 24 pp.); IV, pp. 1–24 (with
carbon copy, 24 pp.). Mostly typed on quarto paper, but some pages are of
various sizes. Text is of the version published in 1933, with some slight
changes. On the title page of Scene I there is signed in ink: 'S. O'Casey.
Hillcrest, Deanway, Chalfont St. Giles, Bucks'. There are a few corrections
and additions in ink.

(7) Draft of revised version of Scene I of the play (entitled 'Stage Version
Act I'), pp. 1–21. Text is that published in 1949 in *Collected Plays*, vol. II.

(8) Draft of revised version of Scene II of the play (entitled 'Stage Version
Act II'), pp. 1–17. Text is that published in 1949 in *Collected Plays*, vol. II.

(9) Draft of a revised version of Act III of the play (entitled 'Revised Version
for the Stage'), pp. 1–18. Text is that published in 1949 in *Collected Plays*,
vol. II.

(10) Draft of a revised version of Act IV, (entitled 'Revised Version for the
Stage'), pp. 1–19. Text is that published in 1949 in *Collected Plays*, vol. II.
Each of the above typescripts of the revised version of *Within the Gates*
has a few minor corrections in ink in the text.

(11) Carbon copy of typescript of *Within the Gates* ('Stage version'), typed by
Ethel Christian typing agency. Act I, pp. 1–32; II, pp. 1–25; III, pp. 1–25;
IV, pp. 1–27, plus title-page and 2 pp. There are minor alterations in ink in
O'Casey's handwriting. The text is that published in 1949 in *Collected Plays*,
vol. II.

(12) Typescript carbon copy of 1933 text, reproduced by Madden Play
Company, New York. Contents: 128 pp. with the four scenes separately
paginated as follows, 33 pp.; 26 pp.; 29 pp.; 33 pp. O'Casey's Chalfont St

Giles address appears on the title-page. The script was the property of George Bushar and John Tuerk, the New York producers of the play, and there are pencilled notes on costumes, stage directions, etc. interspersed throughout the text. (Theatre Collection, New York Public Library.)

(13) Typescript carbon copy identical to item (12) above, but without the notes. Contents: 128 pp. (Theatre Collection, NYPL.)

5   (TS) END OF THE BEGINNING

The following typescript is listed separately from *Windfalls*, in which volume the play first appeared, because it is a somewhat altered text from the published one. Other typescripts of the play, closer to the printed form, are recorded under *Windfalls* (E36).

(1) Draft typescript, entitled 'Power House God' (early title for the play), pp. 1–16 typed on paper of various sizes. There are considerable changes from and additional material to the published text. There is also one additional character, Alice Lanigan. Corrections and additions in ink are in the author's hand.

36 (TS) WINDFALLS

There are four collections of typescript material, as described below. The first two batches recorded here, which comprise substantial portions of the book (148 pp. and 131 pp., respectively), were found among the playwright's papers and are now in the Berg Collection. Item 3 is also in the Berg, having been acquired among the Lady Gregory papers. The fourth entry is a typescript of 'The End of the Beginning' that is part of the George Jean Nathan archive at Cornell University.

(1) Original typescript draft (carbon copy) of poems, stories, and plays, 148 pp.
   Contents: Poems, 40 pp.; Stories, 72 pp.; Plays, 36 pp. This draft was found in an envelope on which O'Casey had written: 'First Typescript of *Windfalls*'. There is some material additional to that published in the book in 1934. There are corrections and additions by the author in ink in the text.

Detailed contents:
Poems:
'A Walk with Eros', stanzas I–LXXXIII, pp. 1–17 (this poem includes several stanzas deleted in the published version); 'Chosen Things', 2 pp. (published as 'Chosen Life'); 'Wisdom and Life', 1 p.; 'Sunshadows', 2 pp.; 'The Summer Sun is Tightly Folding', 1 p. (not published in *Windfalls*, but posthumously printed in *The World of Sean O'Casey*); 'Margarita', 1 p. (not published); 'Bonnie Mary', 1 p.; 'The Garland', 2 pp.; 'Fragment', 1 p. (not published); 'Travels of the Sun', 1 p. (not published); 'The Dreamer Dreams of God', 2 pp. (plus another carbon copy of this poem in a different version, 2 pp.); 'Gold and Silver Will Not Do', 4 pp.; 'She Will Give Me Rest', 1 p.; 'The Grand Oul' Dame Britannia', 2 pp.

Many of these poems contain alterations from the versions finally printed in *Windfalls*; four of the poems were not, finally, included in the book and three have never been published.

Stories:
'I Wanna Woman', pp. 1–31; 'The Job', pp. 1–12 (plus rough early draft, 4 pp.); 'The Star Jazzer', pp. 1–13 (plus another complete copy, pp. 1–6); 'Mollser', 6 pp. (story published under title of 'A Fall in a Gentle Wind').
In the typescripts of 'I Wanna Woman' and 'Mollser', there are several slight changes from the versions printed in *Windfalls*, and both typescripts contain phrases deleted in the book.

Plays:
'Pound on Demand', pp. 1–14 (plus title-page and list of characters, 2 pp.); 'The End of the Beginning', pp. 1–19 (plus one extra page, numbered 7a).

(2) Typescript of revised version of *Windfalls*. This text, with minor alterations is that published in 1934: the typescript bears the printer's marks. Some poems found in typescript (1) above, have been omitted while others ('A Walk with Eros', for instance) have undergone alteration. The typescript totals 131 pp.: Preface, 2 pp.; Poems, 35 pp.; Stories, 56 pp.; Plays, 38 pp. There are occasional entries in ink by the author.

Detailed contents:
Preface, 2 pp.
Poems:
'Wisdom and Life', 1 p.; 'A Walk with Eros', pp. 1–17; 'Chosen Things', 2 pp.; 'Sunshadows', 2 pp.; 'The Garland', 1 p. (subsequently printed in a slightly different version in *The World of Sean O'Casey* (B53)); 'Thoughts of Thee', 1 p. (another typescript existed separately among the playwright's papers, 1 p. with additional two lines in holograph; this poem was also printed in a slightly different version in *The World of Sean O'Casey* (B53)); 'Bonnie Mary', 1 p.; 'Gold & Silver Will Not Do', pp. 1–4; 'The Dreamer Dreams of God', 2 pp.; 'She Will Give Me Rest', 1 p.; 'The Grand Oul' Dame Britannia', 2 pp.

Stories:
'I Wanna Woman', pp. 1–31; 'The Star Jazzer', pp. 1–13; 'The Job', pp. 1–12.
Plays:
'The End of the Beginning', pp. 1–9, [2]; 'Pound on Demand', pp. 1–15, [2].

In addition, there is a printed copy of 'A Fall in a Gentle Wind' (the story which was originally entitled 'Mollser'), taken from the pages of the journal *Life and Letters* (December 1933, pp. 403–11). This item is not included in the total of 131 pp. which is typescript material only.

(3) Carbon copy of typescript of poem, 'Chosen Things' (printed as 'Chosen Life' in *Windfalls*), 3 pp. with a marginal note in Lady Gregory's hand identifying O'Casey as the author. (Lady Gregory Papers, Berg Collection.)

(4) A typescript of 'The End of the Beginning', typed by Rialto Service Bureau, New York, is among the George Jean Nathan Papers at Cornell University, pp. 1–26; no additions in ink.

(TS) I KNOCK AT THE DOOR

There are typescripts of chapters from the first volume of autobiography in two library collections. The main bulk of twenty-two chapters was found among the playwright's papers and is now in the Berg Collection. The typescripts of two chapters in the Houghton Library were probably copies submitted to the *Yale Review* by the author; the journal printed 'The Dream School' in June 1937 but O'Casey asked that 'A Child of God' not be printed in the magazine once *I Knock at the Door* had been accepted for book publication by Macmillan; see his letter to Horace Reynolds dated June 28, 1938 in *The Letters of Sean O'Casey* (A46).

(1) Typescripts of 22 chapters (each separately paginated); with chapter six, 'His Father's Funeral', missing. There is a carbon copy of chapter 13, 'The Dream School'. There are a few corrections in ink in the text. Total: 253 pp. (plus 18 pp. of carbon copies).
(2) Typescript of story, entitled 'Dream-school', 9 pp. This was the text printed in *Yale Review*, June 1937 (C192), which shows various changes from the chapter 'The Dream School' published in *I Knock at the Door*. (Houghton Library, Harvard University.)
(3) Typescript of 'A Child of God', 24 pp. (with additional typescript copy, 22 pp.). There are some changes from the chapter with the same title printed in the first volume of autobiography. (Houghton Library, Harvard University.)

(TS) THE STAR TURNS RED

(1) There is no typescript material relating to this play among the playwright's papers. The following text was almost certainly sent to George Jean Nathan by the playwright, however. It is a carbon copy typescript of the play typed by the Rialto Service Bureau, New York. Act I, pp. 1–32; II, pp. 1–27; III, pp. 1–18; IV, pp. 1–25. There are no corrections in ink in this copy but there are a number of additions and other changes to the text first published in 1940. For instance, each scene in this version is given a time of day: Act I is one o'clock in the afternoon; II is eight o'clock in the evening; III is nine o'clock in the evening and the fourth act opens an hour later. The Old Man was originally called Nimmo, the name of an obnoxious character in O'Casey's second play, *The Harvest Festival*. Kreencuss is here the Railwaymen's Delegate in Act II instead of, as in the printed version, Brallain. There are other changes in the stage directions and dialogue. This typescript is among the George Jean Nathan Papers at Cornell University.

(TS) PURPLE DUST

Of the following five typescripts, the first two were among the playwright's papers and are now in the Berg Collection. The third and fourth items are in the Nathan Papers at Cornell University. The song is in the F. D. Murphy Collection at the library of the University of California, Los Angeles.

(1) Typescript in a dark blue binding. This was typed by Hart Stenographic Bureau, New York. Act I, pp. 1–38, II, pp. 1–34; III, pp. 1–36. Some corrections and additions in ink are by O'Casey (one on p. 38, for instance), but there are also corrections in another hand.

(2) Typescript, typed by Ethel Christian Ltd (London): Act I, pp. 1–42; II, pp. 1–36; III, pp. 1–37 (with a complete carbon copy of this version). There are no alterations by the author.

(3) Another typescript, typed by Ethel Christian Ltd, is among the George Jean Nathan Papers at Cornell University: Act I, 47 pp.; II, 41 pp.; III, 39 pp. with many corrections in ink by the playwright and additional material pasted into the typescript.

(4) Another typescript of the play among the Nathan Papers at Cornell has the following pagination with no additions in ink: Act I, 44 pp.; II, 37 pp.; III, 37 pp.

(5) Typescript of song entitled 'The Ruined Rowan Tree', 1 p. with holograph corrections and additions in ink. The author has written at the bottom of the page: 'Song written for a *Purple Dust* production that never came to London. It goes to the air of "Carrigdhoun", a lovely old tune'. Written in 1953, the song was printed in *Chanticleer*, summer 1956 (C455) and included in the 1957 printing of *Purple Dust* (A21*b*). (F. D. Murphy Collection, UCLA Library.)

E40   (TS) RED ROSES FOR ME

Of the following six typescripts in library collections, the first four are from the playwright's papers and are now in the Berg Collection; the fifth and sixth items belonged originally to George Jean Nathan. *Red Roses for Me* was revised at various times before and after its first publication in 1942. The following typescripts reflect many of these changes. It should be noted that there are four different published versions: the first edition of 1942, the text published in *Collected Plays* (A29), that published in New York in 1956, and, finally, the version printed in *Three More Plays* (A42). The latter, though it appeared after the dramatist's death, was personally supervised and approved by him.

(1) Typescript (carbon copy) of the play, originally entitled 'A Rich Bunch of Red Roses', with minor alterations and additions by O'Casey in ink. The text is that published in 1942. Act I, pp. 1–21; II, pp. 1–20; III, pp. 1–17; IV, pp. 1–22.

(2) Typescript with brown binding and title printed in silver lettering on the cover: typed by Hart Stenographic Bureau, New York. Act I, 33 pp.; II, 25 pp.; III, 17 pp.; IV, 23 pp. There are some entries in O'Casey's hand but these are not extensive.

(3) Stencilled copy with light blue cover, and on the cover, in O'Casey's handwriting, the words: 'Red Roses for Me – Correct Final Draft'. Act I, 33 pp.; II, 26 pp.; III, 21 pp.; IV, 23 pp. There are several changes in O'Casey's hand in the text.

(4) Typescript, typed by Ethel Christian Ltd (London), with the words 'Final Form' in the author's hand on the front cover. No other entries by O'Casey. Act I, 30 pp.; II, 24 pp.; III, 18 pp.; IV, 22 pp.

(5) Earlier carbon copy typescript, typed by Rialto Service Bureau (New York), is among the George Jean Nathan Papers at Cornell University. Act I, 28 pp.; II, 22 pp.; III, 17 pp.; IV, 24 pp. There are no additions in ink.

(6) Another typescript (carbon copy) of the play among the Nathan Papers at Cornell has the following pagination (again, there are no additions in ink): Act I, 30 pp.; II, 25 pp.; III, 19 pp.; IV, 24 pp.

(TS) DRUMS UNDER THE WINDOWS

Only one brief typescript draft of material for this book existed among the playwright's papers and is now in the Berg Collection.

(1) Rough incomplete early typescript draft of one chapter from the book. It is entitled here 'Green Skies and Buff', but was published as 'The Bold Fenian Men', 12 pp. (foolscap).

(TS) OAK LEAVES AND LAVENDER

There are five typescripts in library collections. The first two described below were among the playwright's papers and are now in the Berg Collection. The third and fourth texts, one typed by the playwright, are in the Theatre Collection of the New York Public Library. The fifth item is among the George Jean Nathan Papers at Cornell University.

(1) Incomplete typescript of rough draft of Prologue and opening scene of 'Roll Out the Barrel' (earliest title for the play), pp. 1–10, typed on paper of various sizes.

(2) Typescript entitled 'Warald on Wallpaper' (later, the play's sub-title), with a number of corrections and additions in ink by the author. The text is that of the published version of 1946 (New York, 1947) with only a few words changed. Act I, pp. 7–42 (Act I itself is complete, but the play's 'Prelude' is missing); II, pp. 43–64; III, pp. 65–84.

(3) Typescript carbon copy entitled 'Warald on Wallpaper'; various pagings with extensive cuts and additions on almost every page; several pages are original typed copies. Contents: Act I, pp. 1–42 (together with title-page and additional page, 27A); II, pp. 43–84 (together with title-page and two additional pages, 49A and 78A). There are holograph corrections by the author. (Theatre Collection, NYPL.)

(4) Typescript copy of 'Warald on Wallpaper', incorporating changes made in typescript (3) above, and with a note on the title page 'Retitled "Swords and Old Lavender" – "Oak Leaves and Lavender".' Almost certainly typed by Hart Stenographic Bureau of New York; presented to NYPL by Edward Choate. Contents: 2 pp. preliminaries; Prelude, 7 pp.; Act I, 42 pp.; II, 28 pp.; III, 27 pp. (Theatre Collection, NYPL.)

(5) Typescript entitled 'Warald on Wallpaper', typed by the Hart Steno-graphic Bureau of New York. Contents: Prelude, 7' pp.; Act I, 42 pp.; II, 28 pp.; III, 27 pp. (G. J. Nathan Collection, Cornell University.)

E43 (TS) INISHFALLEN, FARE THEE WELL

The first two items of typescript material for this book come from the author's papers and are now in the Berg Collection. Item three is in the library of SUNY, Buffalo.

(1) Typescript of fragment of early draft of autobiographical chapter, 'Girl I Left Behind Me', typed on the verso pages of printed news bulletins, 3 pp. (numbered pp. 11–13). These are foolscap pages, whereas almost all O'Casey's other typescripts are quarto sized.

(2) Typescript (carbon copy) of eighteen biographical chapters – the complete book – with some corrections and additions in ink by the author. Each chapter is paginated separately. There is also a duplicate carbon copy of one of the chapters, 'Mrs. Casside Takes a Holiday', 19 pp. Total: 262 pp. (plus duplicate chapter, 19 pp.).

(3) Typescript of chapter entitled 'The Raid', with corrections by O'Casey, 14 pp. (SUNY, Buffalo.)

E44 (TS) COCK-A-DOODLE DANDY

The first two typescripts, now in the Berg Collection, come from the play-wright's private papers; the third (mimeographed) typescript is in the Theatre Collection of the New York Public Library.

(1) Rough early draft, entitled 'Cock-a-doodle-Doo'. Scene I, 25 pp.; II, 26 pp.; III, pp. 1–23. This draft is very different from the final printed version of the play. There are many changes and some additional dialogue in ink in O'Casey's hand.

(2) Typescript of later draft of the play: Scene I, 23 pp.; II, 21 pp.; III, 22 pp. (with carbon copies of each of these three scenes: 23 pp.; 21 pp.; 22 pp.). This draft is entitled *Cock-a-doodle Dandy*, and is similar to the printed text. There are considerable alterations and additions in ink in the author's handwriting.

(3) Mimeographed typescript entitled *Cock-a-doodle Dandy*, very similar to printed text; each of the three scenes is paginated, 1–35 pp. O'Casey's Totnes address is typed on the title-page. (Theatre Collection, NYPL.)

E45 (TS) HALL OF HEALING

The two typescripts existing in library collections are both from the play-wright's papers and are in the Berg Collection.

(1) Typescript (dated 'March 25, 1949' on the title-page), typed by Ethel Christian Ltd (London), 37 pp. There are corrections and additions in ink in the author's hand.

(2) Identical carbon copy of the above typescript, 37 pp. What is worth noting, however, is that the author's corrections and additions in ink are not

uniform with those made in the original typescript. Compare pp. 32 and 36 in each text, for example.

(TS) BEDTIME STORY

Of the three following typescripts in library collections, the first two were among the playwright's papers and are now in the Berg; the third copy originally belonged to George Jean Nathan.

(1) Typescript typed by O'Casey, with minor changes in O'Casey's hand in the text, 26 pp. (with an identical carbon copy, also containing changes in the author's hand, 26 pp.).
(2) Typescript of the same play, typed by Ethel Christian Ltd (London), 30 pp. There are no corrections or changes by the author.
(3) Another typescript, typed by Ethel Christian Ltd, and with the same pagination (30 pp.) is to be found among the George Jean Nathan Papers at Cornell University. There are many changes in ink made by the author and a sub-title, 'An Immorality Farce in One Act' (not eventually used in the printed text), is crossed out by him.

(TS) TIME TO GO

(1) The only copy of this play in a library collection is a typescript (sub-titled 'A Morality Comedy in One Act'), typed by Ethel Christian Ltd (London), and found among the George Jean Nathan Papers at Cornell University. It numbers twenty-six pages and there are corrections in ink by the playwright.

(TS) ROSE AND CROWN

The following batch of typescript chapters was originally among the playwright's papers and is now in the Berg Collection.

(1) Typescript of sixteen chapters from the book (chapters 1–7 and 9–17); the missing chapter (eight), entitled 'A Gate Clangs Shut', is represented by a printed copy torn out of the magazine *Irish Writing* (issue for December 1950, pp. 7–18). Total: 238 typescript pages. Each chapter is paginated separately. There are considerable corrections and additions in ink in several of the chapters.

(TS) SUNSET AND EVENING STAR

Similarly, the following single collection of typescript material was found among the author's papers and is now in the Berg Collection.

(1) Complete typescript of the fourteen chapters in the book. Each chapter is paginated separately. Some additions and corrections have been made in

ink. In addition there is a draft of an incomplete chapter entitled, 'Crossed Guns Crossed Keys', which appears to be an early draft of Chapter 7, 'Heavily Hangs the Broad Sunflower', pp. 1–7 (with one carbon copy, 7 pp.) Total, 279 pp.

E50 (TS) THE BISHOP'S BONFIRE

The first three of the following six typescripts in library collections are from the playwright's papers in the Berg Collection. The fourth item is also in the Berg, having probably been acquired from the author's literary agent in the United States. The fifth entry is to be found in the F. D. Murphy Collection in the library of the University of California, Los Angeles, and the sixth is among the George Jean Nathan Papers at Cornell University.

(1) Early draft typescript, incomplete, typed by O'Casey. 'Act I, Scene I', 34 pp.; 'Act III, Scene I', 27 pp.; with 1 p. (holograph) *Dramatis Personae*; and 1 p. (typed) 'Lyrics of Songs of the Play'. There is no extant copy of Act II in this draft, which is typed on the back of used typing paper; on the other side of some of the pages are parts of chapters from early drafts of *Sunset and Evening Star*. There is also a typescript entitled 'Suggestions for Scene 2', 2 pp. This concerns a possible change in the second act.

(2) Later draft typescript of *The Bishop's Bonfire*, typed by O'Casey, with corrections in ink in his hand. Act I, 30 pp.; II, 25 pp.; III, 29 pp.

(3) Still later draft (incorporating earlier alterations), typed by Ethel Christian Ltd (London). This version was used for the published text, and the typescript has the printer's marks on it. Act I, 45 pp.; II, 34 pp.; III, 38 pp. Minor corrections by the author in ink.

(4) Carbon copy typescript, typed by Ethel Christian Ltd (London), 118 pp. There are many holograph corrections by the author throughout. Contents: Act I, pp. 1–43; II, 1–34; III, 1–37. (New York Public Library, Theatre Collection.)

(5) Typescript entitled 'McGilligan's Daughter. Act 2. Music for the Bishop', 17 pp. with holograph corrections and additions. The material has been typed on the blank sides of various manuscripts and letters. Letters to the playwright are to be found on the verso of six pages; typescript 'Alterations in The Silver Tassie' with some holograph changes in ink are on the verso of another four pages (pp. 1–4); two pages from a typescript of the 'Chalfont' chapter of *Rose and Crown* are on the verso of two other pages; two pages from a typescript of the 'Rebel Orwell' chapter in *Sunset and Evening Star* (one entitled 'Pull that Green Flag Down, Boy'); and one chapter from 'Cambridge' in the same book is on the verso of another page. Total, 17 pp. (F. D. Murphy Collection, UCLA Library.)

(6) A carbon copy typescript, typed by the Rialto Service Bureau (New York), 124 pp. Contents: Act I, 47 pp.; II, 36 pp.; III, 41 pp. There are no additions in ink. (G. J. Nathan Papers, Cornell University.)

E51 (TS) THE GREEN CROW

Ten typescripts associated with *The Green Crow* were found among the playwright's papers at his death and are now in the Berg Collection of the New

York Public Library. These are items 4 to 12 in the following list. The first three items and the fourteenth (one holograph and three typescript copies) are among the F. D. Murphy Collection at the library of the University of California, Los Angeles. Item fifteen is in the Baker Library, Dartmouth College, New Hampshire.

(1) 'The Flying Wasp', one page holograph. 'Draft for "Contents" to *The Green Crow*' appears at the bottom of the page in O'Casey's handwriting. (F. D. Murphy Collection, UCLA Library.)

(2) 'The Green Crow', carbon copy typescript, 1 p. with handwritten comment at the bottom of the page: 'Prefacing remarks to *The Green Crow*'. (F. D. Murphy Collection, UCLA Library.)

(3) 'Foreword', carbon copy typescript, 6 pp. (with additional material pasted on to the last two pages). The author has added a note in ink at the top of the first page: 'Written for *The Green Crow*'. (F. D. Murphy Collection, UCLA Library.)

(4) 'Overture', pp. 1–12 (with minor changes in ink in the text).

(5) Typescript note introducing 'The Public Death of Shakespeare', 1 p.

(6) Typescript note introducing 'National Theatre Bunkum', 1 p.

(7) Typescript of 'Critica Silentio Luna', pp. 1–14.

(8) Typescript of 'Bonfire Under a Black Sun', pp. 1–24.

(9) Typescript of 'Tender Tears for Poor O'Casey', pp. 1–10 (slight differences from article printed in *The Green Crow*).

(10) Typescript of 'A Whisper about Bernard Shaw', pp. 1–8.

(11) Typescript of 'St. Pathrick's Day in the Morning' (here entitled 'Irish Through the Tare and Ages'), pp. 1–6.

(12) Typescript of 'Come to the Fair', pp. 1–14 (some pages of irregular size).

(13) Typescript of 'A Whisper about Bernard Shaw', 6 pp. (foolscap). An item of especial interest in that it bears the handwriting of both Bernard Shaw and Sean O'Casey. Shaw's correction in ink is on p. 4. There are several alterations by O'Casey, and a note in his hand says that it was 'Written for the Ministry of Information ten years ago'.

(14) Another typescript of 'A Whisper About Bernard Shaw', here entitled 'Aha, St. Bernard Shaw', 6 pp. with a few manuscript corrections by O'Casey in pencil. An accompanying letter would date the typescript as approximately 1946–7. (F. D. Murphy Collection, UCLA Library.)

(15) Typescript of 'Artist's Place in Life' (printed as 'Always the Plow and the Stars'), with O'Casey's corrections, 7 pp. (Dartmouth College Library.)

2 (TS) THE DRUMS OF FATHER NED

This play was entitled, in different drafts, 'The Night is Whispering', 'Green Geese' and 'The Rainbow Ends'. The first eleven items described below were among the playwright's papers and are now in the Berg Collection. The last entry, number twelve, seems to be identical with items 8 and 9; it is also in the Berg and was probably acquired from the author's literary agent in the United States.

(1) Holograph notes, characters and snatches of dialogue for the play, 9 pp.

(2) Typescript of early draft of 'Prerumble' to the play, pp. 1–9.

(3) Typescript of early draft of 'Scene 1: Night is Whispering', pp. 1–2 and 5–26.

(4) Typescript of early draft of 'Act 3' of 'The Night is Whispering', pp. 1–22; there are many additions and changes in ink in the text.

(5) In addition, there are also 3 pp. of dialogue for Act 3 of the play, with six loose parts of pages of dialogue (different sizes of paper).

The above four items (numbers 2–5) were found in an envelope which was labelled by O'Casey: 'Rejected Parts of *The Night is Whispering*'.

(6) Typescript of 'Prerumble' to 'Night is Whispering', pp. 1–8, with three introductory pages (plus carbon copy, 11 pp.).

(7) Draft typescript of the play without the 'Prerumble'. There are a number of differences from the published edition. Additions and changes are pasted into the text and some pages are irregular in size as a result; there are many additions in ink in the author's handwriting. Act I, pp. 1–27 (plus carbon copy, 27 pp.); II, pp. 1–20 (plus carbon copy, 20 pp.); III, pp. 1–19 (plus carbon copy, 19 pp.).

(8) Typescript typed by Ethel Christian Ltd (London) in light blue cover with red spine. On the cover there is written in ink: 'Amended Version'. There are many changes and additions in ink in the text and some additional material is pasted into the typescript. Introductory material, 5 pp.; Prerumble, pp. 1–12; Act I, pp. 1–33; II, pp. 1–29; III, pp. 1–29.

(9) Carbon copy of typescript (8) above, with identical pagination, similar changes and additions in ink in the text. The typescript is in a light fawn cover with a red spine.

(10) Draft typescript of revised version of the play, retyped by Ethel Christian Ltd in a red cover with a black spine. There are minor additions in ink in the text. Introductory material, 5 pp.; Prerumble, pp. 1–12; Act I, pp. 1–33; II, pp. 1–30; III, pp. 1–29. This version is that published in 1960.

(11) Carbon copy of typescript (10) above, with minor alterations in ink in the text, and with printer's marks throughout. The pagination is as in (10) above; the pages are loose, having been torn from a grey cover.

(12) Typescript identical with (8) and (9), above, typed by Ethel Christian, bound in buff with dark blue rexine spine, 74 pp. 'The Night is Whispering' is crossed out on the cover and the finally approved title typed in. 'Final Design' is added in ink. There are numerous corrections and additions in ink throughout and some typed corrections are pasted into the text. Contents: Prerumble, Act I, pp. 1–12; II, 1–33; III, 1–29, plus five separate sheets of music and chants for the play, of irregular sizes, with the author's additions in ink.

E53 (TS) FIGURO IN THE NIGHT

The following two typescripts are both from the playwright's own papers and are now in the Berg Collection.

(1) Typescript of early draft, typed by O'Casey, with many changes in ink in the text. Scene I, 13 pp.; II, 11 pp. There is also a carbon copy of Scene I, 13 pp.; but not of Scene II.

(2) Later typescript, typed by Ethel Christian Ltd, with considerable changes and additions in O'Casey's hand. Scene I, 19 pp.; II, 17 pp. This text is much closer to that of the printed version.

(TS) BEHIND THE GREEN CURTAINS

Each of the following seven items (two holograph and five typescript drafts) is from the author's personal papers and is now in the Berg Collection.

(1) 'Dark Kaleidoscope': stage direction and snatch of dialogue for Act II of *Behind the Green Curtains*, 2 pp. holograph.

(2) Notes for *Behind the Green Curtains* (one entitled 'The Jittering Gate'), 2 pp. holograph.

(3) Draft typescript entitled 'Behind Green Curtains: 1st. draft', pp. 1–8. In fact, this draft is only part of what is now Act II of the printed version of the play.

(4) Draft typescript of early version of the play, in three scenes. 'Scene I. The Jittering Gate', pp. 1–17; 'Scene II' ('Act II' is written on another page of the text), pp. 1–21; 'Scene III: Afterglow', pp. 1–20. There are many additions and corrections in ink added to the first scene, and several changes and deletions in the second scene too. The end of Scene III is different from that of the published version.

(5) Later typescript typed by Ethel Christian Ltd (London), in light fawn cover with red spine; Scene I, 23 pp.; II, 29 pp.; III, 28 pp. There are a few minor corrections in ink. Again, the end of Scene III is different from the published text.

(6) Identical typescript (also typed by Ethel Christian Ltd), but with many additions in ink and an additional scene and extra dialogue pasted into the text. The typescript is bound in a light blue cover with a red spine. A note in ink on the cover says: 'Semi-Final Copy, Sent to Printers afterwards amended. Oct. 1960. S. O'C.' Another note in ink says: 'Final Draft. Revised'. Pagination is the same as in typescript (5) above, (Scene I, 23 pp.; II, 29 pp.) with the exception of Scene III, where an additional episode has been added to the end of the play; Scene III in this version totals 29 pp. The copy bears the printer's marks on it.

(7) Identical typescript (typed by Ethel Christian Ltd), in red cover with black spine. On cover is written in ink: 'Final Draft. Revised', with 'A few final changes – Beoman who was said to be married, is so no longer', etc. Pagination, changes and additions are the same as in typescript (6), above. In addition, 3 pp. of notes and prefatory matter have been written in ink on the title-page and the two spare pages at the beginning of the typescript: these quotations preface the play in its printed version.

(TS) THE MOON SHINES ON KYLENAMOE

Both these typescripts are from the dramatist's papers and are now in the Berg Collection.

(1) Early draft, originally entitled 'The Pale Moon was Shining'. Typescript typed by O'Casey, with many changes in ink, 25 pp.

(2) Later typescript, typed by Ethel Christian Ltd, with blue cover, signed by the author on the front cover: 'Semi-Final Copy, Sent to Printers,

Afterwards Amended. Oct. 1960. S. O'C.' 33 pp. The copy has the printer's marks on it, and some corrections in ink by the author.

E56 (TS) FEATHERS FROM THE GREEN CROW

Typescripts of the two plays that were included in this anthology – 'Kathleen Listens In' and 'Nannie's Night Out' – are listed earlier as they were staged more than forty years before publication (see E31 and E32). Only one typescript associated with this book was among the playwright's personal papers; it is now in the Berg Collection.

(1) Typescript of 'Sound the Loud Trumpet', typed by Robert Hogan, with O'Casey's comment in ink at the end of the article: 'An antique article', pp. 1–6.

E57   (TS) UNDER A COLORED CAP

Twenty-five typescripts of material for this collection of articles, stories and a song were found among the author's papers and are now in the Berg Collection.

(1) Typescript of Prefatory material, 6 pp.
(2) Typescript of *'Under a Colored Cap.* Part I: An Army with Banners', pp. 1–24 (with carbon copy, 24 pp.).
(3) Typescript of *'Under a Colored Cap.* Part II: Reverie in the Dusk', pp. 1–20 (plus carbon copy, 20 pp.).
(4) Typescript entitled 'Resurgam', pp. 6–29, with 'Cancelled' written in ink on the front page. The first three pages of this draft were later incorporated into *'Under a Colored Cap,* Part II'; the rest of the article appears not to have been published (plus carbon copy, pp. 6–29).
(5) 'The Green Bushes' (a song), 1 p.
(6) Incomplete typescript entitled 'Sob Stuff': a rough draft of the essay which was later printed under the title of 'The Green Crow Caws', pp. 1–6.
(7) Early draft typescript of 'The Green Crow Caws', pp. 1–34. There are corrections in ink in the text.
(8) Revised version of 'The Green Crow Caws', with alterations in ink, pp. 1–30.
(9) Draft typescript of 'Under a Greenwood Tree He Died', originally entitled 'Dear Son of Memory', pp. 1–26 (plus a carbon copy, 26 pp.). There are minor changes in ink in the typescript.
(10) Typescript of 'Under a Greenwood Tree He Died', revised version typed by Ethel Christian Ltd. This typescript has no corrections by the author, but does contain the printer's marks on it, pp. 1–38 (plus carbon copy, 38 pp.).
(11) Typescript of 'The Lark in the Clear Air Still Sings', pp. 1–7.
(12) Typescript of 'The Lark in the Clear Air Still Sings', typed by Ethel Christian Ltd, pp. 1–9 (plus a carbon copy, 9 pp.).
(13) Incomplete draft typescript of 'Immanuel', 12 pp. (plus carbon copy, 12 pp.).

(14) Typescript of 'Immanuel', pp. 2–41.

(15) Typescript of 'Immanuel', typed by Ethel Christian Ltd, bearing printer's marks, pp. 1–69 (plus carbon copy, 69 pp.).

(16) Incomplete draft typescript of 'Immanuel', with note by author 'Draft only—cancelled', pp. 1–10.

(17) Draft typescript of 'Merrical of Miracles', pp. 1–8.

(18) Typescript of 'Merrical of Miracles', typed by Ethel Christian Ltd, and bearing the printer's marks, pp. 1–13 (plus a carbon copy, 13 pp.).

(19) Typescript of 'The People and the Theatre' pp. 1–6.

(20) Another typescript of 'The People and the Theatre' containing printer's marks, pp. 1–6.

(21) Typescript of 'Culture Incorporated', pp. 1–37 (plus two carbon copies, 2 × 37 pp.).

(22) Typescript of 'Culture Inc'., pp. 1–31. This copy contains the printer's marks.

(23) Typescript of 'Out, Damned Spot', containing printer's marks, pp. 1–6.

(24) Typescript of 'Purple Dust in Their Eyes', pp. 1–17 (together with seven odd pages of typescript of this article, described by the author as 'Redundant Pages', 7 pp.).

(25) 'Alteration of Sentences in *Under a Colored Cap*', 2 pp.

(TS) MISCELLANEOUS TYPESCRIPT MATERIAL

With three exceptions, the following one hundred and eighteen typescripts of articles, book reviews, poems and miscellaneous writings were found among the author's papers and are now in the Berg Collection. (The three exceptions are items 44, 72, and 118, the first two of which are in the F. D. Murphy Collection in the library of UCLA, Los Angeles; item 118 is in Dartmouth College Library, New Hampshire.) Although many were printed in periodicals, they were not published in any of his books during his life time. Whenever possible, publication details are provided. The list is alphabetical by title, save for item 118 (appended here at a late stage).

(1) Typescript notes and comments, entitled 'The Abbey Theatre'. The typescript remains unfinished and has the first page missing, pp. 2–13.

(2) Unfinished typescript of a satirical short story (in fantasy form) entitled 'Agaliamh St. Patrick & Peter Paul McUrnee', 16 pp. With some corrections and additions in ink.

(3) Carbon copy of typescript of article, 'Art is the Song of Life', 5 pp. Published in *Literaturnaya Gazeta*, Apr 5, 1960 (C527); first printed in English in *Blasts and Benedictions* (A44).

(4) Typescript of article entitled 'Ashes and Sparks' (or 'Writers' Opinions'), with minor corrections and additions in ink, 12 pp. Some of this material was used in *Under a Colored Cap* (A41).

(5) ['Autobiography'], typescript of untitled autobiographical fragment *(I Knock at the Door* period, but not used in the book) typed on the verso pages of old letters, 2 pp.

(6) Photocopy of typescript programme note entitled 'Badtime Story', 3 pp. Published in *Blasts and Benedictions* (A44).

(7) Typescript of fragment of an article, entitled 'Beat Beat Beat', 2 pp.

(8) Typescript (carbon copy) entitled 'Bertrand Russell and The Yogi', 4 pp. Published in *Forward*, Oct 13, 1945 (C313).

(9) Typescript (carbon copy) of article, 'The Black Flag of Fascism', 2 pp.

(10) ['Blasphemy and *The Silver Tassie*'], photocopy of untitled typescript, 3 pp. Published in this version in *Blasts and Benedictions* (A44). Written in 1935, this article was first printed in *Sean O'Casey: the Man Behind the Plays* (B45) as 'A Stand on *The Silver Tassie*'; reprinted in *The Letters of Sean O'Casey* (A46).

(11) Typescript (carbon copy) of short article, 'Britain with her Back to the Screen', 3 pp. Published in the *Listener*, July 27, 1932 (C127).

(12) Typescript (carbon copy) of short story entitled 'A Bull of Bashan' (afterwards 'Toreador'), 7 pp. Published in *Time and Tide*, Dec 2, 1933 (C137). Reprinted in *Blasts and Benedictions* (A44).

(13) Typescript (carbon copy) of article, 'Cardinal Griffin's New Recruit', 2 pp.

(14) Typescript of book review entitled 'Choir & Tempest', 2 pp.

(15) Carbon copy of typescript of article entitled 'The Church Tries to Close the Gates', 5 pp. Written 1934–5; first published in *Blasts and Benedictions* (A44).

(16) Typescript (carbon copy) of a short salute to the Soviet Union, 'A Clap from Hands in an Irish Home', 1 p.

(17) Carbon copy typescript of article, 'Coal and Kingfisher', 3 pp.

(18) Photocopy of first page of typescript entitled 'Cock-a-doodle-Doo', 1 p.

(19) Typescript (carbon copy) of article, 'Coloured Ribbons in the Cap of Youth', 6 pp. Published in *Komsomol'skaya Pravda*, Aug 8, 1958 (C501).

(20) Typescript (carbon copy) of article entitled 'Crimson in the Tricolour', 2 pp.

(21) Carbon copy of typescript of an unfinished article entitled 'A Crow for Cock-a-doodle Dandy', 20 pp. Written 1947–9.

(22) Typescript (carbon copy) of article entitled 'Culture and Comradeship', 2 pp.

(23) Typescript (carbon copy) of article, 'Darkness this Side, Light on the Other', 5 pp.

(24) Photocopy of typescript entitled 'The Day the Worker Blows a Bugle', 7 pp. Published in *Novoe Vremya – New Times*, May 1958 (C495) in an abbreviated version. Full text printed in *Blasts and Benedictions* (A44).

(25) Typescript (carbon copy) of article entitled 'The Dead Awakened', 2 pp.

(26) Typescript (carbon copy) of book review, 'Distant Point', 2 pp. Published in *Labour Monthly*, Jan 1942 (C266).

(27) Photocopy of typescript article, 'Empty Vessels', 3 pp. Published in *Irish Freedom*, May 1942 (C272). Reprinted in *Blasts and Benedictions* (A44).

(28) Typescript (carbon copy) of anti-Hitler poem, 'Ere Autumn Leaves Fall', 2 pp.

(29) Typescript of broadcast talk headed 'Essay 3: Radio Eireann' (dated April 7, 1955), 6 pp. Some pages slightly torn; corrections and additions in ink.

(30) Carbon copy typescript of article, 'Exmouth Ship, Ahoy!', 2 pp.

(31) Typescript (carbon copy) of article, 'The Flaming Sunflower', 5 pp. Published in *Izvestiya*, Apr 21, 1960 (C529); extract quoted in Preface to *Blasts and Benedictions* (A44).

(32) Typescript (carbon copy) of article, 'From a Little Window on the World', 2 pp. Published in *Book Find News*, 1949 (C369).

(33) Typescript (carbon copy) of article, 'The Gathering of Growing Life', 4 pp.

(34) Typescript (carbon copy) of article, 'God Rest you Merry, Polish People', 3 pp.

(35) Typescript (carbon copy) of article entitled 'Green Searchlight', 16 pp. One of a series of articles with this title, written during the Second World War for readers in the Soviet Union. Dated July 22, 1943.

(36) Carbon copy of typescript entitled 'Green Searchlight', 12 pp. This article is quite different from the other four articles with the same title listed here. 'Green Searchlight' was the pen-name that O'Casey used as a free-lance correspondent in Russian newspapers, 1943–5. In this copy of the article, p. 2 is faded and almost illegible.

(37) Carbon copy of typescript entitled 'Green Searchlight', 8 pp.

(38) Typescript (carbon copy) of article entitled 'Green Searchlight: Controversy', 7 pp.

(39) Typescript (carbon copy) of article entitled 'Green Searchlight: Flag of the Soviets', 10 pp.

(40) Untitled typescript of a fragment of a lecture given at St Catharine's College, Cambridge, 2 pp. The author's autobiography tells us that the talk was entitled 'The Holy Ghost Leaves England'. First printed in *The Letters of Sean O'Casey* (A46).

(41) Typescript (carbon copy) of article, 'How the War Hits O'Casey', dated 1941, 1 p.

(42) Typescript of article, 'How to Succeed as a Playwright', 3 pp. Published in *The Holiday Book* (B20).

(43) 'Ireland, Boys, Hurrah!' Typescript article (carbon copy) signed 'Sean O'Casey Totnes, Devon' in ink on title-page, 14 pp. The type has faded badly on some pages and is difficult to read; p. 14 is torn. Although only a carbon copy of this article can be found among O'Casey's papers, it is almost certain that this article remains unpublished. It was most probably written late in 1947 or early 1948.

(44) Another typescript of item 43, above, with the title 'Ireland, Boys, Hurrah!' crossed out in ink and a new title, 'Minding Me Own Business', substituted by the author, 23 pp. (with other holograph changes). This typescript is among the F. D. Murphy Collection in the library of the University of California, Los Angeles.

(45) Carbon copy of typescript book review, 'Ireland's Black-headed Boy', 3 pp. First published in *Our Time*, Nov 1945 (C314); reprinted in *Blasts and Benedictions* (A44).

(46) Typescript of note entitled 'For Irish Drama – Critics', 1 p.

(47) Typescript of fragmentary draft of article entitled 'Irish Literature', 5 pp. (numbered pp. 3–6, and p. 10). This is an early version of the essay, 'Literature in Ireland', originally published in abbreviated form in *Internatsional'naya Literatura*, Dec 1939 (C227).

(48) Typescript (carbon copy) of article entitled 'An Irishman's Plays', 2 pp.

(49) Carbon copy of typescript obituary, 'Jim Larkin's Gone', 6 pp.

(50) Photocopy of typescript entitled 'John Millington Synge', 7 pp.

Published in *Britansky Soyuznik*, June 23, 1946 (C327); first published in English in *Blasts and Benedictions* (A44).

(51) Carbon copy of typescript entitled 'Lenin', 3 pp. Probably article published in *Inostrannaya Literatura*, Apr 1960 (C526).

(52) Typescript (carbon copy) of article, 'Lenin Logos of Russia', 4 pp. Probably article published in *Literaturnaya Gazeta*, Apr 23, 1960 (C530).

(53) Typescript (carbon copy) of article 'Let's Write a Play', 4 pp. Published in *The Writer*, May 1952 (C408).

(54) Typescript of extract from 'Life is More than Meat', 6 pp. (together with carbon copy, 6 pp.) This passage from a chapter in *I Knock at the Door* was used for O'Casey's second phonograph recording for the Caedmon company, recorded on December 26, 1963.

(55) Photocopy of typescript entitled 'Literature in Ireland', 14 pp. Published in abbreviated form in *Internatsional'naya Literatura*, Dec 1939 (C227). Full text printed in *Blasts and Benedictions* (A44). An early fragmentary version of the essay is described under the title 'Irish Literature' (E58(TS)47).

(56) Typescript of article (carbon copy), 'Look-out Twenty-six years Ahead', 2 pp. First published in an abbreviated version in *Daily People's World*, Jan 13, 1962 (C564); fuller text printed in *Look*, Jan 16, 1962.

(57) Carbon copy of typescript, 'March Towards a New Era', 4 pp.

(58) Typescript (carbon copy) of book review, 'Mayakovsky Immortal', 3 pp. Published in *Anglo-Soviet Journal*, spring 1946 (C325).

(59) Photocopy of typescript entitled 'Melpomene an' Thalia Beggin' for Bread'. 3 pp. First published in *New York Times Magazine*, Nov 9, 1959 (C515); reprinted in *Blasts and Benedictions* (A44).

(60) Photocopy of typescript entitled 'Melpomene in Ireland', 7 pp. Published in *Tribune*, Jan 31, 1947 (C336); reprinted in *Blasts and Benedictions* (A44).

(61) Typescript of 4 pp. of quotations entitled 'Miscellaneous'.

(62) Typescript draft of notes for article entitled 'Mr. Wesker's Goody Wine' (later called 'Mr. Wesker's March Past'), 4 pp. Written 1962–3; first published in *Blasts and Benedictions* (A44).

(63) Typescript (carbon copy) of article, 'My Friend, Chekhov', 2 pp. Published in *Voks Bulletin*, Mar 1954 (C425).

(64) Typescript of unused fragment entitled 'Nation-Builders of Babylon', 5 pp. (4 pp. of which are foolscap). This unpublished piece of auto-biography – O'Casey working on the Railway – is typed on the verso pages of printed war-time news bulletins of the early 1940s.

(65) Typescript (carbon copy) of article, 'New Chance for a People's Theatre', 4 pp.

(66) Typescript entitled 'O'Casey by O'Casey', 1 p. Programme note for the Mermaid Theatre productions during the Mermaid's O'Casey Season in 1962 (C570).

(67) Photocopy of typescript entitled 'O'Casey in Hungarian Costume', 2 pp. Published in Hungarian magazine, *Tájékoztató*, Dec 1957 (C482). First published in English in *Blasts and Benedictions* (A44).

(68) Photocopy of typescript entitled 'O'Casey's Drama–Bonfire', 4 pp. Published in *Zvezda*, Jan 1958 (C483). First published in English in *Blasts and Benedictions* (A44).

(69) Typescript of unfinished article entitled 'O'Casey Versus the Abbey

Theatre', 39 pp. This article started as a letter to Ronald Ayling (dated 'August 1958'); later it developed into a long essay, some of the material of which was later incorporated into the play, *Figuro in the Night* (A42), and in essays in *Under a Colored Cap* (A41). There are corrections and additions in ink in O'Casey's handwriting. On p. 6 there is the note 'All Cancelled'. A short quotation from the article appeared in the *Kilkenny Magazine*, spring–summer 1964 (C591).

(70) Typescript (carbon copy) of article entitled 'The Oddest Neutrality', 3 pp.

(71) Typescript of poem, 'Oh, Women, guide our feet into the way of Peace', 2 pp.

(72) Typescript of programme note for a production of *Red Roses for Me*, entitled 'The Okay and the One Who Wrote It', 2 pp. On the second page is a letter dated October 26, 1963 to Robert H. Hethmon of the Department of Theatre Arts, Los Angeles, signed in ink with a short holograph post-script. The programme note was published in the *UCLA Playhouse Programme*, May 15, 1964 (C596). This typescript is among the F. D. Murphy Collection at the library of the University of California, Los Angeles.

(73) Photocopy of typescript entitled 'One of the World's Dramatists', 4 pp. Written in 1944 for Russian readers, this essay was first published in full in *Blasts and Benedictions* (A44); it had earlier appeared in abbreviated form in *Culture and Life*, Sep 1966 (C626).

(74) Typescript of poem, 'O Women, Gracious and Gallant, be Braver Now', 1 p. Published in *Daily Worker*, Apr 3, 1948 (C360) as 'O women, be braver now'.

(75) Typescript entitled 'Poem', with corrections in ink, 1 p.

(76) Typescript (carbon copy) of book review, entitled 'Poor Puzzled Ireland', 3 pp. Published in *Tribune*, Feb 22, 1957 (C466).

(77) Typescript of 'Pound on Demand', 15 pp. This is an unpublished short story with the same plot as O'Casey's play of that title (A16); both were written in 1932–3.

(78) Typescript (carbon copy) of article 'Red Envoy to Outer Space', 2 pp.

(79) Typescript (carbon copy) of book review, 'Red Grave in Burma', 3 pp. Published in *Daily Worker*, Oct 21, 1944 (C304).

(80) Typescript (carbon copy) of article 'Red Star over the Red Hand', 2 pp.

(81) Typescript (carbon copy) of article, 'Red Thoughts in a Green Shade', 12 pp. Most probably written spring 1943; some of this material used later in *Sunset and Evening Star* (A31).

(82) Typescript of article entitled 'Resurgam' (alternative title: 'L'Envoi'), 7 pp. With corrections and additions in ink in O'Casey's handwriting. First published in *Blasts and Benedictions* (A44).

(83) Typescript of extract from autobiographical chapter, 'R.I.P.', 5 pp. This passage from *I Knock at the Door* (A19) was prepared for use in the second phonograph record O'Casey made for Caedmon; it is typed on the verso pages of a typescript early draft of the 'Cambridge' and 'Childermess' chapters from *Sunset and Evening Star* (A31). It was not finally included in the contents of the second phonograph record, perhaps because of limitations of time.

(84) Typescript (carbon copy) of article entitled 'Rise O' The Red Star', 14 pp. Published in *Anglo-Soviet Journal*, spring 1946 (C324).

(85) Carbon copy of typescript of article entitled 'The Rose of Youth', 3 pp. Published in *Novy Mir*, July 1957 (C473).

(86) Carbon copy of typescript of article, 'The Shadow of the Vatican', 6 pp. Published in *Daily Worker*, Mar 23, 1944 (C299) as 'Shadow of the Vatican'.

(87) Typescript of extract from 'Ship in Full Sail', 5 pp. This extract from a chapter in *Rose and Crown* (A30) was used for O'Casey's second phonograph recording for the Caedmon Company, recorded on December 26, 1953.

(88) [*The Silver Tassie*], untitled typescript notes, answering Irish criticisms of *The Silver Tassie*, 3 pp. Almost certainly written in 1935.

(89) ['*Soviet Literature*'], untitled typescript containing 'a few general words about Soviet Literature', 2 pp. Published in *Komsomol'skaya Pravda*, June 5, 1958 (C498), with two extracts printed in the Preface to *Blasts and Benedictions* (A44).

(90) Photocopy of typescript entitled 'A Sprig of Rosemary among the Laurel', 3 pp. Essay printed as the Foreword to *Selected Plays of Lady Gregory* (B44). Reprinted in *Blasts and Benedictions* (A44).

(91) Carbon copy of a typescript entitled 'Star Ascending', 5 pp.

(92) Typescript of short dialogue entitled 'Television Interview', 2 pp.

(93) Fragmentary typescript notes and comments entitled 'Theatre' (ideas for articles), pp. 10–16 and pp. 21–3. The typescript remains unfinished.

(94) Photocopy of typescript entitled 'The Theatre and the Politician', 4 pp. Published in *Common Wealth Review*, Jan 1946 (C320). Reprinted in *Blasts and Bendictions* (A44).

(95) Typescript of poem, 'Tidy the Nazis up for the Dead', 2 pp.

(96) Carbon copy of typescript entitled 'The Time the Lilac Blooms', 2 pp. (one page torn).

(97) Typescript (carbon copy) of book review entitled 'Tolstoy Tunes In', 3 pp. Published in *Tribune*, Nov 28, 1947 (C348).

(98) Carbon copy of typescript of poem entitled 'To Maire', 2 pp. With corrections in ink. Probably written during the period 1917–22, the poem is addressed to the woman who inspired the poems that appeared in the 'First Fall' section of *Windfalls* (A16); a version of the poem was first printed in *The World of Sean O'Casey* (B53). A holograph draft, entitled 'To Mary', is to be found in the Fergus O'Connor Papers in the Berg Collection (E3(MS)21).

(99) Typescript (carbon copy) of article, 'Trumpeters in Man's March', 3 pp. Probably the message published in *Inostrannaya Literatura*, Mar 1959 (C507); extract quoted in the Preface to *Blasts and Benedictions* (A44).

(100) Carbon copy of a typescript of an article entitled 'Undying Stars', 4 pp.

(101) Typescript (carbon copy) of article, 'Vatican and Jugo-Slavian Red Star', 5 pp. Published in *Daily Worker*, Dec 12, 1946 (C335) as 'Vatican and Red Star in Yugoslavia'.

(102) Typescript (carbon copy) of article entitled 'Vatican's Rage at the Red Star of Yugo-Slavia', 4 pp.

(103) Typescript (carbon copy) of 'Virtue and Erin Censorship', 3 pp. Published in *Irish Freedom*, Jan 1943 (C285).

(104) Typescript (carbon copy) of article, 'Voice of the Vatican', 2 pp.

(105) Photocopy of typescript entitled 'What Thou Seest, Write in a Book', 4 pp. Published in *Blasts and Benedictions* (A44).

(106) Carbon copy of typescript, 'When the News Came to Dublin', 4 pp. Published in *Inostrannaya Literatura*, Nov 1957 (C479).

(107) Carbon copy of typescript of article, 'Wherever the Place may be, the Time is Now', 2 pp. Published in *Daily Worker*, Sep 24, 1942 (C277) as 'Further they Go, Nearer they Come'.

(108) Typescript of an incomplete fragment entitled 'William Archer Buries the Elizabethans', 3 pp. Probably written 1935–6.

(109) Fragmentary typescript draft of unfinished article, 'William Archer Defends the Gap of Danger', 2 pp. Probably written 1935–6.

(110) Photocopy of typescript entitled 'Within the Gates and Without', 4 pp. First published in *Blasts and Benedictions* (A44).

(111) Typescript (carbon copy) of a dialogue entitled 'Women's Reveille', 2 pp.

(112) Photocopy of typescript entitled 'A Word before Curtain-rise', 2 pp. Published as an introduction to *Selected Plays of Sean O'Casey* (A32). Reprinted in *Blasts and Benedictions* (A44).

(113) Carbon copy of typescript entitled 'The Word En-Masse', 2 pp.

(114) Typescript notes and comments (written 1956–7), entitled 'Words', 19 pp.

(115) Typescript (carbon copy) of article entitled 'Year of Victory and Work', 4 pp. Most probably written January–February 1945; the article is addressed to Mme L. Kislova (Soviet Union).

(116) Typescript (carbon copy) of article, 'Young Shoots on Life's Tree', 5 pp.

(117) Typescript (carbon copy) of article, 'Youth is the Bugler', 4 pp.

(118) Typescript of review, 'Bernard Shaw and Mrs Patrick Campbell', with holograph corrections, 4 pp. Published in *New York Times* (C416) and *Blasts and Benedictions* (A44), this typescript is now in Dartmouth College Library.

III PROOF MATERIAL

59 THE SILVER TASSIE

(1) Copy of the 1928 edition used as page proofs for the revised edition printed in *Collected Plays*, vol. II. The pages are torn loose from the cover and bear the printer's marks; 140 pp. There are several minor changes and a few instructions to the printers in ink in O'Casey's hand.

60 WINDFALLS

(1) Incomplete page proofs, marked 'First Page Proof' and '17 August 1934'; pp. i–x; 1–53; 13–63; 121–201 (and with duplicate copy of pp. i–x). There are several minor corrections in ink by the author.

61 THE STAR TURNS RED

(1) Copy of the 1940 edition of the play used as page proofs for the revised edition published in *Collected Plays*, vol. II. The pages are torn loose from the cover; four pages are missing; pp. 1–158; 163–84. There are a few additions and changes in ink by the author.

E62   DRUMS UNDER THE WINDOWS

(1) Uncorrected proof copy (in brown cover) marked 'First Page Proof' and
dated '4 April 1945'; pp. 1–148; 151–330. Note in ink on cover (in
O'Casey's hand) says: 'Page 150. Song of the Fishhawker silenced.
Macmillan's didn't like it.' Yet pages 149–50 are missing from this copy.
Duplicate copy, without cover, and without corrections; pp. 1–330. The
ballad was a bawdy one that originally was planned to appear in the chapter
'Song of a Shift'.

E63   COCK-A-DOODLE DANDY

(1) Galley proofs, sheets numbered 1–37; marked 'First Proof' and dated
'10 April 1948'. Some of the sheets are torn and tattered. There are minor
corrections and additions in ink by the author.
(2) Page proofs, marked 'First Page Proof' and dated '4 December 1948';
pp. i–vi; 1–104. There are a few minor corrections in ink.

E64   COLLECTED PLAYS, VOLUME I

(1) Page proofs, stamped 'First Proof' and dated '21 February 1949' (incomplete); pp. 1–90; 155–314 (pp. 91–154 are missing; the missing portion
contains almost the whole of *The Shadow of a Gunman*).

E65   COLLECTED PLAYS, VOLUME II

(1) Page proofs, marked 'First proof' and dated '23 March 1949'; pp. 1–354
(plus 4 pp. of music), with minor corrections and additions in ink.

E66   COLLECTED PLAYS,   VOLUME III

(1) Page proofs, stamped 'First proof' and dated '8 February 1951'; pp.
1–274. Minor corrections in ink by author.

E67   COLLECTED PLAYS, VOLUME IV

(1) Uncorrected page proofs marked 'First Page Proof' and dated '13 March
1951'; pp. i–v; 1–294.

ROSE AND CROWN

(1) Galley proofs, stamped 'First proof' and dated '8 October 1951'. Sheets numbered from 1–97, with 3 pp. of typed additions to the text and very many changes and additions in ink.

(2) Page proofs, stamped 'First Page Proof' and dated '28 March 1952'; pp. 1–307. There are a few slight corrections in ink by the author.

SUNSET AND EVENING STAR

(1) Galley proofs (numbered 1–103) marked 'First Proof' and dated '25 November 1953', There are many alterations and additions made in ink by O'Casey. In addition there are three sheets of galley proofs (nos 99, 100 and 103), used for phonograph recording made by O'Casey. These three sheets contain various marginal notes and additions in ink.

(2) Page proofs marked 'First Page Proof' and dated '24 March 1954'; pp. 1–312. There are several corrections and additions in ink.

THE BISHOP'S BONFIRE

(1) Galley proofs (numbered from 1–35) and stamped 'First Proof' and '13 November 1954'; there are very many corrections and additions in ink in O'Casey's hand.

(2) Page proofs, stamped 'First Page Proof' and dated '16 February 1955'; pp. 1–124. A few slight changes recorded in ink.

THE DRUMS OF FATHER NED

(1) Galley proofs (sheets numbered 1–31) stamped 'First Proof' and '9 September 1959', with many minor corrections in ink by the author.

(2) Page proofs, marked 'First Page Proof' and dated '9 December 1959'; pp. i–x; 1–109. There are no corrections.

BEHIND THE GREEN CURTAINS, FIGURO IN THE NIGHT and THE MOON SHINES ON KYLENAMOE

(1) Galley proofs marked 'First Proof' and '13 October 1960' (sheets numbered 1–47). There are many corrections and additions in ink by O'Casey, including a different ending for Act 3 of *Behind the Green Curtains* and extra dialogue for 'Figuro in the Night'.

(2) Incomplete page proofs, pp. 1–74 (*Behind the Green Curtains*); 125–57 (complete text of 'The Moon Shines on Kylenamoe'), plus 4 pp. of music. The text of 'Figuro in the Night' is missing and so are pp. 75–84 of *Behind the Green Curtains*. There are a few corrections in ink by the author.

E73 UNDER A COLORED CAP

(1) Galley proofs (two sets), complete except for the last article in the book, 'Purple Dust in Their Eyes'. Both sets stamped 'First Proof' and marked '9 July 1962' and '11 July 1962'. The sheets are numbered 1–83. Both sets of proofs contain corrections in ink made by Sean and Eileen O'Casey.

(2) Page proofs, marked 'First Page Proof' and dated '24 September 1962'; pp. 1–277.

First Stage Productions and Major Revivals

Checklist of world stage premières and of first productions (whether amateur or professional) in Ireland, England and the United States. Notable revivals are also acknowledged. The plays are listed alphabetically by title. Films of O'Casey's plays (but not television versions) are given at the end of Section F.

F1 BEDTIME STORY

An Anatole Burlesque in One Act

John Jo Mulligan
Angela Nightingale
Daniel Halibut
Miss Mossie
Policeman
Nurse

Director:
Designer:

a. *World première*
   May 7, 1952
   Yugoslav-American Hall,
   New York

   Robert Donley
   Anne Jackson
   John McLiam
   Osceola Archer

   Joseph Papirofsky
   May Callas

b. *Irish professional première*
   June 27, 1972
   Peacock Theatre, Dublin
   (Abbey Theatre Company)

   Donal Neligan
   Michele Lohan
   Clive Geraghty
   Máire Ní Ghráinne
   Niall O'Brien
   Fionnuala Kenny

   John Lynch
   Gerard Crossan

There is no record of a professional London production.

F2   BEHIND THE GREEN CURTAINS

	a. *World première*	b. *European première*
	December 5, 1962	November 20, 1965
	University of Rochester,	Theatre der Stadt, Cottbus,
	New York State	German Democratic Republic
		(translation by Jorg Wehmeier)
Dennis Chatastray	Rick Rahn	Helmut Schellhardt
Reena Kilternan	Joan Wescott	Renate Kohn
Martin Beoman	Jerry Livadis	Eckart Strehle
Noneen Melbayee	Elaine Magidson	Maja-Rosewith Riemer
Bunny Conneen	Jeffrey Fine	Martin Richter
Jack McGeetish	Jon Mezz	Rolf Dietrich
Wycherley McGeera	Bayard Ewing	Walter Wickenhauser
Leslie Horaum	Robert Ferguson	Werner Knodel
Christy Kornavaun	James O'Smith	Hansdieter Neumann
Lizzie Latterly	Sonya Raimi	Ruth Festersen
Angela Carrigeen	Anne Senning	Leonore Holland
Dan Basaun	Dan Walkowitz	Waldemar Reinhold
Verger	Stuart Ritching	Rolf Winkelgrund
First Man	Thomas Rush	Fred Puls
Second Man	Thomas Durham	Werner Hohlfeld
Third Man	Edward Delaney	Lothar Wenzel
The Older Woman	Jo Chandler	Margret Stange
The Younger Woman	Felice Elias	Hannelore Kreutze
Director:	Robert Hogan	Friedrich Siebert/Rolf Winkelgrund
Designer:	Robert Hogan	Walter Bohm

c. *Irish Première*
July 22, 1975
Project Arts Centre,
Dublin

Dennis Chatastray	Tim McDonnell
Reena Kilternan	Ruth Hegarty
Martin Boeman	Eamonn O'Dwyer
Noneen Melbayee	Martina Stanley
Bunny Conneen	Frank Melia
Jack McGeelish	Eoin White
Wycherley McGeera	Ronan Patterson
Leslie Horaun	Stephen D. Brennan
Christy Kornavaun	Sean O'Briain
Lizzie Latterly	Biddy McGrath
Angela Carrigeen	Patricia McMenamin
Dan Basawn	Arthur O'Sullivan
Verger	Denis O'Neill
First Factory Girl	Patricia McMenamin
Second Factory Girl	Michelle O'Connor
First Man	Denis O'Neill
Second Man	Jerry Lundberg
Third Man	Joe McParland
Other Citizens of Ballybedhust	Maureen Mythen
	Michelle O'Connor
	Jerry Lundberg

Director: Frank Murphy
Designer: Rúairí O'Broin

There appears to have been no English production of the play.

F3   THE BISHOP'S BONFIRE

A Tragi-Comedy in Three Acts

a.   *World première*
February 28, 1955
Gaiety Theatre, Dublin

b.   *English première*
July 26, 1961
Mermaid Theatre, London

	World première	English première
Dick Carranaun	Seamus Kavanagh	Godfrey Quigley
Richard Rankin	Tony Quinn	Howard Goorney
Councillor Reiligan	Eddie Byrne	David Blake Kelly
Very Rev. Timothy Canon Burren	Paul Farrell	Paul Farrell
Manus Moanroe	Denis Brennan	Derek Young
Daniel Clooncoohy	Aiden Kerrigan	Terry Scully
Keelin Reiligan	Maureen Cusack	Annette Crosbie
Codger Sleehaun	Cyril Cusack	Davy Kaye
Fr. Boheroe	Patrick Leyde	Hugh Sullivan
Fooraun Reiligan	Sheila Brennan	Celia Salkeld
Lt. Michael Reiligan	Godfrey Quigley	Joe Lynch
A Railway Porter	Harry Hutchinson	Harry Hutchinson
Director:	Tyrone Guthrie	Frank Dunlop
Designer:	Michael O'Herlihy	Tony Carruthers

There appears to have been no United States production.

F4   CATHLEEN LISTENS IN

A Phantasy in One Act

a.   *World première*
     Abbey Theatre, Dublin
     October 1, 1923

Meehawl O'Houlihan	F. J. McCormick
Sheela O'Houlihan	Maureen Delany
Kathleen	Eileen Crowe
Thomas Thornton	Barry Fitzgerald
Jimmy	Michael J. Dolan
The Man in the Kilts	Gabriel J. Fallon
The Free-Stater	Arthur Shields
The Republican	Tony Quinn
The Business Man	U. Wright
The Farmer	Maurice Esmonde
The Doctor	Eric Gorman
The Man with the Big Drum	Peter Nolan
Two Men	Walter Dillon
	P. J. Carolan

Producer: Lennox Robinson

Revived at the Abbey Theatre (in a slightly revised version), March 3, 1925. The play does not appear to have been staged in England or the United States.

F5 COCK-A-DOODLE DANDY

A Fantasy Drama in Three Scenes

	a. *World première* December 10, 1949 People's Theatre, Newcastle upon Tyne	b. *U.S. première* January 30, 1950 Theatre '50, Dallas, Texas (Theatre-in-the-Round)	c. *New York première* November 12, 1958 Carnegie Hall Playhouse	d. *London première* September 17, 1959 Royal Court Theatre
The Cock	Peter Andrews Collier	Bill Bray	Carlo Mazzone	Berto Pasuka
Michael Marthraun	Jack Percy	Louis Veda Quince	Will Geer	J. G. Devlin
Sailor Mahan	Tom Rutherford	Ben Yaffee	Ian Martin	Wilfred Lawson
Lorna	Helen Paterson	Mary Finney	Rae Allen	Pauline Flanagan
Loreleen	Margaret Wilson	Margaret O'Neill	Gaby Rodgers	Joan O'Hara
Marion	Nancy O'Kane	Peggy McCay	Anne Meara	Etain O'Dell
Shanaar	James Garbutt	Edwin Whitner	Paul Shyre	Eamon Keane
First Rough Fellow	Allan Law	Charles Braswell	Dennis Drew	Alex Farrell
Second Rough Fellow	Alan Brown	Larry Hageman	David Faulkner	Colin Blakely
Father Domineer	John Lilburn	Richard McCook	George Ebeling	Patrick Magee
The Sergeant	Geoffrey Branson	Joe Sullivan	John Aronson	John Kelly
Jack (The Lorry Driver)	Ronald Nible	Bob Cotten	Paul Hinxmann	Robert Arnold
Julia	Irene Godfrey	Virginia Robinson	Carroll Conroy	Jeanne Hepple
One-Eyed Larry	Arthur Allsop	Don Howell	Frank Groseclose	Bill Keating
The Messenger	W. R. Nicholson	John Denney	Jack Betts	Norman Rodway
A Porter	Robin Page	Phil Slater	M. David Samples	Charles Wade
A Mayor	Wallace P. Coxon		Sidney Kay	John Kelly
A Macebearer	George Leach		Howard Lee	Stephen Dartnell
Julia's Father	Nicholas Whitfield		M. David Samples	Robert Arnold
The Bellman	Jack Willis		Sidney Kay	Stephen Dartnell
Villagers	Lorna Fawcitt Joyce Archer Myra Watson Hazel Burdikin Dick Rimmer James Baird		Ailsa Dawson (A Nun)	

Director:	Peter Trower	Margo Jones/	Philip Burton	George Devine
Designer:	W. R. Nicholson	Jonathan Seymour	Lester Polakov	Sean Kenny

e. First professional production in Ireland, at the Lyric Theatre, Belfast, opened on November 5, 1975; It was directed by Tomás MacAnna. Earlier, the Irish première was an amateur production staged by the Tipperary Dramatic Society in the Gaiety Theatre, Tipperary, on November 28, 1972.

A Mickrocosm of Ireland

	a. *World première* April 25, 1959 Little Theatre, Lafayette, Indiana	b. *European première* November 8, 1960 Queen's Theatre, Hornchurch	c. *Irish première* June 6, 1966 Olympia Theatre, Dublin
Characters in the Prerumble			
Officer of the Black and Tan	Walter Richter	Patrick O'Connell	Robert Carlile Jnr
First Black and Tan	Anthony Tommasi	James Mellor	Gerry Alexander
Second Black and Tan	Alan Burdick	Michael McKevitt	Seán McCarthy
Third Black and Tan	Burnham Carter, Jr.	Norman Bennett	John O'Flynn
Fourth Black and Tan	Willian Tatum	Christopher Dunham	
Binnington	Robert Hogan	David Blake Kelly	Ronnie Walsh
McGilligan	Bernard Shiffman	Kevin Fitzgerald	Arthur O'Sullivan
Characters in the play			
Alderman Binnington	Robert Hogan	David Blake Kelly	Ronnie Walsh
Elena Binnington	Hilary Smith	June Watson	Anna Manahan
Micheal Binnington	John Tully	Gawn Grainger	Bill Golding
Councillor McGilligan	Bernard Shiffman	Kevin Fitzgerald	Arthur O'Sullivan
Mrs. Meeda McGilligan	Joan McLeod	Shela Ward	Beryl Fagan
Nora McGilligan	Geraldine Gray	June Watts	Deirdre Purcell
Bernadette Shillayley	Patricia Hensley	Doreen Keogh	Maura Hastings
Tom Killsallaghan	James Bilyeu	Michael McKevitt	Robert Carlile Jnr
Oscar McGunty	Robert Feichter	James Mellor	Gerry Alexander
Man of the Musket	William Hoffmann	Christopher Dunham	Seán McCarthy
Man of the Pike	Nicholas Bielenberg	Patrick O'Connell	John O'Flynn
Rev. D. Fillifogue	Robert Corbin	Duncan Lewis	Martin Dempsey
Alec Sherighan	Stuart Main	Will Leighton	Joe Lynch
Mr. Murray	Richard Jaeger	Norman Bennett	Jim Norton
Tostal Helpers and Villagers	Margaret Reuszer Linda Veach, Pamela Drake Jean Ricklefs, William Darnell, Barry Gray, Mark Griffin	Julia Blake Jackie Harskin Daphne Saunter Ian Strachan	Tony Corcoran, Tom Sheedy, Patrick Dawson, Niall Buggy, Frances Moran, Ethna Quinn, Elizabeth Walsh, Maureen Aherne, Mary Frawley
Echo	Jay Paul Minn/Niki Minn		Thomas Studley [in this production the Echo was called 'Voice of Sean O'Casey']
Bugler	Tore Ramstad		
Director:	Jeanne Orr/Robert Hogan	David Phethean	Tomás MacAnna
Designer:	Michael Brown	David Jones	Tomás MacAnna

d. The London première was a non-professional production, at Canonbury Tower, which opened on May 21, 1965.

F7 THE END OF THE BEGINNING

A Comedy in One Act

	a. *World première*	b. *English première*	c. *U.S. première*
	February 8, 1937	October 16, 1939	(one performance)
	Abbey Theatre,	'Q' Theatre, London	February 25, 1942
	Dublin		Court Square Theatre,
			Springfield, Mass.
Darry Berrill	P. J. Carolan	Edgar K. Bruce	(Cast list unobtainable)
Lizzie Berrill	Maureen Delany	Beatrix Fielden-Kaye	
Barry Derrill	F. J. McCormick	John Laurie	
Director:	Arthur Shields	Beatrix Lehmann	Eddie Dowling

London Revival: May 22, 1953, at Unity Theatre.

F8 FIGURO IN THE NIGHT

	a. *World première* May 4, 1962 Hofstra University Playhouse, New York	b. *New York (professional) première* October 30, 1962 Theatre de Lys	c. *Irish première* August 14, 1975 Peacock Theatre, Dublin
Young Girl	Carol Sica	Nancy Reardon	Jeananne Crowley
Old Woman	Joyce Cohen	Margaret Brewster	Aine Ni Mhuiri
Old Man	Charles Ludlam	Jerome Collamore	Niall O'Brien
First Old Man (Mr. Murphy)	David Frankel	Howard Claney	Eamon Kelly
Second Old Man (Mr. Tynan)	Jon Schweitzer	James Kenny	Micheal O Briain
Blind Man	Bennett Yahya	Louis Beachner	Ray Hardie
Deaf Man	Ronald Walken	Raymond Allen	Gerry Walsh
Young Man (Jimmy)	Barry Michlin	Joseph Daly	Bryan Murray
Birdlike Lad		James Cahill	John Clohan
Young Dubliners		Sylvia Selby Michael Henry Judy Jordan	
Director:	Mirim Tulin	John O'Shaughnessy	Tomás MacAnna
Designer:		Robert L. Ramsey	Bronwen Casson

F9   HALL OF HEALING

A Sincerious Farce in One Scene

	a. *World première* May 7, 1952 Yugoslav-American Hall, New York	b. *European première* November 26, 1952 Skegness Grammar School, Lincolnshire	c. *London première* May 22, 1953 Unity Theatre	d. *Irish (professional) première* February 28, 1966 Abbey Theatre, Dublin
			(Cast list unobtainable)	
Alleluia	Benedict MacQuarrie	Brian Amesbury		Harry Brogan
Old Woman	Osceola Archer	Ann Walkerley		Eileen Crowe
Red Muffler	John McLiam	Nigel Harris		Deasúin Mac Dhaibhidh
Doctor	Gilbert Green	Carl Jones		Micheál O hAonghusa
Apothecary	Kenneth Manigault	Donald Hallam		Niall O Briain
Jentree	Michael Lewin	Frank Applewhite		Seathrún O Goili
Black Muffler	Michael Howard	Bryan Law		Cladhbh MacOireachtaigh
Young Woman	Peggy Bannion	Pamela Cragg		Deirdre Puirseal
Green Muffler	Robert Donley	Michael Vardy		Micheál O Briain
Lad	Ronald Hamilton	Derek Whittington		Niall Buggy
Grey Shawl	Melanie York	Aileen Hill		Caitlín Ní Bhearáin
Townspeople	Peadar Noonan Vita Cox ⎱ Ted Rowan ⎰ Liam Lenihan Toni Tonley Maurice Winters	John Lockwood (Blue Muffler)		Proinnsias O Greidhm (A Patient)
Director:	Joseph Papirofsky	M. P. Bound	David Dawson	Tomás MacAnna
Designer:	May Callas	M. Bamforth	⎱ Kate Amaral ⎰ Robert Dyson	Brian Collins

A Tragedy in Three Acts

	a. World première March 3, 1924 Abbey Theatre, Dublin	b. London première November 16, 1925 Royalty Theatre	c. U.S. première March 15, 1926 Mayfair Theatre, New York
Residents in the Tenement:			
'Captain' Jack Boyle	Barry Fitzgerald	Arthur Sinclair	Augustin Duncan
'Juno' Boyle	Sara Allgood	Sara Allgood	Louise Randolph
Johnny Boyle	Arthur Shields	Harry Hutchinson	Barry Macollum
Mary Boyle	Eileen Crowe	Kathleen O'Regan	Isabel Stuart Hill
'Joxer' Daly	F. J. McCormick	Sydney Morgan	Claude Cooper
Mrs Maisie Madigan	Maureen Delany	Maire O'Neill	Eleanor Daniels
'Needle' Nugent	Michael J. Dolan	J. A. O'Rourke	Ralph Cullinan
Mrs Tancred	Christine Hayden	Kitty Kirwan	Kate McComb
Jerry Devine	P. J. Carolan	David Morris	Lewis Martin
Charlie Bentham	Gabriel J. Fallon	Eric Page	Charles Webster
First Irregular	Maurice Esmonde	Barney Mulligan	J. Augustus Keogh
Second Irregular	Michael J. Dolan	E. J. Kennedy	Wallace House
First Furniture Remover	Peter Nolan	Edmund O'Grady	G. O. Taylor
Second Furniture Remover	Tony Quinn	Edmund O'Grady	Emmet O'Reilly
Coal-Block Vendor	Tony Quinn	Christopher Steele	Emmet O'Reilly
Sewing-Machine Man	Peter Nolan		G. O. Taylor
Two Neighbours	{ Eileen O'Keely / Irene Murphy	{ Joyce Chancellor / Mollie Mackay	Mildred McCoy
Director:	Michael J. Dolan	J. B. Fagan	Augustin Duncan

The London première ran for 202 performances, the longest professional run for an O'Casey play. One of the most notable revivals was Laurence Olivier's production for the National Theatre at the Old Vic, London, which opened on April 26, 1966.

Note: For details of the film version see F23.

KATHLEEN LISTENS IN

See CATHLEEN LISTENS IN (F4)

The play was first staged under the latter title but was printed as 'Kathleen Listens In'.

F11   THE MOON SHINES ON KYLENAMOE

a. First performed on Irish television (Radio Telefís Éireann,
    Dublin) November 4, 1962. With Dermot Kelly, Harry
    Brogan, Seamus Kavanagh, Paul Farrell, Bríd Lynch, Frank
    O'Donovan and May Cluskey.

	b. *World stage première* October 30, 1962 Theatre de Lys, New York	c. *Irish stage première* August 14, 1975 Peacock Theatre, Dublin
Sean Tomasheen	Raymond Allen	Bryan Murray
The Guard	James Kenny	Micheal O Briain
Lord Leslieson	Grant Code	Gerry Walsh
Boy	Louis Beachner	John Olohan
Girl	Nancy Reardon	Bríd Ni Neachtain
Cornelius Conroy	Ewing Cherry	Eamon Kelly
Martha Conroy	Margaret Brewster	Aine Ni Mhuiri
Andy O'Hurrie	Jerome Collamore	Niall O'Brien
Woman Passenger	Sylvia O'Brien	Jeananne Crowley
		Ray Hardie
		(Another passenger)
Director:	John O'Shaughnessy	Tomás MacAnna
Designer:	Robert L. Ramsey	Bronwen Casson

F12 NANNIE'S NIGHT OUT

	a. *World première* September 29, 1924 Abbey Theatre, Dublin	b. *U.S. première* March 13, 1961 Little Theatre, Lafayette, Indiana
A Ballad Singer	F. J. McCormick	Robert Corbin
Polly Pender	Maureen Delany	Jeanne Orr
Oul' Johnny	Barry Fitzgerald	Stuart Main
Irish Nannie	Sara Allgood	Patricia Hensley
Oul' Jimmy	Michael J. Dolan	Charles Helmetag
A Young Girl	Eileen Crowe	Kathy Hogan
Oul' Joe	Gabriel J. Fallon	Don Ream
Robert	Gerald Breen	Bobby Hogan
The Young Man	Arthur Shields	Tom Marshall
Policemen		{ Tom Dowling { Jesse McKinney
Crowd	{ Seaghan Barlow { F. Ellis { W. O'Hara { M. Judge	
Director:	Michael J. Dolan	Robert Hogan

There is no record of an English production of the play.

	a. *World première* November 28, 1946 Helsingborgs Stadsteater, Sweden (translation by Ebbe Linde)	b. *English première* May 13, 1947 Lyric Theatre, Hammersmith
First Lady Dancer	Annika Tretow	Ann Brooke
First Gentleman Dancer	Erland Josephson	Spencer Hale
Second Lady Dancer	Anne-Marie Berg	Audrey O'Flynn
Second Gentleman Dancer	Rune Turesson	Robert Urquart
Young Son of Time	Gunnar Ekström	John Foster
Third Lady Dancer	Vanja Rodefeldt	Patricia Brent
Third Gentleman Dancer	Bertil Sjödin	Conrad Phillips
Feelim O'Morrigun	Sture Ericson	Fred Johnson
Monica Penrhyn	Margareta Bergfelt	Sheila Sim
Mark	Björn Berglund	Charles Lamb
Jennie	Lisskulla Jobs	Joyce Marwood
Joy	Siv Thulin	June Whitfield
First Special Constable Sillery	Gunnar Nielsen	Reynor Healy
Second Special Constable Dillery	Curt Edgard	Kenneth Brown
Drishogue	Erland Josephson	Edward Golden
Edgar	Rune Turesson	Alec Ross
Mrs Watchit	Marianne Nielsen	Marjorie Ziedler
Dame Hatherleigh	Elsa Widborg	Mary Hinton
Michael	Bertil Sjödin	Bertram Shuttleworth
Mrs Deeda Tutting	Dagny Lind	Janet Borrow
Third Home Guard	Bengt Magnusson	Oliver Burt
Abraham Penrhyn	Otto Landahl	Robert Urquart
Mr Constant	Gunnar Ekström	Robert Urquart
A Man	Willy Keidser	John Whiting
Pobjoy	Curt Edgard	Nellie Sheffield
An Old Woman of Seventy	Svea Dalqvist	James Neylin
Foreman in Factory	Gunnar Nielsen	
Boy	Bengt Schött	
A Seller of Lavender	Marianne Nielsen	June Whitfield
Director:	K-H. Edström	Ronald Kerr
Designer:	Per Falk	

This play has not been produced in the United States or Ireland.

F14 THE PLOUGH AND THE STARS

A Tragedy in Four Acts

	a. *World première* February 8, 1926 Abbey Theatre, Dublin	b. *English première* May 12, 1926 Fortune Theatre, London	c. *U.S. première* November 27, 1927 Hudson Theatre, New York
			Irish Players production with Arthur Sinclair and Sara Allgood.
Jack Clitheroe	F. J. McCormick	David Morris	
Nora Clitheroe	Shelah Richards	Eileen Carey	
Peter Flynn	Eric Gorman	J. A. O'Rourke	
The Young Covey	Michael J. Dolan	Sydney Morgan	
Fluther Good	Barry Fitzgerald	Arthur Sinclair	
Bessie Burgess	Maureen Delany	Sara Allgood	
Mrs Gogan	May Craig	Maire O'Neill	
Mollser	Kitty Curling	Joyce Chancellor	
Captain Brennan	Gabriel J. Fallon	Felix Irwin	
Lieut. Langon	Arthur Shields	Harry Hutchinson	
Rosie Redmond	Ria Mooney	Kathleen Drago	
A Barman	P. J. Carolan	E. J. Kennedy	
The Voice	J. Stephenson	Barney Mulligan	
Corporal Stoddard	P. J. Carolan	Edwin Ellis	
Sergeant Tinley	J. Stephenson	Christopher Steele	
A Woman	Eileen Crowe		
Director::	Lennox Robinson	J. B. Fagan	George C. Tyler
Designer:		Simpson Robinson	

On transfer to the New Theatre, Kathleen O'Regan (who was prevented by illness from appearing in the original London presentation) replaced Eileen Carey, and Fred O'Donovan replaced David Morris as Clitheroe.

The production ran for 133 performances in two theatres.

Note: For details of the film adaptation see F24.

F15 A POUND ON DEMAND

A Sketch in One Act

According to O'Casey's correspondence (letter to Gabriel Fallon, dated March 23, 1936), the first productions were by the Irish Literary Society and Darlington Grammar School, Durham, early in 1936 (dates and casts unobtainable).

a. *London première*
October 16, 1939
'Q' Theatre

A Girl	Irene Handl
Jerry	John Laurie
Sammy	Edgar K. Bruce
A Woman	Beatrix Fielden-Kaye
A Policeman	Alan Wheatley
Director:	Beatrix Lehmann

b. *New York première*
December 19, 1946
International Theatre
(American Repertory Theatre)

Cavada Humphrey
Philip Bourneuf
Ernest Truex
Margaret Webster
Eugene Stuckmann

Victor Jory

London revivals include a production at the Mercury Theatre, with Fred Johnson and Liam Redmond directed by Denis Carey, opening September 18, 1947 and the Mermaid Theatre production, in 1967, which featured Jack McGowran and Shivaun O'Casey. The Irish Festival Players staged the play in Wexford in 1957 (details unobtainable).

F16 PURPLE DUST

A Wayward Comedy

	a. *World première* December 16, 1943 People's Theatre, Newcastle upon Tyne	b. *U.S. (non-professional) première* December 6, 1944 Boston Tributary Group New England Mutual Hall, Boston	c. *Professional première* October 31, 1945 Liverpool Playhouse (Old Vic Company)	d. *New York première* December 27, 1956 Cherry Lane Theatre
First Workman	Terence McElderry	(The leading players, according to the *Boston Herald* for December 7, were: Frederick Farley, George Doughty, Robert Milam, Edward W. Mundo, Margaret Roberts, Pauline Dockery, William Otis, Richard Kilbride, Edward J. Finnegan, Edward P. Goodnow and William Mason.)	James Cairncross	Mike Kellin
Second Workman (Philib O'Dempsey)	Jack Percy		David Garth	Stephen Elliott
Third Workman	Dennis Eves		Harry Locke	Robert Geiringer
Cyril Poges	Geoffrey Branson		Maurice Jones	Harry Bannister
Souhaun	Shelagh O'Hanlon		Joan Geary	Mary Welch
Barney	Robert Morrison		Charles Keogh	James Kenny
Avril	Elizabeth Kelly		Sheila Mullin	Kathleen Murray
Basil Stoke	Leonard Scott		Cyril Luckham	Paul Shyre
Cloyne	E. Burn		Lucille Steven	Betty Henritze
O'Killigan	William Scott		Kieron O'Hanrahan	Alvin Epstein
Yellow-Bearded Man	J. Alfred Simpson		Alfie Bass	Sandy Kenyon
Rev. George Canon Creehewel	Bertram Waights		Stanley Howlett	P. J. Kelly
Postmaster	W. J. Priestley		Edward Burnham	Stefan Gierasch
Figure	J. Alfred Simpson		Peter Varley	Alan Bergmann
Director:	Peter Trower	Eliot Dunvey	Eric Capon	Philip Burton
Designer:	{ Geoffrey Branson William Southern	Paul Cadorette	Kathleen Ankers	Lester Polakov

F16 PURPLE DUST (continued)

	e. London première August 15, 1962 Mermaid Theatre	f. Irish professional première April, 1973 Lyric Theatre, Belfast	g. Dublin professional première January 30, 1975 Abbey Theatre
First Workman	James Grout	Louis Rolston	Philip O'Flynn
Second Workman *(Philib O'Dempsey)*	Robert Mooney	Seamus Newham	Patrick Laffan
Third Workman	Russell Hunter	Clem Davies	Robert Carlile
Cyril Poges	Ronald Fraser	Pitt Wilkinson	Pitt Wilkinson
Souhaun	June Tobin	Linda Wray	Kate Flynn
Barney	Gordon Rollings	Michael Duffy	Edward Golden
Avril	Annette Crosbie	Denise McKenna	Máire Ní Ghráinne
Basil Stoke	Peter Bowles	Robert French	John Kavanagh
Cloyne	Phyllida Law	Maureen Dow	Billie Morton
O'Killigain	Ronald Hines	Pat Brannigan	Desmond Cave
Yellow-Bearded Man	Harry Hutchinson	Maurice O'Callaghan	Geoffrey Golden
Rev. George Canon Creehewel	Paul Farrell	Jack McQuoid	Micheál O hAonghusa
Postmaster	Harry Hutchinson	Peter Templar	Bill Foley
Figure	Dermot MacDowell	Maurice O'Callaghan	Ray Hardie
Fourth Workman		Peter Templar	{ Martin Corcoran Conal Kearney
Director:	Peter Duguid	Tomás MacAnna	Tomás MacAnna
Designer:	David Myerscough Jones	John L. Stark	Brian Collins

The first Irish production was a non-professional one by the Sundrive Players, Dublin; it opened on February 27, 1972. The Director was Una Parker.

Staged by the Berliner Ensemble in East Germany on February 14, 1966 and in Paris the same year by Théâtre National Populaire.

F17 RED ROSES FOR ME

	a. *World première* March 15, 1943 Olympia Theatre, Dublin	b. *English première* March 25, 1943 People's Theatre, Newcastle upon Tyne	c. *U.S. première* March 3, 1944 Tributary Theatre, Boston	d. *London première* February 26, 1946 Embassy Theatre	e. *New York première* December 28, 1955 Booth Theatre
Mrs. Breydon	Ann Clery	(Cast list unobtainable)	(Cast List unobtainable)	Ethel O'Shea	Eileen Crowe
Ayamonn Breydon	Dan O'Herlihy			Kieron O'Hanrahan	Kevin McCarthy
Eeada	Sheila Carry			Nora O'Mahony	Ann Dere
Dympna	Gertrude Quinn			Sheila Carty	Katherine Hynes
Finnoola	Cepta Cullen			Norrie Duff	Virginia Bosler
Sheila Moorneen	Sheila May			Maureen Pook	Joyce Sullivan
Brennan o' the Moor	John Stephenson			Eddie Byrne	E. G. Marshall
A Singer (Sammy)	John Richards			Dermot MacDowell	David McDaniel
Roory O'Balacaun	W. O'Gorman			Alex Dignam	Eamon Flynn
Mullcanny	Seamus Healy			Victor Wood	Casey Walters
Rev. E. Clinton	Michael Walsh			Tristan Rawson	Michael Clarke Lawrence
First Railwayman	Pat Nolan			Robert Mooney	James C. Kelly
Second Railwayman	Gerrard McCarthy			Michael Healey	Lou Frizzell
Inspector Finglas	Austin Meldon			Harry Webster	Shamus Locke
First Man	Joseph O'Dea			Dermot MacDowell	Furrell Pelly
Second Man	Patrick Nolan			Meric Dobson	Page Johnson
Third Man	Luke McLoughlin			Michael Healey	Vincent Dowling
Samuel	John McDarby			T. J. Hurley	Whitford Kane
Dowzard	Wilfred Brambell			Charles Blair	Jock McGraw
Foster	John Allen			Terry Wilson	Barry Macollum
A Lamplighter				Robert Mooney	David Ryan
Citizens, Strikers, Etc.	Miss Mignon Rumbold, Messrs Burke, S. Burke, Byrne, N. Byrne, Bloomfield, Carroll, Healy, Larkin, Merrigan, Morris, O'Neill, Penston, Quinn, Scanlon, D. Smyth, M. Smyth and Tobin				David McDaniel, Paul Sanasardo, Jeff Duncan, Beatrice Seckler, Judith Coy, David Gold, Sandra Pine, Jack Moore and Eve Beck
Director:	Shelah Richards			Ria Mooney	John O'Shaughnessy
Designer:	Ralph Cusack			Henry Bird	Howard Bay

F18 THE SHADOW OF A GUNMAN

A Tragedy in Two Acts

	a. *World première* April 12, 1923 Abbey Theatre, Dublin	b. *English première* May 27, 1927 Court Theatre, London	c. *New York première* October 30, 1932	d. *New York revival of note* November 20, 1958 Bijou Theatre (Actors' Studio Company)
Donal Davoren	Arthur Shields	Harry Hutchinson	(By the Abbey Theatre Players on tour. The cast included Barry Fitzgerald, Arthur Shields, F. J. McCormick, Michael J. Dolan and Eileen Crowe.)	William Smithers
Seamus Shields	F. J. McCormick	Arthur Sinclair		Gerald O'Loughlin
Maguire	G. V. Lavelle	Tony Quinn		Bruce Dern
Mr. Mulligan	Eric Gorman	Felix Irwin		Daniel Reed
Minnie Powell	Gertrude Murphy	Eileen Carey		Susan Strasberg
Tommy Owens	Michael J. Dolan	Brian O'Dare		Stefan Gierasch
Mrs. Henderson	Christine Hayden	Sara Allgood		Zamah Cunningham
Mr. Gallogher	Gabriel J. Fallon	J. A. O'Rourke		Arthur Malet
Mrs. Grigson	May Craig	Maire O'Neill		Katherine Squire
Adolphus Grigson	P. J. Carolan	Sydney Morgan		George Mathews
Auxiliary	Tony Quinn	Edwin Ellis		James Greene
Passersby				{ Jack Allen Tammy Allen Hilda Brawner Tom Wheatley
Director:	Lennox Robinson	Arthur Sinclair		Jack Garfein
Designer:				Peter Larkin

THE SILVER TASSIE

a. World première
October 11, 1929
Apollo Theatre, London

Sylvester Heegan	Barry Fitzgerald
Mrs Heegan	Eithne Magee
Simon Norton	Sydney Morgan
Susie Monican	Beatrix Lehmann
Mrs Foran	Una O'Connor
Teddy Foran	Ian Hunter
Harry Heegan	Charles Laughton
Jessie Taite	Billy Barnes
Barney Bagnal	S. J. Warmington
Soldiers:	Charles Laughton, Ian Hunter, Barry Fitzgerald, Jack Mayne, G. Adrian Byrne, S. J. Warmington
The Corporal	Sinclair Cotter
The Visitor	Iva Dawson
The Staff Wallah	Alban Blakelock
Stretcher-bearers	Norman Stuart, Oswald Lingard, Charles Schofield, Barry Barnes
Casualties	Clive Morton, James Willoughby
Surgeon Forby Maxwell	Hastings Lynn
Sister of the Ward	Audrey O'Flynn
The Croucher	Leonard Shepherd
The Trumpeter	Emlyn Williams
Guests, etc.	Ethel O'Shea, Maureen O'Beirne, May Brooks, Ann Holland, Lloyd Bennet, James Willoughby, Queenie Russell, Jack Mayne, Barry Barnes, Seymour O'Farrell, Alban Blakelock, Emlyn Williams, Clive Morton, Norman Stuart

Director: Raymond Massey

Designer: G. E. Calthorp (Acts 1, 3 & 4)
Augustus John (Act 2)

b. U.S. première
October 24, 1929
Irish Theatre, New York City

Sylvester Heegan	Sean Dillon
Mrs Heegan	Emma Conrow
Simon Norton	Eddie O'Connor
Susie Monican	Margaret Barnstead
Mrs Foran	Kitty Collins
Teddy Foran	Ralph Cullinan
Harry Heegan	Sherling Oliver
Jessie Tate	Allyn Gillyn
Barney Bagnal	David Keating
The Croucher	Schuyler MacGuffin
First Soldier	James Metcalfe
Second Soldier	John Ferris
Third Soldier	Ned Lane
Fourth Soldier (Teddy)	Ralph Cullinan
The Corporal	Francis Kennelly
The Visitor	Abram Gillette
The Staff Wallah	L. H. Dennison
First Stretcher-bearer	Pendleton Harrison
Second Stretcher-bearer	Harry Wallace
Third Stretcher-bearer	John Wynne
Fourth Stretcher-bearer	Dajalna Montana
First Casualty	Patrick Glasgow
Second Casualty	Leonard Austin
Surgeon Forby Maxwell	Bertram Millar
The Sister of the Ward	Ennis Clare

Director: Miceal Breathnach

Designer: Charles Friedman

THE SILVER TASSIE (continued)

c. *Irish premiere*
August 12, 1935
Abbey Theatre,
Dublin

Notable revivals:

d. September 10, 1969
Aldwych Theatre, London
(Royal Shakespeare Company)

e. September 27, 1972
Abbey Theatre, Dublin
(earlier Dublin revivals
were staged in June
1947 and in 1951)

Sylvester Heegan	Barry Keegan
Mrs Heegan	Ann Clery
Simon Norton	Michael J. Dolan
Susie Monican	Eileen Crowe
Mrs Foran	May Craig
Teddy Foran	P. J. Carolan
Harry Heegan	F. J. McCormick
Jessie Taite	Aideen O'Connor
Barney Bagnal	Fred Johnson
Soldiers:	Denis O'Dea
	J. Winter
	Cyril Cusack
	J. Hand
The Corporal	P. J. Carolan
The Visitor	J. Stephenson
The Staff Wallah	Edward Lexy
Stretcher-bearers	Tom Purefoy
	W. O'Gorman
	M. Finn
	M. Clarke
	B. Carey
Casualties	W. Redmond
	Edward Lexy
	Tom Purefoy
	Truda Barling
Surgeon Forby Maxwell	
Sister of the Ward	
Director:	Arthur Shields
Designer:	Maurice McGonigal

F20 THE STAR TURNS RED

World première
March 12, 1940
Unity Theatre, London

(Two anonymous casts played on alternate nights)

Director: John Allen
Settings: Lawrence Gowing
Music: Alan Bush

This play has not been performed in Ireland or the United States. It was revived at Unity Theatre, London, on July 24, 1946. It was staged in Sydney, Australia, in 1948, in Budapest in 1959 and in Paris in 1962.

F21   TIME TO GO

A Morality Comedy in One Act

a. *World première*
May, 7, 1952
Jugoslav-American
Hall, New York

b. *English première*
May 22, 1953
Unity Theatre,
London

c. *New York revival*
March 22, 1960
Theatre de Lys

(Cast list unobtainable)

(ANTA Matinee Theatre
Series produced by
Lucille Lortel)

Bull Farrell	Clifford Carpenter
Flagonson	Leonard Yorr
Young Man	Arnold Walton
Young Woman	Melanie York
Widda Machree	Adelaide Bean
Mrs. Flagonson	Edith Wade
Barney O'Hay	John McLiam
Cousins	Michael Howard
Conroy	Stefan Gierasch
Kelly	William Marshall
Sergeant	John Regan

Director: Albert Kipton   Ivor Pinkus
Designer: May Callas   Kate Amaral and Robert Dyson

WITHIN THE GATES

A Play of Four Scenes in a London Park

	a. *World première*	b. *U.S. première*
	February 7, 1934	October 22, 1934
	Royalty Theatre, London	National Theatre, New York
The Dreamer	Basil Bartlett	Bramwell Fletcher
The Bishop	Douglas Jefferies	Moffat Johnston
The Bishop's Sister	Gertrude Sterroll	Kathryn Collier
The 1st Chair Attendant	Walter Herbage	Barry Macollum
The 2nd Chair Attendant	Jack Twyman	John Daly Murphy
A Girl	Diana Sinclair Hill	
The Atheist	Richard Caldicott	Morris Ankrum
The Policewoman	Molly Tyson	Jessamine Newcombe
The Man in Plus-Fours	Gerald Gibbons	Ralph Sumpter
The Scarlet Woman	June Lawson	Mirium Goldina
The 1st Nursemaid	Isobel Scaife	Vera Fuller Mellish
The 2nd Nursemaid	Daphne Scorer	Esther Mitchell
A Guardsman	Ronald Waters	James Jolley
The Gardener	Alan Wheatley	Barry Kelley
The 1st Evangelist	Edward Mervyn	Edward Broadley
The 2nd Evangelist	G. R. Schjelderup	Arthur Villars
The Young Whore	Marjorie Mars	Lillian Gish
A Young Salvation Army Officer	Patrick Barr	Byron McGrath
The Foreman	Denis Alban	Ralph Cullinan
The Old Woman	Marie Ault	Mary Morris
The Man in the Trilby Hat	Ernest G. Cove	Charles Angelo
The Man in the Bowler Hat	Edward Mervyn	Stanley G. Wood
The Man with the Stick	Leonard Shepherd	Phil Bishop
The 1st Platform Speaker	Leonard Shepherd	Gordon Gould
The 2nd Platform Speaker	Edward Mervyn	Dodson Mitchell
The Man in the Burberry	Richard Caldicott	Charles Keane
Group of Down and Out,	⎰ Audrey Dunham, Zara Gray,	⎱ Mildred Albert, Suzanne Black, Mary Brandt,
Strollers, Salvationists,	Phyllis Hayward, Jane Kidner,	Kathryn Curl, Martha Eaton, Betty Gladstone,
Chorus of Young Men, and	Violet Lynch, Joyce Peters,	Anne Goddard, Dorothy Higgins, Marjorie Hyder,
Girls, and Dancers	Sylvia Rye, Denzil Bond,	Ellen Love, Elizabeth Morgan, Evangeline Raleigh,
	Reginald Gittings, Patrick O'Moore,	Ursula Seiler, Edith Shayne, Virginia Spottswood,
	Charles Schofield	Pauline Stokes, Peggy Strickland, Teddy Williams,
		George Augustin, Tony Barone, Mordecae Bauman,
		Victor Bryant, Kenneth Bostock, Serge Gradoff,

F22 WITHIN THE GATES (cont.)

a. World première (cont.)

Group of Down and Out,
Strollers, Salvationists,
Chorus of Young Men, and
Girls, and Dancers

A Boy
A Young Man
Symbol of the Seasons
Woman Who Feeds the Birds

Director: Norman MacDermott
Designer: Norman MacDermott
Music: Herbert Hughes

b. U.S. première (cont.)

Tomes Chapman, Frank Gabrielson,
Serge Inga, Robert Kerr, Stanley Klein,
Gifford Nash, William Trieste, Rodifer
Wilson, Karl Kohrs, Ram Meyer, Clyde
Walters, William Williams

Alexander Lewis
Arthur Gould Porter
Margaret Mower
Ellen Larned

Melvyn Douglas
James Reynolds
Milton Lusk

The New York production had a run of 101 consecutive performances and, after a short tour, a further run of forty performances. The first presentation in Ireland was an amateur production by the Sundrive Players, Dublin, in May 1977 (directed by Una Parker).

F23 JUNO AND THE PAYCOCK (*film*)

Released early in 1930 after first London showing at the Regal Cinema, Marble Arch, on December 30, 1929

Mrs Madigan	Maire O'Neill
Captain Boyle	Edward Chapman
'Joxer' Daly	Sidney Morgan
Mrs Boyle ('Juno')	Sara Allgood
Johnny Boyle	John Laurie
Jerry Devine	Dave Morris
Mary Boyle	Kathleen O'Regan
Charles Bentham	John Longden
The Mobiliser	Dennis Wyndham
Mr. Kelly [*Nugent in the original play*]	Fred Schwarz

(Barry Fitzgerald was one of the extras in the film.)

Production Company	British International Pictures
Producer and Director	Alfred Hitchcock
Photography	J. J. Cox
Art Director	J. Marchant
Assistant Director	Frank Mills
Sound Recordist	C. Thornton
Scenario	Alma Reville
Musical setting arranged and conducted by	John Renders
	British International Symphony Orchestra
Distributed by	Wardour Films Limited

F24   THE PLOUGH AND THE STARS *(film)*

Released for general viewing in March 1937 after its first screening in New York in January 1937

Nora Clitheroe	Barbara Stanwyck
Jack Clitheroe	Preston Foster
Maggie Gogan	Una O'Connor
Fluther Good	Barry Fitzgerald
The Covey	Denis O'Dea
Bessie Burgess	Eileen Crowe
Padraic Pearse	Arthur Shields
Peter Flynn	J. M. Kerrigan
Mollser Gogan	Bonita Granville
Rosie Redmond	Erin O'Brien-Moore
Captain Brennan	F. J. McCormick
General Connolly	Moroni Olsen
Lieutenant Langon	Neil Fitzgerald
Corporal Stoddart	Cyril McLaglen
Sergeant Tinley	Brandon Hurst
The Barman	Robert Homans

Production Company	R.K.O. Radio Pictures
Director	John Ford
Associated Producers	{ Cliff Reid / Robert Sisk }
Screenplay	Dudley Nichols

A copy of the screen play is in the Library and Museum of the Performing Arts, the New York Public Library at Lincoln Center.

SECTION G

Adaptations

G1 I KNOCK AT THE DOOR

Concert reading

An adaptation of *I Knock at the Door* designed for a concert reading by six voices was prepared by Paul Shyre. It was first presented at the YM-YWHA Poetry Center (Kaufmann Concert Hall), New York, on March 18, 1956 directed by Stuart Vaughan. The same production was presented at the Belasco Theatre, New York, on September 29, 1957. The adaptation in two acts was published by Dramatists Play Service on July 2, 1958 at $1.50.

Reader

A version of *I Knock at the Door* for the use of the sixth form in secondary schools, prepared by O. Truevtseva and L. Shifulina, was published in 1959 in Leningrad by the State Text Book Publishing House of the USSR Ministry of Education.

G2 PICTURES IN THE HALLWAY

Concert reading

An adaptation of *Pictures in the Hallway* designed for a concert reading by six voices was prepared by Paul Shyre. It was first presented at the YM-YWHA Poetry Center (Kaufmann Concert Hall), New York, on May 27, 1956 directed by Stuart Vaughan. The same production was presented at the Playhouse, New York, on September 16, 1956. The adaptation in two acts was published by Samuel French, Inc., on April 24, 1957 at $1.00. A recording by the cast of the September 1956 production was issued by Riverside Records. Another adaptation, by Patrick Funge and David Krause, was staged at the Lantern Theatre, Dublin, on August 4, 1965. The Funge–Krause adaptation has not been published.

G3 JUNO AND THE PAYCOCK

Musical play

In 1956 Joseph Stein had the idea that *Juno and the Paycock* would make a good musical play and began an exchange of letters with O'Casey. He visited the dramatist in England with an outline of the book, showing scenes and places for some of the songs. In April 1957 Stein approached the composer Marc Blitzstein suggesting a collaboration on a musical based on O'Casey's play. By August, part of the music and the songs were ready. O'Casey wrote two songs for the musical. In the accompanying letter to Joseph Stein dated October 8, 1956 he said: 'I'm afraid, I've little talent for this special work, but I present them to you as (I think) the best I could do.' The musical *Juno* opened 'on the road' in Washington, D.C., with Shirley Booth (Juno), Melvyn Douglas (Captain Boyle) and Jack McGowran (Joxer) playing the principal parts. On May 19, 1958, O'Casey wrote to Jane Rubin, 'I've listened to the musical Juno—record sent by Joe S[tein]. Breon and Eileen and Shivaun think it good; I'm not so sure, finding it hard to get my ear to go with the modern rhythms.' The play underwent many revisions, and the director, Vincent J. Donehue, was replaced by José Ferrer in an attempt to have a strong play ready for the Broadway début. It opened at the Winter Garden Theater, New York, on March 9, 1959. Reviews generally were unfavourable; Brooks Atkinson in the *New York Times*, March 15, 1959 remarked on the failure to capture 'the biting humor and the blistering tragedy' of the original. The closing notice, effective at the end of the week, was posted on Monday, March 16, 1959. On April 4, 1959 O'Casey wrote to Jane Rubin concerning the closing, 'I'm afraid the result (folding of musical) wasn't unexpected by me and I feel the critics were mainly right.' A copy of the final revised script is in the New York Public Library. The musical saga was taken a stage further when an adaptation of Blitzstein's *Juno*, entitled *Daarlin' Juno*, was given a trial production by the Williamstown Theatre Festival (Virginia) in the Summer of 1974; it was revived at the Long Wharf Theatre, New Haven (Connecticut) from May 14 to June 11, 1976. The adaptation, made by Richard Maltby Jr and Geraldine Fitzgerald, contained additional lyrics by Maltby and the music was arranged and adapted by Thomas Fay. Further details of this adaptation and its relationship to both O'Casey's play and Blitzstein's original musical adaptation are given in the notes to *Juno and the Paycock* (A11).

G4 DRUMS UNDER THE WINDOWS

Concert Reading

An adaptation of *Drums Under the Windows* designed as a kaleidoscopic dramatisation for seven actors was prepared by Paul Shyre. It was first presented at the Cherry Lane Theater, New York, on October 13, 1960, directed by Paul Shyre. A first draft rehearsal copy, in typescript, without the cuts or changes included, is in the New York Public Library. The adaptation in two acts was published by Dramatists Play Service, Inc. on September 14, 1962 at $1.50. Another adaptation by Patrick Funge and David Krause, was staged at the Lantern Theatre, Dublin on July 21, 1970. The Funge–Krause adaptation has not been published.

THE PLOUGH AND THE STARS

Opera

The Plough and the Stars, a three-act opera based on the O'Casey play with music by Elie Siegmeister and libretto by Edward Mabley. *Dublin Song* was the name given to an early version which employed much spoken dialogue and which was first performed at Washington University, St Louis, on May 15, 1963. A revised version set entirely to music had its première at Louisiana State University, Baton Rouge, on March 16, 1969. The European première took place at the Grand Théâtre Municipal, Bordeaux, on March 13, 1970. Drafts, libretto, piano–vocal score, designs, sketches and other manuscript material are in the Library of Congress, Washington, D.C.

INISHFALLEN, FARE THEE WELL

Concert reading

An adaptation for the stage of *Inishfallen, Fare Thee Well* by Patrick Funge and David Krause was presented at the Lantern Theatre, Dublin, on July 24, 1972. It shared the stage with the authors' adaptations of *Pictures in the Hallway* and *Drums Under the Windows* in a production which lasted for six and three-quarter hours. This adaptation has not been published.

SECTION H

Recordings

SEAN O'CASEY READING FROM HIS WORKS

Caedmon TC 1012. 2 sides. 33⅓ rpm.
Side 1: Opening scene from *Juno and the Paycock*. Final scene from *Juno and the Paycock*. 'The Death of Mrs. Casside' from *Inishfallen, Fare Thee Well*.
Side 2: The second half of Chapter 2 ('Cat 'n Cage') from *Pictures in the Hallway*.

The recording was released sometime between June and October 1953. Recorded at the O'Casey home in Totnes, Devon, on November 12, 1952.

The excerpts vary from the published texts, and were obviously adapted and 'cut' for the readings.

2   JUNO AND THE PAYCOCK

A Tragi-comedy of Dublin. Angel Records 3540B (ANG 35275–76). 4 sides. 33⅓ rpm.
Introduction by O'Casey. Starring Siobhán McKenna, Cyril Cusack, Maire Kean and Seamus Kavanagh. The Angel Records issue has programme notes (12 pp.) in a container which includes a note on the play by Alan Dent, biographical sketches of the actors, text of the preamble spoken by the author, and synopsis (B30).

The recording was released in 1956. Recorded by Cyril Cusack Productions, Ireland, in Dublin, June 1955. Released in the United Kingdom on EMI's HMV series; issued by Angel Records (35275–76) on February 27, 1956; reissued by Seraphim Records (IB6014) on May 29, 1967.

3   PICTURES IN THE HALLWAY

Adapted by Paul Shyre. Riverside Records RLP 7006/7. 4 sides. 33⅓ rpm.
Starring Aline MacMahon, Staats Coatsworth, Rae Allen, George Brenlin,

Robert Geiringer and Paul Shyre. Recorded in New York, March 14 and 29, 1957. Critical notes by Paul Shyre on slipcase.

H4   SEAN O'CASEY READING VOLUME TWO

Reading from I Knock at the Door, Rose and Crown, Sunset and Evening Star and Singing The Wearing of the Green. Caedmon TC 1198. 2 sides. 33⅓ rpm.

Side 1: A selection from the chapter 'Life is More than Meat' from *I Knock at the Door*. A selection from the chapter 'Ship in Full Sail' from *Rose and Crown*.

Side 2: A selection from the chapter 'Outside an Irish Window' from *Sunset and Evening Star*. A selection from the chapter 'And Evening Star' from *Sunset and Evening Star*. 'The Wearing of the Green' traditional song sung by O'Casey.

The recording was released in September 1969. Recorded at the O'Casey home in Totnes, Devon, on December 26, 1953.

Typescripts of 'Life is More than Meat' and 'Ship in Full Sail' especially prepared for the reading are included among the O'Casey papers in the Berg Collection, New York Public Library.

H5   SEAN O'CASEY'S WORLD

A famed playwright reviews his life & Irish theatre. Center for Cassette Studies, Inc., 010–3107.

The recording was released in 1970. This is the sound track of the television programme 'A Conversation with Sean O'Casey and Robert Emmett Ginna' broadcast on January 22, 1956 by NBC–TV.

H6   DYLAN THOMAS READING FROM THE WORKS OF DJUNA BARNES AND SEAN O'CASEY

Caedmon TC 1342. 1 side. 33⅓ rpm.

Contains excerpts from the chapter 'Watchman, What of the Night?' from *Nightwood* by Djuna Barnes, and excerpts from the chapter 'First the Green Blade' from *I Knock at the Door* by Sean O'Casey. Backed by 'Dylan Thomas Reading from His Work'.

The recording was released in January 1971.

H7   AUTOBIOGRAPHY

Die komplette Autobiographie in einer Kassette. Einmalige Sonderausgabe. Diogenes, 1973.

Radio and Television Broadcasts

THE PLAYWRIGHT AND THE BOX OFFICE

On June 25, 1938 the British Broadcasting Corporation broadcast a discussion between Sean O'Casey and Maurice Browne entitled 'The Playwright and the Box Office', in the series 'The Theatre'. The text of the discussion was published in the *Listener*, July 7, 1938 (C204) and reprinted in *Blasts and Benedictions* (A44).

GEORGE BERNARD SHAW – AN IRISH PORTRAIT

On August 13, 1954 the BBC Third Programme broadcast 'George Bernard Shaw – An Irish Portrait', produced by Maurice Browne. O'Casey contributed reminiscences of Shaw to the programme. Transcriptions of this and the 1938 programme are in the Sound Archives of the BBC, to which the public does not have access.

SEAN O'CASEY TALKS

O'Casey gave three talks for Radio Éireann in 1955 which were broadcast under the general title, 'Sean O'Casey Talks: The Playwright Looks at the Ireland of his plays and at the Ireland of To-day'. The talks were transmitted on May 15, 22 and 29.

A CONVERSATION WITH SEAN O'CASEY

On Sunday, January 22, 1956 (2.00–2.30 p.m.) the National Broadcasting Company (NBC-TV) presented 'A Conversation with Sean O'Casey and Robert

Emmett Ginna' in its Wisdom Series. The programme was filmed at the O'Casey home in Torquay, Devon, and produced and directed by Robert D. Graff. Photography was by W. Suschitzky. Released as a documentary film by Encyclopaedia Britannica Films in 1958. A cassette recording of the sound track was released by the Center for Cassette Studies, Inc. in 1970.

J5 THE EXILE

On February 6, 1968 (10.25–11.25 p.m.) BBC 1 (TV) presented 'The Exile' in its 'Omnibus' series. 'A study of Sean O'Casey by Don Taylor, with glimpses of the aged O'Casey himself, lively, passionate and invincibly gay, memories of him by all sorts of people involved in his life and work, and moments from his plays', *The Times*, February 7, 1968.

SECTION K

Motion Pictures

Two motion pictures of plays by O'Casey were made during the playwright's lifetime; the cast lists of these films – *Juno and the Paycock* and *The Plough and the Stars* – are recorded in an appendix to Section F: see F23 and F24.

SEAN O'CASEY

National Broadcasting Company, released by Encyclopaedia Britannica Films, 1958. A release of the film of the NBC-TV programme 'A Conversation with Sean O'Casey', originally broadcast on January 22, 1956.

CRADLE OF GENIUS

Directed by Paul Rotha. Plough Productions, Dublin, 1959. Released in the United States by Irving Lesser Enterprises, 1961. Commentator, Frank O'Connor; photographer Wolfgang Suschitsky; produced by Tom Hayes and Jim O'Connor.

Includes a conversation between O'Casey and Barry Fitzgerald, the former Abbey actor, who created the role of Captain Boyle in *Juno and the Paycock* and of Fluther Good in *The Plough and the Stars*.

3 YOUNG CASSIDY

Directed by Jack Cardiff; screenplay by John Whiting. Sextant Films, London. Released in the United States by Metro-Goldwyn-Mayer, 1965. Producers: Robert D. Graff and Robert Emmett Ginna. Cast: Rod Taylor, Julie Christie, Michael Redgrave, Edith Evans, Flora Robson and Maggie Smith. A copy of the script is in the Wesleyan University Library, Middletown, Conn. A John Ford film, released March 1965.
Based loosely on certain portions of *Mirror in My House*, O'Casey's early years.

Index

Titles of books and pamphlets by Sean O'Casey in the English language are capitalized; other book and periodical titles are italicized. Titles of poems, essays, etc. are set in quotation marks. For Section A a lower case *n* following the number indicates the reference is to an item in the *Notes* section; a lower case *r* following the number indicates the reference is to an item in the *Reviews* section. An italicised number indicates the item where the fullest description of a major work may be found.